Competitive Diving

The Complete Guide for Coaches, Divers, Judges

Curiosity – Imagination – Creativity – Perseverance

Hobie Billingsley

World's Greatest Diving Coach
Five Time Olympic Diving Coach
Two Time Olympic Judge
132 National Champions
Founder of World & American
Diving Coaches Associations
23 Big Ten & 6 NCAA Team Championships

Trius Publishing
San Diego

Competitive Diving

The Complete Guide for Coaches, Divers, Judges

Published in the United States of America by:
Trius Publishing, 6382 Lake Dora Ave., San Diego, CA 92119

The author of this book, and other written materials does not dispense medical advice or prescribe the use of any technique as a form of treatment for physical or mental problems without the advice of a physician, either directly or indirectly. The intent of the author is only to offer information of a general nature to help you in your quest for diving performance improvement. In the event you use any of the information or methods and cues in this book for yourself or to help others is your constitutional right, the author and publisher assume no responsibility for your actions.

This is the most complete guide for establishing and developing competitive diving programs. You can learn methods and skills to evaluate programs, facilities, coaches, divers, and judges. Mechanical principles and techniques are offered to help teach and judge competitive dives and organize and administer programs. Communication and safety practices are also covered for one and three meter, and tower/platform diving.

To learn more, place book orders, find stories and pictures about this sport's icon, go to his secure website: https://HobieBillingsley.com

ISBN: 978-0-9986357-2-9 paperback $29.95

Order other Hobie Billingsley publications at http://HobieBillingsley.com

Challenge: How to succeed beyond your dreams

Hobie's autobiography. An entertaining page-turner, his life and worldwide influence on history of competitive diving.

ISBN: 978-0-9986357-0-5 paperback 7x10 375 pages $29.95

Competitive Diving Illustrated – Coaching Strategies to Perform 134 Dives

Illustrated numbered sequence drawings with detailed explanations how to perform 134 of the more common competitive dives.

ISBN: 978-0-9986357-1-2 paperback 7x10 304 pages $29.95

Competitive Diving – The Complete Guide for Coaches, Divers, Judges

The most complete guide for establishing and developing competitive diving programs. You can learn methods and skills to evaluate programs, facilities, coaches, divers, and judges. Mechanical principles and techniques are offered to help teach and judge competitive dives and organize and administer programs. Communication and safety practices are also covered for one and three meter, and tower/platform diving.

ISBN: 978-0-9986357-2-9 paperback 7x10 328 pages $29.95

Hobie's Heroes 25th Anniversary Edition

A film by Steven Montgomery, Barbara Wolver, and Tony Gucchiari. Documents young divers overcoming their fears to learn a full list of new dives on one meter and three-meter for the first time at Hobie's famous summer camps. Updates divers 25 years after the making of the film.
DVD color 29 minutes $19.95

About Hobie Billingsley

Against all odds to be a success, Hobie overcame insurmountable odds to become the World's Greatest Diving Coach in the history of the sport.

At the young age of 3 his father walked out on the family leaving him and his older brother and mother penniless during the Great Depression. He fought through hunger and homelessness with the help of two men who mentored him at the Erie, Pennsylvania YMCA.

At an early age, he taught himself to swim and when the team needed a diver he tried out and liked the challenge. Eventually he would also become a gymnast and cheerleader for the high school.

As his diving skills improved to become the Pennsylvania state high school champion, the coach suggested he compete at the National AAU Championships. There, the top Ohio State University divers gave him pointers he could take back to his coach, and he became the first high school diver to place in the finals of a national championship.

He enrolled at Ohio State and became the first All-American for all four years. World War II called him into service in Okinawa where the war with Japan ended and he resumed his college diving career, and head athletic cheerleader on the sidelines for all the football games.

After college, Hobie and Bruce Harlan formed a popular clown diving act performing at schools, hotels, and country clubs all over the United States. After a short high school coaching stint, he became only the 2nd diving coach ever hired by a college or university.

In 1959, he came to Indiana University to start an unequaled diving dynasty that continues today. He started with very poor facilities and no committed divers with any skills. Then Rick Gilbert came to Indiana when they moved into the new Royer Pool facility. Rick became his first national champion his freshman year that attracted other great talent to the school.

He was the first to coach women in any sport and did so without pay well before Title IX guaranteed equal rights for women athletes in 1972.

Along with head swimming coach, Doc Counsilman, together they won 23 Big Ten Championships and 6 NCAA Division I titles.

Hobie was selected as the Olympic Diving Coach 5 times and coached 132 National Champions. After retiring in 1989 he gave diving clinics and judged major competitions all over the world, and in 1996 was selected to administer the Olympic Oath to all the judges at the Atlanta Olympics - a great honor.

His leadership was evident by forming the World Diving Coaches Association and the United States Diving Coaches Association. In 1983, he received the high honor of being inducted into the International Swimming Hall of Fame.

He continues to have a profound effect on the diving community publications, clinics, and lectures to divers in summer camps, high schools, and collegiate athletic programs.

Hobie is an icon in all of sport, and a great entertaining speaker.

CONTENTS

3. The Diver

4. The Diving Coach

14. Judging competitive diving

PROLOGUE

THE PURPOSE FOR WRITING THIS BOOK

In the making for over forty years, this book was written with the purpose of making the sport of competitive diving easier for the reader to understand how to teach and coach divers in achieving a higher level of performance. I believe that to meet such goals requires one to have some idea of where the sport came from, where it is at the present time, and where it may be heading in the future. Having lived through much of the development and growth of the sport, a lot of the history presented here by the author is given first hand.

I believe that the reader can more easily grasp the value of this book by relating how it was that I could take a non-existent program when arriving at Indiana University and build it into one of the finest diving programs in the world in a period of three years. With the suggestion of several diving coaches, I wish to offer a short story on how it was done with the hope that it will inspire other coaches to improve their diving programs.

When I arrived on the Indiana campus in the fall of 1959, the swim team had no divers, a dingy pool with four lanes, seven feet of water, and a ceiling eight feet above the one-meter board which jetted out from the side of the pool. I started my career at Indiana with two divers, who had transferred from Ohio University where I coached for two years, two incoming freshmen from a nearby town, and a freshman swimmer who was cut from the swim team and decided to be a diver. None of the divers, who were at a low competitive level, were qualified to dive varsity for a year, because the two divers from Ohio were ineligible due to transferring schools, and the N.C.A.A. prohibited athletes in all sports from competing in any sport until they were sophomores.

To prevent the divers from diving on top of the swimmers that practiced during the day, I had to coach them in the pool during the evening hours after working them out on the trampoline in the gymnasium and from a sand pit board in the field house during the day. Since we were never in the pool when the swimmers practiced, they never knew they had a diving team for the first year I coached at Indiana. Most of the swim team members still didn't know that they had a diving team for most of the second season because when competing in dual meets, the swimmers left the pool for a meeting with Doc Councilman during the diving event in all of the meets. Our presence was so insignificant, that the divers and I were not invited to the Indiana swimming banquets at the end of the first two seasons.

During my second year at Indiana, the football coach was caught cheating for the second time in a year and the N.C.A.A. placed all sports at Indiana on probation for four years which meant no one could compete in the N.C.A.A. National Championships. Of course, this made it nearly impossible to recruit anyone to take part in our diving program which was basically non-existent. Aware of our nearly impossible position,

Doc Councilman and I decided to look for another job but changed our minds a couple of weeks later and decided to ride out the probation.

Unbelievably, while coaching under such poor conditions, Doc Councilman and I developed the best swimming and diving teams in the world, while still on probation. Doing so in such a short time was a miracle, and with the aid of this text, I would like to pass on some information on how it was possible to produce two Olympic Diving Champions in 1964 when under such adverse conditions.

Such an accomplishment occurred when, after arriving on campus, I decided to set some realistic goals and objectives for myself and, hopefully for the divers on the team. Knowing how difficult it would be to recruit a good diver when the school was on probation, I decided to see what it would take to create a good diving program. Starting from nothing, I first decided to make myself the kind of coach for which a dive would want to dive. I started by quitting to smoke, stopped frequenting local bars, and refrained from using any foul language or telling dirty jokes. I also began to dress as a professional by wearing a sport coat, shirt, and tie in and out of the pool and classroom and started attending the national diving conventions. Though believing it was a useless task, I began to write letters to high school divers around the country that I believed had good diving potential.

Though progress in developing a diving program at Indiana started out real slow, one day near the beginning of my second season, one of the divers mentioned that he had heard about a good diver who was a senior in high school and lived in Lancaster, Pennsylvania. Having nothing to lose, I decided to write him a letter but got no response. Refusing to give up on him, I continued to drop him a line a couple of times a week and after about three months, Rick Gilbert finally wrote back which started a correspondence that continued for about four months. During that time, I had no idea of how good of a diver he was, so I finally asked him if he could send me a film of his diving. After viewing the film, I was surprised to see that he was a much better diver than what I had expected.

Soon after, Gilbert decided to compete in the Senior National A.A.U. Diving Championships at Yale University in April of 1961 and placed seventh in the one-meter event which was a rare accomplishment for a high school diver. Coaches were not permitted to talk to any recruits in person at that time so when the meet was over, he was immediately mobbed by divers from several universities, especially from Ohio State. Later he visited five different colleges that showed great interest in him which included Indiana. Believing, he didn't have any interest in attending Indiana University because we were on probation, the program had no reputable divers, the diving program was lousy, and I was a new coach with no reputation, I decided to phone him on the first night that scholarships were offered to find where he had decided to attend school. After he told me how impressed he was with the diving programs at two other universities he had visited, I was flabbergasted when he told me that he decided to attend Indiana.

When asked why he turned down the two best diving programs in the country to go with the worst, he said that he believed in me and what I stood for. With a new pool built at Indiana before his arrival on campus in the fall of 1961 and with no three- meter experience, he learned to perform a full list of dives from that height in two months. After placing fourth in the one- meter competition, he went on to win the National A.AU. three-meter championship on April 7, 1962 in Bartlesville, Oklahoma by beating four Olympians and three national champions with the highest score and by the widest margin ever made in his first attempt at competing from that height. His unbelievable victory over some of the best divers in the world was made possible because he had learned to perform his dives using mechanical principles based on the laws of motion.

My introduction to using a scientific approach to coaching diving occurred during the spring before Gilbert arrived on the campus. One day, Doc Councilman asked me who Isaac M. Newton was and if I knew what I was talking about when coaching. On the same day, one of my divers, who had transferred from Ohio University, explained to me how a diver should perform an inward dive in the layout position when using Newton's Third Law. The suggestions from these two people led me to immediately realize that I didn't know anything about diving and that there was a much better way to coach the sport then in the way I had been using.

Doc Councilman had just gone through the same experience of coaching swimming the same way as did the better coaches. One day he decided to change his coaching by using scientific principles which led him to writing the book "The Science of Swimming." This book changed the thinking of coaches throughout the world and has continued to be the best source for coaching competitive swimming up to the present time.

When Gilbert arrived on the campus, I immediately started to coach diving using basic mechanical principles of motion that I found in books written by two great bio-mechanics experts: Geoffrey Dyson and George Rackham. I tried out this new approach to coaching when first analyzing simple dives and, as my confidence grew, I gradually applied the scientific principles to more difficult dives. This made it possible for me to form a solid base for analyzing all dives regardless of how difficult they were to perform. Coaching diving in this manner was not only stimulating and challenging but actually fun. I found that analyzing dives with a scientific approach was almost like working a crossword puzzle, particularly when trying to figure out how divers generate multi-somersaults and fast twisting motions. Naturally, there were times when questions arose that were questionable and confusing, but they were usually answered when turning to Newton.

Although changing to a scientific approach when analyzing and coaching dives was a challenge, it was also obvious that it offered a quicker and far better way to coach diving in the direction of perfection then by copying others or by using trial and error methods. Using such an approach was also much like using formulas when working out mathematical and scientific problems. I also was amazed to find that this new approach to coaching greatly reduced the effort when searching for solutions to the proper performance of dives.

Obviously, Gilbert's quick claim to fame encouraged other divers to attend Indiana University even though we were still on probation for three more years. The new divers soon found that I was not saying the same things over and over or offering next to nothing that was new to motivate or stimulate them . . . or myself. I was also no longer doing the same thing all other coaches were doing which was copying the movements made by other good divers or using methods believed to improve their dives, while not knowing how or why the movements worked.

Every college coach knows that the success of a sport requires some financial help. When I first arrived at Indiana, the swimming teams in the country were given twenty scholarships for a four-year period. I was given one of those scholarships each year for men's diving. Nothing was given for a women's diving team because there was no program offered by Universities for female athletes at that time. The first collegiate diving programs started with Coach Bruce Harlan at the University of Michigan and by me when at Ohio University in 1958. When title IX was introduced in the 1970's the number of scholarships for males was reduced to eleven, one of which I received every four years. The women's swimming and diving programs received eighteen scholarships from which I received two every four years. Unlike previous years when scholarships were only offered to males, scholarships for both male and females could be broken down so that more than one person could receive a portion of the scholarship which was not possible before Title IX.

This short story is given with the purpose of encouraging those who wish to succeed in coaching to form goals that at times appear to be hopeless and impossible to achieve. They should not be afraid to question themselves and make changes in their teaching and coaching methods. Coaches and divers should develop a curiosity for why things happen in a dive and be creative by trying different methods in correcting errors while keeping the scientific principles in mind. And if they don't work, try something else. Coaches should also not underestimate the talents and the abilities of their divers or themselves which often take time to surface.

I truly believe that any coach who learns to use mechanical principles based on the laws of motion can form a sound scientific base that will make it possible for them to answer every question and solve every problem found in the execution of any dive. There is no limit to what coaches and divers can accomplish if they are willing to take the challenge with an open mind. I also believe that the reason I was able to succeed so quickly when under such adverse conditions, was because I decided to take the challenge and change the way I saw the sport.

ACKNOWLEDGEMENTS

The following persons are recognized for offering their assistance, knowledge, and experience that has made it possible for this book to be written.

Robert Clotworthy - Olympic gold medalist in 1956 who recently wrote the history of competitive diving and offered historical and scientific information for this text.

Geoffrey Dyson - (England) the brilliant bio-mechanics expert who introduced Isaac M. Newton's Laws to the sports world which included diving.

Jan Gabriel - one of my first female divers who is totally dedicated to the sport and continues to endlessly work with U.S. Diving in making diving better for all of us. Her dedication and knowledge has been priceless in making better coaches and teachers.

Jerry George - showed the diving world how moves in gymnastics could also be applied to diving.

Dennis Goldman - shared many bio-mechanical principles that are used in diving, giving us a better understanding of the sport.

Bruce Harlan - Olympic gold medal winner in 1948, first diving coach ever hired on the college level. Harlan introduced several dives now performed in competitions and was just beginning to understand the need for physics in diving when he was killed in a tragic accident in 1959.

Mark Lenzi - 1992 Gold medal Olympic champion who helped show me the way to coaching the sport and never lost faith in me on his way to becoming the world's best.

Doris Miller - (Canada) outstanding bio-mechanics wizard who has contributed invaluable information relating to the movements used in the performance of dives.

Peter Panai - (Australia) diving coach and bio-mechanics expert who was one of the first to recognize the importance and need for basic physics in teaching and coaching diving.

George Rackham - (England) - showed how Newton's Laws of Motion apply to springboard and platform diving which opened the doors for a new and better way of analyzing, coaching, and teaching diving.

Fred Schlicting - one of my first collegiate divers who turned my world of coaching completely around when he introduced me to Newton's Laws of Motion.

Sam Slovinoff - (Russia and U.S.A.) a well-educated teacher and coach in the science of diving who has shared his knowledge with many coaches and divers.

Ulla and Matti Turnpeinin - (Finland) both have an excellent understanding of the sport of diving and have produced several studies related to the science of the sport. They stand with the best in the world in revealing how people should perform dives using scientific principles.

Derek Travis - (England) his lectures on mechanical principles, philosophy, and psychology have shown the diving world that there is a better way of teaching and coaching the sport

Grunde Vegard - (Norway) famous diver and coach with a bio-mechanics background who gave me some vital information concerning twisting somersault dives.

Special tribute is given to the following for taking an active part in helping me write this text. They spent countless hours editing and proof reading the book and that was started in 1965. Thank you for your untiring efforts and priceless comments.

Sheilagh Boudia,
Cary Finneran,
Gretchen Hirsch,
Holt and Debra Manis,
Sean McCarthy,
Jody Riskowski,
John Wingfield

ABOUT THE AUTHOR

Hobie Billingsley is simply the most influential person that the sport of diving has ever known! His coaching successes are legendary. Hobie's innovations, no-nonsense approach and use of mechanical principles transformed the sport from the dark ages to the science that it is today. His organizational skills brought order to a sport that, at one time, offered little leadership.

A five-time Olympic coach, he was the third coach to ever coach women in any sport at the college level. Having coached divers who won 115 national titles, he was National Diving Coach of the year 11 times and was inducted into five different Halls of Fame. He also gave the official's Oath at the 1996 Olympics in Atlanta, an honor never before given to a diving coach.

His organizational skills and ability to bring people together led to many groups that are essential to diving today. Hobie formed the World Diving Coaches Association in 1968 which brought all the diving coaches together from all over the world to exchange ideas, philosophies, and share diving information. This led to global friendships and the forming of many diving competitions that helped in the growth of world diving. He also formed the American Diving Coaches Association in 1971, now known as the Professional Diving Coaches Association (P.D.C.A.), which has greatly helped organize and bring better cooperation to coaches and divers.

Hobie's innovations didn't stop here. They extend to books, training aides, and diving equipment. He even inadvertently invented the Port-A-Pit. With his divers receiving injuries while practicing hurdles and landing in a pile of sawdust, Hobie decided to dig a pit in front of the board and fill it with foam rubber to make the landing much softer. Someone in California saw this new innovation in the newspaper and decided to package the idea which is now used in such sports as gymnastics and in track events that allows the performer to land without injury. He has also designed several diving wells one of which was the IUPUI natatorium in Indianapolis which is believed to be the best in the United States.

Hobie ran a diving camp for youngsters at Indiana University for over 25 years from which a movie was made "Hobie's Heroes" that won many film festivals and placed second in the Academy Awards for documentaries. Hobie was a showman as well! He toured all over the United States for 15 years doing a one hour seven-act show with his two close friends, 1948 Olympic Champion, Bruce Harlan, and later with the University of Michigan's diving coach, Dick Kimball. They performed at country clubs and professional water shows throughout the United States and other parts of the world.

A very compassionate and personable person, Hobie served his country in other areas other than diving. He is a veteran of World War II after serving in the Army Air Corps where he escaped death many times mostly from the poor shooting by the enemy on Okinawa. On a personal note, I am honored that he picked me to attend Indiana University where he taught me the mechanics of diving, mentored me, and made me a better man. I am also honored to be the last "Hobie's Heroes" when he retired. Thank you, Hobie for letting me be a part on your life!

Mark Lenzi – Two-time World Champion, 1992 Olympic gold, and 1996 bronze medal winner.

CHAPTER I

AN INTRODUCTION TO COMPETITIVE DIVING

Competitive diving is a unique sport that offers individuals the chance to enhance their motor development and kinesthetic movements resulting in happier, healthier, adolescents. The diving program offers divers the opportunity to develop a competitive spirit and improve performance through instruction by coaches who communicate with others at all levels, from the beginner to the most elite.

Several other sports may be more popular than diving, but few can match the beauty that is portrayed by its participants. A diver combines the skills of a gymnast with those of a ballet dancer, all within a mere one and eight tenths of a second. Using many elements of airborne acrobatics, a diver can perform somersaults and twists while expressing subtle and graceful movements with ease before entering the water. When performed properly from the tower and the springboard, diving proves to be a thrilling experience for both the performer and the spectator. Competitive diving is basically a "one on one" sport where the talents and athletic abilities of one diver are matched with those of another. Few will dispute that competitive diving is an art "and" a science. An art in respect to the great amount of time and practice needed to develop and express certain aesthetic movements; and a science in respect to applying certain mechanical principles to basic and intricate actions that are essential for a successful performance of the dive.

Whether diving for recreation or competition, participants often find a challenge in attempting something they don't believe they can do; yet, through proper instruction and some practice, accomplish the unbelievable. Normally, persons who learn to dive as a form of recreation are satisfied with learning basic dives that require fundamental skills, little form, and limited acrobatic ability. They also find the activity challenging, interesting, and at times, scary. A beginner diver can experience as much satisfaction in learning to perform a basic dive, like a front jackknife, as an accomplished diver when learning to perform a triple twisting one and half somersault. Whether a beginner or an expert, divers soon realize that their performance is completely dependent on their own individual movement patterns.

How much a person can accomplish in competitive diving depends much on their physical ability, age, training, type of program, kind of instruction, available diving facilities, personal habits, psychological and physiological make up, emotional stability, environment, and time allotted for the sport. Whatever, if a person has the desire and perseverance to learn and participates in a program that has reasonable facilities, teaching aids, and offers some guidance and instruction, he or she will learn how to dive to some degree. The diver will also learn that practice is necessary if improvement is to occur. Like learning to play a musical instrument, very little is accomplished when the student plays only when taking a lesson.

Those wishing to dive competitively must start from the very beginning by first mastering the forward approach and the back take off from the springboard. The divers then learn to perform basic dives that involve body control, grace, and a limited amount of acrobatic movement. To learn how to perform these basic dives, and all other dives, requires divers to first create a basic concept (mental picture) of how the dive is to be performed, which is usually formed by watching others. With the aid of a teacher or coach, the divers can then be guided through certain fundamental movements performed in sequence during the learning process. Once the basic dives are successfully performed, they can then move on to learning dives that are more difficult and challenging: In following this procedure, divers find that dives are performed in one of four directions and are divided into six different groups:

1. *Forward-* dives that rotate in a forward direction when leaving the end of the board in a forward direction.

2. *Backward* - standing backward on the end ofthe board or platform and rotating in a backward direction.

3. *Reverse* - facing forward when leaving the board or platform and rotating backward on the take off.

4. *Inward* - standing backward on the board or platform and rotating forward on the take off.

5. *Twisting* - dives performed from any of the first four groups that rotate at least 90 degrees on the longitudinal (long) axis while the body rotates at least 180 degrees on the horizontal (somersaulting) axis

6. *Arm stand* - dives that are performed from a handstand starting position on a platform of the diving tower.

Divers learn to perform simple and difficult dives by mastering certain movements that are normally performed in progression. For example, when learning to perform a back dive in the layout position, the diver must first learn how to properly stand on the board in balance and fall backwards while landing on his or her head. The movement is usually performed with the use of a teaching aid which is usually the instructor or coach holding the diver during the process. The next move is to learn to perform the movement without the aid of the mentor or teaching aid. The diver then moves on to performing a back dive while taking a little jump, etc. Such progressions are found in Chapter 3 which offers a course in teaching basic dives.

Competitive diving used to be an easy sport because there was little more involved in practice than the coach instructing the diver to perform the dives on the springboard and/or tower which did not give cause for long work outs. However, major changes in the sport over the last seventy years, now demand more time and energy and better instruction to offer elite performances by divers than ever before. Competitive diving now involves goals that cannot be achieved without diving programs that provide all of the basic fundamentals that are needed to compete at any level. Even at the basic competitive level, the diving program can be very complicated due to the many different related activities that must be addressed in preparing a diver for competition. In other words, the whole competitive diving program has become a very complex matter that constantly demands total dedication from the divers and coaches if top performances are to be achieved.

Though most people already engaged in competitive diving feel they are organized and really understand the sport, many, in reality, are in sad need of forming realistic goals and knowledge from sources that can best aid them. In working with divers and coaches over the years, I found that everyone in diving is subject to certain weaknesses and strengths in various areas and not consciously aware of them. Some coaches can communicate well with their divers but have a limited knowledge of mechanical principles used in the execution of dives while others may be strong in both areas but have no idea of how to motivate divers. One of the most common weaknesses found among today's coaches is in offering the "correct" information to the divers when analyzing their movements. It would be wise for some coaches to make as great an effort to improve their own coaching techniques as when trying to improve those of their divers. It appears that many of the problems that concern both parties could then be solved with some guidance and direction much of which is offered in this text.

Moving into its second millennium, the sport of diving has grown to such unbelievable proportions that it has surpassed everyone's wildest dreams. Because such growth has made the sport very competitive, divers must be in excellent physical, mental, and psychological condition to perform through intensive training programs that necessitate a great amount of instruction, time, energy, and equipment. To execute dives that were seemingly impossible only a few years ago, divers must now become familiar with various segments in diving that relate to technology, physics, and psychology. This approach to competitive diving has often caused some to be confused and frustrated when attempting to reach desired goals. Therefore, it is hoped that some of the answers to the various questions and problems facing divers and coaches at the present time can be solved with some guidance and direction from this book.

With this in mind, divers and coaches may better understand what it takes to achieve better performances in competitions by:

* Improving communication between the diver and the coach.

* Being aware that diving skills are learned through instruction and imitating others.
* Helping to recognize fundamental diving concepts based on scientific principles.
* Creating and exercising sound administrative principles, standards, and objectives in a diving program.
* Learning to properly analyze the movements used in the performance of dives.
* Recognizing the safety factors and legal concerns related to competitive diving.
* Learning how to instill confidence in a diver through the coach.
* Becoming aware of the basic weaknesses and strengths that many divers and coaches possess in various areas of the diving program.
* Using various teaching aids that can be used when training divers.
* Developing a sound training program that is conducive to the needs of the divers.
* Encouraging divers to develop a good competitive attitude and a sound thinking pattern when performing dives.
* Recognizing the difference between " teaching" and "coaching" and how to do both.
* Recognizing the range in which a coach and teacher can instruct competitive divers.
* Being aware of the difficulty in recognizing talent and evaluating a diver's potential to dive.
* Developing a sound competitive philosophy and a positive attitude by the divers and coaches.
* Showing an open mind and willingness to change when new ideas and diving techniques are offered.

HISTORY OF COMPETITIVE DIVING

Origin of Competitive Diving

In the latter part of the nineteenth century, acrobatic diving appeared from an outgrowth of Swedish Ling and German Turnverein gymnastics which included tumblers performing stunts from docks, boats, piers, and other swimming areas on lakes and rivers. Though the depths of the water differed, it offered a far better landing cushion than gymnasium mats and floors. With the use of gadgetry, such as wagon springs under the fulcrums, primitive wooden boards were used to give better spring when performing difficult stunts.

The oldest swimming club in Germany, the Berliner Schwimvin, which was also known as the "Neptune" introduced international diving contests in 1881 which included divers from Sweden. These contests were derived from arguments between various athletic clubs that claimed to have the best divers. Diving contests soon after occurred in England which spread to Canada around the 1880s. and with the organization of the A.AU. in 1888, diving contests were started on the East Coast of the United States.

Diving was first introduced in the Olympics in 1900 in Paris where divers gave exhibitions in the Seine river. Diving tables for dives were created and published in 1882 followed by the first recorded diving contest which was held in the United Kingdom as the "Championships of Scotland" in 1889. Strangely, the forming of any diving rules did not occur until 1891. The first world diving championship meet made its debut at the 1904 Olympics which was staged in Saint Louis, Missouri and included only two countries - the United States and Germany.

As fancy diving spread throughout England, another form of diving competition called "Graceful Diving" emerged that required divers to perform a plain front dive, known as the "Swallow Dive" and later as the "Swan Dive." This dive was repeated several times from different heights and the diver who performed the dive the best was declared the winner. The competition was only performed from facilities outdoors that ranged from heights of five to ten-meters as no indoor facilities were available at that time. Annual "National Graceful Diving Championships were staged for a number of years then replaced with a similar event called "Plain High Diving" which was very similar to graceful diving. This contest had divers perform two Swan dives from the five-meter and two Swan dives from the ten-meter platforms with the winner being the one who best performed the four dives. Believe it or not, this event was introduced in the 1912 Olympics and continued until the completion of the 1924 Olympics, when it was dropped due to the loss of public appeal. Throughout these early years, another form of competitive diving emerged in Sweden known as "Fancy High Diving that soon spread to England. This contest involved the performance of simple dives that rotated forward, backward, and inward. Though this event was soon discarded like the others, it did have some influence in categorizing dives into different groups used in the 1924 Olympics and now in all modern-
day diving contests.

Diving in The United States

Diving contests were introduced in the United States from England at the tum of the century with the first recorded diving contest ever staged in this country between the University of Pennsylvania and Harvard University. The sport received the attention of spectators worldwide when Dr. George E. Sheldon, an American, won the first Olympic gold medal in his home town of Saint Louis, Missouri. How Sheldon won the contest has been questionable over the years because it is not clear if the contest was from the springboard or high platform. Whatever, research has proven that there was only one diving event in the Olympics which involved two countries and five contestants; two from the United States and three from Germany. Right from the very first diving event in an Olympics, a great controversy occurred over the judging when it was seen that all three of the judges were from the United

States. Unbelievably, they discussed the performance of each dive with one another *before* giving their scores - and this resulted in Dr. Sheldon winning the contest. Believing they had the best divers, the Germans felt they had been robbed of a rightful first place finish and protested the outcome. Unfortunately, competitive diving did not have diving referees in those days, so the protest was presented to the director of the aquatic events, James E. Sullivan, who, being an American and was not present at the contest, rejected the German protest. This gentleman is still well recognized for the "Sullivan Award" which is given annually to the best amateur athlete in the United States. Unfortunately, controversies over the judging of diving have continued to occur right up to the present day.

Starting on the East Coast, swimming and diving competitions gradually spread throughout the country and by 1924, contestants from clubs, colleges, and universities were taking part in dual and championship meets. Interest and development of diving on the West Coast came to pass through the efforts of Ernest Brandstein who was a member of the 1908 Swedish Olympic diving team and migrated to America where he became the swimming and diving coach at Stanford University in 1912. His ideas and methods of teaching and coaching diving were so impressive that he was recognized as the pioneer of the sport in the United States and was later selected as the first American to ever coach diving at an Olympics which was in 1924. With the Olympic Games continuing to be the ultimate goal for all amateur athletes, the divers from Germany and Eric Bergval of Sweden continued to dominate competitive diving in the world until 1920 when the American men and women divers stepped into the lime light when winning three Olympic gold medals. From that time on, the Americans continued to develop most of the world's best men and women divers on the springboard and tower until the completion of the 1988 Olympics in Seoul, Korea - spanning World and Olympic dominance in the sport for nearly seven decades.

Beginning with the 1952 Olympic Games, other countries such as Russia, East Germany, Mexico, Canada, Sweden, and Italy began to produce excellent divers that challenged America's world supremacy over the next twenty years. America ' s dominance was challenged by Chinese male and female divers who entered the competitive diving arena in the late 1 970' s. They immediately stunned the world with their divers performing the most difficult dives with flawless motion and phenomenal entries from the springboard and tower. What astounded everyone even more was the youth of their divers who averaged thirteen or fourteen years of age. China has since shared much of its success in competitive diving with divers from Russia, and more recently with Canada, who have also consistently fared well in international contests. Even with the fantastic divers developed by these countries, no single diver has ever made more of an impact on the sport of competitive diving than the American, Greg Louganis. Throughout his brilliant career, Louganis proved over and over to be the greatest competitive diver of all time. His outstanding performances in winning four Olympic, five World Cup, six Pan American, and nearly fifty national championships attracted the attention of sports enthusiasts world-wide as he became the hero of nearly every person who has ever had the desire to dive. Having qualified to compete in the 1980 Olympics staged in Moscow, Russia, and having won a silver medal at the 1976 Olympics at the age of 16, had it not been for the boycott made against the Russians by the United States that prevented all American athletes from competing, Louganis probably would have won six gold Olympic medals.

Female Divers

Though some females trained using college facilities for many years, no competitive program was available for them, so they were not able to represent their schools. Unfortunately, some of the greatest female divers in the United States, Pat McCormick, winner of four gold Olympic medals, Cynthia Potter, member of three Olympic teams and winner of twenty eight national championships while at Indiana; Lesley Bush, the Olympic Tower champion while in high school who continued her career at Indiana University where she won many titles at all three levels of competition; and Micki King, the 1972 Olympic Springboard champion from the University of Michigan , never competed for their universities . Their position in the sport changed when Title IX was passed in 1972 and women athletes were given an equal opportunity to participate in sports at colleges and universities.

The move to include women in collegiate sports was not very popular for it meant that the facilities, budgets, training programs, administration departments, and everything else related to men's athletics was to be equally shared with the female programs. Since nothing in the athletic programs was ever planned to include female participation, sharing half of everything was a tough pill to swallow for male athletes, coaches, and administrators. Once in motion, Title IX was very helpful in developing female athletic programs at the higher learning institutions, but it was also a disaster for many non-revenue male programs which are still being discontinued in nearly every college and university in the country.

Since the law requires females to have the same number of scholarships as males, it has not proven to be fair to those in the men's programs because eighty-five of the scholarships for males are given to football teams. Since there is no such team requiring that number of scholarships for a women's sport, the athletic

programs have either dropped some of the men's non-revenue programs or added more women's sports to make the number of scholarships equal in both programs. Finding it less costly to eliminate sports for men's programs than to add more sports for women, athletic departments have dropped many of the men's non-revenue sports. It is frustrating to see a men's swimming team, such as UC.LA, place third in the N.C.A.A. Swimming and Diving Championships only to be dropped from their athletic program the next year. It may also be noted that nearly all of the female sports programs created by Title IX were first coached by males, but this has gradually changed to where most female sports are now coached by females.

Governing Bodies

In the early years when competitive diving became popular, it was obvious that the sport needed some rules and regulations to organize, direct, guide, and control the competitions. As previously mentioned, the first rule book for competitive diving was created in 1889 by representatives from different clubs in England. The rule book was very general in nature offering little more than a few dives that could be used in competition along with some simple rules concerning the administration, conduct, and judging of the contests. In 1908, the Federation International de Natation Amateur (F.I.N.A.) was formed as the governing body for all international aquatic contests in the world including diving rules. As competitive diving progressed, more governing bodies were formed for the purpose of running local and national contests. Many of these governing bodies offered their own rule books with most of the information adopted from the F.I.NA. rule book. Some of the governing bodies for competitive diving now found in the United States include: National Interscholastic Athletic Association (N.I.H.S.A.A.), National Collegiate Athletic Association (N.C.A.A.), Amateur Athletic Union (A.AU.), and United States Diving (U.S.D). The F.I.N.A., A.AU., and the U.S.D. are the governing bodies that direct contests outside the jurisdiction of the learning institutions.

Competitive diving that offers meets for divers in the United States is currently divided into three age group levels : The age group has competitions ranging from nine and under up to eighteen years of age; the senior level , which is for advanced divers that age from twelve years and older; and the masters level program, that starts at the age of twenty five and has had divers perform who are well into their nineties, has proven that one is never too old to dive. Naturally, the rule books had to revamp their rules to meet the needs of the three different age levels of competition.

THE TREND OF WORLD COMPETITIVE DIVING

To follow the trend of competitive diving as it is seen by the world today requires one to go back to its origin and note how diving changed over the years in each of its stages of development. This relates to the philosophy of competitive diving, the changes in diving equipment, the growth of diving conditions, the increase in the number of dives, divers, and coaches, the development of different teaching and coaching aids, and the growth in technology and sports science.

The philosophy regarding the format of the competition

In examining competitive diving from its beginning, it is recognized that a basic philosophy concerning how the judges were to determine the best diver was never offered and because of its absence, changes the rules were constantly and erratically made over the years particularly in the selection of specific diving positions for certain compulsory dives. For example: the rules required the forward dive to be performed in a pike position for two or three years, then changed to the layout position for a year or two only to again be changed back to the pike position. Other radical changes were made in the 1939 National A.A.U. rule book that required compulsory dives performed on the three-meter springboard to include a flying forward somersault; a back- dive pike; a reverse dive layout; an inward dive layout; and a back dive with a half twist layout. A year or two later, the dives were changed back to a front dive, back dive, reverse dive, and a front dive all performed in the layout position except the inward dive which was done in the pike position. Divers had no choice in the position for which the compulsory dives were to be performed and no explanation for the changes was ever offered by the rule's committees.

At least some direction was offered when the rules were changed that required the divers to perform a certain number of simple dives plus a number of difficult dives to determine the winner of the contest. The simple dives, none of which rotated more than 180 degrees, were listed in the rule books as "compulsory" or "required" dives and were listed as the easiest dives that could be performed from each of the five diving groups. At first, the easiest dive from group three, the "!sander" and later changed to the "Half gainer" and currently referred to as the "reverse" dive was not required to be performed due to the danger of the diver hitting the board that was then elevated, by the rules, at least two inches from the back end to the tip (photo 6, Page 117). The compulsory dives were also performed in the order of the diving groups which meant that everyone had to perform the front dive first, the back dive, second, and so on. Though never stated by the rules, the rationale for everyone performing the same dives in the same order and in a particular position was to permit the judges to compare the performance of one diver with that of another when performing the same dive. The same procedure was also used for the performance of voluntary dives but had little merit for comparing dives because the divers often selected different dives from each of the five groups that could be performed in different positions.

The purpose for performing compulsory dives in each of the five groups was never explained. Therefore, it must be assumed that the intent was to offer the divers the opportunity to display grace, beauty, and body control when performing simple dives involving basic moves. The assumed purpose for performing more difficult dives was to express acrobatic ability, strength, explosive power, and physical awareness with the control of certain body movements. With the exception of the compulsory dives, all of the other dives in the rule books could be used as "optional" dives with at least one dive performed from four of the five groups. Again, a dive from the third group was usually avoided because it was considered dangerous in hitting the board. The format of four compulsory and four optional dives in a contest on the one-meter and three-meter springboards was used until 1929, when the rules were again changed to include five compulsory (required) and five optional (voluntary) dives with one dive from each group. Unbelievably, performing the compulsory dives in order and in a specific position continued for forty years which left many of the dives offered in the rule books never to be performed by anyone.

In 1947 and 1948, the F.I.N.A. and A.A.U. rule books required that all divers perform a front dive with a full twist in the layout position as a compulsory dive which was used in the 1948 Olympics. Following the Olympics, the half twist replaced the full twist as a compulsory dive with no explanation offered. It is apparent that all of the chaos created by changing the required dives nearly every other year could have been avoided if a philosophy had been established in the early stages of the sport that simply expressed the basic objectives of the diving contest that would best determine the winner of the contest.

Another radical change made by the rules committee in the late 1940s that only lasted for a year or two, required divers to perform *seven* voluntary dives. The format had the divers perform three required and two optional dives in the preliminaries, two required and one optional dive in the semi-finals, and one required (the reverse dive again) and four optional dives in the finals. This contest of 13 dives meant that a diver could actually perform three voluntary dives from the same group. With such a small selection of dives found in the first four groups of dives, divers who were proficient in performing twisting somersault div s had a tremendous advantage over those who were not proficient twisting divers. Needless-to-say, the divers who performed good twisting somersault dives usually won the contest. Fortunately, this rule was quickly changed back to divers performing only five required and five optional dives.

One national championship meet staged in Louisville, Kentucky, in the early 1970's resulted in a change of several rules. The one-meter event had over 120 divers performing the same compulsory dive in the same order. The event took nearly eight hours to complete which left everyone in a state of total exhaustion. This was particularly evident for the judges who had to judge 120 front dives in a row followed by a 120 of the other four compulsory dives in order. The divers also performed the optional dives in the same order though some dives differed from diver to diver. A year or two later, that meet caused the rules to be changed that allowed divers to perform optional dives in any order they wished. Incidentally, the meet also resulted in the creation of qualifying meets staged around the country that drastically reduced the number of divers that could qualify to participate in the national championships.

A new format was later presented to jazz up interest in competitive diving by permitting divers to select any dives from the five groups where the total degree of difficulty of the five dives did not exceed a certain limit. This rule permitted divers to perform the dives in any order which was eventually adopted by the F.I.N.A. and the rest of the world. From that time on, it was not uncommon for a diver to perform a simple dive like a front dive, while another diver executed a double twisting 1½ somersault both of which were used as compulsory dives in the preliminaries. This new version of performing a great variety of compulsory dives, some of which had never been used before in competition, made the diving contest more interesting though it deviated from the unwritten philosophy that all divers perform the same simple dive, so the judges could compare the performance of one dive with that of another.

Not long after, another big change in the rules was made when a sixth optional dive was offered for men's contests from the one-meter springboard and for both men and women on the three-meter springboard. The rule did not permit women to perform a sixth dive on the one- meter springboard because the number of dives that women could perform from that height was very limited due to their perceived "lack of strength." This rule, still in effect, allows those who must perform six dives, to select the sixth dive from any of the five groups which is usually from the group they favor the most. Since the fifth (twisting) group provides a greater variety of dives, most divers select the sixth dive from that group. Again, no explanation was ever given by the rules committee for adding the sixth dive.

The induction of new competitive dives

Starting from around 1932, competitive diving went through an era of about twenty-five years when a new dive was rarely added to the rule books. Not until after World War II was there any activity regarding the addition of new acrobatic dives. Up to that time, divers could not perform dives in competition that were not in the F.I.N.A. rule book. Since all diving rule books world-wide adopted the rules presented by F.I.N.A. from it forming in 1908, there was no incentive for divers to create new dives, though many were created with the use of the trampoline.

This "dive barrier" limiting the dives that could be performed in competitions by the F.I.N.A. diving rule book prevented little to no growth in the sport during this period. The dive barrier was finally lifted in the early 1980s when a formula was created by a gymnast, Robert Bollinger of Rockford, Illinois. The formula was his thesis for obtaining a college master's degree which presented a system that offered a calculable scale for the degrees of difficulty of any stunt performed in gymnastics including any skill not yet performed in competition. Of course, this new system was immediately adopted by the World Gymnastics Federation.

Soon after, Constantine Domilov, a top gymnastic coach from Russia who was appointed as the Russian diving coach for the 1972 Olympics, decided to try and convert the formula from gymnastics to competitive diving. His bold attempt was in the form of a book that was very difficult to read so it made no impact on competitive diving for years. In 1979, Herb Flewelling, the Canadian who later invented the bubbler system, came to the rescue by having the book translated from Russian into English. This new translation was reduced to the size of a booklet and was accidentally brought to the attention of Bob Bollinger while he was visiting my home. After making some minor adjustments, Bollinger' s formula was finally made accurate enough to be used for competitive diving. First rejected by F.I.N.A, it was eventually accepted for competitive diving in the early 1980s after it was used by divers in the United states for a couple of years. From that time on, dives that were not in the F.I.N.A. rule book could be performed in competition if a member of the F.I.N.A. rules committee viewed the performance of the dive and assigned it a degree of difficulty by using the formula. The new formula has resulted in the addition of many new dives now found in the F.I.N.A. rule book.

International competitions

Before World War II, American divers rarely competed in contests outside the country. Then after the 1948 Olympics, American swimmers and divers began to visit other countries, giving exhibitions and acting as goodwill ambassadors for the United States. These exhibitions were eventually changed to competitions which encouraged countries around the world to form their own governing bodies, under the control of F.I.N.A. Such events as the European Championships, Asian Games, Pan American Games, the World Championships and many others are now common events offered for diver. With all of this activity, the Olympic Games have remained the proving ground for the world's best athletes which, of course, includes diving.

An event that further unified those involved with competitive diving and encouraged the formation of more international competitions occurred on October 26, 1968 at the Olympic Games in Mexico City, Mexico where the World Diving Coaches Association (Wo.D.C.A.), pronounced "Vodka", was formed. Up to that time, divers and coaches at meets usually regarded the other competitors as the enemy and avoided each other which did little to encourage any growth in the sport. The creation of Wo.D.C.A. changed that attitude by gathering diving coaches from all over the world with the purpose of becoming friends and exchanging diving information, experiences, and philosophies that could help the sport grow. When the United States and other diving powers of the world had competed in only one or two major competitions each year, this new, cosmopolitan alliance encouraged countries to invite divers and coaches from other countries to share friendly competitions in their meets such as the Swedish Cup, the Grand Pre, F.I.N.A. cup, and many others which are now offered all over the world nearly all year round.

Amateurism versus professionalism

In the beginning, nearly every person who coached or competed in diving throughout the world was an amateur. In other words, no one got paid for their coaching or diving and participated out of their love for the sport. With the rejuvenation of the Olympic Games in 1896, all of the competitors had to be amateurs to compete. Most of the coaches and trainers were also amateurs which made the competitions fair for all. Avery Brundidge was the president of the International Olympic Committee for many years and staunchly supported amateur sports throughout his whole life. He forbade professional athletes from taking part in the Olympic Games and was greatly pressured over the years to change his convictions that stood fast until his death soon after the 1972 Olympics. Following his passing, sports began to fade more and more from amateurism as athletes and coaches in many sports turned professional.

Diving coaches in the United States began to emerge out of clubs in the 1950s where they coached various age groups and received no or very little pay for their services. Then in 1954, diving coaches began to be hired by colleges, universities, and high schools. Swimming coaches who also attempted to coach diving found that, due to the rapid growth of their swimming teams, they no longer had time to coach both sports so were forced to either employ a diving coach, or simply ignore that portion of their program which encouraged many swimming coaches to try and eliminate diving as part of the swimming program. As the need for diving coaches increased, they soon began to get paid for their services which encouraged many diving coaches to seriously consider coaching as a profession.

During this period of professional growth, most of the athletes and coaches behind the "Iron Curtain" were subsidized by their governments which off-set the fairness of many competitions performed in the Olympic Games and other international contests. Few believed that it was fair for some countries to pay their athletes and coaches while others in the rest of the world maintained the standard of amateurism. The United States seemed to straddle the fence on this issue because many of the athletes who participated in sports at the college level received scholarships for their efforts and all of their coaches were professionals.

By the time the 1980 Olympics Games were held in Moscow, Russia, athletes were being paid to compete in many different sporting events. It did not take long for the world to realize that the chances of an amateur athlete beating a professional in the Olympics, or any other important competition, were very slim. With the aid of television, world-wide interests in sports at that time was escalating so rapidly that it became a multi-million-dollar business and has now reached a point where it is at the multi- billion-dollar annual level. One only needs to look back to the American basketball "Dream Team" that performed in the 1992 Olympics in Barcelona, Spain to recognize how difficult it would have been for any amateur team to beat those who were the best in the world and earning millions of dollars a year for their efforts. The Spanish athletes who competed in Barcelona were awarded $1,000,000 for a gold medal, $800,000 for silver, and $600,000 for a bronze medal. It was no wonder that so many of their athletes "choked" when trying to perform. It is also interesting to note that the United States seriously considered awarding $50,000 for gold, $35,000 for silver, and $25,000 for bronze to the American divers in the 1996 Olympics as an incentive for them to work harder and remain committed to the sport. Since that time, the whole concept of amateurism in sports has changed or has been ignored. It now appears that the only sports that entertain amateur athletes are those that are non-revenue. This point is illustrated when one observes how rare it is to find a non-revenue sport shown on television.

The rise of diving coaches

In the United States

In the sport of diving, the manner in which persons learned to dive in the United States during the first fifty years of the twentieth century was through the efforts of a hand full of teachers and coaches who were affiliated with clubs. These coaches were poorly informed about the sport but were willing to give their all to those who wished to learn. During that time, the instructor often learned as much about diving as did the student. Those wanting to learn had few educational sources that related to diving, so taught themselves by trial and error and by copying the movements of others who were successful in performing certain dives. Most of what was learned about diving came from diving enthusiasts who were first curious of how to perform a dive, and when unsuccessful in attempting a dive, often became confused and frustrated and would attempt to perform the dive a different way or quit trying. As the sport gradually grew and became more popular, more people began to take an interest in diving and took on the task of teaching and coaching others. As progress was made, those who were good at teaching people to dive later developed into the best coaches, because they could offer the best information from a basic progressive learning perspective.

Very few diving coaches were found in the world during the first half of the twentieth century. A little more than a half dozen persons coached diving in the United States who knew much about competitive diving. Ernest Brandstein had installed the most complete training quarters for diving in the United States which was proven by the string of divers he produced in the 1920s and 1930s that included such national and Olympic champions as Clarence Pinkston, Al White, Pete Desjardins, Marjorie Gestring, and others. Fred Cady, another diving coach from Philadelphia and later from the Los Angeles Athletic Club, produced such greats as Georgia Coleman, Micky Riley, Harold "Dutch" Smith, Dorothy Poynton and a host of others. Cady's divers placed 1st, 2nd and 3rd at the 1932 Olympics in the men's springboard and platform contests; 1st, 2nd, and 3rd in the Women's platform, and 1st in the Women's springboard contests. Other great divers during that period were Aileen Riggen and Helen Meany who won most of the national diving titles between 1920 and 1928.

Most of the teachers and coaches were either associated with a club or were swimming coaches in high schools or colleges who were trapped into coaching diving as a part of the swimming team. The premier swimming and diving coach on the college level at that time was Mike Peppe, of The OhioState University. He started his coaching career in 1931 and consistently produced the nation's and world's best divers from 1937 until the early nineteen sixties. Starting with Jim Patterson, some of his greatest divers included Al Patnik, Earl Clark, Miller Anderson, Frank Dempsey, Charlie Batterman, Hobie Billingsley, Bruce Harlan, Fletcher Gilders, Don Harper, Dr. Ron O'Brien, Bob Clotworthy, Tom Gompf, Lou Vitucci, Jerry Harrison, and many others.

Bruce Harlan was the first diving coach ever hired by a university which occurred in 1954 at the University of Michigan. Hobie Billingsley, who in 1957 was hired at Ohio University as the second college diving coach, was followed by Dick Kimball who in 1959 was hired by the University of Michigan after Harlan's tragic death. At that time, the diving coaches at the University of Michigan and Indiana University were instrumental in breaking up Mike Peppe's diving dynasty of 25 years before he retired in 1962. Ron O'Brien started his college coaching career at the University of Minnesota during this time and soon moved on to his alma mater, the Ohio State University, where he coached for several years before again moving on to Mission Viejo where he created a very powerful club team. Many colleges and universities began to hire diving coaches in the 1960s because they became aware of the value of divers winning meets for swimming teams. Diving coaches also began to crop up in high schools for the same reasons they were hired by the collegiate swimming coaches. Hundreds of professional diving coaches are now found in high schools, colleges and universities, and clubs throughout the United States.

I believe that it is safe to say that Lyle Draves, Dick Smith, Dr. Ron O'Brien, Dick Kimball, Glenn McCormick, and Hobie Billingsley produced most of the senior national, Pan American, Olympic champions and top divers in the United States from 1962 to 1996. Most of the elite divers are now developed in the mid-west, southwest, and southern part of the country, but none of the recent coaches have dominated the sport nationally or internationally as the six coaches mentioned. Some of the coaches who have been most successful up to the writing of this text include, Kenny Armstrong of Woodlands, Texas, Jeff Huber of Indiana University, John Wingfield of I.U.P.U.I, Vince Panzano of Ohio State University, Jeff Schafer of Auburn University, and Randy Ableman of Miami University, Miami, Florida just to name a few.

In foreign countries

Amateur diving coaches also came into existence in Europe and other foreign countries in the early 1950s, all of which were affiliated with clubs. Countries such as Great Britain, Austria, Sweden, Norway, Denmark, Japan, Canada, Australia, France, Mexico and many others were slow to develop good diving programs because very few of their diving coaches and programs were paid for their services. Many of the problems in achieving competitive excellence also arose because competitive diving was a non-revenue sport and few people were willing to pay money to watch a diving contest - a condition that has remained unchanged up to the present time.

In 1985, I took a sabbatical leave from Indiana University to make a world tour giving lectures on competitive diving and observing diving programs everywhere. In visiting twelve different countries over a 3 ½ month period, I found the biggest problem with world-wide diving programs to be the fact that their diving coaches were amateurs and receiving no pay for their efforts. This meant that their coaches could not make a total commitment to competitive diving without it interfering with their regular jobs and family responsibilities. Taking on such an assignment made it extremely difficult for a coach to work eight hours a day at a job, then coach two, or three hours pro-bono before going home to the family only to find that they had already eaten dinner and the children had been put to bed. This kind of life left no doubt in the minds of most coaches that they could not produce divers that could successfully compete with divers and coaches from other countries who were professionals. Since that tour, nearly all of the countries with diving problems have hired professional age group and senior level coaches who have done much to improve their diving programs.

Starting with the great emphasis placed on all kinds of athletic activities in such countries as East Germany and Russia, where the coaches and athletes were supplemented by their governments, Ingred Kramer, of East Germany, broke into the United States ring of worlds supremacy in women's diving when she won the 3-meter and IO-meter events at the 1960 Olympics in Rome. Her performance was followed by the Russian divers who came on strong in the world. Growth in competitive diving continued in many other countries such as Italy, West Germany, and Mexico all of which produced several world class divers who showed their merit by winning several gold medals at the Olympic Games. Much of the success of these countries was due to the governments paying their coaches and divers.

The challenges to the world of diving changed when the Chinese divers entered the competitive arena in the early 1970s and showed immediate success against the Russian and American divers who continued to offer very strong opposition. It is apparent that the tremendous success of the Chinese and Russian divers in recent years can not only be attributed to the talents of the divers but also to the great devotion and dedication their coaches have given to the sport. It is a certainty that many of them made a great study of competitive diving and developed diving styles and techniques relating to mechanical principles and other foreign diving programs.

A closer look at the style and technique used by the Chinese and Russian divers has shown a great similarity to those created by the American divers and coaches. When the Chinese coaches were asked where they obtained their information for their diving programs that resulted in such great success the first year they competed internationally, they said they received it from the Russians. When asked where the Russians got their information, they said that they learned it from the Americans and since the Americans were trying to copy the Chinese methods, which originally came from the Americans, they believed us to becrazy.

In moving into a new century, many Chinese and Russian diving coaches have left their homelands to coach and live in other countries that offer better living conditions and more freedom to coach. How influential and how much impact these coaches have and will make working with foreign diving programs is yet to be determined. With Chinese coaching, the Australian team at the 2004 Olympics secured several medals including a women's gold and a men's silver in the tower events, which may indicate the impact of this recent trend.

The Use of Technology in Competitive Diving

One of the most important and frequent problems confronting coaches throughout the world today concerns their knowledge and concern to use scientific principles when coaching the performance of their divers. In plain words, most coaches do not know how to adequately analyze dives with an accurate understanding of the laws of motion. Consequently, when one has limited knowledge concerning the science that relates to the sport, it becomes questionable as to whether or not they can accurately determine the difference between good and poor movements used in the execution of dives. Up until the early 1960's, few coaches were aware of Newton's Laws and how they could be applied to the movements of athletes. When one considers that it took over forty years for those in competitive diving to figure (out how to perform more than one twist when performing a forward somersault, it became quite obvious that no one in diving knew much about the physics used in human movement. Thankfully, some coaches world-wide have begun to take notice of a more scientific approach to teaching and coaching different sports and have found their efforts to be well rewarded when not relying on the trial and error method and/or copying the movements made by other athletes.

The American Problem

The United States supremacy in international competition reached its peak at the 1984 Olympics staged in Los Angeles, California when all seven divers earned a medal, with Greg Louganis winning two gold. Since then, the American divers have gradually faltered on the international scene which has created great concern from diving enthusiasts throughout the land. Such a rapid decline in supremacy has been hard to believe when it is noted that adequate diving facilities, a very strong and healthy national age group program, money to develop good divers through excellent educational and developmental programs, adequate coaching, and a self-governed association (diving was controlled by the swimming organization for nearly sixty years) is available for all divers. In other words, the diving programs in America have appeared to be very sound at all levels with all the means for developing top divers. Yet, today's American programs have not only failed to perform well in the Olympics, but also in most international meets staged since 1988.

The question is "What happened to cause such poor performances in international competitions when all the means to uphold the tradition of supremacy in the world of diving are available?" Looking back at the sport over the past few years, one problem that has greatly affected the performance of American diver's concerns ***"time".*** When comparing the American diving programs with those of other countries that have superior divers, one finds that they have had the time to train and develop their divers to a top level. The families of their top divers are also supported by their government which offers great incentives for their divers to perform well. This kind of support has not been available in America because the government does not finance the diving programs though many of those attending colleges receive compensation through scholarships. It is also found that at least eight hours of each day are used by American divers to attend school and/or work at jobs after which they engage in social or domestic activities leaving them with little more than two or three hours a day for training and practice.

To be a top diver requires one to learn and perfect dives that are extremely difficult to perform. To successfully master such dives with consistency requires preparation and practice that demand a great deal of the diver's time. Top class divers must engage in training programs that develop flexibility, conditioning, and strength; perfect dives that require the use of various teaching and training aids such as the trampoline, dry land board, video, mats, etc.; practice lead up dives in preparation for the execution of difficult dives; practice line up dives to develop "rip" entries and finally practice the dives to be used in meets.

Another problem involving time is in the number of dives that must be practiced for diving events. Years ago, divers competed on the one-meter and three-meter springboards while some divers also competed on the ten-meter platform in meets held in the summer. During that period, nearly all of the divers in America competed on the one-meter springboard while the rest of the world did not compete at this level. The American divers who went to college were expected to compete on the one- and three-meter springboards, in order to help the swimming team's score points in swimming meets. Tower diving was later added to the college programs which added more needed time to the divers' practice schedule. Now, even more time is needed for those who wish to participate in synchronized diving which has been added to the competitive criteria outside of the learning institutions. The addition of this event has doubled the number of events used in national and international contests which has not yet aided the American divers in their quest for supremacy.

Though not a college event, synchronized diving is now performed from the three-meter springboard and tower levels in all national and international meets. The time that it takes learning and practicing dives needed to compete in all of these events, and the time allotted each day to engage in all of the activities that are needed to learn and perform difficult dives with consistency and perfection, clearly indicates why our divers are having great difficulty trying to stay up with their advisories. It has been found that divers who are not totally dedicated to the sport do not have much chance of beating divers from other countries who are totally dedicated.

A major development in divers from foreign countries has recently occurred that is causing even Greater concern from the Americans. It now appears that the Russian, Chinese, and divers from other countries are beginning to compete in only one event, with an occasional exception where a diver may participate in two events if he or she is exceptionally talented. In many of these cases divers are competing in one individual event and a synchronized event.

The strategy used for making these decisions is based on giving the divers more time to practice and focus on fewer dives which obviously develops greater perfection and consistency.

Such a strategy places the American divers in a precarious position for it is easy to see that when foreign divers practice forty or more hours a week to dive in one or two events and most American divers, pointedly those in college, practice only twenty hours a week in preparation for two or more events, the chances of getting beat by the opposition is monumental. Also, if foreign divers practice dives for only one event, they can use the same dives to compete in synchronized events with no need to practice any extra dives which leaves more time to practice for synchronized events.

Perhaps one of the most controversial subjects concerning competitive diving today is found in the divers and coaches who attempt to copy the unique style of the Chinese divers. The whole world was in total awe of their divers when they first came on the scene in the late 1970's. Everyone wanted to dive like them by cloning their style and technique. This has led to several countries employing Chinese coaches with the purpose of teaching and coaching their divers the Chinese methods. Though some of these coaches, most of which are knowledgeable and experienced in the sport, have proven to be helpful in many diving programs, none have been able to teach the American divers to perform well enough to beat the Chinese who practice eight hours a day, every day, performing conditioning exercises and practicing diving skills.

Some solutions to the American problem

So, the big problem is "How in the world can the American divers train in an environment that demands so much effort, time, and energy and still have the time to enjoy a normal life. I do not believe that any of the American divers want to become fanatics by diving all day long just to prove a point. Most youngsters participate in many activities outside of diving and enjoy various forms of cultural and recreational experiences that contribute to their normal growth. Granted, other sports such as gymnastics, swimming, and ice skating are as demanding of their athlete's time as diving and also require a great sacrifice from those who participate. But in this respect, time is the ultimate factor and our need for it to be successful creates a huge problem.

If one can accept the fact that time is of major concern in training, then an attempt must be made by the coaches and divers to assess the quantity and quality of the time at hand and dedicate every effort to use it where it will best improve the performance of the divers. To take such an approach requires the divers and coaches to recognize the strength and weakness of the diving program, fix those things that are amiss, establish priorities in terms of importance to the divers, form short term and long term goals with objectives that are realistic and well within their capabilities, and then try to develop a program that is workable and can satisfy the needs of each diver and coach within the available time frame.

The designing of such programs must be suited for the *individuals* rather than for groups because some activities may not be helpful for everyone. For example, if a program is set up to include exercises that improve flexibility of a diver, it is of little use and a waste of time for those who are flexible to participate in that phase of the program. However, if a person is in need of developing strength, then it would be helpful for the person to participate in the strength program. In similar' fashion, a diver who knows how to rip entries need not spend a great amount of time practicing this exercise though some time should be used to occasionally practice entries to maintain excellence in the skill.

The diving program should be set up for those who plan to dive at the national or international level with the intent of diving in only one or, at most, two events which may or may not include synchronized diving. The divers can then focus and concentrate on the dives needed to obtain top performance and not get bogged down and become fatigued by practicing too many dives. Though reducing the number of events and the number of practice dives may be difficult for some divers to accept, they must realize that they have less chance of beating the keen opposition if they dive in a lot of events that require practicing a large number of dives in practice. A fewer number of events requires good planning and some sacrifice but by employing quality time over quantity time, the opportunity to practice and focus on a lesser number of dives can affect the outcome of the performance. Thankfully, with the recent elimination of required dives in competitions at the senior level, American divers now have more time to focus on the difficult dives that are necessary to perform in most competitions.

Many believe that the creation of training centers could be the answer to the Americas international problems. This may be so, but such training centers require great leadership and administrative responsibilities for which only a select few of coaches qualify. Most of those who qualify for such a position already have very good jobs with universities and may be reluctant to leave positions that offer limited hours and perks for them and their families. The National Training center in Indianapolis, Indiana has proven that youngsters can be trained to compete with top divers from any part of the world. This training center has selected and started to train young talented divers with great success which clearly points to the fact that the future of American competitive diving depends on how well "young" divers can be trained and developed in a well-organized program with a minimum chance of injury.

I also believe that it is imperative that America offers a training center ***for coaches*** who can be trained to use mechanical principles which can improve their technique in coaching. Such a center could help coaches over the years where they can attend sessions that will help upgrade their coaching in many different ways that would include communication and psychological information. The center would also offer direction to perfection with everyone learning to coach in the same direction when applying technology and scientific knowledge.

Looking at the present and to the future

- As was found with the elimination of compulsory exercises in ice skating, competitive diving seems to be leaning toward the elimination of compulsory dives. It appears this has come about because the difference in the range of total points scored by divers performing compulsory dives has had little effect on the outcome of the diver's placing in the contest. Many believe that the execution of compulsory dives takes up too much time and has proven to be very boring for all involved. Though competitive diving may be moving away from the original "unwritten" philosophy that compulsory dives are necessary to determine the best diver, a change in this direction may be necessary to prevent the sport from becoming extinct.

- Other forms of competition such as synchronized diving, are gradually working their way into diving programs with the purpose of stimulating more interest in diving. Other forms of competition such as "team" diving may also offer more variety and interest in the sport. Team diving is where two divers compete with other pairs by each performing three compulsory dives to include dives from the five groups of dives, and six optional dives to also include one dive from each of the five groups. The sixth compulsory dive would be selected from group five which offers four simple dives that can be performed with a half twist. This contest allows divers to perform dives they favor and can perform well which will improve the quality of the competition. The divers would also need to perform only six dives which would greatly reduce their practice time.

- The second half of the twentieth century brought major changes in many areas of competitive diving which was made possible through the improvement of diving facilities, the use of new teaching aids, and the recognition and application of technology. All of these changes have aided in developing better divers performing dives that were not believed possible during the first half of the twentieth century.

- Nearly all of the optional dives performed by divers from the 1 and 3-meter springboards and various levels of the platforms on the tower before the 1960s have been replaced with more intricate dives. Many of the new difficult dives performed by male divers are also being executed by female divers. The increase in difficult dives, and our ever-developing litigious society, has also encouraged the induction of more safety rules to protect the divers from injury and the coaches and divers from law suits.

- Apparently, a point has been reached where little improvement can be made on the diving equipment and teaching aids which have accounted for the great improvement in competitive diving. The standard heights from which competitive diving occurs will not change due to the great cost in modifying the facilities world- wide.

- It now appears that diving is moving in the direction of providing training centers around the country with the purpose of developing young divers with the use of technology computers, and other scientific aids. It is imperative that such training centers focus on divers of a very young age using teaching aids that prevent injury.

- The Chinese, Russian and Canadian divers have not only become the supreme divers in the world in recent years, but also masters in training methods, technology, and body mechanics. It is, therefore, necessary for coaches and divers from other countries to concern themselves with training methods and scientific techniques that offer the best results within a given amount of time.

- International contests were rarely offered in the first half of the twentieth century but due to the rapid growth of diving, diving programs and competitions have emerged world-wide for divers at all ages and competitive levels. The forming of the World Diving Coaches Association was responsible for most of this growth by unifying diving coaches world-wide that resulted in the induction of many international contests now offered all year long.

- It would be helpful for competitive diving if an effort be made to revive W.D.C.A. and make it a center for better communication and competition. This organization could establish an International Hall of Fame for all the divers, coaches, and administrators who have risen above mediocrity and contributed so much to the sport. An actual "Hall" could be made available in a country where everyone could visit and view the history, development, and accomplishments of those from all the countries that have given so much to the sport.

- With the fall of the Russian Empire, many Russian divers are now able to dive in major International contests representing their Russian satellite countries.

- It appears that, with present diving equipment, the creation of new difficult dives is nearing a limit. However, with the innovation of the "Diving Formula" divers can still create intricate dives not yet listed in the rule books and use them in competition.

- It is not yet clear if competitive diving should be a professional sport. It does appear that competitive diving will continue to move in the direction of professionalism where divers will be paid to compete, and coaches will be paid to coach. Countries that are professional will continue to beat the countries that remain amateur.

- Though the United States has fallen from its supremacy in competitive diving, I believe that they will work their way back to be a threat to the rest of the world if they are willing to make some major changes in their philosophy and goals.

- Title IX will continue to force non-revenue sports for men in the colleges and universities out of existence and in so doing, men's swimming and diving teams will return to be a club sport.

- Chinese and Russian diving coaches will continue to leave their countries to coach m other countries where living and coaching conditions are more favorable.

- The judging of competitive diving will move upward to meet all of the changes and improvement that has been made in competitive diving by discarding the judging system that has not changed in more than 100 years and will move to using quarter points that will broaden the range of scoring and create a greater accuracy in the judgment of dives. This new approach will allow dives to be evaluated up to a $1{,}000^{th}$ of a point which will go far in preventing ties in a contest.

- Schools will be offered to educate and certify those who wish to be diving coaches. Besides offering courses on diving, the schools will also offer times for up-dating coaches with information concerning new and different coaching techniques. Judges will need to be certified to judge major meets for all competitions level by passing written and practical tests.

CHAPTER 2

THE DIVING PROGRAM AND HOW TO EVALUATE IT

One would think that every diver involved in competitive diving is connected to a diving program, but this is not always the case. Some divers practice without a coach and compete unattached because they are not associated with a team. When this occurs, it is safe to say that the diver is not involved in a diving program. But the moment the diver engages a coach, the diver is then in a program. Therefore, a diving program may be defined as an operation that offers divers assistance with the intent of improving their performance. Obviously, the quality of the diver's performance not only depends on the ability and t lent of the diver but also on the kind of diving program available. Some programs are so limited that it is not possible for a diver to develop his or her talent. Other programs may provide everything needed to promote a champion, but the diver may not have the talent or be able to take advantage of it to reach his or her intended goals. So, if one wishes to evaluate a diving program that can develop a top performance by the diver, according to his or her ability, then it is necessary to first find what constitutes a diving program. Therefore, a program is offered in this chapter that may be used as a guideline for other programs from which changes and adjustments can be made.

The composition of a diving program

An easy way to construct a quality diving program is to divide it into four different categories consisting of the diver, the coach, the facilities, and the environment. Though the first three categories are a part of the program's environment, the fourth includes everything in the program that is not directly related to the first three. The functions of these four categories depend much on how they can fulfill certain responsibilities, needs, goals, and objectives. Some of the characteristics found in one category may overlap with those found in one or more of the others. Whatever the case, each category outlines goals and objectives that can offer direction and motivation to the diver and coach (Figure 1).

The goals and objectives in the program are usually recognized as long term and short term. For example, a long-term goal for a diver may be to win the state high school championship. To do so may require the learning of certain optional dives, which may be seen as short-term goals. A long-term goal for the coach may be to develop the best diving team in the league. To fulfill this desire may require the recruiting of certain talented divers - a short term goal. Installing a three-meter complex in the pool would be a long-term goal and finding the funds for such a need may be seen as a short or long-term goal. In reference to the environment, a long-term goal may refer to creating a strong parent association for the diving club. The recruiting of certain parents who possess willingness, desire, and leadership to help form the club may be seen as a short-term objective. Obviously, goals could change in importance to a point where a long-term goal could be made into a short-term goal and vice versa. Other goals and objectives may relate to all four of the sections which may help develop the best possible performance from a diver and/or coach.

AREAS CONCERNING
A COMPETITIVE DIVING PROGRAM

Diver **Coach** **Facility** **Environment**

Short Term **Long Term**

State of Performance

Success **Failure**

Diver Coach

The Diving Program
Figure 1

The state of performance

On the surface, it appears that the sole objective of competitive diving is for the diver to win the contest. As a coach, I believe the primary purpose of the diving program is for the divers and coaches to give their best possible performance with consistency when in a competitive environment. Winning may appear to be the ultimate goal but Greg Louganis stated many times during his career that it was more important for him to give a good performance than it was to win. This may have been true in Greg's case for he rarely ever lost a contest regardless of the merit of his performance. But, for the average competitive diver, 'winning" is the most important goal and if a good performance is made along with the victory, then the conquest is even more gratifying.

Those who have been involved in the sport for any length of time eventually realize that not every diver is going to be a winner. Some divers try for years to qualify for the state or national championships but fail in their efforts no matter how hard they try. So, it is questionable why they continue to participate when their chances of winning are hopeless. Thousands of runners who compete in the Boston Marathon know they cannot possibly place in the top ten thousand runners and yet they continue to try. Obviously, there must be other reasons for their participation or they would quit the activity and try something else. One good reason for participating may be in their desire to perform as well as their talents and abilities will allow regardless of where they finish in the contest. It has often been stated that "winning" isn't everything ... it's the only thing". This statement does not bear any truth when relating to divers who perform in a setting that is above their ability level. They may never win but they continue to try. Many have found winning to be a fallacy when they may be good enough to win when competing at one level but not good enough to win at a higher competitive level.

Some athletes are never satisfied until they achieve a high level of performance while others seem to be content with a mediocre performance because they simply like to participate. Having coached close to a thousand divers in my career, I would say that a great majority of them dived with the purpose of giving a good performance rather than the need to win. I also believe that most coaches will agree that the performance of their divers is as important, if not more so, as their winning.

Whatever the reason for wanting to perform well, it is helpful if one understands what is involved in attempting to give a top performance. First, one must be aware that a top performance is not a maximal performance for the latter requires the diver to perform where there is no possible room for improvement. A maximal performance can, therefore, occur if every factor and condition is ideal at a given moment which is highly unlikely because conditions are constantly in a state of change. So, a competitor's success depends much on certain factors that directly or indirectly affect the performance which are located in the four different areas of the diving program.

Perhaps a clearer picture of how the state of performance works within the four areas can be shown in (Figure 2). In reference to "Potential Levels" and "Level of Performance" the range of performance is portrayed from "A" through "D" with the letter "A" indicating a high level and "D" a low level. So, persons with a potential level of "C" (as compared to others competing at the same level) can perform only to that level no matter what positive factors influence their performance. More simply stated, a diver may give a great performance "A" at his or her "C" potential level. This means that a diver with a limited talent at the "C" level and performs near the top of his or her ability, may never come close to beating those in an elite "A" or "B" level of competition though he or she may be outstanding when diving at a lower level of competition. Likewise, with the aid of those factors found in the top program, the diver may be able to give an "A" performance according to his or her potential which may be good enough to win at one competitive level but not at another. Therefore, the purpose of the program is to attempt to develop the diver to a point closest to his or her potential in terms of performance which may determine the level at which the diver should compete.

One may observe a couple of examples to further clarify the "state of performance" shown in (Figure 2). In this sample, a diver with the potential to perform at the "B" competitive level trains with a coach who is at the "C" coaching potential level. They are training in an ideal facility that offers outstanding equipment including all of the teaching aids which qualify as an "A" facility. However, the diver must travel 75 miles each way to practice which was a negative environmental factor. With these different levels of influence, the diver may never dive near his or her potential "B" level because the coach can only offer "C" services.

State of Performance

Diver Coach Faculty Environment

Potential Levels
A B C D

X- Factors

Positive Adverse Missing

Level of Performance
A B C D

Figure 2

The state of performance by the athlete depends much on what and how much information he or she has learned from the instructors and/or coaches in the program.

A diver with great talent ("A" potential level) may constantly perform poorly **("D"** performance level) if the pool is available for practice only a half hour a day three days a week **("D"** environment level), has only a one meter stand and a regular Duraflex board in the pool **("D"** facility level), and is coached by one who has had little experience or possesses little knowledge about diving.

Years ago, I was invited to Japan to coach their top divers and found the very talented, but none could come close to reaching their potential when there were only four indoor pools in the whole country. This meant that the divers could not practice in any of the pools during the winter due to their school and domestic work and because the distance to the pools were often in different cities far away from where they lived. To me, these divers showed a potential to be nearly as good as the Chinese divers, but they could not reach that competitive level because they could not train in the winter time due to the absence of an indoor pool in their vicinity.

The "X" factor

With the program divided into four different developmental categories, certain factors located in each of these, influence the performance of the diver and the coach. Some factors are adverse, positive, or missing and it is very important to identify which factors favor a good performance and which contribute to an unfavorable performance. In observing the various factors in each category, the coach and diver involved in the program easily distinguish what is and what is not desirable to aid the diver in giving a desirable performance. It is also easy to observe what factors are missing in any of the four categories which may require adjustments, if possible, that will change the program to fit the divers and coach's needs. Obviously, some adjustments are not possible to make so the coach and diver must accept what is available. The term used to distinguish between the factors desired, not desired, and those that are not available may be identified as the "X' factor.

Understand the "X" factor and the role it plays in the success or failure of a diving program requires one to be clear on how it works within each of the categories. In a hypothetical program where a diver with virtually unlimited talent is being tutored by a coach with superior ability and experience and is training in a superior facility that offers an outstanding environment, the end result would obviously be "successful" because there would be little or no opposing factors preventing the diver and coach from reaching their set goals and objectives.

In the same manner, if there are certain factors missing, or unfavorable in any of the four categories, the chances of the coach and/or diver reaching their goals and objectives may be questionable. Pointedly, if a superior coach works in an excellent facility under a favorable environment with a diver who is very limited in ability and talent, the chances of the diver meeting the potential goals and objectives set by the coach and the program are very slim. Though the diver may be working near the peak of his or her potential, certain physical factors involving strength, power, flexibility, coordination, ability to take instruction, etc. may be adverse or missing and could prevent the diver from meeting the standards set by that particular program. Likewise, divers with all of the talent needed to be champions may never come near to developing their potential if coached by a person who is limited in coaching potential.

Some adverse conditions are mentioned here to further display some of the conditions that coaches and divers may have to overcome in order to fulfill their desires to be successful.

1. Environmental

- Poor diving facilities - stands, springboards, platform, water spray, absence of teaching aids such as trampoline, dry land board, mats, no hot tub or close warm showers, etc.

- Absence of teaching aids such as the trampoline, dry land board, mats, exercise equipment, the bubbler, etc.

- Poor pool conditions which include- room and water temperature, design, ladders, deck level, water depth, grates on the pool bottom, deck space.

- Bad lighting - too dark, light glare, sharp contrasts, bad lighting in the ceiling.

- Poor meet or training administration and management involving schedules, workouts, and pool time.

- Television invasion during meet regarding commercial times, recording equipment placed in inappropriate positions.

- Noise - loud music, poor acoustics.

- Over-crowded workouts and practice sessions, not enough board or practice time.

- Unqualified judges.

- Inadequate transportation to and from pool.

- Diving boards located in the center of the pool requiring the coach to instruct the divers from behind the boards.

2. Adverse personal performance conditions

- Not physically or mentally prepared to perform well.
- Diving first on the diving roster when competing, making error on the dive sheet, forgetting or losing your suit.
- Starting off the competition with a poor execution of a dive.
- Following Greg Louganis when he just scored tens on a dive.
- Having performed a dive poorly every time in practice before the meet.
- Not enough or too much confidence.
- Not up to competing well.
- Having difficulty spotting dives.
- Placing the dives to be performed in the wrong order.
- Uncontrolled fear while competing - fear of losing: missing a dive: letting down your coach, family, team members and yourself.
- Having difficulty with focusing on how to perform a dive.

3. Other Influences

- Conflict with coach, team member, girlfriend, boyfriend, or member of the family prior to the competition.
- Comments from a diver, coach, or someone who wishes to "psych" you out.
- Late for practice or team meetings.
- Feeling that the diving judges are not scoring you fairly.
- Feeling that the judges are over paying your opponents
- Poor or no coaching - coach plays favorites, yells or puts you down after poor performance of a dive, plays the performance of one diver against that of another.

- Starting off the competition with a poor execution of a dive.
- Following Greg Louganis when he just scored tens on a dive.
- Having performed a dive poorly every time in practice before the meet.
- Not enough or too much confidence.
- Not up to competing well.
- Having difficulty spotting dives.
- Placing the dives to be performed in the wrong order.
- Uncontrolled fear while competing - fear of losing: missing a dive: letting down your coach, family, team members and yourself.
- Having difficulty with focusing on how to perform a dive.
- Late for practice or team meetings.
- Not physically or mentally prepared to perform well.

While some factors in the four different categories of a diving program are more important than others, some important factors may not be found in any of the categories which affect the performance of the dives. For example, if a program does not possess a trampoline or dry land facility or other teaching aids, it does not mean that the divers in that program cannot be successful. But it does indicate that the absence of certain teaching aids could affect the total success of the diving program. Further, an age group program with a poor parent's association may or may not affect the performance of the divers and/or coach in the program, but it certainly can make it uncomfortable for those involved in it.

The absence of certain factors or the presence of certain weak factors in a diving program can often be overcome by strong factors. A coach who lacks the knowledge to analyze dives due to a poor understanding of mechanical principle may be able to overcome the deficiency to some degree by using a strong persuasive personality that convinces divers to attempt dives over and over even though they experience pain with every attempt. In this situation, the missing factor (the absence of knowledge of mechanical principles) and the adverse factor (poor analyses of the dives) are both somewhat compromised by a positive factor which is the coach's strong persuasive personality. It may be possible to educate the coach in analyzing dives properly, but it may not be possible to change the personality of the coach if he or she is not strong in this area. As seen in all phases of life regarding personality, some have got it and some do not and never will get it because it is just not there. Fortunately, some who do not have certain desirable traits, can obtain them with some effort while other factors can never obtain them no matter how hard they try.

In evaluating a diving program, it is not advisable to select only those factors that are helpful to the diving program while disregarding those that are damaging because some factors may prove damaging under one condition but not under another. Such a situation may occur when a coach teaches certain techniques to a diver on the one-meter springboard and then experiences total disaster when trying to teach similar techniques to a diver on the ten-meter platform. For example, when teaching a diver the inward dive in the layout position, the moves used when taking off from the springboard are very different than the moves used when taking off from the platform. If not aware of such differences, the coach's instruction could seriously cause injury to the diver.

When examining the four categories in the diving program, divers and coaches should try to find which parts of the program cause a problem. How easily such problems can be spotted depends much on the kind of problem and the experience and knowledge of the coach and diver. Once a problem is identified and evaluated, plans can then be made to correct it. Obviously, not all of the problems can be dealt with through such an examination and evaluation process; but weaknesses in the program caused by the presence and/or absence of certain factors can at least be recognized, corrected, or substituted with more beneficial factors.

With a general idea of how the diving program is constructed, it is imperative that those involved seek out a better understanding of how the various factors influence the different categories in the program. First, one must try to identify the factors in each of the categories then break them down into finer segments which offer a better view of what may or may not be desired in the diving program (Figure 3). Factors for divers, coaches and facilities are discussed in the following chapters. Although the environment is indirectly related to the three categories, a separate chapter is not possible because factors involving the environment are found in nearly every chapter in the text.

FACTOR IDENTITIES

Diver	Coach	Facility	Environment
Physical	Qualifications	Equipment	Diving Program
Psychological	Psychological	Pool type	Location
Physiological	Social		External influence
Social			Internal influence

Figure 3 Factors involved in the four sections of a diving program

Since competitive diving has experienced so much growth in developing good divers in the last four or five decades, I believe it is important to the diver and coach that they be aware of the time it takes to create a successful diving program. With divers from other countries training six to eight hours a day, how long must divers train to keep up with the competition is of great concern in the design offered by many diving programs. With that in mind, observe the following assessment of time to determine where your program is, or perhaps should be, to take on parties from other parts of the world. If your diving program is not concerned with that level of competition, then it is not too important to take time into account. It is, however, still important that coaches and divers know what is involved in the diving program and what amount of time it takes to successfully develop good divers.

The assessment of time needed for a diving program

Number of hours needed for training

Sessions: Winter ___ Summer ___

Number of hours per day

Monday _____

Tuesday _____

Wednesday _____

Thursday _____

Friday _____

Saturday _____

Sunday _____

Number of days per week _____

Number of weeks/ Winter _____ Summer _____Total number of hours _____

Activities in the diving program

Diving workouts – number of workouts for each competition

1. One meter _____
2. Three meter _____
3. Tower _____
4. Synchronized _____ Total number of hours _____

Preparation for dives – hours per week

1. Lead ups _____
2. Line ups _____

3. Video _____ Total number of hours _____

Dry land training

1. Trampoline _____
2. Dry land board _____
3. Dry land platform _____ Total number of hours _____

Physical training – hours per week

1. Flexibility _____
2. Conditioning exercises _____
3. Strength and power _____ Total number of hours _____

Miscellaneous

1. Team and parent meetings _____
2. Travel to meets _____
3. Other ( ) _____ Total number of hours _____

Approximate total number of hours for practice each week _____ Season _____ Year

Equipment available for diving workouts

Diving facilities

One meter springboard(s) _____ Indoor _____ Outdoor _____

Three meter springboard(s) _____ Indoor _____ Outdoor _____

Diving tower

One meter _____ _____ Indoor _____ Outdoor _____

Three meter _____ _____ Indoor _____ Outdoor _____

Five meter _____ _____ Indoor _____ Outdoor _____

7 ½ meter _____ _____ Indoor _____ Outdoor _____

Ten meter _____ _____ Indoor _____ Outdoor _____

Trampoline(s) _____ _____ Indoor _____ Outdoor _____

Dry land board _____ _____ Indoor _____ Outdoor _____

Bubbler system

One meter _____ _____ Indoor _____ Outdoor _____

Three meter _____ _____ Indoor _____ Outdoor _____

Five meter _____ _____ Indoor _____ Outdoor _____

7 ½ meter _____ _____ Indoor _____ Outdoor _____

Ten meter _____ _____ Indoor _____ Outdoor _____

Spotting rig

Trampoline(s) _____ _____ Indoor _____ Outdoor _____

Dry land _____ _____ Indoor _____ Outdoor _____

One meter springboard _____ _____ Indoor _____ Outdoor _____

Video system _____ _____ Indoor _____ Outdoor _____

Tivo _____ _____ Indoor _____ Outdoor _____

The clientele

Coaches

	Number	Male	Female
Age group	______	____	____
High school	______	____	____
College	______	____	____
Club	______	____	____
Masters	______	____	____

Number of divers

	Winter (Indoor)		Summer (Outdoor)
Male divers	_____	_____	_____
Female divers	_____	_____	_____

Parents club

Duties

Organization

Publicity

Help at table, refreshments, etc.

Chaperones

Sponsors

Travel

Headaches

Seasonal training

In order to simplify the training, teaching, and conditioning for diving, it must be assumed that the seasonal training commences with the beginning of the school year which is generally in the first week of September.

Length and number of daily workouts

a. Pre-season – before the competitive season starts, a diver should have at least one workout a day five days a week within a time period of one to two hours.

b. During season - a diver should try to have two workouts a day with each workout not exceeding two hours.
c. Before championships - it is a natural tendency for most divers to practice too long during a championship meet which often results in a poor performance due to fatigue. It is best for the diver to go through the list of dives, no more than two times each, that are to be performed in the meet then rest for the competition.

Suggested procedure for pre-season and seasonal workouts.

a. First two weeks
   (1) One to two hours of strength and stretching exercises.
   (2) Half hour on dry land board and or trampoline.
   (3) Half hour in pool doing basic dives and line ups.

b. Third week
   (1) Half hour to 45 minutes - warm up and strength exercises.
   (2) Forty-five minutes to an hour on trampoline, and/or port-o-pit.
   (3) Forty-five minutes to an hour on basic dives and/or line ups.

c. Fourth week and on
   (1) Twenty-five minutes warm up with stretching exercises and practice approaches.
   (2) Trampoline and dry land board. Usually used for lead-ups and refreshing the basics.
   (3) Performing the compulsory and optional dives - three each.

Diving workouts for beginners and novices

Beginners - The first two or three weeks in the pool should be devoted to practicing approaches, front and back take-offs, and front and back jumps in the tuck, pike, and layout positions. Following the jumps, the five basic dives should be practiced in the layout and pike positions. Once the basic dives are learned, the diver should then learn single somersaults from the first four groups of dives for these are the lead-ups for the more difficult dives.

Novices - It is important that the diver progresses only as he or she learns and masters the fundamentals. That is, after having learned the front dive, the diver should not try to learn a forward double somersault until first learning to perform a forward somersault and 1 ½ somersault; which in this case, are lead-up dives for the double. As the lead up dives are learned with instruction, it is usually safe to gradually eliminate the practice jumps so more time can be devoted to learning the more intricate dives. Once the lead up dives are mastered, the diver than can attempt the dive related to the lead up dive.

The number of dives in a workout for novices should be around fifty dives which include the approaches with jumps from the board, the lead up dives, and the dives learned. If the diver has difficulty with a particular dive, it is best to go on to the next dive after three or four attempts because most often the bad movements used in a dive get worse and can become a habit if the dive is repeated over and over. In this way, the diver will also not tire easily or get frustrated with continual attempts. When championship meets occur, divers might perform each dive two times followed by going through a list of dives once before performing in the meet.

CHAPTER 3

THE DIVER

Physical	Psychological	Physiological	Social
Body makeup	Motivation & confidence	Flexibility	Popularity
Strength	Competitive attitude	Cardiovascular condition	Group dynamics
Stamina	Experience	Nutrition	Maturity
Physical training	Behavior patterns	Rest & relaxation	
	Fear	Body control	

PHYSICAL

Nothing contributes more to the beauty of a well-executed dive than a diver who possesses a well-proportioned body. Some divers can near perfection when performing a dive but display little beauty due mainly to their physical make-up. Greg Louganis unquestionably was the greatest diver who has ever lived. Along with his diving talents, he possessed the perfect body for diving which complimented every graceful and aesthetic movement he made when performing a dive. Watching him soar through the air while executing certain graceful movements was thrilling and exciting; for he possessed every physical asset needed to portray beauty and grace. In fact, it was exciting to look at him when he was just standing on the board. Naturally, most divers are not blessed with such physical features, but it does help for those who wish to become great competitive divers to possess certain physical qualities. It must be recognized that the body continually changes from day to day, especially during the period of childhood. Therefore, no guarantee can be assured to one who wishes to develop into a fine diver during dynamic periods of growth - as such periods produce changes that may help or hinder a desired performance.

Perhaps the most important part of the body that provides the best opportunity for a diver to be successful is the legs. Without strong powerful legs there is little chance a diver can perform the very difficult dives required in most contests staged at any competitive level. Strong legs and other parts of the body can be developed through a weight training program. This can also improve the diver's appearance and performance. Since much of diving involves form, it is important that the diver learns to extend the feet and point the toes. A stretching program that offers exercises to develop flexibility can help divers achieve the form in the foot area necessary for success. Divers have found in recent years that they must also possess strong shoulders and arms because the dives and entries into the water performed in most present competitions offer a much greater resistance from the water than dives that were performed with less difficulty years ago. Also, the "rip" entry requires a great strain on the upper body, so this part of the body should be well conditioned to prevent injury. Nowadays, tower divers use so much tape on their hands and wrists that they look more like boxers than divers.

Of course, it is desirable for a diver to possess a nice-looking physique that is strong and well-conditioned in areas of the back, shoulders, neck, arms, wrists, and hands all of which can be acquired through a conditioning program. Good posture can also affect the outcome of a contest. Divers should be aware that the manner in the way they stand on the board or platform before executing a dive can influence a judge's score. Judges look at divers with more favor when they offer a good appearance than when slouched over in an ugly stance with the neck and the stomach jutted out, feet apart, knees bent... and chewing gum.

Because there are so many events offered and the competition is constantly getting more intense, divers must train for the sport nearly year-round. Even strong divers find it difficult to participate in other physical activities when the training periods for diving require so much time and energy.

PSYCHOLOGICAL

The success or failure of a diver also depends a great deal on his or her psychological makeup. Unlike the diver's physical appearance, how a person may feel or thinks is often very difficult to recognize. At times, divers who appear to be very confident and portray extreme confidence, may actually possess great inner fears and inadequacies that are hidden. Therefore, coaches should be cognizant of a diver's psychological state in search of factors that affect their performance. It is apparent that a diver who possesses self-confidence, is highly motivated, has a good competitive attitude, learns from experience, has positive behavior patterns, and recognizes fear and how to control it, will enjoy a successful diving career. These psychological factors depend on one another and contribute as much, if not more, to the diver's performance than any other form of behavior.

Confidence and Motivation:

Confidence may be recognized as the belief and trust that one has in oneself. It stimulates and breeds hope and faith in achieving certain goals that lead to accomplishments and success. Confidence is something that all coaches like to see in their athletes because it depicts a positive attitude. It has been heard many times that so and so did not win due to the lack of confidence or lost because of being over confident. Confidence appears to play a dominant role in sports and in our lives. If confidence is so important in the success or failure of a performance, divers and coaches should make an effort to obtain it, and if they already have it, they must continue to work to retain it.

The amount of confidence one possesses often depends on how much the person is motivated. When one is confident, motivation is easily acquired and if one is highly motivated, confidence aids in the amount of motivation one creates. In other words, the two traits complement each other. Relating to sports, and particularly diving, "motivation is an inner source from which is derived the means to stimulate and instill the desire to perform well." When an athlete is aware of his or her potential to perform, and the athlete possesses motivation, then short and long-term goals can be accomplished. For instance, if a diver is good enough to compete in the high school championships, he or she will most likely retain the confidence to perform at that level. If success is accomplished and motivation remains high, the diver may then increase his or her confidence to compete at a higher competitive level, such as the national championships. Then again, if the diver competes at higher level of competition and doesn't fair well, a temporary loss in confidence may occur.

Depending on the athlete, competing at a higher level may or may not motivate him or her to train and practice harder. Whichever way, confidence in one's self may determine the way the diver will perform at a given competitive level. Hypothetically, if two athletes have identical talents and abilities in all categories, the difference in their performances and the level of competition they wish to compete in could depend greatly on how confident and motivated each is in his or her quest to succeed.

Divers learn from experience that to obtain high levels of performance, requires intensive training that includes proper physical conditioning, consistent and well-planned workouts, ample competition, a positive environment, and ideal supervision and coaching. Occasionally, an athlete will come along who has the confidence, motivation, and talent to perform well without engaging in such training methods. However, the level of the performances desired by athletes in nearly every competitive level today makes such an athlete a rare exception. Unfortunately, less talented divers, who are highly motivated and confident may push their training to the very limit and still not achieve their intended goals. Such failure to succeed often causes them to lose their confidence and change their goals to one less challenging or direct their energies and interests in some other direction. Whatever the goal, motivation affects the performance of divers which results in a loss or gain of self-confidence. Conversely, the gain or loss of self-confidence normally affects the motivation of the diver in obtaining certain goals.

How to motivate athletes to perform well is a question that plagues all coaches. And if coaches had the pat answer to that question, they all would be masters of their trade. However, there are some means that can be helpful in recognizing and understanding how divers can be motivated to give good performances. First, it is known that athletes may be motivated by positive or negative reinforcement, but it is not always possible to know which approach will work. What may motivate a diver to perform well at one moment may not motivate the same diver under similar conditions at another time. To be more specific, a coach may holler and scream (negative reinforcement) at a diver during practice or during a contest and the diver may respond with an outstanding performance. The coach may then use the same tactics at another time and under similar conditions only to find the diver perform poorly.

Obviously, positive reinforcement does not always produce positive motivation because it can be artificial, an obvious act, or be applied too often and too much to have any meaning or effect on the athlete. This often occurs when a coach tries to "psych-up" an athlete when it is obvious that the coach does not really mean what he or she is saying. Some coaches give the same praise regardless of how poor or outstanding the performance may be which often results in no measurable increase in their motivation or performance level. Similar reactions (or lack of reaction) from the diver can also occur when receiving negative reinforcement so it is difficult to determine what kind of reinforcement should be used at a given time to motivate the diver. Stated another way, is it better to praise and reward or punish and/or criticize a diver to obtain the desired performance? There is no standard answer to the question, but studies have proven that, more often than not, positive reinforcement gets better results in a diver ' s performance than negative reinforcement. This is particularly true when working with beginners and intermediate divers.

Strangely, there are times when a diver performs extremely well when subjected to negative reinforcement. This generally depends on the personality of the coach, the conditions at hand, and the manner in which the enforcement is given. Coaches must be very careful when using negative reinforcement on a diver because they could end up losing the diver or be sued for harassment. As is known, athletes in diving do not receive the same rewards given to those who participate in revenue sports. which may reflect on how some coaches use reinforcement to motivate their athletes.

An example of using negative reinforcement by one who coaches a college revenue sport is seen when the coach may constantly badger and harass the players who, more often than not, responded with a positive performance. They know that if they can endure such negative behavior from the coach, they may receive professional contracts, outstanding press and television coverage, peer identity, spectator approval, and many other rewards. Why a coach yells or corrupts an athlete after a poor performance in any sport has often baffled me because it is obvious that the athlete didn't perform badly on purpose. Heaven knows he or she is aware of the poor performance so why must a coach take it out on the performer. I can only guess that the coach shows his dissatisfaction for the performance to get the athletes attention or to let off steam for his or her disappointment.

There are also times when a diver needs to be motivated and times when motivation is not needed to inspire the diver for a desired performance. Let it be said that there are times when a coach should try to push certain buttons to motivate a diver and other times when such tactics are not needed. An illustration of how to push a button on a diver can be seen when one of my former divers was competing on the one-meter board at the N.C.A.A. national championships at Brown University. During the preliminaries, he got lost in the air while performing a double twisting 1 ½ somersault and received an average of one's from the judges for the dive. The outcome of the event placed him in 83rd place out of 84 divers. Normally, I would have given him a tongue lashing for his poor performance. Instead, knowing that he could handle criticism, I put my arm around his shoulder and told him that since he had at least beaten one diver I was sure he would place higher on the three-meter event the next day. He did place higher by winning the contest which shocked everyone who was there... including me. Afterwards, I often wondered how well he would have dived had I given him a chewing out.

The next year he was defending the same title at Cleveland State University. When coming down to the last dive, he needed scores of nine or better to win the contest. Wondering what I could possibly say or do to motivate him, I finally walked up to him just before he was to perform a triple twisting 1 ½ somersault. Reminding him on how he went from 83rd in one event to first in another at Brown the year before. I told him that everyone at that meet believed it was a ' fluke' that he won the title. Then I asked him if he thought it was *really* a fluke and walked away. He received three tens and three nine and halves on the dive and won the contest. This example suggests that it is very difficult to predict what may or may not motivate a diver at a given time but pushing buttons has proven to be a great way to get results from my divers... most of the time.

At the Olympic tryouts in 1964, I had two divers make the Olympic team but was terribly disappointed to see Rick Gilbert, my first great diver, place fourth and not make the team. After the contest was over and being upset over Gilbert not making the team, I told my team to suit up for a practice on the ten-meter platform which was the event on the next day. The team gathered together and informed me that they were tired and didn't wish to practice. Being the coach, I disagreed and after waiting on the deck for several minutes, only one diver came out of the locker room to inform me that the team had left and gone back to the hotel to rest. Saying nothing to them until the next day, when they came out to practice just before the tower event, they found me sitting in the stands and asked me to come down and coach them. I informed them that since they didn't need my help the day before, they didn't need my help for the tower event either, so I sat there and said nothing to any of them throughout the entire meet. To my amazement, everyone dived better than they had ever dived before. Looking back at that time, I can't believe that I used such a tactic at such an important event and got away with it.

From that time on at meets, I would inform the divers that I would sit in a particular place and if they felt a need for assistance, to come over to me for coaching hints. This kind of coaching at meets worked better than any other method I had ever tried before. It allowed the divers to focus better on what they were taught to do rather than me trying to feed them information that could cause them to forget or miss other movements in the dive. The *absence* of trying to motivate divers at certain meets proved to be very successful because they were already motivated to compete and needed very little information from me on how to perform a dive.

Many times, when in a stressful environment, a coach will blurt out a lot of instructions which often bewilders the diver and causes a negative effect on his or

her performance. This is often a time when a coach thinks he has made comments one way, but the diver hears the comments in another way which may have been better if the coach had said nothing at all. As a coach, I found that there was no way to 'plan' a way of motivating a diver when he or she was under stress or in a critical moment during the competition. Again, what may motivate the diver at one moment may
not be a motivating factor at another moment. My suggestion for the coach is to wait until the occasion arrives and then go by gut feeling as to what, if anything, should be tried to motivate the diver.

Some athletes perform better when the intensity of the competition increases for they thrive on the challenge ... the head on engagement with the other divers. Such a case was seen at the 1992 Olympics in Barcelona, Spain, when Mark Lenzi stood on the three-meter board ready to perform his last dive, a reverse 3 ½ somersault. Everyone was shocked to see him grinning at the referee and judges knowing that this dive would decide whether or not he would be the winner. This intense moment did not seem to bother him for he went on to perform the dive flawlessly and win the gold medal. Incidentally, Lenzi showed no sign of fear when performing before an audience of seven hundred million spectators for he had total confidence, focus, and control of his faculties which permitted him to perform better as the pressure of the competition mounted. Just before the event started, Lenzi was asked by a newspaper reporter if he minded diving in the shadow of one of his teammates which infuriated him so much that he used the comment to help him focus better on his dives and increase his desire to win the contest.

Then, there are athletes who seem to "choke" when things get tough and usually perform worse as the pressure of the competition mounts. In such cases, the athlete tries too hard to perform better than the way he or she does in practice. Such poor performances can usually be traced to their lack of confidence which increases the fear factor-fear of losing, fear of letting down teammates, parents, and the coach, all of which result in the diver's inability to control and/or focus on the given moment. When such performances occur, it is suggested that the coach make an attempt to help the diver with his or her insecurity by offering a lot of positive reinforcement. If such an approach doesn't work, the coach might try negative reinforcement which is what I tried on Lenzi at the 1996 Olympics when he was in 26th place with three dives to go in order to qualify for the finals. Meeting him in the locker room, I told him, among other things, that if he didn't hit the next three dives, he was history, and nobody would cry over it- including me. He got the message and went on to qualify and take the bronze medal.

Another cause for "choking" can be found when a diver becomes overly nervous and reaches a point of stress. Like fear and anxiety, getting nervous before a contest can add to a good performance if the nervousness is under control. However, if the diver becomes overly nervous and loses self-control, he or she may perform poorly.

Therefore, the diver may perform better as nervousness increases but once it reaches a certain peak, the diver will lose self-control and the performance will worsen as the fear and stress sets in. One of America's diving coaches, Alan Goldberg, states that divers express their nervousness in three different ways. "The first is physically - where the body changes in muscle tension, rate and depth of breathing, blood flow within the body, heart rate and blood pressure, all of which invites frequent trips to the bathroom, caused by a feeling of nausea, and other physical discomforts. The second is when the diver mentally breaks down and goes through an inability to concentrate, entertains self-doubts, starts forgetting things, and the mind begins racing and has difficulty focusing on the dives to be performed. The third expression is the diver may become hype reactive, withdraw from others, talk continuously, get giggly, and entertain several other nervous habits. A solution to ultra-stress, fear, anxiety, and nervousness that causes one to panic or choke is sometimes as simple as the diver taking three or four deep breaths. In doing so, the air passes through the diaphragm and feeds oxygen throughout the body which relaxes the muscles in the chest and abdomen and permits the diver to focus on positive thoughts and retain self- control.

These cases are offered to show how delicate things can get when attempting to motivate divers to improve their performance when competing. Sometimes a pat on the back, a wink of an eye, a scolding or a hug from the coach, watching others perform, an insult from another teammate, and a million other silly things may or may not motivate a diver. What motivates an athlete may come from within, from others, or from an incident in the environment which can cause the diver to respond in a positive or negative fashion. The time, the place, and the situation often dictate the kind of motivation that may influence the performance of the athlete. Whatever it takes, to make an athlete perform well is often a mystery to the coaches because there is no way of knowing when a diver will get too nervous, develop great fear or anxiety, lose confidence, panic, or lose self- control. When reaching such a state, some divers, unbelievably, may suddenly tum completely around from being in a state of despair and perform far better than they had performed before.

There is also evidence that too much motivation can result in an athlete or team reaching a state of panic that can impair performance or stop performance altogether. When motivation becomes that intense, fear and self-control can become a major factor which makes performance very complex and often impossible. Such a case happened to the University of Wisconsin's football team a few years ago when after a terrible lashing by an opponent, a psychologist was brought in to examine their pitiful performance. The doctor publicly stated that the whole team had been so "psyched up" that they had reached a point well beyond their ability to function.

Perhaps the worst approach in attempting to motivate a diver is for the coach to offer no reinforcement at all, that is, to ignore the diver altogether. Though there have been instances when divers have given an outstanding performance with no aid from anyone, it is still the coach's job to at least offer encouragement then leave it up to the diver as to whether he or she wants help or not at a given time. This approach is not to be confused with the method I used when I said little to the divers before competing in the Olympic tryouts. They were never ignored but rather left alone to feather their own nest. They knew they could seek help from me at any given time before or during their performance but chose not to. They were always given positive reinforcement before a contest and often were reminded, in a positive way, what was expected of them during the meet. My objective was to give them the freedom to depend on themselves when performing and not have to rely on the coach.

Unfortunately, not enough self-motivated and self-disciplined athletes are found these days. Much of this can be blamed on the technical advances that encourage youngsters to watch too much television, spend hours with video games, do drugs, or drive around in cars instead of knocking themselves out performing in some sport. In all fairness, many young people are exposed to great educational challenges that require many hours of preparation and study that often leaves them exhausted and with little time for social and physical activities. On the other hand, many athletes become motivated because of peer pressure, acceptance by others, publicity, awards, professional contracts, fantasies and dreams, and much more. Sometimes athletes become motivated because of a negative incident such as the death of a close friend, disappointment, revenge, jealousy, and selfishness. They can also become motivated due to positive incidents relating to love, hero worship, loyalty, or patriotism.

Technique and how it affects the performance of a dive

Diving technique refers to the movements that are made in a sequential manner when performing a dive. Technique can be related to the hypothesis "No move should be made in the execution of a dive unless it contributes to the performance of the dive." When a diver performs a dive and makes improper moves or makes moves that do not contribute to the performance of the dive, it may be said that the diver is using poor technique. Technique refers not only to the movement used in the dive but also to the timing of the moves and the place where the movements occur. For example, a diver may perform a reverse dive in the pike position and make the desirable moves when touching the feet with the hands but does so well off the vertical line or after the dive has dropped two or three feet from its peak. Making the right moves is good technique but making the moves at the wrong time or in the wrong place is poor technique. Therefore, the success of the dive depends much on the diver making the right moves at the right time and in the right place. This approach to perfection is further discussed in other chapters.

There are times when divers perform a dive in the exact same manner then, suddenly, one diver appears to perform the dive the same way but somehow, it appears different than the others. The difference can usually be found in the diver's physique, coordination, grace, and smoothness of the movements. In other words, the diver performed the dive using a better technique than the others. Such differences are usually taught by coaches who are experienced, knowledgeable, and well-versed in mechanical principles that control human movement.

Experience

Certainly nothing is more important to an athlete than experience. When one has already passed down that competitive road a few times, he or she has gained the ability to make right decisions and anticipate what is to happen. This offers the coach a great advantage over those who have never been exposed to such experiences. A diver with little or no experience in the sport is at a great disadvantage when competing with an experienced diver because the latter is more familiar with the obstacles, tricks, techniques, strategies, pressures, and crowd influence all, of which could be new to the less experienced competitor. The experienced diver knows how to pace himself or herself, perform with the proper timing, place the dives in the proper order, execute and correct certain moves when necessary, knows where and when to save a dive, control fear and anxiety, make good decisions, analyze and evaluate the opponent and above all knows how to compete.

The experienced diver also knows how to train, prepare, and relax. He or she can build strategies for a meet, is more aware of his or her strengths and weaknesses and knows how to correct that which needs to be corrected. Experience also aids the diver in learning to control his or her temper, get along with teammates, and create realistic goals. All of this does not mean that a novice cannot compete with a veteran athlete, for many inexperienced divers learn very quickly, but it does suggest that an experienced diver usually has an advantage over a novice diver who may possess similar abilities.

Talent

Talent is the natural ability to physically and/or mentally perform a given task better than the average person. Not all men are created equal in the talent department. Talent is a special gift that is available for some but not for others. Talent is something a person is born with much of which is often hereditary. For example, some people are born with a musical talent to play a piano or violin when only toddlers. Few would deny that geniuses are born and not made. Most often, people are born with or without certain talents and possess certain characteristics that may vary in quality and quantity. How, when, or where these talents are exploited depends a great deal on circumstances and environment. Those born with great mental, musical, and physical talents may never use their blessings if they are not recognized and nurtured. What a shame that so many are born with hidden talents that are lost or never discovered because they were not in the right position or in the proper environment to have such gifts recognized. Even if they aren't particularly talented, some people become successful in their endeavors because they work hard enough to overcome their lack of talent. But few ever accomplish more than those who are naturally gifted.

Nearly most of my life, I loved to watch Fred Astaire and Gene Kelley dance so, in later life, I decided to take tap dancing lessons out of my appreciation of their talents. However, when attempting to perform the easiest dance steps possible, I found myself exhausted and covered with sweat from my feeble attempts. When looking around at the other members in my class, I found them physically fresh as they learned the steps that I found extremely difficult. Every week after class I would swear that I would not return to again suffer such humiliation. As reluctant as I was to go back and fearing that nothing I was doing was ever going to improve, I continued to go back anyway. After finishing the course, I found that I had never learned to tap dance worth a lick, but I did learn to appreciate and respect the talents of the experts and those that took the course.

In the world of diving, there is no possible way that any of us could ever dive like Greg Louganis even if we remained young for a hundred years and practiced eight hours a day. He was born with every faculty, ability, and talent needed to be a great diving champion. Therefore, the best that can be done for young divers who wish to be like Louganis is to provide them with a diving program that will help draw out and develop whatever talents they possess. In making such an effort, a diver may become another Mark Lenzi who portrayed next to nothing by way of talent when he first embarked on a diving career at the age of eighteen. However, with hard work and desire, he eventually became the best diver in the world.

Self-esteem

Another characteristic identified with confidence is self-esteem. Self-esteem may be seen as how a person sees oneself from a positive view. People who possess self-esteem are achievers, are well organized, have self-control, and have the discipline to accept challenges and push forward. They feel they can do great things and are willing to pay the price to obtain their goals. Self-esteem isn't something inherited but rather something that one has to work for. They may have occasional doubts and question themselves, but they get up again when knocked down. They learn to be good losers and work harder when confronted with defeat. They don't sulk and blame others when things don't go their way. They find that they can get those "lucky breaks" that others obtain if they have faith in themselves. Nearly all of the divers on my team over the years who had self-esteem were usually the best divers on the team. They had little doubt about themselves and portrayed confidence every time they stood on a diving board or platform.

On the other hand, people with low self-esteem are usually underachievers who don' t feel good about themselves. They usually are temperamental, undisciplined, poor organizers, discontented, moody, quick to blame others for their mistakes, and only see the darker side of life. Non- achievers fool themselves when thinking they can create self-esteem by doing nothing. They don't wish to identify their weaknesses and try to correct them but rather find it easier to blame others for their misfortune and always have excuses when things don't go their way. Above all, they don't want to make decisions that would make them feel better about themselves because in doing so, it would take dedication, courage, discipline, and consistency to do so. As a coach, it is very difficult to coach divers with low-esteem because they never feel they are good enough to win, don't take criticism or instruction well, and can influence the rest of the team in a negative manner. Those with low-esteem rarely reach their full potential as a diver because of the way they see themselves.

Fear

Whether a beginner or a champion every diver experiences fear at one time or another when diving and/or competing. Fear is perhaps the strongest emotion divers and other athletes experience in their careers. Fear has kept many potential divers from pursuing greatness. After suffering pain from an attempted a dive some beginning, and novice divers develop such a great fear that they never attempt to dive again.

So, what is this chilling and uncomfortable state that affects us all in so many ways and what causes it? In respect to those who dive, fear may be recognized as a state of apprehension experienced by one who, when placed in an unknown, unfamiliar, or foreign position, believe they will experience personal harm. Fear is an alarm system that goes off when one senses danger. All sorts of fears crop up when there is a possibility of a person being injured or harmed. It is forever present when learning such things as new dives and performing dives from various heights. There are actually two kinds of fear: rational and irrational. Rational fear is one with which a person can identify with such as the parachute not opening when jumping out of a plane or diving from a ten-meter platform for the first time and landing flat on the surface. An irrational fear is one that is believed to exist but may not be real such ashaving a tooth ache and believing that the tooth will have to be extracted. Fear can suddenly appear before a contest, diving on television, or competing before large audiences or after performing badly, having to confront the coach, teammates, and parents who had high expectations for a great performance.

Fear is an emotion that can be an instinctive reaction to possible danger. Such a reaction can be internal, external, or both. Fear is a measurable form that comes in different shapes, forms, and sizes and can change in proportion at any given moment which causes people to react accordingly. While some experience little fear of some things and great fear of others, it appears to be a great mystery to most people because it often appears and disappears in split seconds or remains with them for long periods of time that may last for a lifetime.

To understand how fear can affect a person, let's consider that you have to take a written test that you must pass to remain in school. Realizing the importance of the examination, you study very hard but no matter how prepared you think you are, you still enter the class room with a certain amount of anxiety. The fear increases as you sit down, and the teacher reminds you of the importance of the exam as she passes the test out and places it face-down on your desk. A state of panic almost occurs when the teacher states that there is a time limit for taking the test and you suddenly realize that you are a slow reader. Obviously, nearly all of the fear experienced up to that time is related to the unknown, not knowing what is on the test.

On a signal from the teacher, you tum the exam paper over and begin, finding your hands shaking and your heart beating like a steam engine. When looking at the first question on the test, you begin to panic for it looks like it is written in Greek, beginning to wonder if you are in the right classroom, you look at the next question which doesn't look much different than the first.

Suddenly, you find a question that you can answer, followed by another, which offers a small feeling of relief. Once going over all of the questions, you then go back to the beginning of the exam and find that the questions you could not answer the first time around are not written in Greek after all. After completing the exam, regardless of how well you faired, you suddenly realize that you are no longer experiencing any form of fear because the unknown is now known. Believe it or not, as a school teacher for many years, I have seen students feint or become ill from fear when placed in a similar situation.

Every person who has ever dived has had to contend with fear. How much fear one experiences depends much on the conditions at hand. Some persons have fears that appear to be inborn while others derive fear from outside sources. The origin of innate fear is sometimes difficult to identify because people develop fears from almost anything that cannot be anticipated. Some people develop fear of the food they eat; thunder and lightning; of people they know or don't know; or even such things as germs, spiders, and snakes. Seemingly, for some reason, people develop fears to the point where they can't leave their house, drive a car, ride on an elevator, or fly in an airplane. These fears may take on other forms with names like "phobias" or "compulsions" but whatever the names, they are still fears. Sometimes fear is created within people through their imagination or psychological makeup. Fears are often created from experiences encountered at certain times in a person's life when they are not conscious of the situation. Such fear may cause an immediate reaction, or it may manifest itself over a long period of time before surfacing.

Some people become fearful of something they have seen or heard. Watching a person crash when performing a dive has prevented many persons from ever wanting to learn to dive. After September 11, 2001, when the terrorists attacked the World Trade Center in New York City, it is safe to say that every American who viewed the attack on television, read about it in the newspapers, or were physically present, immediately developed some kind of fear. The amount and kind of fear affecting the American people reached both ends of the spectrum. Some people responded with controlled fear because they believed that the incident would not endanger their personal lives while others throughout the country reacted with panic believing that the terrorists might blow up their homes, place of business, the schools, or poison the water. Such fantasies of what could happen affected everyone in many different ways none of which are found to be measurable for the fear would increase or diminish from day to day due mainly to the news media. That tragedy changed all of our lives. But in doing so, it also taught us to accept, and control our fears of such madmen while continuing to live civil but cautious lives.

Fear can cause great confusion and frustration when it suddenly appears for no apparent reason. When approaching middle age, I suddenly became afraid to fly in a small aircraft, ride on a Ferris wheel, look down from tall buildings, or ride on a roller coaster. Having been an amateur and professional tower diver for over twenty years, heights had never bothered me much. Then, out of the blue, I became terrified of heights but only when I knew that there was a possibility that I could jump and self-destruct. Strangely, I could fly in a commercial plane or look through the window of tall buildings and experience no fear of jumping, but when I believed that I could jump, I immediately became afraid.

This fear remained with me for about ten years until one day I decided to face it and finally talked myself out of it. What I feared most was the impulse of wanting to jump and self-destruct when placed in a position where it was possible to do so. The physical reaction to this kind of fear included clammy hands, dizziness, fast heartbeat, little awareness of things around, little sound, and a feeling of helplessness - none of which ever occurred when I was in a position where I knew I could not jump. As crazy as it may seem, I finally reasoned that this feeling was caused by the devil who was after my soul and was tempting me to do his will. Believing this, I decided to reject his intention to trap me which immediately eliminated my fear and it has never come back. As ridiculous as it may be, this approach proved to be the solution to my problem, but it may not work for someone else. It made it clear to me that such fear is created in the brain and it is possible for one to control or eliminate certain fears if he or she is willing to seek out a solution.

After I felt I had cured my fear of jumping from heights, I decided to test myself and my new- found courage. Jumping from an airplane seemed be an ideal test so I went to a local airfield and took four hours of instruction. They then stuffed me into a jump suit, boots, and helmet and gave me two parachutes; one to put on my back and the other one on my chest which was to be used as a back-up chute in case the main chute didn't open. When the jump master asked me if I wanted to pack my own chutes, I replied "Are you crazy? I would surely get killed if I packed my own." At this point, my real fear was whether or not I could unbuckle the chute in mid-air and plunge to my doom. Oddly, the fear of the chute opening never occurred to me. When the jump master assured me that it was not possible for me to get out of the chute without assistance, much of the anxiety I was experiencing diminished.

When I jumped from a small round disk attached to the strut of the plane four thousand feet in the air, I immediately experienced some apprehension for I did not know what was going to happen until the chute opened which was done with the use of a static line. Never looking up to see if the chute had opened, I enjoyed a thrilling ride safely to the ground. That jump changed the way I felt about myself because I developed some self-esteem in the fact that I was not a coward and could face fear and control it within myself. The reaction from that jump also changed the manner in the way I coached and taught and how I regarded people, which was truly amazing.

As stated, fear is found in all of us. The kind of fear and how it affects us is a dilemma for it depends much upon so many different circumstances. It is also important to know that there are two kinds of fears. It can be a friend, protecting us from danger, or it can be a foe by hurting us. Water can help keep us alive by satisfying our thirst or it can kill us by drowning. Likewise, fire can protect us from the cold or it can bum us. Those who recognize fear and try to work and deal with it, find that it can be a source that helps rather than one that hurts us.

Under certain conditions, those who are unable to function when in a state of panic or experience great fear, can suddenly become very calm, begin to think clearly, evaluate the situation, and then take control of the fear. This may happen when a person is trapped and panics when attempting to find some means to escape. One such occasion occurred to one of our top diving coaches who was involved in a plane crash on the island of Pago Pago located in the South Pacific. While the plane was landing late at night in a rain storm, the coach looked out the window to find the wings of the plane clipping off the tops of palm trees in the jungle. Miraculously, the plane landed in the jungle and appeared not to be damaged or anyone injured. Suddenly the plane burst into flames and everyone, but the coach panicked and ran to the front door of the plane to get out. Unfortunately, the front door was one that required it to be pulled back and slid side-wards to be opened. With the passengers in a state of panic, they crowded the door area which prevented it from being opened. With the plane in flames and people screaming trying to get out, the coach opened the emergency door next to his seat in the middle of the plane only to face hot flames blocking his escape. Realizing his predicament, he crawled on the floor to the other side of the plane and opened the other emergency door but was again confronted with fierce hot flames. In a high state of fear, he realized that he was about to die by inhaling a poison toxic gas given off from the burning plastic seats.

Suddenly, a calm came over him and he reasoned that his only chance of survival was to take a pillow lying under the seat, cover his face, and dive head first out the emergency door and into the hot flames. In doing so, he landed on his head on the wing of the plane and bounced off onto the ground. He then got up and ran as fast as he could away from the plane while expecting it to blow up at any second which, thankfully, did not occur. With the people still trapped in the plane and screaming for help, four badly burned people miraculously managed to escape the fire and walk away panicked and pushed on the front door so hard that it could not be opened. Three of the people who walked from the plane were so badly burned that they later died in the hospital. Thankfully, our heroic coach suffered nothing more than a bump on the head and a couple of slight burns on his face. He later said that due to his diving background, he was able to control his fear which saved his life. After that episode, he would never fly in a commercial plane unless he was given a seat next to the exit door.

It can be seen from this coach's ordeal that one just does not know how they would react when faced with such a fearful ordeal at any given time. The coach was placed in a position that, by choice, he could either save his life, experience great harm to his body, or die. How he would decide to react was not possible to know for at one moment he may have decided to react one way but, at another moment, react another way. When placed in such positions of fear, the choice could make a person appear to be a hero or a coward. When divers used to perform on television after climbing a narrow ladder as high as 170 feet to perform certain dives from a small circular disk, some were so afraid that their voices would change to a higher octave. Others would freeze with fear and decide not to perform a dive from that height and climb down. Having refereed the event for several years and having dived from ten meters for nearly twenty years, I knew that I would not climb to the top of the ladder and, much less do a dive, for any amount of money.

All of us have known of situations where, through fear, people have performed unbelievable feats which were far beyond their capabilities. Some have heard of the mother who heard her son screaming with pain from under a car that had fallen on him while changing a rear wheel tire. Seeing her son in such great pain and perhaps facing death, she picked up the back end of the car high enough for her son to crawl out. On the other hand, some people like to feel that if they saw a burning building, they would run in and get the people out or perform some other great feat in a state of emergency when in reality, they may not do anything.

Fear has been greatly reduced or eliminated in our lives because of safety devices. For instance, traffic signals take away much of the fear associated with crossing busy streets. By regulating the flow of vehicles, they make dealing with traffic a relatively predictable experience which is all too often taken for granted. Likewise, the use of the bubbler when learning new dives eliminates most of the fear of being injured by landing flat on the surface of the water. If the coach understands fear and uses various teaching aids to control it, he or she also finds that the time needed to learn new dives and certain skills is greatly reduced.

Most divers at some time in their careers experience some moments of pain or discomfort which may not be physical but rather psychological. If a coach or teacher can explain to a diver how to avoid pain by making certain moves when performing a dive, the diver can develop an understanding of what and what not to do and avoid much of the fear when performing the dive. Therefore, when a diver is in a good diving program and encounters good instruction, facilities, teaching aids, and safety equipment, he or she will endure little physical or psychological damage and gain more confidence and motivation. Some coaches are heard to say that they do not want a bubbler system in their pool because they can teach and coach without one which may be so. I believe that such reasoning is naive because it involves the coach's ego. Therefore, it is strongly suggested coaches put a bubbler in their pool for they are not only playing with the diver's physical welfare but also their psychological makeup which may have long lasting consequences.

Those who wish to learn to dive, particularly at the novice stage, should do so in a group. Although individual lessons may offer more attention to the student, they also create more fear because the student has no way of knowing what is going to happen when attempting a dive. He or she has no models to look at and can easily imagine the worst. A group setting offers the opportunity for divers to see others perform dives in a learning situation which helps reduce fear. Repetition offers the diver experience in performing certain dives and the opportunity to correct moves in a dive. Some instructors and coaches request the diver, when experiencing pain after performing a dive, to repeat the dive right away because he or she will not have the nerve to attempt the dive again at a later time. This is unwise advice because if the diver repeats the dive and again gets hurt, the fear of the dive is compounded to a point where he or she will never attempt the dive again or may even quit diving. However, a diver who lands flat and does not suffer any injury should be encouraged to attempt the dive again, but only after corrections for the miscues are made by the coach, so the diver does not experience the same experience again.

The transition from fear to confidence

There seems to be a physical and mental similarity in the reaction to those who reach the ends of the fear-confidence spectrum (Figure 1). When some persons develop fear to a state of panic or possess a tremendous amount of self-confidence, they often find themselves unable to respond or react to a given situation. So, they simply "choke" or "freeze" which causes the body and mind to shut down. An explanation of the terms used in Figure 1 may help us better understand the impact that fear and confidence can have on individuals.

* Panic - uncontrolled thinking, confusion, little or no function of mental or physical facilities, no awareness or perception of what may or may not happen, and a threat of danger of their self-preservation.

* Fear- rational and irrational anxiety of that which is not known such as, illusion, fantasy, confusion, vacancy of familiar experience, and disorganized thinking .

* Control of fear - ability to accept the reaction of fear through internal induction and external forces, such as taking deep breaths, which induces positive reaction.

* Confidence - organized thinking, belief in oneself, positive reaction to a given situation.

* Over confidence - bewilderment, illusion, unrealistic dreaming of what may happen without fact or evidence, little or no thought of consequences.

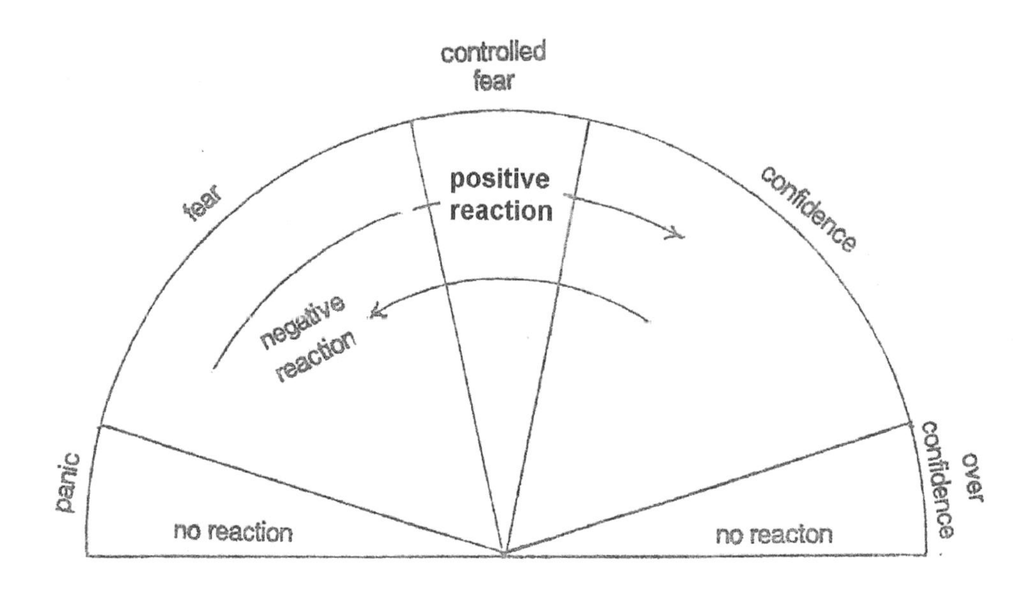

The Transition between fear and confidence
Figure 1

Competitive Attitude

My oldest daughter decided to go out for the swimming team when she was a little tot. Her first competitive race was the fifty-meter breaststroke and like any father, I walked along the side of the pool encouraging her to swim faster. When she neared the end of the pool, she suddenly stopped and stood up on the bottom of the pool. A little surprised, I told her to touch the wall, so she would take third place and her reply was "Dad, I don't want to beat anybody." When I helped her out of the pool, I told her that I understood, but that was the end of her competitive athletic career. Nancy is now in a business that is very competitive, and I wouldn't want to compete with her because she is one of the best in the business. These stories point out that some people may not be competitive in certain areas or at certain times in their lives but can suddenly become very competitive in other areas or at other times. It seems that some are born with a competitive attitude which may blossom at a certain time or under certain circumstances while others learn to be competitive in different settings later in life.

Usually, at an early age, youngsters aren't aware that they are competing with someone or for something. As they grow and enter the school environment, they become more aware of the need to compete with others in order to obtain their desires. They immediately begin to compete in games on the school playground, which involve skipping rope, tag, and hopscotch, and also compete in the classroom for grades, the teacher's attention, acceptance and approval of their peers and other attention getters. This sort of competitive behavior continues to be active before and after school. Most of these competitive patterns are recognized as "simple behavior" because little if any of the competition is planned. They simply behave in a competitive manner because of the surrounding environment. During this period, some youngsters respond out of a natural competitive instinct, while others don't so they have to be coaxed, badgered, awarded or motivated by some other means to get them to compete. Studies have shown that highly competitive children are usually the most popular with their peers.

Once children advance to the high school level, the mode of competition changes from a simple form to one of complexity, which is brought on by the intensity of formal competitive events. Athletes get involved in organized activities that usually include more than one person. They plan and prepare strategies that offer such behaviors as dedication, leadership, teamwork, discipline, self-control, loyalty, and making short term and long-term goals. They also learn to take instruction, make sacrifices, develop patience, and confidence...quite a change from competing for mom's attention. How well the athlete will compete at this higher competitive level depends much on the motivation, confidence, focus, physical and mental prep-a ration, and instruction they receive. A good instructor or coach can direct the competitor to a high state of performance if good communication takes place and the competitor accepts the environment in which he or she is placed.

Obviously, the desire to compete is based on the individual's wants, needs, and goals. Strangely, it is found that some individuals don't need the aid of others in order to compete because they will do so within themselves or when competing against such things as the clock. It is also found that the intensity of the competition often depends on how important the prize or goal is to the one competing. For example, if Notre Dame was to play Ann Arbor High School in a game of football, it is doubtful that the Notre Dame players would be too excited about the contest. They probably would do little preparation for the game showing as much enthusiasm as when watching the movie "Heidi". However, in observing the preparation of the game by the Ann Arbor High School team, we would probably find the whole town spending months preparing for the game with great zeal, spirit and excitement.

In perspective, the Ann Arbor ball players would be yawning a lot before the game due to fear, excitement, and anxiety while the Notre Dame players would also be yawning because of boredom and lack of zeal. Therefore, the quality of competition for Notre Dame would be very poor and require little motivation while the Ann Arbor team would be highly motivated and feel this to be the greatest challenge in their lives. Regardless of the outcome of the game or who competes well or poorly, there is going to be a winner and a loser which is very important to those competing at the time. The most important factor is not which team wins or loses, for it is obvious who will win, but how well they perform which will offer more reward or disappointment to the players than anything else. Either way, most will find the activity healthy with the Ann Arbor players and spectators never forgetting the game for the rest of their lives while the Notre Dame contingency forgetting the whole episode within a few short days.

In sports, one of the big goals when competing is to win; to be number one. But it may be asked just what is really gained by winning; and for that matter what is lost or gained by losing? Normally, the athlete who wins reaches certain goals for the moment and often relaxes and/or becomes complacent over the victory. Self-confidence is certainly maintained or increased but usually the only motivation derived from winning is in trying to win again the next time around. The thought of dominance over others may also be motivating, and sometimes addictive, because beating others often provides a sense of "being better" than the opposition which can offer personal satisfaction and self-esteem. One only needs to observe Tiger Woods when he is playing good golf to recognize this point. But what of the loser?

A person often can learn more from losing than from winning; he or she may become more motivated and focused in defeat. The challenge to win may become more pressing and important than ever before. In defeat, the athlete may question his or her abilities, talent, training habits, attitudes, and goals. If self-confidence can be retained, the desire to compete better may improve and be stronger than before. Unfortunately, some athletes become despondent over losing which can affect their entire view of their abilities and talents. Such a reaction may only be temporary or may be long lasting. Whatever the case, the decision as to which way to handle a loss is entirely up to the individual. As a coach, I often reminded my divers when they lost, it was only a game, and even the New York Yankees don't win every game.

PHYSIOLOGICAL

The need for a physical conditioning program

A diver can have all of the abilities and talents needed to be a good diver, none of which will matter if the athlete is not in good physical condition to perform the dives. Divers who can flawlessly perform a list of dives, that have low degrees of difficulty, with outstanding grace, rhythm, and form have little to no chance to compete with divers who perform dives with high degrees of difficulty. This is due to the dramatic increase in the number of difficult dives performed in recent years that require great strength, flexibility, and endurance. It also should be noted that competitive diving is gradually moving away from performing simple graceful dives because they do not appeal to the spectators and do little to change the outcome of a contest. Such a change requires divers today to take part in some sort of training program that will equip and prepare them to perform dives with higher degrees of difficulty if they wish to compete with any success.

There was a time when no diving coach would ever consider coaching a person who had been a gymnast because of their poor form. Then in the late sixties, gymnastics went through a great transition period that emphasized form and difficulty. The change attracted diving coaches who began to look for gymnasts who possessed the strength to perform difficult dives. The addition of synchronized diving to many competitive programs worldwide and the introduction of tower diving in college conference and national meets has placed even greater emphasis on the need for proper conditioning and training which requires a tremendous amount of strength, energy, and time from the divers and coaches.

Today's competitive diving arena requires divers to remain in peak physical condition nearly all year long with little more than a month to relax and rest between seasons. Divers who compete at the high school level don't experience the same demand for rigorous training as those who compete in other programs because they compete in only one season and in one event. However, college divers normally compete in two springboard events and, with the addition of tower diving, now compete in three events. Divers who compete in meets outside of the learning institutions not only compete individually in springboard and tower events but also in synchronized events from the springboard and tower which means they may need to train for five events. Such a schedule requires most divers to train in the pool and in the gym prior to the season and then adjust their physical training during the competitive season.

Normally, divers have a maximum of three to four hours to train daily, which includes physical training and diving time. This doesn't seem appropriate when some countries train up to eight hours a day. To make up the difference in training time, it has become necessary for the training schedules for American divers to be very car fully planned with every moment used as prime time in the pool or gym. This means, that in the physical training sector of the diving program, the exercises used must be those that best fit the needs of the individual because there is no time to indulge in exercises that do not contribute to their improvement. Another point worth mentioning is that the physical training must be consistent to be effective. Otherwise, those who train only on occasion to physically condition themselves will not fare well in this sport.

Naturally, the purpose of the physical training program is for divers to develop the qualities needed to compete with other divers at their competitive level. These qualities involve:

* Agility - to be able to change directions quickly and accurately while in a state of motion.

* Balance - to develop equilibrium while engaged in static and dynamic activities.

* Coordination - to learn to synchronize body parts that will provide body control.

* Speed - to train the limbs and torso to move as quickly as possible when in motion in order to create more force.

* Muscular strength - to develop muscles, connective tissue, and joints to produce the force and power needed to perform difficult dives.

Development of these qualities requires the selection of exercises in the training program that prepare the athlete to perform dives that lean toward great difficulty. The need to perform exercises that identify with basic simple dives is dwindling because they are no longer being used in most competitions above the age group level. The endless source of exercises that can be used to develop the diver's body is often confusing to divers and coaches because they have difficulty deciding which ones best meet their needs.

Most of the exercises can be found in books, training manuals, videos, films, and articles. The exercises are of an isometric, isotonic, concentric, plyometric, aerobic, and anaerobic nature which can be chosen specifically for the development of certain parts of the body and certain movement patterns. Care should be taken in the selection of exercises and the manner in which they are used to prevent injury and to obtain the best results. Exercises that do not meet a necessary and specific need should be replaced with those that do. Some exercises are found to overlap in their use and value to condition the body. For example, an exercise may help strengthen a certain area of the body, but it may also be used to better the diver's cardio vascular condition by increasing the number of repetitions of the exercise.

Physical qualifications required to participate in a training program

Before undertaking a training program, the coach should require all divers to obtain medical approval which will confirm that they are physically fit to take part in the program. This assurance should be in the form of a written release especially if the athlete has or has had an injury or medical problem. It cannot be assumed that the diver is healthy and devoid of physical handicaps. This decision can only be made by the person that qualifies to confirm their physical condition which is usually a medical physician.

Should a diver perform exercises that create any form of pain, he or she should cease performing the exercise. If the pain occurs again after a rest period, the diver should stop training and inform the coach of the problem. Under no circumstance should the diver continue to execute that exercise until permission is given by the coach or a medical professional. Young divers require a lot of guidance when performing training exercises that require weight and/or repetitions because they can easily injure themselves if not properly monitored. Periodical programs should be set up by the coach to make sure the athletes are exercising properly. It is suggested that a program offer a lot of callisthenic exercises for the very young and beginning divers until they are physically conditioned enough to encounter other forms of exercise that offer more emphasis on resistance.

In recognizing the importance of a physical training program, divers should take a quick look at the kind of training needed to physically develop the body in the three mentioned areas which are flexibility, cardio vascular conditioning, and strength. Obviously, it is not possible to go into detailed training methods to be used by each diver because every training program is different than another with none using the same exercises to reach the divers objectives. It also should be kept in mind that since the program to physically train and condition divers is only one segment of the diving program, it must fit within the time frame that is allotted for such training.

Flexibility

Flexibility of the diver ' s body is acquired through the use of stretching exercises that increase the range of motion of muscles, ligaments, facial sheaths, and tendons around the joints. Stretching is based on the principles of joint mechanics, neurophysiology, and the adaptation of neuromuscular tissue. Care must be taken when performing exercises that relate to flexibility because over stretching can cause stress or injury to the areas involved. The connective tissue responds to tw o forms of stretching: dynamic stretching, which is the tissue that is stretched, like a rubber band and returns to its natural state after the stretching force is quickly released, and static stretching. This when the tissue remains in its stretching state and does not return to its normal form before being stretched. The latter stretch reacts like stretching modeling clay. Stretching exercises that create flexibility should be designed to produce static deformation in order to develop a permanent range of motion which has been shown to be the most desirable for divers.

How exercises affect flexibility

* Extend the muscles and connective tissue of the body to induce flexibility.
* Increase and maintains complete range of motion of a joint.
* Prevent injuries such as cramping, pulled muscles, or muscle strain by maintaining muscle balance with freedom of motion.
* Relieve muscle soreness. If severe injury should occur, complete rest should be used before pursuing further activity.
* Aid in developing coordination.
* Help improve the capacity for activity. Stretched muscles require less energy for the completion of movements.
* Assist in decreasing unnecessary neuromuscular tension by promoting general body relaxation and the reduction of emotional stress.
* Stretch the muscles up to no more than 1.6 times its normal length before tearing the muscle.
* Increase angular velocity while rotating about the axis by reducing the radius of some portion of the body. It also aids in decreasing the splash when entering the water by creating a straighter body.
* Aid in muscular warm-up to promote circulation.

* Add optimal strength gain potential when combined with a strength training program. Nearly all of the stretching exercises from which divers can select will increase the range of motion in joints but static stretch is consistently superior to the others.

It is strongly recommended that when stretching any part of the body, the area stretched should be warmed to around 104 degrees and stretched slowly to avoid the "stretch reflex" to be effective.

Some limits to stretching depend on:

* Joint structure, particularly ball and socket joints, which determine the range of motion.
* A large increase in muscle bulk may adversely affect the range of motion. This may be avoided by using the full range of motion of both the agonist and antagonist muscles or by altering the training program.
* Awareness that young people tend to be more flexible than older people and females are usually more flexible than males.

When to stretch

Stretching exercises should be performed daily from ten to twenty minutes before and after the workout or competition to develop a better range of motion and to decrease muscular soreness. Stretching before practice and a competition can aid in the prevention of injury. The diver should also remember that the range of motion for particular exercises should be increased progressively throughout the season

The regions of the body to be stretched

* The shoulder girdle using the tricep stretch, backward stretch, circular shoulder stretch, arm extensor stretch, and arm adductor stretch.

* The trunk using the abdominal and hip stretch, upper back stretch, lateral trunk stretch, lower back and hip stretch, rotational trunk stretch, and trunk extensor stretch.

* The pelvic girdle and the legs that involves stretching the groin, hamstring, quadriceps, ankles, thigh flexors, and thigh extensors.

Effects of stretching

The degree of stretch plays a more important role than the mode of the stretch. Begin the stretching activity by increasing the range of the stretch slightly, and then increase the stretch after the body begins to relax.

* Ballistic stretching involves moving joints rapidly and powerfully from one end of their range of motion to the other, by using bobbing and bouncing forces. This method can often cause pain and possible muscle or tendon tear and rupture. Ballistic stretching is more dangerous than the others and should be avoided.

* Slow-dynamic stretching is a reduced version of the ballistic method. The joint is moved slowly rather than quickly through a range of motion. It can be combined with static stretching by holding the stretch for ten or more seconds at the extended end of the range. The diver should remember that the range of motion for particular exercises should be increased progressively throughout the season.

* Static stretch should take place to the point of discomfort but never to the point of pain. Partner-assisted stretching is a means of static stretching with the pressure applied by another person. This permits a greater degree of stretch and more range of motion. It is recommended that when applying held-stretching or contact-relax stretching that the elongate state be maintained from six to sixty seconds. Anytime longer has proven to have no effect. In general, this method of stretching should be avoided because the partner may stretch the other person's muscles and connective tissues beyond the tearing point and rupture them. rupture them. However, the partner method is very effective in improving ankle flexibility with little danger of injury.

* Passive stretching is recommended when there is a need for extreme range of flexibility in certain joints. This system should be started in the pre-adolescent period when possible. When using this technique, the diver should stay in a relaxed state and make no active contribution to the stretch.

As in other forms of training, the overload and progressive principles stretching should be applied without causing pain. Worth mentioning again, trying to perform stretching exercises when at normal body temperature is a waste of time.

Having a large number of divers on my team, I found I could save time in my conditioning program by having some of them take ballet classes at school where they could learn to stretch the lower extremities of the body that included the toes, insteps, ankles, and legs. However, I became very careful in their selection of ballet classes because two of my divers ended up marrying their instructors.

Physical Conditioning

Divers must develop endurance and stamina in order to cope with the strenuous training methods needed to compete in various events. Performing at peak capacity for long periods of time is enhanced by cardiovascular endurance. A person in good cardiovascular condition has a low resting heart rate that will beat rapidly during long periods of time. Then after exercising, the heart will return to its normal rate more quickly.

This type of fitness permits one to work longer at a given task without undue fatigue. Cardiovascular endurance is more important to divers than ever before due to the amount of energy spent in performing more difficult dives. and training for longer periods of time each day.

Cardiovascular conditioning reduces the state of fatigue and increases stamina through a combination of aerobic and anaerobic exercises. As the physical activity increases, the cardiac output also increases through the greater input of oxygen transported to all tissues of the body by way of the heart, blood vessels, and blood. Aerobic classes offered in most high schools and colleges are an ideal means for getting the body in good physical condition for sustained activities. With the aid of music, these aerobic classes offer a continuous series of light resistance exercises that in involve many repetitions for about. an hour. Coaches can save much training time if they can enroll their divers in these classes which offer physical activity enhancing agility, balance, coordination, rhythm, and flexibility. Anyone taking these classes will note that the aerobics instructors all use different exercises that cover every area of the body. Many training programs now provide exercise machines such as the treadmill, stair climber, stationary bicycle, etc. that substitute for the many ways of exercising to improve the athlete' s cardiovascular endurance.

A Physical Conditioning Program

Beyond conditioning the body, a training program is also useful in preventing injuries as well as reducing recovery and rehabilitation time in the event of an injury. Most injuries in diving are spread across the joints of the body; including the fingers, hands, wrists, upper arms, shoulders, necks, feet, ankles, knees, and lower back. The U.S. Sports Committee has developed a list of exercises that can aid in preventing diving injuries which are not listed here due to the lack of space but can be obtained through U.S. Diving educational resources. All of these exercises are relatively simple to execute and can be performed around the pool. None of the exercises require any special equipment and are divided into ten groups with a different group performed each day. After ten days, the cycle should be repeated.

The importance of a good conditioning program is apparent considering the number of diving tasks that divers must accomplish in the diving program. On a daily basis, competitive divers take part in such peripheral diving activities as dry land training that involves the trampoline, dry land board, and gymnastic mats; conditioning and warm-up exercises; lead-up dives; and line-ups in the pool. They also practice a certain number of dives performed from the many levels of the tower and the one-and three-meter springboards. In many cases divers also practice synchronized diving from the platforms and diving boards. Normally, divers will perform each dive at least three times, which could have the divers performing well over a hundred dives in each work-out which, I believe, is not practical. Then, additional time is needed for divers to review video feedback and consult with the coach. Ideologically, it would take nearly 24 hours a day to thoroughly go through a training period where the divers ta e part in every phase of the program. This predicament makes it necessary for the divers and coaches to carefully divide the activities over the days of the week and give priority to the important areas of development.

Current divers would have enjoyed competing forty or fifty years ago, when all that was required in a diving workout was to warm up with about five minutes of exercises on the deck, practice three or four approaches on the board, perform a list of ten dives - doing three each, and then taking a shower before going home. "Whew" what an exhausting workout!

Selecting exercises

Due to the seriousness and importance of planning a conditioning program that includes the necessary exercises to be used in a conditioning program, coaches and/or divers who are unsure of their program should investigate and seek aid from other diving programs and outside sources. With hundreds of exercises available that can be used for conditioning the various parts of the body, the coach and the diver should select those that are believed to be the most effective for each individual. The exercises selected should also be used in the program within the allotted time. If certain exercises do not suit the diver or not show any affect, the coach should replace the exercise that is to be used for the same areas of the body. Nearly all of the exercises that can be used may be categorized as:

* Isometric - exercises that involve muscular contractions against resistance without movement of the joint. Isometric exercises appeal to those who do not wish to exert themselves or work up a sweat. An example of isometric contraction is when placing the hands against a wall and pushing against it as hard as one can for a designated period of time. People with high blood pressure or have a heart condition should refrain from doing these kinds of exercises. Tend to hold their breath so the duration of the muscle contraction should be relatively short which is no more than six seconds (some isometric exercises such as some wall sit sessions may last as long as three minutes). These exercises work well in yoga training. People who have broken or sprained any body parts find that isometric exercises are the only ones to prevent atrophy of certain muscles enclosed in a cast.

* Isotonic - a strength exercise performed with a constant weight. This kind of strength exercise is the most commonly practiced. Those exercising in this manner are likely to accelerate the weight rapidly after the initial inertia is overcome which results in the momentum becoming the primary force throughout the remainder of the movement. This can be easily observed when a person performs a clean and jerk exercise with barbells bar-bells. Because muscle action is only

necessary to begin movement in the exercise, strength is not developed in other segments of the exercise.

* Isokinetic - a muscle contraction exercise in which the muscle shortens at a constant velocity. Resistance training equipment allows one to set the speed of the movement within the range of motion to the same degree as the start of the movement. When a muscle changes length at a constant rate of velocity, loading varies or remains constant, but the velocity remains constant.

* Plyometric - an explosive muscle recoil exercise that takes advantage of eccentric contractions of muscles to facilitate performance. A movement is performed to stretch a muscle quickly and then contracts to prevent the muscle from being strained or torn. Such exercises consist of jumps, hops, leaps, lunges, and skips. Plyometric depth jumping is the is the most popular form of eccentric exercise performed by a person dropping from an elevation and upon landing, immediately jumps to another elevated platform. The act of landing then preparing to jump again involves eccentric contractions and muscular strength gains. We see this action when one performs the hurdle and after landing on the board immediately jumps up again in performing the takeoff. Caution to avoid injury should be followed concerning the height from which a person jumps and when any added weights are used when jumping.

* Concentric and eccentric - concentric exercises are known as those of positive work while eccentric exercises are those which produce negative work. The negative work is usually discounted and not calculated. This can be seen when one lifts a weight which can be calculated as work, but no work is calculated when lowering the weight.

* Aerobic - physical work done in the presence of oxygen such as when running and swimming. It refers to the ability to exercise at moderate or heavy intensities for prolonged periods of time. This is why distance runners and swimmers train over long distances in the early part of the training season. This type of training does little to promote explosiveness and strength.

* Anaerobic - physical work done in the absence of oxygen. These are activities that involve high intensity outburst within a short duration such as used when sprinting a short distance.

All of these forms of exercise can be hazardous if improperly used so people who have disability, weight, or posture problems should learn what exercises they can perform safely.

The structure of a conditioning program

The difficulty in setting up a conditioning program is found in the amount of time needed to perform all of the exercises used to condition the divers while also engaging in all of the training tasks practiced in the diving program during the diving seasons. Therefore, a program should be offered that allows alterations and changes when needed. One can grasp a better understanding of the training dilemma when viewing the categories that are subject to the physiological needs of the divers. These areas include:

* The age, gender, competitive level of each diver, and the number of divers that are involved in the program. Evaluating these factors is important when forming appropriate training groups.

* Available facilities - may include the training area in a gym, separate room, or near the pool that offers trampolines, dry land diving equipment, gymnastic mats, weights, balls, charts, and others.

* Tests of the divers to determine their physical weakness and strengths in the areas of flexibility, endurance, and strength. There is no need for divers to spend a lot of time, for example, building up strength in particular areas of the body if they are weak in those areas. If they are not weak in the body, they should then work on some other area where weakness is present. That doesn't mean, for example, that divers should completely avoid strength exercises, but "time" is being wasted if they are trying to develop an area that is already developed. This is particularly found with divers who are naturally flexible but are doing stretching exercises which do little to improve their flexibility.

* The kind and number of instructors qualified to implement the conditioning exercises.

* A list of exercises that refer to flexibility, vascular conditioning, and strength that will improve the diver's physical condition. This should include the type and purpose of each exercise, the number of repetitions, high and low intensity workouts and it may also include those that can be used as a warm-up exercise before starting to dive.

* It is also suggested that the coach take an inventory of the equipment available to determine what types of exercises can be performed in the program. In some cases, equipment can be built with little cost and be efficient and satisfy the need. Example, a three or four-foot steel pipe can be inserted into two one-gallon cans which can be filled with cement to form a bar bell.

* Chart indicating the training schedule before, during, and after the competitive seasons.

* Time schedules for daily dry land training and time for diving practice.

* Short and long-term goals and objectives that can be achieved through the application of the principles and the selection of exercises related to particular goals.

* Administrative supports for the program which may include logging and charting each performance of the training workouts, evaluating the diver's progress, keeping records, promoting activities, and others.

* Determine improvement by evaluating the training performances of sessions, eating habits, importance of rest.

* Monitoring of eating habits, rest periods, circadian rhythm, etc.

The purpose of a conditioning program

1. Raise self- esteem.
2. Obtain proper body weight.
3. Increase capacity to endure stress.
4. Endure long periods of physical activity.
5. Obtain better balance.
6. Improve general fitness.
7. Use exercises that will fit specific training needs.
8. Control the cholesterol and cardiovascularsystem.
9. Develop better body control and mental awareness of body movements.

Caution should be taken when first beginning to condition the body because it is not ready to withstand a great amount of stress when exercising. This is particularly true when performing weight training exercises for exercising too much too soon could cause bodily harm and chronic fatigue. One should start out slow and gradually work up to a point where the exercises are conducive to the planned goal. Exercising the 639 muscles in the body can produce strength and store energy through an extended period of time. This is referred to as muscular endurance. Shortening the muscles at varying rates is called speed of contraction and stretching or extending the elasticity of the muscle is referred to as flexibility. A combination of these qualities creates muscular power.

A physical conditioning program offers

1. Exercises for flexibility - increase muscle length that affect motion around single and multiple joints.
2. Aerobic training - produces muscular and cardiovascular endurance that reduces fatigue and supplies energy to the muscles.

Aerobic interval training is ideal for pre-season training because the diver can focus on reaching certain goals by building up more stamina and endurance and getting the entire body in better shape. Such an interval program has the body exposed to short but repeated periods of stress with timed rest periods. As the diver progresses in the program the period of stress should be increased as the rest periods are decreased which is known as interval training. Some of the goals that may be set by the diver are:

a. Increasing the number of dives in a session.
b. Speed up the movement of the muscles.
c. Increase energy through the muscle system.
d. Improving the cardiac response to specific exercises that entertain fatigue.

3. Balance and coordination exercises - creates muscle and nerve response to activities that are related to specific skills

4. Speed training - involves the exercises that may aid in a dynamic pattern of movement.

5. Strength training - increases the muscle force of output at various speeds of muscle contraction.

Performing such exercises improves sports performance, decreases the potential of injury by conditioning the athlete to absorb normal and abnormal forces associated with diving, and reduces the recovery of exercises that produce fatigue. A physical conditioning program also offers a means for divers to warm up before practice.

Some physical conditioning programs offer cardiovascular benefits through exercises that require repetitions that change the heart rate while, conditioning various parts of the body. Conditioning exercises firm up various parts of the body so that the diver can maintain form, proper alignment of the body for head first entries, withstand the impact when entering the water head first, and prevent injury to the shoulders, neck, back, and arm and leg extremities.

Strength

Strength in competitive diving was not a major concern until the early nineteen sixties when most senior level divers in the world began to perform voluntary dives that involved multi- somersaults and twists. The new difficult dives required a great amount of angular momentum that depended greatly on the strength of the diver's legs. The upper body also needed to be strengthened to absorb the impact of the water and the diver's angular rotation as the divers made their entries.

Exercises used to improve the diver's strength and power normally involve weight training of core muscle groups around ligaments, bones, and connective tissue. Strength exercises are needed to require quick powerful movements that relate to the high velocity of the body parts when performing dives. Such exercises are primarily kinetic or isotonic rather than low velocity isometric training. In performing the exercises, the diver should be aware that the time to stop is when reaching the "break" point that produces pain and/or discomfort.

Though there is not complete agreement on exactly what is the best procedure for building maximum muscular strength, the best policy to follow at the beginning of a strength-building program is for the diver to choose weights that can be used to perform no more than ten repetitions without undue strain. The diver should also choose exercises that relate to the area of the body that needs to be developed. Whatever exercises used by the diver, the strength training session period should not be less than thirty to forty-five minutes or more than ninety minutes. How long the conditioning period should last when starting the training program depends much on the physical condition of the diver and how well he or she recovers from the exercises selected. The strength program should begin with the diver using light weights and gradually increasing the weight based on the athlete's comfort when performing the exercise.

Pre-season and seasonal physical training

The program should be designed to get divers into top shape through the adjustment and consistency in training methods before, during, and after the competitive seasons that will develop and maintain a competitive edge. The pre-season is the best time for intensive conditioning because more time can be focused or reaching certain strength and power goals. The intensity should be lowered during the season to allow the diver to perform diving skills after which intensive training can be resumed. How much one should adjust their physical conditioning program during the season depends on the amount of time available for training each day. With the American divers training two or three hours a day, it is quite difficult to employ a physical conditioning program that can be effective within a short period of time. Of course, this is no problem for those countries who train up to eight hours a day.

The value of rest

A few years ago, I attended a clinic sponsored by the U.S. Diving Olympic team. as one of the expert clinicians, I observed two divers - obviously dedicated to the sport - who displayed training efforts that were much more intense than the other divers. It seemed every move these two made was made with all of the intensity to qualify for the Olympic team as they continued to train on their own after the scheduled workouts of the clinic were finished. They went on, in the rain yet, to practice dives from various heights, perform exercises on the trampoline, dry land board, and mats, then finished with an hour of line-ups and lead-ups from the different platforms while seemingly never stopping in their relentless desire to improve.

After observing these two divers for a few days, I approached them and mentioned that I believed they were over extending themselves in their training workouts. Reminding them that they were not Chinese, and it was highly unlikely that they could train at their pace, they should reduce the intensity of their training to avoid what could result in serious consequences. I suggested that they consider taking short and long rest periods from time to time to allow their bodies to rest and rejuvenate. I also reminded them that it was not possible to put such continual stress on the body without it in some way rebelling and breaking down. Unfortunately, the warning and suggestions were not taken seriously or they came too late because both divers soon after suffered serious physical and psychological problems that kept them from diving and training for a very long time. It was found later that the diver who suffered a major physical injury had not been treating his body properly due to poor eating habits and not getting the proper rest.

These two experiences exemplify the need for the body to obtain proper rest when placed under great physical and/or mental stress. Divers should be aware that training programs requiring long periods of intense physical training should also include short and long periods of rest. Such rest allows the body to recharge its physical and psychological elements which make for better performance and less chance of injury or some other form of body breakdown. This can be more easily understood when we observe boxers who take a minute rest between rounds to reduce the fatigue caused by the activity. When divers find themselves tired from training, they should take a day or two off to allow the body to rest and relax so as to regain strength and endurance. They may also consider taking off a week or two when the body is not responding to such intensive workouts. Such rest will not offer a negative effect in their training.

Divers should train by engaging in high pressure workouts, where the body experiences fierce physical and mental activity. These should be followed with low pressure training periods that permit the body to relax and recover from stress and fatigue. I strongly believe that such an approach to training is important for it has been successful in conditioning athletes in other sporting activities such as swimming and track. In observing "Doc" Councilman's greatest swimming teams over the years, I found that the swimmers "tapered" only for the important meets. It became obvious that the greater the intensity of the workouts, the better the taper worked. One year, Doc decided to reduce the intensity of the workouts to see how much it affected the swimmers taper. Needless to say, Doc never tried that method again for it did nothing to improve their performance which resulted in losing an important meet. I found that divers also need to taper for an important meet by reducing their conditioning program and the number of dives after several intensive practices. Such a taper was found to help divers retain their strength, reduce fatigue, and keep their minds focused on the dives to be performed in the up-coming meet.

The length of the rest period may also be determined by the intensity in which the diver trains and for what period of time. A diver who trains with little intensity or trains hard for a short period of time can expect little benefit from resting regardless of the length of the rest period. But the diver who trains consistently with great intensity for a reasonable time can adjust the length of the rest period in accordance to the state of his or her physical and/or mental condition. Physical tension subsequently impairs performance while mental tension, caused by excessive thinking, worry, and fear, affect the diver's concentration and can also cause poor performance. Most often the athlete knows when it is time to stop resting and get back to training because the body starts to feel strong and relaxed while the mind wants to get back to the action.

Understanding the value of rest, I have often wanted to rest the divers for four or five days before an important contest then have them warm with a few practice dives before competing to see what kind of performance they would offer. Unfortunately, I never gathered the nerve to try it.

In summary, the physical state of the diver in competitive diving is more of a concern to divers and coaches than ever before due to the difficulty of the dives performed in present competitions and the training it takes to participate in so many events and competitions. The keenness of the competition has also continued to improve from year to year in the last few decades which has included use of more difficult dives. Dives that were not thought possible to be performed in meets on the ten meter-platform only a few years ago are now performed by both males and females.

Nutrition

A top performance in competitive diving requires divers to not only be in excellent physical condition regarding strength, flexibility, but also in terms of fitness and lean body mass which may be obtained through proper nutrition. A simple definition of nutrition may be stated as a science that is concerned with properly nourishing the body. The kind and amount of food that one should eat everyday may not seem to be very important, but it is. In competitive diving, divers should be aware of their eating habits which can often determine how well they will perform at a given time or even through their entire diving career. To clarify this point, I had a diver from Europe on my team who I thought could win the 1976 Olympic Gold medal on the ten-meter platform because all of his workouts showed that he had the ability to do so. Suddenly, a few days before the event, he started to dive poorly which got worse every day as he showed no power in any of his practice sessions. One afternoon, I decided to have lunch with him in the village to check out what he was eating and was astounded to find that the only thing he was eating was strawberries. When questioned about his eating habits, he admitted that he loved strawberries and had eaten nothing else since he arrived at the village - nearly a week beforehand. Naturally, this nonsense was immediately stopped, but it was too late for him to regain the strength to compete well enough to even make the finals. A similar occurrence happened with a female Russian diver - favored to win the gold - who decided to eat everything in sight in the village cafeteria causing her to put on about ten pounds before her event that caused her not to medal.

Athletes who follow a diet to help them remain in good physical condition normally perform better than those who take little notice of their nutritional habits. Divers should not suddenly change their eating habits just before an important contest because an unfavorable reaction may occur. For example, some believe they should eat candy bars or eat honey to obtain greater strength which, studies have shown, does not occur. Eating such items before a meet when not in the regular diet should be avoided. Some never realize that they should be as concerned about their eating habits as they are with their physical training program. Other than those who only compete and train during the high school season, most divers must train ten months of the year because they compete in two different seasons. This requires them to adopt eating habits that help them maintain a desired weight while supplying their bodies with substantial energy that will develop strength and keep them healthy.

Recent studies have shown four different attitudes that people have toward eating:

* Gregarious eater - eats many different types of food based mainly on taste.
* Vegetarian - eats food that is not meat orientated, unprocessed and natural.
* Meat eater - eats all kinds of meat with little regard for health requirements.
* Health conscious eater - selective in choosing healthy foods and diet.

How nutrition works

To better understand how nutrition affects athletes while training and dieting, one should first become more acquainted with what is involved in its contribution to supplying energy to the body. The pursuit of excellence in the performance of athletes requires strong cohesion and balance between exercise and nutritional elements that consist of carbohydrates, fats, proteins, vitamins, and minerals. The body receives its nutrition from the ingestion of food and nutrient supplements that permit it to function through a process of digestion and absorption which occurs in a water solvent in the body that also acts as a cooling system when the body is highly active. The body functions best when the energy is generated from food items that provide carbohydrates, fat, and fuel from proteins. When eaten, the food and supplements are broken down into small bits with some of the nutrients absorbed from the food. The cells of the body then utilize the absorbed nutrients as they are transmitted and circulated about the body by way of the blood stream in the form of energy which creates the actions of the body. When taking part in an active sport like diving, essential nutrients are particularly needed in appropriate quantities which depend primarily on the age and physical condition of the athlete and the level of the physical activity in the training program.

The importance of water to the athlete

No other compound is more important than water for without it, life cannot exist. Obviously, water contains hydrogen and oxygen and makes up between 45 to75 percent or the human weight. The content of water is higher in young men and thin people with the amount between male and female dependent upon the amount of body fat a person possesses. Due to the high specific heat (1 calorie per gram) and evaporation (80 calories per gram) water prevents rapid fluctuations in the body temperature and permits small amounts of water (perspiration) to control body heat during exercise. Water also aids in the body by removing waste products in the form of urine, feces, perspiration, and evaporation by heat.

The intake of water should balance out with the amount of water output for the body has no water reserves such as found in camels. When exercising, the amount of water in the body is reduced by about one or two percent which causes the individual to become thirsty. If one reaches the point of dehydration, the heat tolerance of the body can be affected to the point of causing a heat stroke which can be recognized by experiencing headaches, nausea, dizziness, excessive sweating, and cramps. When any of these symptoms occur, it is strongly suggested that the diver immediately drink water slowly to reduce the body temperature. If dehydration becomes intense, a person can undergo unconsciousness, go into a coma, or even die.

Energy-yielding Nutrients

The ways nutrients give energy to the body:

1. Carbohydrates - are either sugar or starches and fibers that are distributed in a variety of plants, grains, vegetables, and fruits which provide humans with 40 to 80 % of energy intake. These carbohydrate food materials, first in the form of glucose then starch and fiber are produced in plants by photosynthesis from carbon dioxide and water while exposed to sunlight and the plant chlorophyll. The digestion of most carbohydrates is initiated with salivary amylase which occurs in the acidic environment in the stomach. It is found It is found that one gram of carbohydrates provides an average of 4 calories to the body.

A. Sugar-chains that compromise carbohydrates are the most abundant components of living matter. The most common sugars are identified as mono - saccharine and disaccharides glucose (blood sugar), fructose (sweetest sugar), and lactose (a component of milk sugar).

1). Mono-saccharine - often called "simple sugar" includes such ingredients as fruit juices, honey, hydrolysis from cane sugar, and milk sugar.

2.) Disaccharides - are two simple sugars linked together such as is found in many unprocessed foods including cane and beet sugar, brown sugar, sorghum cane and molasses, maple syrup, pineapples, and carrots.

B. Starch - are large polymers of glucose formed from polysaccharides which contain many mono-saccharine units that are found in coarsely ground or chewed cereals, uncooked potatoes and legumes. Most of these are not completely broken down when consumed and passed on to the large intestine. The amount of starch breakdown varies on the food physical form so that\ a substantial amount escapes digestion in the small intestine before being passed on to the large intestine and colon. The cooking of starch foods not only improves the flavor but also facilitates the digestive process.

C. Dietary fiber - includes cellulose and is known as indigestible carbohydrates. These fibers contribute to the bulk in the diet and maintain gastric motility. Its nutritional importance is found in preventing gastro intestinal diseases related to chronic conditions, such as heart disease and diabetes.

2. Lipids (fats)- fats in the diet are referred to as saturated and unsaturated which relate the nature of the component fatty acids in the food fat. Saturated fats refer to solid fats such as meats, poultry, seafood's, and dairy fats while unsaturated fats are in liquid form found in olives found in olives, olive oil, vegetable corn, cauliflower, etc. The fatty substances that are organic and do not dissolve in water. Americans who consume an excessive amount of these lipids can be easily identified by observing their abdominal, thigh, hip, and buttock regions. Less obvious are the internal body organs, supplying energy for active muscles, keeping the heart muscle going and keeping the lungs operating regularly. Lipids contain carbon, hydrogen carbon, hydrogen, and oxygen with three fatty acids attached to the three carbon bases of glycerol. Fats are the most energy dense class of nutrients with the body converting one gram of fat to an average of nine calories. Fats function by carrying and storing fat-soluble vitamins A, D, E, and Kin some foods that contain fat. Such fats are shared with glycogen in the liver and muscle and with glucose in the blood to prevent tissue protein from disintegrating.

Fats in the diet are referred to as saturated and unsaturated which relate to the nature of component fatty acids in the food fat. Saturated fats refer to solid fats such as in meat, poultry, seafood and dairy fats while unsaturated fats are in liquid form found in olives, olive oil, vegetable corn, cauliflower, etc.

3. Protein - is found in nitrogen containing classes of food and is the last of the three energy yielding macronutrients. Protein supplies the body ' s nitrogen which is found in such foods as meat, fish, poultry, cheese, eggs, and milk. Its major function is building and rebuilding body tissue through the use of amino acid s. Proteins accumulate to allow the body to grow during childhood and then maintain the body throughout adulthood. The proteins eaten, such as chicken fish, and beans, must first be broken down into amino acids then reformed into specific body proteins for body functions. Whether tissue

protein in our bodies or food in our gastrointestinal tract, all protein is made of chemical compounds known as amino acids. Food proteins are broken into amino acids then digested and assembled in the body cells in a certain order so to make specific tissue proteins to be used as building units in such forms as collagen in connective tissues or myosin in muscle tissue.

Most protein foods contain many different kinds of protein some of which are essential while others do not meet the body's needs. Proteins that contain all of the essential amino acids needed in adequate amount for the needs of the body are found in meat, fish, poultry, cheese, eggs, and milk. Most plant foods are not a sufficient source of protein for they do not contain a sufficient quality of amino acids needed by the body. Such foods as vegetables, legumes grains, seeds, and nuts are all low in certain amino acids, but adequate protein quantity and quality can be obtained by consuming certain foods that complement the amino acids present in these types of protein sources. Protein digestion starts in the stomach with the aid of enzyme pepsin which is effective due to the presence of hydrochloric acid.

The Needed Diet When Training to Compete

The competitive level of springboard and tower diving not only requires divers to be strong, flexible, and agile but also to be as physically fit as possible while creating and maintaining a desirable lean body weight. The last two objectives may be reached by following a diet that controls the quality and quantity of food eaten. Eating properly is particularly important when one is still in the period of growth, for the body is in a constant stage of change - requiring certain nutritional ingredients that offer energy and strength to acquire a top physical development. Physical changes not only depend on what foods are consumed but also how and when the food is eaten.

During their careers, some divers lose lean muscle mass while others gain it. we Some divers have little or no difficulty with maintaining proper lean muscle mass for their bodies respond according to their natural growth. When divers become too thin or too heavy, it obviously affects their performance capacity. In most cases the diver's physical composition can be traced back to their eating habits or psychological views related to diving. An optimal body fat component is probably close to 10% in males and 18 % in females. One of the most perplexing situations for divers is when they are born stocky or obese due to their genetic disposition passed down to them from their parents or grandparents. Some of these poor souls find that no matter how much they diet or exercise, they still have great difficulty in controlling their weight.

Overweight and extremely underweight people are often associated with ill health. With over sixty percent of the adults and fifteen percent of the children in the United States found to be obese, much of the problem can be attributed to poor eating habits and the lack of exercise. Most of the obesity seems to be identified with fast food diets that involve fats, salt, sugar, and oils that contain excessive amounts of calories. Overeating, eating sweets and white bread, and drinking alcohol to access does not offer a firm and healthy body. When the number of calories taken in by the body exceeds the number used up, an increase in body weight can be expected. Though putting on body weight may not directly reflect the eating habits of all divers, it does appear to have some influence on their physical condition. Divers must realize that for every ounce of fatty weight they carry above their normal stature, the more difficult it is to project the body upward from the springboard or tower to perform maneuvers that require great strength and well-conditioned bodies.

Granted, some divers can burn off a great number of calories than is gathered when eating. But due to the physical make up of some divers, this does not occur. For example, many persons drink and/or smoke for forty or fifty years with no sign of adverse effects while others do not have the tolerance to accept such abuse so develop all kinds of diseases many of which result in death.

Obesity

Recently it has been found that the chief cause of preventive deaths in the United States is smoking which some believe will soon be replaced with the obese condition of the young and old. Obesity of the American people has risen to such a state that it threatens to wipe out all the progress made in fighting cancer, heart disease, and other ailments combined.

It appears that female divers are more susceptible to obesity than male divers and have more difficulty working with the problem because they appear to eat more than males while being physically less active. Many females take drastic steps to refrain from gaining weight by indulging in anorexic and bulimic practices that often place them in great physical danger. Some divers can control their weight easier than others while some have great dietary difficulty in trying to establish a good diet routine because they will violate all eating rules when they get hungry. In fact, many find food to be more addictive and difficult to control than those who drink or smoke, and also find it more difficult to quit the habit. In controlling body composition, the kind and amount of food consumed must be related to its nutritional needs. One will not have much success dieting without some form of exercise and conversely, exercise to extreme levels will not cause a loss of a fatty mass if certain bad eating habits are not changed and controlled.

The cause for most people to be overweight concerns two aspects in their eating habits:

1. Energy (calories) provided by food in various forms.
2. Chemicals (vitamins, minerals, etc.) in the food.

Those who are concerned with obesity should pay particular attention to the amount of food they consume when eating food that contains relatively high calorie count. If a person commits to a diet that allows approximately 2000 calories per day, it is quickly recognized that this is not possible if he or she indulges in high energy foods. A short list of high energy and low energy foods that may affect a person's composition is presented here to show how difficult it is to retain a daily 2000 calorie diet. To accept such a diet is not easy when most people love to eat sweets, fried foods, white bread with jam or jelly, ice cream and other dairy products. Potato chips, salted peanuts, beer and other forms of alcohol, much of which is consumed before, during, and after eating calorie-adequate meals does little to reduce one's weight.

Calories in some high energy foods

1 Chump chop	200
2 slices of pork	350
1 pork sausage	250
1 square inch of cheese	140
1 slice of buttered bread	150
1 lb. of chocolates	2500
1 pint of homogenized milk	360
1 teaspoon of oil or fat	30
9 dried dates	260
2 Brazil nuts	100
1 small slice of cake	200
1 glass of beer	150
1 glass of lemonade	100
1 dip ice cream cone	100

Calories in some low energy foods

½ grapefruit	25
1 apple	60
1 orange	50
1 head of lettuce	30
1 whole cucumber	20
1 helping of spinach	25
2 tablespoons of fresh beans	15
12 oysters	100
1 lean veal chop	100
1 egg	70

People are constantly informed, through the media, of thousands of ways they can solve their weight problems if they purchase amazing supplements and drugs that will cause them to lose an outstanding amount of weight within a few short days. Most of these alluring ads also state that there is no aftermath of physical danger in using products and also no need to exercise. Similar pressures are put on the public to buy amazing exercise machines that, after using them for twenty minutes a day three times a week, they will immediately become Miss or Mister America.

Of course, some of the supplemental products and exercise machines have merit but many are also found to be damaging to a person's health due to the rejection of the supplements by a person's system and the failure to use the exercise equipment with any consistency for a period of time. All in all, it adds up to people spending billions of dollars a year trying to obtain a "quick fix" for a healthy body without any physical work. These who believe they can buy their health artificially while continuing to eat the wrong kinds of food, smoke, drink alcohol, and do drugs with their bodies never breaking down live in a dream world. If this approach was effective, everyone in America could become healthy nearly overnight and with little chance of disease.

Most people know that it is just not that simple to obtain and/or retain optimal health. Realistically, the body is a very complex machine that must be treated properly and physically tuned to stay healthy and functional. This requires the body to receive proper nourishment and exercise over a period of time that will produce a sound and healthy product. If one wishes to lose weight, they should do so by aiming to lose three or four pounds a week through a good diet and adequate exercise. Some believe that taking a Turkish bath or spending time in a sauna will reduce weight quickly by perspiring. They are correct until they drink some water which -immediately restores the body's water balance and weight.

A suggestion to those who seek out supplements when attempting to lose weight is to seek professional help from a physician or dietician who can offer direction that is safe. This is particularly important when supplemental information is offered via the web site and other forms of media. Articles can be found that can support their contents with scientific facts and laboratory testing offered by professionals.

Underweight

Divers who are underweight generally experience the problem of not being able to project the body from the board high enough to perform difficult dives that require strength and certain acrobatic skills. Though most under weight problems are concerned with diet, one finds that many divers are genetically thin because of the genetic structure inherited from their families. In cases where divers have difficult gaining weight, some solutions are offered here that may be helpful in fixing the problem:

1. Seek professional help from a physician or dietician.

2. Be aware of high calories and high energy food and eat as much as the digestion will allow.

3. Engage in a physical weight training program that can offer the development of more strength along with an increase in weight.

4. Avoid mental stress and try to relax and rest as much as possible.

In reference to being thin, nearly all Chinese divers are thin due to their rice diet and their intense physical training program that involves around eight hours of strenuous exercise every day. Most Chinese do not indulge in a lot of sweets or drink alcohol, so they have no problems with muscle mass, being overweight, or attracting diseases.

Creating a healthy diet for a diving program

1	package of English muffins, whole wheat or 3 wheat bagels
1	loaf of thick sliced grain bread
2	corn or brand muffins
1	package of whole wheat pita
1	box of Rye Krisp
1	box of stoned- wheat or other whole grain crackers
1	box of fruit and fiber, Grape Nuts or high fiber cereal
1	quart of orange; grape, or cranberry juice
2	12-ounce cans of V-8 juice
1	cantaloupe
1	pint of blueberries or strawberries
3	peaches, apples, pears, or nectarines
¾	pound of grapes
1	kiwi or plum
2	bananas
1	lemon
1	ear of corn
1	bunch of fresh broccoli
2	large tomatoes
1	cucumber
1	green pepper or other vegetable for a salad
1	large carrot
1	bunch of scallions
1	head of garlic
1	large baking potato
1	pound of spaghetti, fettuccine, or rotini
1	small can of pizza or spaghetti sauce
1	can of chick-peas in water
1	jar of natural peanut butter
1	7 ounce can of salmon
1	½ ounce cans of tuna
½	gallon of low-fat milk
2	8-ounce yogurt low fat (vanilla, lemon, or plain)
6	ounce feta cheese
1	stick of margarine
1	small bottle of safflower oil
1	bottle of low sodium soy sauce
1	bottle of salad dressing – low calorie
1	bottle of ketchup

When creating a healthy diet for training, it makes good sense to add concentrated vitamins and minerals to the diet with particular focus on Vitamin " C". This vitamin depletes quicker than any of the others during growth and training. The diver should also include high carbohydrates and low-fat food which is not easy to find in a convenience store so try the supermarket.

When creating a healthy diet for training, the meals should offer maximum nutrition with minimum effort and should be well balanced with around 60 percent carbohydrate, 20 percent protein, and 20 percent low fat. For most diver's body types, such a diet is not a weight loss program for each meal contains around 700 calories and a total of 2000 calories for the day with males eating more calories than females. Small people should eat less than those who are large, and the adjustment of hunger can be adjusted after dieting a few days.

***Some foods that are nutritionally rich in calories from which divers can choose is offered by* Nancy Clark, Author of "The Athletes Kitchen"**

Nearly all of these items can be eaten within five or six days. Please note that there is no meat in this list of diet foods.

An example of some foods that may be used in a diet for the day may be:

Breakfast

a. Fruits such as bananas, watermelon, cantaloupe, orange juice, different kinds of citrus

   fruit juice.

b. Yogurt and low-fat milk.
c. Cereal such as Grape-nuts or other high fiber cereal.

Lunch

a. Tuna salad - cheese, tomato sandwich- cup of broccoli -feta pasta.
b. 2 slices of bread- large tomato - cup canned tuna-½ large cucumber tips.
c. 2 ounces low-fat cheese - ½ cup of cottage cheese - 1 tablespoon of Dijon mustard - 4 ounces of grapes.
d. Large peach- scallions to taste - ½ chopped tomatoes - 1 ½ carrot sticks.
e. 1 can of V8-juice - spoon into 6-inch pita - 1 kiwi - frozen banana.
f. ½ cup of berries - 1 cup of low-fat milk - 8 stoned wheat crackers.

Dinner

a. Salmon salad (1/2 cup of lettuce, ½ carrot, ½ cucumber, ½ green pepper) broccoli - feta pasta -spicy chicken - English muffin pizza.
b. ½ apple - 1 ½ cup pasta - 7 ounce chicken breast- 2 English muffins (four halves)-½ canned salmon 1 slice of bread - 1 large backed potato with two spoons of yogurt or cottage cheese- 2 ounces of feta cheese - ½ cup of chick peas

- 12 ounces of orange juice mixed with club soda - 1 six inch pita bread - 2 tablespoons of low cal dressing - ½ frozen banana.

Other beverages

Coffee	Diet drink
Decaf coffee	Decaf or herbal tea
Tea	Spring water or club soda

Bran muffin ingredients

1 box of Bran Flakes or Raisin Bran cereal
1 egg
1 small bottle of molasses
1 small bag of whole wheat flower
1 box of baking soda
1 small box of sugar

Great eating menus

Breakfast

1	cup of orange juice
1	English muffin
4	teaspoons of peanut butter
1	cup of low fat milk

Lunch

½	cup of low-fat cottage cheese
½	cup of berries
1	large muffin (with cottage cheese or cinnamon)
1	snack – 3 stoned wheat crackers and 1 cup of low fat milk

Dinner

6	ounces of oriental steamed fish
2	cups of spinach (cooked)
1	large ear of corn on the cob
1	pat of margerine

Eat out

Japanese - soups with noodles, sushi, chicken and fish dishes.
Chinese - hot and sour soup, sautéed vegetables, mu shu chicken.
Italian - minestrone, pasta with marinated sauce (avoid oil or creamed based sauces).
Salad bar - thick slice of hearty whole gram bread and soup (not creamed based).

Avoid dairy products which may not be low fat, and oily salads.
Deli - a lean meat sandwich, not over stuffed, on thick sliced whole grain bread, with mustard (not mayonnaise).
Other possibilities - salads with wedge of lemon instead of dressing, baked potato without butter or sour cream, and grilled chicken or fish with no creamy sauce.

The "Egg" Diet

This is a scientifically computed diet that is high in protein, vitamin, and mineral content, but enables everyone to peel off fat with relative ease. This is called the "egg" diet with the eggs cooked in any manner except fried and which is consumed in every meal including breakfast, lunch, and dinner. Nothing but pure water, fruit juices, and tea or coffee without sugar or cream can be drunk if the diet is to be effective. An obese person may eat any reasonable quantity desired as long as the number of calories is in the low range category.

One should participate in the diet until the desired weight is met before making changes that will enable the diver to keep the weight stationary. No more exercise than pushing away from the table is needed in this diet but it is suggested that one do moderate exercise for at least twenty minutes a day. Divers should go on this diet during the "off' season. Suggestions for food to be eaten in the "egg" diet for one week are suggested here. Choices can be made for each meal a day except for those foods specifically stated.

Breakfast
1 eggs
1/2 grapefruit, orange,
1/4 cantaloupe, berries pure water, tea, coffee (no sugar)

Lunch
2 eggs
tomato, celery, cucumber, lettuce, spinach, fruit salad,
1 piece of cold chicken for one meal a week.

Dinner
2 eggs
Salad combination of fruit and lettuce
2 vita wheat biscuits
grapefruit,
1 small grilled or broiled steak without fat for two different days a week
natural uncooked vegetables such as celery, carrots, tomatoes, etc.
cottage cheese (not cream cheese)
cooked cabbage
1 fish (broiled or grilled) on Friday

1 piece of chicken for one dinner
vegetable soup
pure water, fruit juice, tea, or coffee

Vitamin tablets can be added if desired. Repeat this cycle for at least two weeks or until the excess weight is gone. Once the desired weight is met, it can be maintained if the dieter cuts bread and butter out completely and has fruit occasionally at lunch. Breakfast or lunch should not be skipped for this makes one irritable and hungrier.

Controlled Weight

Divers who do not find weight influencing their performance often give that part of their program little concern. What many of them do not realize is that in eating the wrong foods or drinking the wrong fluids can make a difference in their performance depending on what, when, and how the food and fluid is consumed.

When divers are training or competing in a contest, they should be aware of the kind of food and drink they put into their bodies. Food that is hard to digest such as certain meats, peanuts, apples, potato chips, etc. should be avoided prior to a competition or a training session. Most divers believe they should eat sweets like candy bars and honey for energy before competing. This is not so, for such energy sources are difficult to digest. Probably the best way to prepare for a diving contest with relation to food is to eat a meal high in protein at least two hours before the contest so as to give the food a chance to digest and for the body to rest. Drinking milk shakes or eating things not normally in your eating habits is not a good idea and should be avoided.

Digestion

Allowing for proper digestion of food eaten for much of the value of the food is lost if not properly digested. The best way to digest food is to eat the food "slowly" and chew the contents well before swallowing it. In this way, the acids in the mouth and stomach help in digestion. Eating a meal should take at least fifteen minutes or more. No matter how good the food may taste, it should be eaten in a digestible way which takes time. Like dogs, many people gulp food down so fast that they cannot taste it.

Naturally, certain foods appeal to some people but not to others. Per individual it helps to select nutritious food that is pleasant to the person's tastes. People should not eat when in a stressful state for it is very difficult for food to be digested. It is also not a good idea to read or watch television while eating because it takes a lot of energy for the body to be working in two different ways at the same time.

Many contests have been lost because of upset stomachs due to eating too close to the time of the competition when the diver begins to experience stress and tension prior to the contest. Divers should eat nutritional food that is easy to digest: and not require a lot of energy for digestion. Strenuous activity should also be avoided prior to a contest so as not to fatigue the body. If the divers eat anything before the contest, it should be food that is as close to its natural state as possible. That means fruit and vegetables that are not cooked or sweetened.

Some guidelines for dieting

As offered by "Guidelines for Americans", seven suggestions are given for individuals and groups who wish to create a diet that offers health and helps prevent diseases.

* Eat a variety of foods: The greater the variety, the less likely the person is to develop a deficiency.

* Balance the food you eat with physical activity: Exercise in some form at least twenty to thirty minutes a day to help reduce excess body fat and strengthen muscles.

* Choose a diet with plenty of grain products, vegetables, and fruit: This will not only help supply more of the needed starches for energy but also provide many essential nutrients from plant foods that offer vitamin B and C, foliate, and dietary fiber.

* Choose a diet low in fat, saturated fat, and cholesterol: Americans have traditionally consumed a high - fat diet which has led many to become obese and develop health problems.

* Choose a diet moderate in sugars: The major health hazard when consuming too much sugar is tooth decay though it goes to say it does not aid in keeping the weight off the body.

* Choose a diet moderate in salt and sodium: The main source of dietary sodium is ordinary table salt. Excessive salt is not healthy for anyone especially for those who experience hypertension. Many processed food products contain considerable amounts of salt and sodium compounds.

* If you drink alcohol, do so moderately: Drinking alcohol to excess has placed many at risk while endangering others, especially when driving a vehicle. Drinking alcohol excessively has also led people to heart and chronic liver disease, neurological disorders, and throat and neck cancer.

* Face the challenge of abstinence and avoid the lure of the availability of food.

CHAPTER 4

THE COACH

Coaches Identities

Physical	Psychological	Social
Voice	Experience	Personal habits
General health	Ability to communicate	Association
Hygiene	Emotional stability	Maturity
	Level of personal standards	

What kind of coach are you - lousy, good very good, excellent?
What kind of coach do you want to be?
What does it take to be a good coach?
What competitive level do you wish to coach?

How to become a diving coach

There was a time when all it took to become a diving coach was to step out onto the pool deck and start yelling at someone on the diving board. No one needed any diving knowledge, experience, or credibility whatsoever. Many of these self-made experts often found their instruction unfounded which often resulted in pain and bewilderment for the divers while offering little improvement in the diver's performance. A remark often heard in such situations was "The diver learned the dive the hard way" implying that the diver experienced painful trial and error methods when learning to perform the dive. To be a diving coach in America still does not require a person to have any academic preparation since there are no educational institutions that offer classes on how to *coach* competitive diving. It is also very rare to find any school that offers classes that *teach* competitive diving. Universities have frequently hired diving coaches, many of whom do not have a college degree. It is terrifying to think that people will allow themselves to be instructed by someone who has little to no qualifications or experience in teaching or coaching a contact sport such as diving, which could have an enormous impact on the welfare and safety of the student.

Before the middle of the 1980s, anyone in America could be a diving coach if they wanted to be. There were no requirements. After more than 80 years of permitting anyone to teach and/or coach with no qualifications, United States Diving was formed, and soon offered a safety certification manual that required those, who wished to coach had to pass a test on the material in the manual. The manual contained all of the safety aspects related to diving but offered very little information on how to teach or coach diving. Primarily, the purpose of passing the safety certification test was to protect coaches from law suits involving diving accidents. The certification also protected the diver from being coached by anyone who was not familiar with the safety features involved with competitive diving.

A short time later, the certification was revised to include risk, rescue procedures, and spinal injury management combined with traditional water safety and physical rescue demonstrations related to CPR and First Aid. At this writing, there are nearly fifty qualified instructors around the country who can administer these tests to those who wish to qualify as diving coaches. Unfortunately, the tests have no bearing on a person ' s ability, experience, or aptitude to teach or coach diving. Therefore, in spite of the certification process developed by USA Diving, a person who passes the Safety Certification tests can be certified as a diving coach even if he or she may have never seen a diving board, let alone been involved in the sport

How people become diving coaches has been an interesting question. Many of those who profess to be diving coaches have been self-taught or have been instructed by their parents who have had little or no background in the sport. Others have been coached by their husbands or wives who were former competitive divers, while some have remained in the sport after retiring from competitive diving or gymnastics. Although there is some similarity between competitive diving and competitive gymnastics, they are two different sports which do not qualify anyone who has coached one to coach the other.

Sources from which diving coaches have drawn their information to coach are often gathered from their own experience as divers, obtaining information from their coaches, observing others who coach, watching divers perform, studying video tapes, and reading some of the few available books on diving. In all, diving coaches have accumulated their knowledge by association, copying others, and by trial and error. However, there are many questions concerning how much of their acquired information is authentic and accurate. Therefore, it is critical that coaches know how to obtain and apply the correct information to safely instruct divers.

It would seem natural for one who wishes to coach diving to first look in the diving rulebooks beginning with the F.I.N.A. rulebook which governs most of the national and international diving competitions throughout the world. Unfortunately, the only information in the F.I.N.A. rule book that relates to the execution of dives is a series of drawings performed in sequence that were offered in 1912 some of which were so badly portrayed that neither God or Superman could execute them. Some other drawings were added to the book in the 1970's many of which were an improvement. With the exception of the forward header (front dive in the layout position), no rulebook has ever offered any written or descriptions of how dives should be performed.

The reason why the forward header was described in the F.I.N.A. rule book was for an event called "Plain Diving" which was presented in the 1932 and 1924 Olympics. This event required a diver to perform two front headers from the five-meter and two from the ten-meter platforms. Unbelievable, the diver who performed the four dives the best won an Olympic gold medal. Since at that time no one was sure how the dive was supposed to be executed, a vague written description of the dive was provided and remained in the F.I.N.A. rule book for over thirty years... even though the event was dropped following the 1924 Games. Essentially, the sport of diving has operated over the years with no authentic concepts or guidelines on how dives should be properly performed or in what desirable fashion.

If authentic and accurate information on diving is to be offered, it must first be recognized, evaluated, and changed to prevent any bias or prejudice issues. Even when found to be wrong, the concepts and ideas that have been so strongly engrained in the minds of coaches throughout their careers are very difficult to change or delete. To change or eliminate such coaching information requires the coach to have a curious and open mind and a willingness to try new methods and ideas before forming any judgment of their worth.

Qualifications for those who wish to be diving coaches

It is fairly obvious that some sort of a qualification program should be required for a person to become a diving coach in the United States. Incompetent coaching can and does result in poor performance that often results in diving accidents, some of which can be serious. A required course on how to coach competitive diving would go far in improving the kind of instruction a coach could provide for competitive divers. The course may take a week or more to be effective because the student would be engaged in activities involving the setting of the class room and diving well.

Should such a curriculum be offered, it could also include times when the coach could return to be upgraded in various diving areas. Anyone seriously interested in coaching diving could find the time to take advantage of such a program.

Until a coaching program of this nature is offered, the progress of competitive diving in America may continue to dwindle as it has for the last two decades.

The competitive diving level in which the coach wishes to coach

Like school teachers, whether it be kindergarten, elementary, junior high school, senior high school or the university level, coaches also work at different levels in competitive diving. Many coaches cannot coach at the level they prefer because of the environment they are in and the amount of time they have to coach. The coaching environment can greatly affect a coach's chance to gain experience and knowledge. Others may be qualified to coach at a high-competitive level but feel more comfortable coaching divers at a lower level. When coaches attempt to coach divers who can perform at a higher level than that of themselves, little if any improvement by the diver occurs which often confuses and frustrates both parties. This is a time when the coach should make some decisions pertaining to the welfare of the diver.

A simple guide for the kind of dives one should be able to teach and coach at various levels is offered here to help one decide at which level they should take part. This guide is based on the *teaching* abilities of the coach. If the coach cannot teach the dives properly, then it is questionable he or she can successfully coach. Many of these dives may be taught at a different level and may not be mentioned in any of the levels. It is therefore, dependent on the coach as to what dives the divers are safely able to attempt. A bubbler should be used to protect the diver from injury and to build confidence from knowing that very little pain will result if a dive is incorrectly performed.

Beginner level - Teaching simple and basic techniques used in the forward approach, the take-off from the board, and basic dives requiring head first and feet first entries from the one-meter springboard. This includes the easiest dives from each of the five groups of dives which are the front, back reverse, and inward dives in any of the tuck, pike, and layout positions; single somersaults in the tuck position from the first four groups; the forward 1 ½ somersault in tuck position; The diver should also learn to perform a front somersault save from the side of the pool and off the one-meter board. This level of learning usually involves young children but can be taught at any age.

Novice level - After teaching all of the dives at the beginner level, if available, the coach should teach the five basic dives from the three-meter springboards in the tuck, pike, and/or layout positions. Returning to the one-meter board, teach forward 1 ½ somersaults in pike position, and: the forward; backward, inward 1 ½ somersault, tuck position: and back and reverse dive with a half twist; and a front somersault with a full twist.

Intermediate level - Teaching one somersault in pike position, from Groups two, three, and four; back and reverse somersault in layout position, double somersaults in tuck position from Groups one, two; and three; inward 1 ½ somersault in tuck position; back and reverse somersault with 1 ½ twists; forward somersault with two twists from the one-meter board; forward 2 ½ somersault in tuck position ; inward 1 ½ somersault in pike position; back and reverse somersault with 1 ½ twists; and forward somersault with two twists.

Junior level - teaching forward 2 ½ somersault in pike position; 1 ½ somersaults in tuck or pike position from Groups Two Three and Four; forward 1 ½ somersault with two twists; back and reverse 1 ½ somersault with 1 ½ twists; from the one-meter board. If 3-meter board available, forward 3 ½ somersault, tuck; back, reverse and inwards 2 ½ somersaults in tuck or pike position; back and reverse 1 ½ somersaults with 2 ½ twists, and forward 2 ½ somersault with one twist from the three-meter board.

Senior level - Teaching forward 3 ½ somersaults in tuck position; back reverse, and inward 2 ½ somersaults in tuck and pike position; forward 1 ½ somersault with 3 twists;

back and reverse 1 ½ somersaults with 2 ½ and 3 ½ twist; inward 2 ½ somersaults tuck and pike position; and forward 2 ½ somersault with one twist from the one-meter board. From 3-meter, forward 3 ½ somersault in pike position; back, reverse, and inward 2 ½ somersaults in pike position, back, reverse, and inward 3 ½ somersaults in tuck position; back and reverse 1 ½ somersaults with 3 ½ twists; back and reverse 2 ½ somersaults with 1 ½ twists, and forward 2 ½ somersaults with two twists.

It must be remembered that those who wish to coach divers at the higher levels, must know how *to teach* the diver to perform the dives performed in competition at that level. Most of the dives, particularly those from the 1-meter springboard, favor the male's competitive levels. Most female divers can perform the dives up to the senior level but, due to their lack of strength, are not able to perform several of the dives from the different groups. However, female divers over the years have progressed to the point where they can almost match the male divers in difficulty when performing from the ten-meter platform.

Divers at the senior level require an experienced instructor or coach when learning highly skilled and difficult dives. Most divers in high schools compete only from the one-meter board so they are not involved with three-meter competition. Nearly all of the diving programs outside of the high schools have divers compete from the one and three-meter springboards and various platform levels on the tower.

The coach's philosophy

Perhaps the first characteristic to evaluate when obtaining a diving coach is to explore his or her personal philosophy concerning competitive diving for this portrays the entire pattern of a person ' s coaching career. A philosophy is developed from ideals, goals, expertise, behaviors, experience, and guidelines all of which have great bearing on how good or how successful a coach may be. A coach's philosophy will vary from person to person and will often affect those with whom the coach works. The coach's philosophy will change from time to time during his or her career because he or she gains experience in the field, recruits and works with divers at different competitive levels, and finds a change in the environment and exposure with the times.

A Coach's philosophy should have goals that are achievable and realistic and not just fantasies or dreams. Common goals should be shared with the athletes, so they too can relate better with the coach and other team members. The coach whose philosophy is based on the welfare of the divers has a much better chance of achieving satisfaction than one whose philosophy is geared toward his or her personal desire for success and fame.

As stated by age group diving coach, Randy Peterson, "Today's success is too often mistaken with winning and I believe that one should examine where this attitude comes from. Yes, parents and media play a large roll in instilling a *must-win* attitude into our youth, but isn't it the coach's job to stress what sports are really all about? -----How far do we go as coaches to produce a champion? · What about those who will never achieve that higher level? Shouldn't our coaching philosophy help build their character regardless of the skill level or what they can or can't do for our country? Such a philosophy should require the diver to help achieve the highest level of performance possible using a system that fosters style and technique through instruction, discipline and learned self-motivation. Such a philosophy may not produce national champions because most divers do not possess the talent to achieve such goals, but they will leave the sport having learned much more important things about themselves."

I believe that the coaches should offer the divers the best of themselves in teaching them to not only be better divers but to be better persons and citizens. The coach should be responsible for the diver's behavior when under his or her supervision and place their welfare before his or her own. I like to think that the coach's philosophy acts as a road map for the divers which will take them over roads that have curves, hills, bumps, and detours from time to time. But if they stay on course, it will lead them safely to their given destination. How comfortable the ride will depend on the kind of philosophy the coach possesses.

For years, Doc Counsilman kept telling me if I wished to develop a positive philosophy for my teaching and coaching that I should read Dale Carnegie's book *How To Win Friends and Influence People.* Fool that I am, it took me until after his death to get around to reading it and like he had said for years, it changed the way I saw myself, my teaching and coaching, and particularly the way I saw people. So, I say to you, if you want to develop a positive philosophy that will bring you success through a better understanding of yourself and your divers, read the book - not once, but several times! Coaches today need to be understanding and personable with the divers and be aware of the changing times to know how to lead them to a better performance on and off the board.

The role of the diving coach

As in every organized sport, the coach is the most important part of the diving program. He or she is responsible for everything in it, whether having started the program from scratch or haven taken over one on that has been in existence for a long time. In any case, the coach is responsible for the failure or success of every function and activity associated with the diving program. Keeping this in mind some of the roles of a coach include being:

1. As an educator

A good coach must also be a good teacher; for teaching the diver creates the base for diver ' s entire performance on and off the board. Teaching varies from coaching in many important ways:

* ***Teaching*** *is directed toward self-satisfying objectives.*

Coaching is directed toward obtaining certain goals that will offer success when competing in an activity.

* ***Teaching*** *introduces the diver to new physical, psychological and emotional experiences that include fear, challenge, self-control, discipline, receiving instruction, patience, and getting along with others.*

Coaching is improving and/or changing physical, psychological and emotional experiences that are already familiar to the diver.

* ***Teaching*** *is concerned with the basic fundamentals needed to successfully accomplish desired goals regardless of how poor the performance of the diver may be.*

Coaching is concerned with offering more defined points of instruction that adds to the form and proper movements used in the performance of the dive.

* ***Teaching*** *is a trial and error activity where there is no guarantee that the diver attempting to perform a dive will not make a mistake that could be painful.*

Coaching is, using mechanical principles based on Newton's Laws of motion as a guide when improving the performance of dives the divers have learned.

* ***Teaching*** *normally involves the use of the part/whole method which is seen when the diver makes primitive movements that will help in performing the dive.*

Coaching is concerned with the diver making more intricate movements that will result in a better performance of the dive.

* ***Teaching*** *is concerned with a "group dynamics" atmosphere which indicates a group taking part in learning to perform a certain skill.*

Coaching is having a "one on one" personal contact with a person without the aid of others.

* ***Teaching*** *greatly focuses on the individual and group learning of basic safety skills that can prevent injury.*

Coaching is working with those who are already familiar with the dangers involved when performing a particular dive. Such divers can apply the needed safety features because they have much more body control than the beginners.

* ***Teaching*** *normally requires a short period of time to reach the objective.*

Coaching often requires a long time to reach certain goals.

Having observed how divers are taught and coached, it should be helpful for the educators to understand how the athlete learns from the educational process offered by the diving program. If the teachers understand how the learning process works, they can more easily prepare information and materials that will offer the best means needed to reach the objectives and goals of both parties. It is therefore helpful for one to not only know what it takes to be a good teacher or coach, but it is also important that that the teacher knows what it takes to be a good student. I believe that the athletes who learn the most in a program are those who are under the influence and guidance of good teachers and coaches who provide information that encourages the divers to *want* to learn.

It is understandable that poor instruction from a teacher or coach will result in little learning by the athlete. In the same token, if the athlete is not capable of learning the information provided by the teacher and/or coach, there is little the teacher or coach can do to help the athlete. Educators often measure their success as a teacher or coach by the response they receive from the divers. Likewise, the divers measure their success in the program by the way they respond to the information and guidance received from the educators. It is believed that the learner has as many patterns to go by as do the teachers and the coaches. Therefore, if teachers and coaches know how to communicate with the athletes, the easier they find it to construct a sound base of information that will successfully educate the athletes

The steps taken in the process of learning usually deal with curiosity, confusion, frustration, then learning. The general steps can be seen in the following pattern (Figure 1). The gradual elevation of the zigzag line steps represent the changes in the progress made as the person learns through instruction. Studies have shown that in the process of learning, the student will begin to improve with instruction, then level off and sometimes digress for a short period before again improving when instruction is given.

Instruction

The pattern of learning
Figure 1

In competitive diving, how effective and successful the instruction depends on the following areas:

1. Diver profile
   a. Age level

b. Ability and talent
c. Gender
d. Experience

2. Teacher profile
a. Qualifications of the teacher
b. Experience level in teaching diving
c. Instruction levels
d. Size of groups and teacher to athlete ratio

3. Kind of facilities
a. Number of diving areas, stands, and springboards
b. Diving heights available
c. Teaching aids available
d. Indoor and/or outdoor facilities

4. Kind of environment
a. Summer and/or winter season(s)
b. Time allotted for daily, weekly, and seasonal practice
c. Schedules for instruction which includes length of course
d. Geographical location
e. Parental and peer influence
f. Competitive levels
g. Recruiting and sponsors
h. Administration and organization

2. As a motivator

A coach who is not motivated cannot instill motivation. Athletes participate in sports for many different reasons, but few are as motivated as the coach needs to be. Every practice requires motivation from the coach in challenging the divers to perform better on every dive. The kind of motivation often depends on how balanced and controlled is the coach. Acting out personal frustrations or displaying a bad temper can hamper the relationship with the coach and teammates. There are many ways to motivate athletes and it is the responsibility of the coach to try and find what it takes to offer the motivation needed for the athlete to perform as well as possible.

As previously mentioned, I believe that a top performance from an athlete is more important than winning. After Mark Lenzi won the Olympic Gold medal in Barcelona, in 1992, he asked me after the contest how I felt about his winning and I replied that I was somewhat disappointed. Surprised, he then wanted to know how I could feel that way since he had just proved that he was the best diver in the world. I told him that the reason why I was disappointed was because he hadn't performed the back and inward 3

½ somersault that he had learned when a freshman at Indiana University. I went on to say if he had performed those two dives, it would have given him the maximum total degrees of difficulty for the contest. I continued to say that though he won, he had not shown me his best performance. Grantland Rice probably said it best when he created the Olympic motto "For when the One Great Scorer comes to write against your name, he marks not that you won or lost, but how you played the game." Whether a person wins or loses was never the major reason why I coached. My goal has always been to get the best performance possible from a diver and if his or her best wasn't good enough to win, then so be it. I never asked more from an athlete when I knew that it was the best he or she could do. After all, winning or losing doesn't indicate whether you live or die. So, winning shouldn't be the primary reason for competing unless it is at the professional level.

Playing on the emotions of a diver by the coach is a difficult approach to make when trying to motivate a diver because there is such a fine line between applying too little or too much motivation too soon or too late to be of value. A fragile emotional state can quickly move a diver away from or nearer to a great performance. Motivation is especially needed when preparing a diver to learn a new dive. Knowing that the diver can develop great fear when attempting a dive for the first time, the coach must tum into a super salesman to convince the diver that the dive can be performed without pain for this is what the diver fears most. Such an explanation requires positive reinforcement, so the diver can develop full confidence in the coach and in his or her taking on a new challenge. During the discussion, the coach should be very focused on how the diver is responding to his or her encouraging remarks.

Another approach to getting a diver to perform a new dive is through the power of suggestion. This is done when the coach may casually mention that the diver may be able to perform a certain new dive but not mentioning it again for a day or two. The coach might then bring it up again when the diver is having a good workout and suggest a date, such as "next week", when the diver might attempt the new dive. This "in the future" approach is made so the diver doesn't miss any sleep worrying about trying the new dive which he or she may believe will result in instant death. Knowing that the fear of learning the new dive will increase as the time nears when to try it, the coach may casually bring up the new dive again a day or two later but this time the coach informs the diver that he or she should try the new dive "now" instead of on the arranged occasion because the coach believes he or she is ready. The sudden change in plans is made so the diver doesn't have any time to build up any anxiety or fear when trying the dive. If at all successful in the first attempt to perform the dive, the diver should be immediately informed that should he perform the dive three or four more times to convince himself or herself that the dive can be successfully performed with little or no chance ofinjury.

3. As a psychologist

The psychology used by a coach is an endless subject due to conditions, situations, personalities, environment, and countless other factors that affect a diver ' s behavior and performance. However, it is evident that the diving program will be a reflection of the coach' s personality, philosophy, experience, and the manner used when communicating with the divers. With this in mind some suggestions are offered here that may help the coach encourage divers to give a better performance, resulting in individual growth.

Before commenting on the psychology used by the coach, one should be aware that the coach will form a very influential image of himself or herself with the divers. Like it or not, the impression the coach transmits is an unavoidable circumstance of the coaching role. The quality of the image reflected will depend on the association and relationship between the coach and the divers. The image will reflect the coach's personality, character, sense of humor, manner of dress, moral standards, ability to communicate, individual interests, leadership, compassion, and many impressions. Personal habits of the coach are also going to be closely weighed by the divers for it is difficult for them to be told not to smoke, drink alcohol, or use foul language when the coach is standing there smoking a cigarette and reeking with the smell of liquor while cussing out a diver. Coaches who tell off-colored jokes can expect an identical response from the divers. The coach should also avoid discussing personal subjects, such as religion or politics, with divers because it can result in dissention between the coach and athlete.

The coach should begin the season in meeting with the divers to discuss plans regarding the training program, workout schedules, planned meets, goals, and many other issues. This should be followed with the coach covering certain rules concerning their behavior and the consequences that will be enforced if any of the rules are broken. It should be made clear to the divers that such rules are necessary to avoid chaos and confusion and also to maintain discipline and control of the program. After presenting the rules, he or she should ask the divers if they agree to the rules and to the consequences and if they believe they are fair. If anyone disagrees with any rule, it should be discussed until an agreement is accepted by all. Such tactics place the responsibility of the diver's behavior on the rules rather than on the coach and once the rules are accepted by the divers, all the coach need do is enforce the rules which makes it possible to maintain control and discipline. If the rules are fair the coaching can then be firm but fair. The coach who has loose rules can expect a loose program which may be accepted by some in one program but not by another. Whatever the program, I believe that the coach has a better chance to develop top quality athletes when developing a healthy and sincere atmosphere.

Another means of maintaining discipline and earning the respect of the team members is found in the coach keeping his or her word. If the coach does this, control and behavior of the team can be achieved which may save a lot of time and energy when trying to correct problems that often crop up. A coach who continually hedges on issues will find that his or her word has little effect on the divers during workouts or at any other time. Therefore, I suggest the coach be fair but firm especially at the beginning of the season. Should the coach start the season by being easy on the divers, the chances of clamping down on them later are highly improbable. The coach must also realize that nearly every diver is confronted with certain fears when diving and also with problems away from the pool. Much of this stress can be controlled or even eliminated if a certain amount of mental toughness and discipline is instilled from the beginning of the season.

In lieu of what has been discussed here, it must be realized that the relationship between the coach and diver is much different today than it was a few years ago. Athletes in the past had to comply with the rules that were put to them whether they agreed with them or not. But in recent years, many changes involving individual's rights have emerged that have dramatically changed the whole social and competitive structure in most sports. With the formation of Title IX, professionalism, and other social issues concerning drugs, gender, etc. many athletes who have not been content with the rules and demands made by their coaches, question their worth and validity. Some coaches have not been able to adjust to the many changes in their athlete's social upbringing which has led to the loss of control in many programs. There is no doubt that the dramatic changes in the sports culture have affected every program one way or the other and must be dealt with in the best possible manner.

4. As a recruiter

Sometimes a coach with limited coaching ability is regarded as a great coach because he or she is a great recruiter. As I have often remarked, "If you want to be a great coach, have a great athlete." This comment can be said about many coaches in the last century and still remains true in this century. On the college level, it is difficult for a truly great coach to recruit athletes when he or she has very limited scholarship funds and/or coaches at a school that hasn't a diving reputation. Personally, I found it quite difficult to compete with a coach from another college that had five full scholarships to work with over a four-year period when I had only one scholarship every four years. That would be like playing poker with one who is dealt twenty- five cards while you are dealt only five cards. To make matters worse, my coaching was often compared with that of the other coach, and people would ask me why I wasn't fairing so well when competing with him.

Recruiting is also much different now than what it was a few years ago. Students without a scholarship were able to attend college by getting a job and working their way through school. However, athletes without a scholarship who wish to work their way through school is nearly impossible. The tuition, especially when from out of state, and the living conditions are so expensive that it is not possible for an athlete to attend school without financial aid. Because most families are finding it very difficult to finance their children's college education, the athlete will usually go to the school that offers him or her the most money regardless of the kind of coaching, facilities available, school's academic standards, or reputation of the school.

What a diving coach is looking for when trying to recruit divers is to find those who really want to dive and compete and have some talent to do so. It doesn't take long for the coach to realize that people do not automatically show up at his or her institution. The real problem in recruiting involves money, facilities, special features, school or club location, the kind of program offered, scheduling, time, reputation, caliber of coaching, competitive environment, trips to meets, and a parent association. Whatever, the coach is responsible for enticing people to join his or her program and if the program doesn't have much to offer, it is unlikely that the coach and the program will be successful recruiting top athletes.

Some recruiting hints that may be helpful to the coach

1. *Clubs* - coaches should contact Y.M.C.A.' s, schools, and other clubs that have diving facilities but not a diving program. Provide them with notices that can be posted on their bulletin boards. Inform the sports editor of the local newspaper and keep him or her posted on your diving team's activities. Be sure to include pictures of your divers and the results of your meets. Speak at local organizations and show videos of your program. Stage local diving competitions and have water shows that will welcome parents to your water activities. Most clubs have parent associations which will help with the domestic needs.

2. *High schools* - Naturally, most of the recruiting of divers will be with students in the school. Publicize your team and activities in the school paper; make announcements of your team's activities over the school public address system, at assemblies and at football and basketball games. Require your athletes to wear their letter sweaters to school on a given day every week and especially on the day of a meet. Make speaking engagements at local clubs and social functions where you can show diving movies of your divers and other great divers who competed at the Olympics. Post pictures of your divers and meet schedules, and results on the school bulletin boards. Put on a water show which includes swimmers, divers, synchronized swimmers, gymnasts, along with choreographed skits and some musical entertainment. Show films of diving at your assemblies and to gym classes when the weather is poor.

3. *Colleges and universities* - recruiting at this level depends much on the school's reputation, courses of study offered, the conference in which the school competes, the geographical location of the school, the reputation of the diving team and diving coach, the quality of diving facilities, and the level of the diving program which may include the summer. To recruit, the coach must attend age group and high school competitions, seek out those who compete in state meets around the country, attend diving clinics and the national convention to make contacts with other coaches, write articles on diving and put them on a web site and have them published in diving

magazines such as the P.D.C.A. (Professional Diving Coaches Association). Also use the web site to seek out divers from other areas that may be interested in attending your university. Get to know the university sports editors of your school and the local newspaper and keep them informed of your activities. Put on water shows to create better relationships with the swimming team and the public. Attend workshops and have clinics for high school diving coaches in your area; and bring in a top coach to update your teaching and coaching techniques.

Recruiting procedures

Successful recruiting generally depends on the impression the diving coach makes on the recruit. Since the recruit could be in your program for years, it makes sense that you spend a lot of time in preparing and planning for his or her visit to your campus. It must be remembered that you don't get a second chance to make a first impression, so the recruit has to see the best of what you have to offer while being with you. Your intention is to convince the diver that you "really" want him or her to attend your school and be a member of your team. Therefore, a few suggestions are offered that may aid you with your recruiting.

* Meet the recruit at the airport or wherever he or she will be arriving. Do not send someone else in your place to pick the recruit up. Make sure the recruit has eaten and if he or she has not, take him or her to a nice restaurant and not like a McDonalds.

* Be well groomed and wear appropriate clothing. Don't wear sandals or blue jeans.

* Be friendly but don't overdo or under do it. Relax and use your personality seasoned with a little humor.

* Take the recruit to his or her staying quarters and give him or her a little time to get settled and get cleaned up.

* Take time to show the campus including your diving facilities, office, and locker room which should be clean and in good shape.

* Make sure that the recruit meets your athletic director and swimming coach.

* Talk about the academic standards of the school and show interest in what the recruit wants to study. If you already know about his or her academic interests, arrange a meeting with the dean or chairman of that particular discipline. Only after you have discussed academics should you talk about your diving program.

* If rules permit, have the recruit visit your home and meet your family.

* Schedule a time period when the recruit can spend some time with your divers without your presence, so they can get better acquainted. It is very important that your divers are briefed on how to handle the recruit making sure that no immoral behavior concerning alcohol, drugs, sex, or any unfavorable activities occur.

* Be honest with the recruit and don't make promises that you can't keep. Explain what is required and expected of him or her in the program. Above all, don't bad mouth any other school or coach. If he or wishes to do so, just listen and try to change the subject.

* If allowed, take the recruit to a social event on the campus and let him or her meet other people some of which may be your friends.

* Before leaving for home, let the recruit know how much you enjoyed and appreciated his or her visit and how nice it would be for him or her attend your school and be a member of the diving program.

* Follow up the visit with a card or phone call thanking him or her for the visit with the hope that they decide to attend your school.

Clubs do not adhere to any regulated recruiting rules. Therefore, the coach can create his or her own methods for persuading divers to join the club. High schools also are not subject to many of the suggested recruiting methods because the athletes are already members of the student body. However, colleges and universities are faced with thousands of recruiting regulations many of which a coach may not have a clue of their existence. A few years ago, the number of N.C.A.A. rules concerning the recruiting of athletes was the size of a pamphlet, and today, the rules are nearly the size of a New York City telephone directory. The rules are also so confusing that all universities' athletic departments have separate divisions that work with interpreting the rules involving eligibility and the recruiting of athletes. If you have any question about what you can or cannot do, contact your athletic department and make sure that you are not violating any rule that could cause concern.

The Transition of the Diver from High school To College

Since many divers who attend college have, at times, great difficulty in adjusting to the life style away from home, an article is offered here that may be helpful to those who are going to make a change from high school to college.

After selecting a college following high school graduation, many of you are very curious as to how college could be any different than what you were doing in high school. After all, you attend class, study, go to practice, compete in meets, hang out....so what's the big deal? I believe you will begin to see the difference soon after receiving your high school diploma and suddenly realize that you are not going back to the ole alma mater to be with your friends, enjoy all of the school activities, and be with the teachers who knew you personally and recognized your ability and accomplishments.

With this, I would like to discuss some of the changes that you can look forward to when you step on the campus of a university for the first time. The first thing you realize is how much bigger the school is compared to your high school. You will be awed by the numerous buildings and dormitories everywhere and it seems like everyone knows where they are going except you. Naturally, you won't experience all of the changes mentioned here nor will you react to the changes the same way others do because you all come from different home and high school environments. These environmental differences may reflect the kind of experience you have had being away from home, and the activity and academic accomplishments you have acquired in high school, etc. One thing for sure, the changes you endure the first few weeks you are in college often frighten, confuse, and frustrate you for nearly everything around you is different. But the lonely feeling you have should be recognized as a normal reaction to change which eventually vanishes.

Family differences

Another difference you find the first week on campus is the food that you eat in the cafeteria. Though usually good, the menu never seems to change, and it just isn't like those good old-fashioned home cooked meals that mom made for you which you took so much for granted. Now you stand in line each day for food that has little taste and very little variety and it is no wonder that you find yourself losing weight after a couple of months on campus.

Another big change occurs when you realize that you are no longer with your family but out there all by yourself. At first you may feel "free" from the confined and disciplined atmosphere found at home. But, somehow, this feeling soon wears off and you start to acquire a little home sickness. You also begin to appreciate Mom and Dad a little more for they were right there to help you with your problems even though at times you felt they were too nosy or didn't fully understand you.

You also begin to realize that they were the ones who provided you with the car and gave you spending money, so you did not have to work while competing on the high school team. They were always there to encourage and support you when you were trying to accomplish greater things. They offered love, compassion, and guidance whenever you needed it and provided counseling and direction when you had problems with love affairs, sex, money, studies, etc. You also begin to remember who shared your moments of success and offered sympathy and understanding in your moments of despair. It finally hits you that your parents were your greatest fans and influenced you the most during your early school years. This is when you begin to understand that you must accept the loss of those who gave you comfort and security and now stand on your own.

Loss of friends

During your senior year in high school, you and many of your peers felt superior to the under classmen, teachers, and even your parents. Many of you felt that the lower grade kids were really stupid, and the teachers were long out of touch and did not know what was going on. You had the tendency to think that if you were an athlete and had risen above mediocrity by placing high in the city, regional, or state championships, you were very special and ranked above the rest of the other students.

A lot of that charisma begins to fade soon after graduation and suddenly disappears the moment you arrive on the college campus for you suddenly realize that you are again a freshman, and no one is really concerned about you or your accomplishments. You normally move into a dormitory as a total stranger and meet your roommate and other people on the floor by questioning them where they are from and what you should do next. Making friends at this time is not difficult for all of you are in the same state of confusion and loneliness. During the first few weeks in college, you usually write and telephone home a lot to your high school sweetheart, friends, and to your parents for you are still very lonely while trying to adjust to your new style of living. The frequency of this kind of communication soon dies down as you gradually become accustomed to your new surroundings.

College roommate

Most universities require that you live in a dormitory for at least the first year after which you can move off campus if you wish. You normally have the option of living in a single room alone or sharing a room with a roommate in the dorms which is cheaper and a lot less lonely. The kind of roommate you have will have much to do with how much you like college and your first year on campus. Due to the drastic changes in your environment, you probably won't like college the first year but once you start to adapt to a new way of living, you will begin to like what you are doing. Having been a college professor and coach for over forty years, I can honestly attest to the fact that one of the prime problems a person encounters as a freshman is getting along with a roommate. Because this issue of living with another person is so important, some suggestions are made here that may be of help to you.

* It is best not to select an old school mate or high school classmate as a roommate. If you select a diving teammate and you have a quarrel, the problem w1ll likely be brought to diving practice at the pool where it will cause more problems. If you select an old friend or high school classmate, you frequently will find some fault with each other that never surfaced when you were classmates. So, what was a good friendship at home can end up in being a very uncomfortable relationship

in college. This is not to say that you cannot get along with a teammate of former classmate for it occasionally works, but not often.

* Try to select a roommate who has similar lifestyles, social interests, and study habits. For example, trying to room with one who smokes, drinks, does drugs, or frequently has an overnight guest sleeping in the same bed makes it quite uncomfortable for a roommate who is not into any of those kinds of lifestyles. If such an occasion occurs, talk with your floor counselor about getting a new roommate and if he or she cannot help you, go to an authority who can.

* Once settled into your new living quarters for a few days, it would be wise that you have a conference with your roommate for the purpose of establishing certain ground rules that involve the way you wish to share your room. Some rules that make it possible for you to live in harmony will include agreements about:

a. Wearing each other's clothes and using personal articles.

b. Playing the stereo or radio loud and watching T.V. during study hours.

c. Having friends come into the room at night (or a "bull session" when one or both of you wish to study.

d. Share in keeping the room clean. Bad feeling can quickly occur when one person has very clean domestic habits and the other is a slob.

e. Using the telephone. Roommates can stay on the phone for hours with little or no regard for the consideration of others.

f. Attempt to recognize, accept, and adjust to each other's personal habits such as cussing, snoring, talking people down, cracking the knuckles, storing food in the room, etc.

Try to be honest with each other and do not be afraid to discuss differences when they occur. Such discussions should be in private and not be anyone else's business. It is dangerous to hold back things that are bothering you then attack the roommate when in a state of anger.

Adjustment to the campus

Perhaps the first couple of weeks on the campus are the most confusing and frustrating because you are not familiar with anything related to the location of buildings, classes, academic resources, eating areas, etc. Everyone has to ask everyone else where to buy books, pay fees, where the freshman meetings are being held, and so on. Usually the feeling of loneliness and anxiety creeps over you, and you don't have any friends to talk to or help you. That feeling of being "big time" that you had a couple of months ago is now long gone and you have to accept the fact that you are nothing but a "greenie" freshman who is starting all over again.

Choosing a sorority or a fraternity

Though having belonged to a fraternity during my undergraduate days at Ohio State, I would not recommend a diver who is really interested in diving to join a fraternity or a sorority because you simply don't have the time. The training that is required of the diver at the present time is overwhelming and you just can't find the time to do your class work, train three or four hours a day and then go spend time socializing at a fraternity or sorority. These social institutions are expensive and demand a lot of your time neither of which most of you have to give. I can assure you that if you join one of the social groups, your chances of flunking out of college in the first year are overwhelming. You may consider joining one later on in your college life, but not until you have adjusted to college life and you have very good grades. These social clubs do offer a means for making lifelong friends and the opportunity to meet members of the opposite sex but in doing so, none of these benefits are free.

Study habits

One big change found in college is the tremendous increase in reading, writing, and studying material that is required by most of the courses you take. You soon find that you can't socialize much and still uphold your class requirements and responsibilities. Trying to study for a couple of evenings in the dorm will convince you that it is not the place to study or get things done unless you can accept the noise and commotion that is constantly found around you. Therefore, you will probably seek out a quiet place on the campus, such as a library, where you can go to do your work without interference. Beware of when at the library, you look for an attractive person to sit across from which will make studying a lot more difficult.

I would suggest that you make your studies your top priority and fulfill all of your course requirements each evening before seeking recreational pleasure such as watching T.V., attending athletic events, movies, playing bridge, or taking part in bull sessions. One of your worst enemies in college is to procrastinate. I have seen student after student put studying off for a later time then find that they are too tired to do their homework which eventually leads them to expulsion from school. Once you learn to allocate your time, you will find how to do other things besides study but until then, do the right thing by putting your school responsibilities first. If you ignore your studies, you will entertain a few "all-nighters" which will not help your physical condition or allow for good diving practice sessions.

5. As a leader

Everyone concerned with a diving program accepts the fact that the coach is the leader of the whole show. He or she is accountable for everyone and everything that occurs in the diving program. The leader is one who:

* Has the ability to gather people together to recognize, discuss, and make decisions on particular issues.
* Has faith and trust in others and never stops trying to make things better with a little cooperation and effort from the followers. He or she meets opposition and problems head on.
* Influences people to move toward some goal.
* Is willing to take on responsibilities and make decisions when others question or hesitate on how it is going to affect them instead of how it will affect others. Faces problems and consequences with courage, determination, wisdom, and confidence and will not compromise.
* Sees people as individuals rather than as objects, obstructions, or groups.
* Is sensitive to the feelings of others and is willing to listen instead of throwing his or her weight around trying to convince others the he or she knows everything that is going on.
* Is one who is honest, fair, and firm in his or her convictions and has the courage to admit it when proven wrong and make sacrifices when needed.
* Is one who stands up for others who deserve the need of support and doesn't expect anyone else to do any more than he or she would do.
* Is high on meaningful goals that are obtainable and will benefit others.
* Is one who is morally sound, possesses a good philosophy and strong character, and has a positive attitude.
* Is a giver; and not a taker.

It appears that some people are natural born leaders while others are led into a leading position for various reasons. Those who lead, do so with certain objectives in mind that makes things better for others and often not better for themselves. Whatever the reason, those who follow such leadership must accept the leader's actions and consequences and decide whether or not they can welcome, tolerate, or reject the leader's efforts.

Leaders in sports are usually accompanied with prestige developed from their physical size and athletic prowess. Most coaches who are leaders in their particular fields are: constant winners, are popular, have outstanding personalities and/or dominating character, are the most outspoken, can form strategies, are diplomatic, offer hero worship, and are the wealthiest if in professional sports. Many are selected for leadership when undertaking responsibilities involving certain activities and groups of people. For example, when one decides to be a teacher or coach, he or she will immediately become a leader whether they want to be or not because the position warrants leadership for many people.

Leadership can be a very delicate and sensitive position when exposed to public opinion. A coach who loses most of his games is looked upon as a poor leader when in fact, he or she may be an outstanding mentor but has poor athletic material with which to work. The coach's leadership may be questioned by his or her assistants who agree or disagree with his or her program or philosophy. It is amazing how one can be a great leader and then quickly lose the leadership by making a simple mistake or saying the wrong thing at the wrong time. A leader is one who stands above mediocrity which makes it easy for others to either love or criticize him or her. Such leaders require courage, the ability to accept criticism, determination, persistency, and self-esteem. They have to know how to cooperate with others and make unpopular decisions that sometime affect the welfare of the family and/or close friends. A leader is sometimes one who is willing to stand alone while attempting to steer the ship to a safe port.

It may be easier to see what makes a good leader in sports by recognizing some qualities that make a poor leader.

* Authoritarian type --- my way is law.
* Has teacher or coach's pets.
* Picks on athletes and constantly offers negative reinforcement.
* Lacks enthusiasm and motivation.
* Shows no interest in individual's problems.
* Expects too much -- gives no praise or credit to the athlete. Takes full credit for any success made by an athlete.
* Unpleasant disposition.
* Offers no insight, imagination, or creativity.
* Is immoral -- lies, cheats, steals, schemes, deliberately hurts others, lacks courage, makes poor decisions, evasive, greedy, lazy, disrespectful, sloppy, cruel, no control of temper, uncooperative, gossiper shuns responsibility, unreliable, unsociable.
* Refuses to accept or even listen to advice given by others.

6. As a physical trainer

Everyone in competitive diving is aware that the kind of performance one can give in a competition depends much on the physical condition of the diver. Emphasis in this respect has become a major issue in recent years due to the needed strength to perform the very difficult dives in a contest and when entering the water head first. It is known that the Chinese start training potential competitive divers at a very young age by providing physical training centers where they take part in strenuous forms of exercise all day long, every day. Nothing in our social culture appears to support that kind of training so one must be very careful when constructing a training program that will produce top quality and physically conditioned divers in the time period that is allotted.

Such a program requires a close relationship between the coach and diver in deciding what exercises should be used to satisfy the diver' s needs. Obviously, certain tests should be taken by the divers to determine the weakness in their physical condition, strength, and flexibility areas. The focus of the coach on this part of the program is essential because the success of the performance of the divers depends on it.

7. As a second parent

In many cases the coach becomes closer to the diver than his or her own parents because the coach spends more time with the diver than do the parents. Most of the time the two spend together is a period when the coach offers instruction to the diver that involves fear, focus, understanding, loyalty, compassion, patience, responsibility, humor, anger, frustration, success and failure, just to name a few issues. It is no wonder that close relationships and dependence on one another develop between the coach and diver. These issues are important to the young divers, and few parents have the time, to discuss them in depth, so the coach becomes an important substitute.

8. As a friend

It is important that the coach be a trusted advisor and friend, but it is equally important the he or she stay out of the diver's personal life unless the diver asks for help or if it concerns the welfare of other team members. The coach should always be a professional and maintain professional distance from the team by not trying to become a member of the team. When a coach tries to be a buddy with the divers at their level, problems emerge that can result in damaging the coach's purpose for coaching. A very good friend of mine who was one of the top swimmers in the world decided to be a coach. He allowed himself to take part in the team's social activities to the point that it was difficult to know who the coach was and as a result, he failed miserably as a coach and was fired.

Being personable but not personal does not mean a coach can't be friends with the divers for he or she should share some social and recreational activities with them. It is also helpful for the divers to know that the coach is there for them but cannot always give them the help they need. It is also helpful if the coach tells stories about his life while keeping his personal life out of it. Therefore, the coach should offer a friendly attitude to the divers while acting in a professional manner that honors and encourages the respect the coaching position deserves.

9. As an organizer and planner

The activities surrounding the sport of competitive diving requires the coach to be a good organizer and planner. The formation of workouts, schedules, teaching and coaching plans, training programs, keeping records, budgeting, and many other duties all call for the coach to not only be a competent organizer and planner, but also be a good business person. This calls for the coach to be a banker, a super salesman, and a person who can make good decisions and judgments. Those affiliated with the diving program should be very thankful to the diving coaches because the salaries they make for taking on all of these tasks and responsibilities are pitiful. If the coach finds that he or she cannot take on all of the demands required by the position, then outside aid must be sought to get the job done.

Qualities that help make a good coach

The kind of diving coach one wishes to be has much to do with character, personality, desire, goal setting, and many other qualities. Though it is not possible to mention all of the qualities that make a good diving coach, a few are mentioned here with spaces that can be marked off that apply to you.

A coach must:

- ✓ Be a role model - be the person your divers want you to be.
- ✓ Be able to take criticism - Criticizing someone else is easy, but can you accept criticism with grace?
- ✓ Be adaptable - be able to adjust to varying situations.
- ✓ Be a do it yourself person - Fix things that need to be fixed. It sometimes takes forever to get someone else to do it and do it well.
- ✓ Be a good politician - Get acquainted with those who can help you and your program: administrators, faculty, alumni, parents, and others.
- ✓ Be a counselor - Offer advice and guidance to divers outside of the pool as well as in it.
- ✓ Be a giver and not a taker - Help others with no expectation of receiving anything in return.
- ✓ Be aggressive - Take the initiative to move your program forward.
- ✓ Be a good communicator- Useclear English that is plain and direct.
- ✓ Be a hard worker - Don't waste your valuable time or the time of others.
- ✓ Be a good public relations coach - Inform the news media of the progress made by your program including meet results, outstanding performances, articles related to diving and others.
- ✓ Be a good leader - Take responsibility and control of your program. Step up and be accounted for. Do what others are afraid to do. Have the courage to make important decisions and accept success and failure with dignity.
- ✓ Be a mister cool - Be calm, relaxed, and show great poise when under pressur. Pull the team together when things go wrong.

- ✓ Be a motivator - Keep offering encouragement and positive reinforcement even to divers who do not perform well in practice or when competing.
- ✓ Be a problem solver - Find new and innovated ways to make things right by applying a little energy and time. If you don't have the solution, then approach the problem from another angle.
- ✓ Be an actor - No matter how bad you feel or what problems you have, walk out on the pool deck as if it was a stage and give the divers your best shot.
- ✓ Be an individual - Don't try to act like or imitate some successful coach. Teach and coach by using your own personality and character.
- ✓ Be a super salesman - Talk the divers into what you want from them. Tell them that they can dive without pain if they follow your instructions.
- ✓ Be a scientist- Center your coaching around mechanical principles based on Newton's Laws of Motion.
- ✓ Be cheerful - A positive easy-going attitude makes for a good workout with progress.
- ✓ Be competitive - Challenge your divers into learning something new in every practice. The team will be competitive if they see their coach is competitive.
- ✓ Be consistent - In your coaching methods and delivery when teaching and coaching.
- ✓ Be cooperative - Give the divers responsibilities and guide them when making decisions.
- ✓ Be creative - Keep trying to improve your program by trying new ideas.
- ✓ Be curious - Try to understand why things happen.
- ✓ Be dedicated - Give your very best effort to the sport every day. Show everyone that you really want them the best they can be.
- ✓ Be dependable - Arrive at practice before the divers so they know that you have their best interests in mind. Being on time makes for the beginning of a good practice. In the thirty years I coached with Doc Counsilman, he never once was late or ever missed a practice.
- ✓ Be dynamic - Go the extra mile. Keep going when people say you can't.
- ✓ Be emotionally stable - Don' t lose control of your temper because of fatigue, abuse, or frustration.
- ✓ Be enthusiastic -Take the chairs off the deck and coach while standing up. Let your team know that you mean business and that they have your undivided attention.
- ✓ Be flexible in your thinking - There is nothing wrong with changing your mind or seeing things in a different way from time to time. Don't believe that things must be done in only one way.
- ✓ Be honest - Level with the divers and don't hedge when making decisions.

- ✓ Be inspiring - Act in a way that encourages others to believe and follow your way of doing things.
- ✓ Be knowledgeable -Learn all you can about the sport, so you can be a better coach.
- ✓ Be in total control of the diving program - Losing control may result in chaos and the loss of the program.
- ✓ Be loyal - Stick with your divers through the tough times as well as the good times. Stand up for them at all times. Do as much as possible for them in and out of the pool. Do not bad mouth or cut your divers throats in public or to other coaches or athletes.
- ✓ Be mature - Have fun, but act as an adult and a professional at all times.
- ✓ Be open minded - Consider both sides of the story before making decisions. Examine and evaluate issues before reacting.
- ✓ Be worthy of respect - Respect is something you earn and once it's lost, it is gone forever.
- ✓ Be persistent - keep trying until you have exhausted all possibilities.
- ✓ Be socially active - take part in social events and activities. Don't make diving the only thing in your life.
- ✓ Be sympathetic - recognize and react to the feelings of others when things go wrong.
- ✓ Be tactful - Think before reacting.
- ✓ Be trustworthy - Coach by the rules. Don't cheat to win. Set an example for your divers. Trust is like a mirror, once broken, it can never be fixed.
- ✓ Be understanding - Don't show bias because others may have different views than yours.
- ✓ Be willing to learn - no matter how much you know about diving, there is always more you can learn.

Other do's and do not's include:

- ✓ Challenge the divers to perform - This is one of the best means of motivating a diver.
- ✓ Don' t play favorites -Treat everyone on the team the same way. It is normal to be more attached to some than others, but you must give everyone fair treatment.
- ✓ Do not lie or talk behind divers back - It is unethical, and you can do irreparable harm to your relationship with the divers.
- ✓ Do not hold grudges - None of the divers will perform the way of your making all of the time-on or off the board. If someone disappoints you, try to let it go and try to see the best in him or her and not the worst.
- ✓ Do not procrastinate- Do what has to be done right away. Putting it off does not help.

- ✓ Give a good personal appearance - try to groom and dress favorable. Remember, once a slob, always a slob.
- ✓ Like people - the easiest thing in the world is to find fault with someone else. Try to ignore their bad sides and look for their good sides.
- ✓ Have a good sense of humor - If you can start your workout with a clean funny joke or story, you set the stage for a good workout.
- ✓ Have a super ego - believe in yourself but don't flaunt it.
- ✓ Show a compassion for others - show people that you care for them and what they do.

Qualities That Do Not Make for A Good Diving Coach

With the aid of the American Swimming Coaches Association, an additional attempt is made here to give another side of coaching that can cause the teaching and coaching performance to be used in the wrong way. One or more of these can change the intent of the coach to such a degree that the whole program could be seriously damaged or lost. Again, a space is provided for the reader to check those which apply to him or her and it is hopeful that no checks are made.

As a coach if you are:

* Insulter- Consistently putting the athlete down. Criticizes and rarely compliments.
* Shouter- Usually does not know much about the technical side of the sport so shouts to replace the lack of knowledge. A shouter usually turns the athlete off.
* Avenger -Lights into the diver after a poor performance and gives him or her undeserving punishment to get even.
* Choker - Communicative in practice but ties up in meets. Can't motivate divers due to nervousness, fear, and frustration.
* Shaker - Forgets things, sweats, shakes, and usually smokes due to being nervous during competitions.
* Tough guy - Challenges divers into trying most anything with little concern of the consequences. Says things like "you're not hurt, do it again" with little or no additional coaching to prevent further pain.
* Molder-Tries to mold divers out of the same cast. Has only one way of doing things and expects divers to do it that way.
* Mumbler - Not articulate when attempting to communicate. Monotonous talker who is very quiet, fast, or slow when talking.
* General Custer - Never changes approach to learning concepts or handling problems.

* Never wrong about anything.
* Copy-cat - Not creative or realistic. Copies the styles and technique from other coaches and divers. Easier for someone else to do the work than to figure it out for him or herself.
* Sad Sam - Total pessimist. "You'll never learn that dive. Don't try that dive because you are not good enough. You'll be lucky to make the finals" Has no confidence in himself or herself or the divers.
* Hero - Always takes credit for the success of the divers. "They did exactly like I told them. I won the nationals. It was superior coaching. Brags about his or her coaching accomplishments.
* Critic - One who criticizes rather than analyzes. Always finds mistakes in divers' performances and offers negative and sarcastic comments. Knows what is wrong with everything and everybody.
* Whiner - Takes mistakes personally. "Here I spend an hour telling you how to do it and you never listen to me? You don't appreciate my coaching". Complains about everything.
* Sloppy Joe - One who is disorganized, inconsistent, and unprepared. Never prepares anything in advance. Never shows up on time, dresses poorly, forgets things, no consistency in workouts.
* Scientist- Goes into great detail and makes the dive complicated and hard to understand. Causes paralysis through analysis. Uses high technical terms.
* Hitler- One who is in total control. Never explains why but says "do it because I said so" is unapproachable. Doesn't want to hear excuses or alibis. Not personable and never deals with emotional matters.
* Liar - Tells you what you want to hear. Makes things up to cover his or her mistakes. Usually a coward and a conniver. Will say nothing to get his or her own way. Breaks promises.
* Motor mouth - Believes the more you talk, the more the diver learns. Talks too much but says little. Confuses the diver rather than simplifying or correcting the problem.
* Rapper- Calls the divers names and uses sarcasm believing that it will create a positive response. Cuts them up and chews them out.
* Black cat - Superstitions about competitions. Eats or wears the same things at meets. Has a winning lucky charm. Indicates the coach is not sure of oneself.
* Rockne - Always gives high inspirational pep talks. When overdone, the talks become ineffective. When diver wins, it was because of his or her pep talk. Gives the same pep talk in all of the practices.
* Super friend - Wants to be one of the boys or girls. Does a lot of back slapping and hugging (especially male coaches with girls.) Leads singing on the bus and talks with divers on all subjects.

* Jailer - Constantly checking the divers out on what they eat, who they date, how they must sacrifice everything to become good divers. Parties and social functions are out which often causes the diver to lie to the coach.
* White cane - Tells the diver what is wrong with a dive but doesn't give the solution. Doesn't know how to analyze dives.
* Sulker- Poor little me. Walks away or withdraws when things go wrong. Becomes cool and unresponsive with divers. Is moody and appears to be in a trance.
* Informer -Tells everyone about the problems on the team. Gossiper. Can't be trusted with personal or confidential information.
* Attention getter - wants everyone to listen to and watch everything he does, like throwing chairs.

Who should coach?

A hard look at the good and bad qualities and characteristics that concern teaching and coaching clearly points out that some have the ability and talent to be good teachers and coaches while others lack such traits. Many find it very difficult to succeed no matter how hard they try which often results in them becoming tormented, confused, and frustrated. One or more of the negative characteristics can affect the performance of the diver and coach to such a point that the whole diving program is damaged. Since the decision to be a diving coach is up to the individual, information is offered here that may be of help in making that decision.

If one cannot teach or coach outside of the negative parameters of behavior and do nothing but constantly criticize the learner with no positive reinforcement, they should accept the fact that coaching is not a desirable undertaking for him or her and try some other field. Then again, like dancing, if someone wants to dance like Fred Astaire or Gene Kelley but realizes that such a feat is not possible, they may learn enough about dancing to appreciate and enjoy the activity and decide that it is worth spending the time and energy to remain in such an endeavor. In making such decisions, it must be realized that coaching is a service that requires helping others improve themselves by unselfishly giving the best of yourself with the possibility of receiving nothing in return.

Coaching covers a great spectrum in life that measures many behavior patterns and includes making important decisions, plans, developing a worthy philosophy, and reaching for many goals. It is a field that requires one to take on responsibilities that are challenging, emotional, questionable and workable from day to day with constant changes that affect people's lives. Regardless of how good or bad a coach is, he or she will affect everyone in contact with him or her one way or the other in the diving program.

How to recognize those who could make good divers

* Hidden talent - Often takes a while to draw the diver's talent to the surface before it can be recognized.
* Strength and power - The difficulty of performing dives today requires the divers to possess these qualities plus flexibility and endurance.
* Great desire - the diver must be enthusiastic and hungry to learn.
* Cooperative - The diver must be attentive and willing to take instruction.
* Durable - The diver must be willing to stick with it, go for the long haul, and accept the hard work.
* Be a good team member - Be willing to get along with others, give instead of take, be loyal to the team and coach.
* Patience - realize that diving is an art that requires a lot of time to develop and perfect certain movements. The diver must keep trying and not get discouraged.
* Willingness to sacrifice - The diver must be willing to give up certain social events, family trips, eating habits, etc.

Some problems with present divers

* Dreamers but not workers - want to be like Greg Louganis but don't want to work for it. They are not dedicated to the sport.
* Sensitive to social pressure - Drugs, T.V., other sports and social activities, love life, etc.
* Disloyal - Jump from one coach to another when not happy with present coach.
* Pampered - Diver is spoiled by a coach who is willing to do anything to satisfy the diver.
* Prickly - Always has conflicts with the coach and team members
* Undisciplined - Diver cares little for rules and obedience.

A BEGINNERS DIVING CLASS

A sample of a diving class that I taught at Indiana University is presented here to help teachers and coaches better understand what is involved in teaching and how it relates to coaching. These classes averaged about sixteen students from ages of seventeen to fifty most of whom had no background in diving. In fact, I had students who could barely swim to the side of the pool after attempting to perform a dive from the one-meter board.

I. Class meeting

A. Objectives
   1. Learn to perform basic dives as a means of recreation that are easy and fun to learn with little chance of injury.
   2. Develop body control, balance, basic actions, kinesthetic, sense, patience, smooth, esthetic movements, courage, etc.
   3. Become acquainted with dives from the five different groups using the three different body positions.
   4. Learn to take a challenge and instruction from the teacher who will have you learn stunts that are seemly impossible to you.
   5. Learn to concentrate, control body movements, and work with fear by mentally disciplining one's self

Dry land procedures used in learning to take one step then lift hurdle leg.

II. First lesson
   A. Orientation and introduction of course
      1. Two 45-minute periods per week
      2. Time of class meeting, locker procedure, showering, exchanging of towels, bathing suit desired.
      3. Practicing before and after class (life guard or instructor must be present) and time when pool is available for the students.
      4. Explanation of the five groups of dives, body positions, dual and championship meets, degrees of difficulty, judging diving, computing
         diving scores, and basic rules in meet competition.
      5. Demonstrate the four-step approach with arms dangling at sides for first
         two steps, the arms then swing forward on third step and backward on
         fourth step after which they swing forward and upward to perform. the
         hurdle.

III. Second lesson
   A. Teach fundamentals of the front approach by explaining and demonstrating:
      1. The proper stance on the board before performing the approach.
      2. Dry land procedures used in learning to take one step then lift the hurdle leg along with the swing of the arms forward and upward to a position outside the width of the shoulder to create balance.
      3. Dry land four-step approach and a hurdle landing on the deck with arms in a fixed " Y" position.
      4. The four-step approach on the board followed with the hurdle by swinging the arms forward and upward to a position outside the

width of the shoulders and slightly in front of the body for balance while lifting the hurdle leg.

5. How to measure the approach on the board. Take five normal steps back from the tip of the board when using a four-step approach.
6. Show how the diver takes off from the board with the arms swinging in a circle from above the head.

IV. Third lesson

A. Demonstrate the forward approach with a front jump from the board in the layout position and land in the water with arms up or down at the sides. Follow this with a front jump in the pike position reminding the divers to reach overhead on the take- off after which they will begin to move down in front of the body as the legs move upward to meet the hands. Touching the feet will be made when the legs are parallel with the water. Remind the divers not to pull the legs up until they reach the peak of the jump for if they pull them up too early, the body could start to rotate backward causing the diver to land on their back. Repeat the dive three times. The same instruction should be given to the diver when performing the front jump in the tuck position when the bent legs are drawn up to the chest where they are clasped by the hands.

B. Teach divers to perform a front dive from the side of the pool. Once perfected, have them do a *front somersault save* which is done by diving in; and, as soon as the body is submerged, the diver ducks under in an open pike position. Best to have a member of the class demonstrate the save.

C. Have divers perform a front dive in any fashion using the forward approach and ducking under as they enter the water. Those who cannot dive using the approach can try the dive the dive while standing on the end of the board starting with the arms over the head.

V. Fourth lesson - All the dives can be demonstrated by the teacher or a competent student.

A. Review forward jumps and front dive three times.

1. Explain and demonstrate the front dive in the pike position.
   a. Stand on end of board and do front dive pike starting with the arms overhead and rapidly pushing them forward and downward as the hips push upward while keeping the eyes on the water through the whole dive.
   b. Divers do the front dive, pike with regular approach three times making individual and group correction of the dives.
2. Explain and demonstrate a back dive with the diver leaning backward from a stand. This should be done by extending the arms overhead,

arching the back, and looking back at the water when falling from the board with no attempt to jump. The teacher should spot the students who have never performed any kind of back dive. The suggested method on how to spot the dive is to have the diver extend one leg to the teacher who holds the ankle with the sole of the foot in his crotch while using the other hand to hold under the leg near the thigh. Then the diver leans backward with an arch in the back and looking at the hands overhead while the teacher pulls in the other direction to create resistance which is used to guide the dive into the water. When the diver has no difficulty performing the dive with a spotter, the diver can then perform the dive without spotter. The teacher must remind the divers to keep watching the hands while leaning back, arching the back, keeping the legs straight and reaching for the water.

VI. Fifth lesson

A. Review the forward jumps two times, a forward dive pike, and a standing back dive with no jump three times.

1. The teacher then shows the diver how to properly walk out to the end of the board, turn around, and make a stance when performing dives that require a back take-off. The teacher has the diver stand backward on the end of the board, lean slightly backward with arms at the sides and looking straight ahead. As the diver begins to lean, he or she should then do a bunny hop keeping the arms at the sides until the feet leave the board (A bunny hop is a very slight jump upward). Once in the air, the diver then swings the arms overhead from the sides while arching the back and looking back for the water with the head. It is very important that the diver does not throw the arms up while on the board for such action will cause the diver to over rotate and possibly land flat on the stomach. No pain will occur if the diver continues to reach back for the water with an arch in the back for if under rotating and landing on the back, a very small area of the back makes contact with the surface of the water which causes little or no pain.

2. The teacher has the diver stand on the end of the board backward and with a slight backward lean, swings the arms overhead while looking back at the water before the feet leave the board. The legs bend and are immediately drawn up to the chest when leaving the board which causes the diver to start rotating backwards in a "flip" position. Flip means that the diver performs a revolution in the air in no specific body position. After rotating one time, the diver can sight the water and straighten the body to land on his or her feet when entering the water. Divers perform the back flip three times.

VII. Sixth lesson

A. Review - one or two jumps forward in the layout, pike, and tuck position; two or three front dives pike; a back dive with no jump; three back dives with a bunny hop; and three back flips.

1. The teacher explains and demonstrates the arm motion used when performing dives that rotate backward. The instruction for the back-dive layout involves swinging the arms up to the shoulder level where they spread out laterally while looking straight ahead after a very slight lean (to keep the feet from hitting the board). Once in the air and the arms are spread out, the diver moves the head back in search for the water. This motion is used by divers who compete, but less effort is put in the jump by beginners to prevent them from going over and landing on their stomach.
2. The diver then performs a back somersault in the tuck position by leaning slightly backward and swinging the arms upward above head. Then when leaving the board, the legs are drawn up to the arms overhead where the hands clasp them slightly below the knees and pull them in close to the chest. This action requires the head to remain in a neutral position for if the head tilts back before the legs are grabbed, the tuck will be difficult to perform properly. The legs can be released and straightened for the feet first entry a short time after the diver assumes the tuck position.
3. The next new dive has the diver stand backwards on the end of the board with the arms extended overhead. The diver then jumps from the board by pushing the seat upward while the arms and upper torso push straight down at the board. The reaction to the arms pushing downward within the width of the shoulders is for the board to push back with the same amount of force in the opposite direction. Caution: The diver should not look at or reach out for the board during this movement because in seeing the board on the take-off leads divers to think they will hit the board which is not true for the body will move on a parabolic arc away from the board. The diver should look straight down at the water during this action then reach for the entry when passing the level of the board.

VIII. Seventh lesson

A. Review - two or three jumps using the forward approach, and three back dives using a full arm swing.

1. The diver performs two inward dives with the arms overhead then uses a full arm swing to perform the dive making sure that the arms push downward within the width of the shoulders to avoid coming close to the board.
2. The diver does three back somersaults in the tuck position then three back somersaults in the pike position. The latter is done by swinging the arms overhead like when performing the dive in the tuck position except this time, the straight legs are drawn to the hands where they are grasped behind the knees and pulled in

toward the chest with the head in a neutral position. The dive will be poorly executed if the diver tries to tilt the head back while attempting to pike. After one somersault is performed, the diver releases the legs and stands up for a feet first entry. The diver can place the arms at the sides or lift them overhead.

3. The divers go to the side of the pool and with the toes curled over the pool side, they squat down in a tuck position and, keeping the head in, roll off into the water a couple of times while doing a somersault under the surface. The divers then stand up then stand up on the pool's edge with the arms extended over the head, take a slight lean forward and rapidly throw the arms and upward torso downward as they thrust the hips upward. Once in the air the divers draw the knees to the chest where the hands grasp the legs below the knees and hold on until a somersault is completed. If the somersaults are not completed in the air, the diver should continue to hold on to the knees until hitting the water. This action should be done three times.
4. The divers then go to the one-meter board where they can attempt a forward somersault from a regular approach or do the dive from a stand on the end of the board with the arms extended overhead. Whichever way is used, the teacher should be ready to call the diver out of the somersault action if rotating so fast as to cause the diver to land on the stomach or face. The diver will adjust the somersault action after a few attempts. Some divers will perform the somersault so well that they may try a forward 1 ½ somersault in the tuck position. Little chance of pain is involved in attempting this dive with one who rotates with little effort.

IX. Eighth lesson

A. Review - Back dive, layout, back somersault tuck and pike; inward dive pike; and forward somersault or 1 ½ somersault tuck from regular approach for those who somersault well. There is little chance of injury in trying a 1 ½ somersault if the teacher tells the diver to hold on to the tuck position until a call is made to come out.

1. Explain and demonstrate the reverse dive. Avoid using the old method of teaching this dive by having the diver walk off the end of the board and kick one leg upward before reaching for the water. I used this method and got tired of having divers hit the board with their hands or fingers. I would suggest that the teacher explain to the student if they can swing their arms completely over their heads and reach backward before the feet leave the board, they will have little difficulty getting around to where the arms will hit the water first. The teacher can have the diver attempt to perform this stunt in any of the three body positions. The easiest position is the tuck but if the diver changes his mind in mid-air, chances are he will land on his back. Going for the layout position is the safest way for

if the diver continues to reach back for the water and goes short, the diver will not experience any pain due to the arch in the diver's back. This dive requires a sales job for the teacher who should encourage the diver by yelling " keep reaching back" while the diver is in the air. Due to the change in direction when coming off the board, many students panic and try to stop and go back the other way instead of continuing with the arm swing. The diver has to decide to accept that challenge and continue with the arm swing. This is also a group-dynamics stunt for once one diver performs the dive, most of the other students will follow suit. The teacher can have great success in teaching this dive by having the diver walk out to the end of the board and do the hurdle keeping the arms over the head through the whole approach.

2. Have the divers attempt the dive three times. If any do not wish to try the dive, encourage them but don't insist they try it. When they see others do the dive at other times, they will all attempt and successfully perform the dive.

X. Ninth lesson

A. Review - back dive layout; inward dive pike; and reverse dive layout (or tuck position) three times.

1. The diver performs a back somersault in the tuck position three times then performs a dive with similar actions, the reverse somersault. This dive is much easier to learn than the reverse dive, but it has been found that if the diver learns the reverse somersault first, first, it is difficult to teach the reverse dive to the student because when getting into the air, the diver has the tendency to pull the knees up and not do the intended dive. The diver finds the reverse somersault not difficult to learn for there is very little chance of hitting the board or being injured when entering the water. Those who perform the dive well can then try to do the dive in the pike position which is performed exactly like the back somersault in the pike position.

2. Another new dive is learned when the teacher explains and demonstrates a back dive in the pike position. This dive is performed by swinging the arms overhead and bringing the legs up where they touch the hands near the peak of the dive. After touching the feet, the head drops back and the arms reach for the entry. Emphasis is placed on the need for the feet come to the hands rather than the hands to the feet for in doing so, the diver will not land short of vertical. The head remains in a neutral position until the touch is made at the peak of the dive.

XI. Tenth lesson

A. Review - back dive layout; back somersault, tuck and pike; reverse somersault, tuck and pike; followed by three inward dives, pike and three forward somersaults, tuck.

1. The teacher explains and demonstrates how to perform an inward somersault in the tuck position making sure that the diver pushes upper torso downward with the arms within the width of the shoulders to grab below the knees for the tuck position.

   Caution; the diver remains in the tuck position until the feet pass the level of the board to avoid any chance of hitting it.
2. The divers then do three back dives pike before the teacher explains and demonstrates the reverse dive pike which is essentially done the same way as the back-dive pike.

XII. Eleventh lesson

A. Review - divers do *all the dives learned* three times.

The teacher then explains and demonstrates how to perform a forward somersault in an open pike position. This should be done with the diver rotating *slightly past* the vertical line which is to make room for the body when it twists in layout position during the somersault. To perform the somersault, the divers are instructed to throw the arms from overhead downward with the body bent at the waist when taking off the board. After leaving the board, the arms then spread out laterally and remain in the position until a somersault is completed at which time, the diver straightens the body when entering the water feet first. The entry can be made by throwing the arms overhead or by pulling them down to the sides of the body. Once accomplished, the teacher explains and demonstrates on the pool deck the arm position that will be used in performing a twist while μever mentioning to the class the intent of the position. The teacher shows how one arm, from a straight position, crosses in front of the body and bends at the elbow as it passes the center of the upper chest. At the same moment, the other arm raises above the head, bent at the elbow, and pulls backward at the same time the lower arm is crossing the chest. The teacher then checks each student for the proper placing of the arms neither of which should touch the body.

Using one of the better students in the class, to perform the front somersault, open pike, when it is apparent that the diver is starting the open pike somersault properly, the teacher hollers "position". In nearly every case if the diver performs the front somersault properly and positions the arms as instructed, a front somersault with a full twist will occur. Note that the word "twist" is not mentioned because if the diver knows that the command " twist" is made by the instructor, he or she will focus on performing the twist action rather than the somersault action which adversely affects the required action to perform the dive.

The dive most divers wish to perform is saved for the last period of the class and that is the front dive, in the layout position or better known as the swan dive. This dive is difficult to perform properly because there is so little motion involved in its performance. When the diver performs the forward approach and is ready to take-off from the board at a slight angle, the arms (slightly outside the width of the shoulders before the take-off) pull down *laterally* from overhead to a position level with the shoulders before the feet leave the board. The head should be erect during this movement until the diver reaches the peak of the dive at which time it may tilt down slightly to allow the diver to see where the entry is to be made. When nearing the water, the arms then move *laterally* from the fixed position to the point of entry. With the diver making only three moves to perform this dive, it is best performed when it is done four or five feet away from the board.

Dives learned in this class in eleven lessons

Front dive, pike	Back dive, layout	Reverse somersault, tuck
Front dive, layout	Back somersault, tuck	Reverse somersault, pike
Front somersault, tuck	Back somersault, pike	Inward dive, pike
Front somersault, pike	Reverse dive, pike	Inward somersault, tuck
Back dive, pike	Reverse dive, layout	Front somersault, one twist

Other dives that could be learned in this class

Forward 1 ½ somersault, tuck	Reverse dive, tuck
Forward 1 ½ somersault, pike	Inward 1 ½ somersault, tuck
Forward double somersault, tuck	Front somersault, two twists
Back dive, tuck	Back somersault, two twists
Back somersault, layout	

CHAPTER 5

THE FACILITY

Even a very competent coach with a potentially talented diver will find that success is very unlikely without a favorable pool or some body of water that offers the proper diving equipment needed for a diver to learn and excel. The progress and growth of diving was very slow before World War II because so many of the facilities found around the country were so primitive. Then, following the war, a tremendous change in the level of the coaching and competitive diving performances occurred due to the construction of better diving facilities and equipment.

Swimming pools

At the beginning of the twentieth century, swimming pools were called 'baths' which was a term used by the Europeans and mainly by Great Britain. But in the United States they were called 'swimming pools'. Nearly all of the indoor swimming pools located in clubs, high schools, and universities in the United States before World War II were rectangular in design and twenty or twenty-five yards long to meet the standards used for swimming competitions at that time. The pools that were twenty yards long usually had a one- meter board at the deep end of the pool while some pools that were twenty-five yards long had two one-meter springboards. Other pools this size also had two one-meter boards separated by a three meter-board (Photo 1).

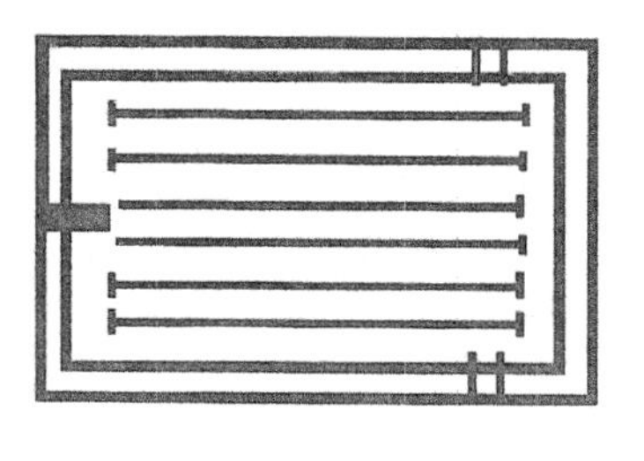

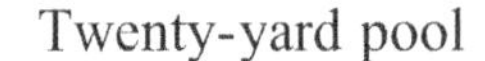

Twenty-yard pool

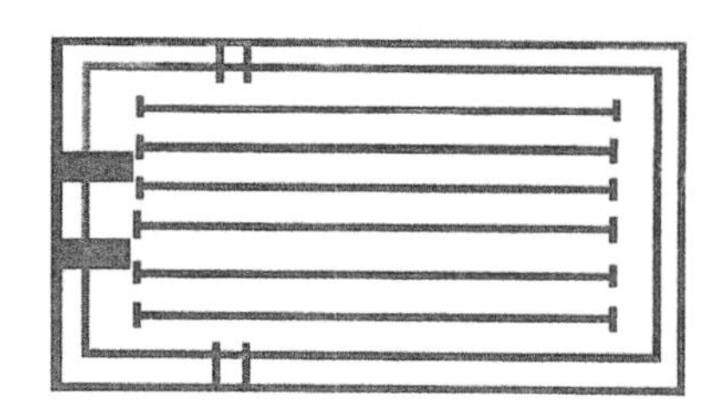

Twenty-five-yard pool

Photo 1

The depth of the water in pools that had one and/or three-meter springboards was usually eight to ten feet and the height of the ceiling from the tip of the board ranged from eight feet for one-meter facilities to twenty-four feet for pools with a three-meter board which made the facility cheaper to heat and easier to light the pool area. Only a few indoor pools in the country had higher ceilings. There were less than a half dozen towers located in indoor pools.throughout the country until after World War II.

Since there were no separate diving wells in swimming pools and only a few diving facilities that possessed separate diving areas in the swimming pools, the divers on a swimming team had to practice diving around the swimmers as they swam laps, or they practiced at a different time than when the swimmers worked out. Diving as an event was not well accepted by swimming coaches because there was not enough time for them to coach both the swimmers and the divers. There was only a handful of diving coaches affiliated with clubs throughout the country and no coaches who coached only diving in high schools and colleges before the second World War. Since the swimming coaches had to coach a large number of swimmers plus a small number of divers, they usually spent nearly all of their time coaching the swimmers. No wonder the swimming coaches in high schools and colleges tried to eliminate competitive diving from the swimming programs for well over fifty years.

Starting in the 1950s, new 25 yard and 25 meter indoor and outdoor pool facilities were built some of which were in a "T" or "L" shape. These designs gave room for a diving facility outside of the swimming area (Photo 2). Similar designs for diving outside of the swimming area in fifty-meter pools were rarely found. The newer pools had depths of nearly 11 feet for one-meter diving and no less than 11 feet 10 inches for 3-meter. Nearly all of the pools built outdoors after the war that had ten-meter towers increased the depth to no less than fourteen feet with most offering greater depths up to twenty feet.

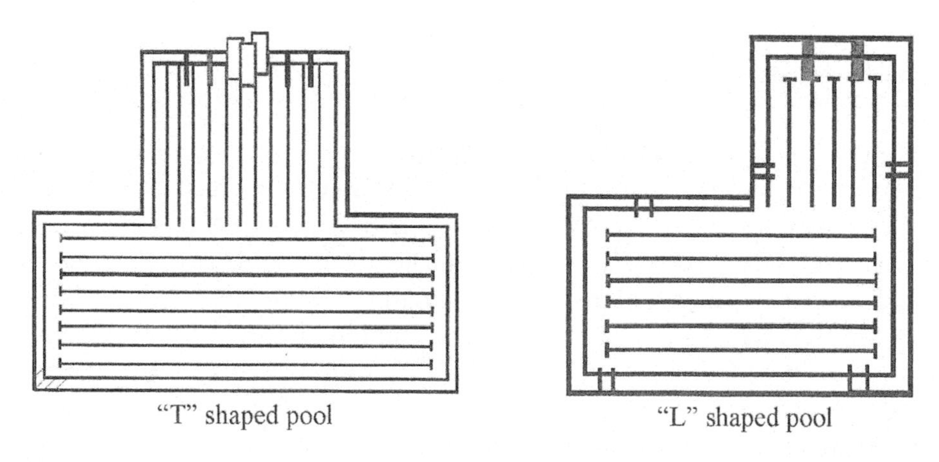

"T" shaped pool

"L" shaped pool

Photo 2

As time went on, new pools were constructed to include separate areas for swimming and diving with some of the diving pools large enough to be used for water polo and synchronized swimming. Many of these new pools include two one-meter boards and two 3-meter boards for synchronized diving. With the introduction of tower diving as an event in collegiate swimming meets, the new collegiate swimming pools are 50 meters in length some of which have separate diving wells away from the swimming pool or have the diving facilities in the swimming pool which are separated by a moveable bulkhead (Photo 3, A & B). At present, there are nearly one-hundred indoor and outdoor diving towers in the United States.

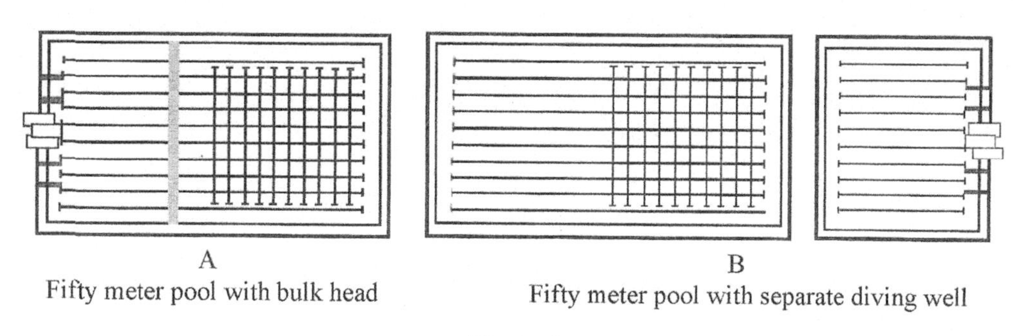

A
Fifty meter pool with bulk head

B
Fifty meter pool with separate diving well

Photo 3

Changes in Diving Equipment

Diving Boards

The first wooden diving boards used for competition were nothing more than that, wooden boards. These primitive boards were usually made of Ash which is a durable and flexible kind of wood. The first diving boards were usually two planks cut in various sizes and lengths attached with wooden slats and wrapped in cocoa matting to keep the diver from slipping (Photo 4 next page).

Then around 1912, Ernest Brandstein, swimming and diving coach at Stanford University, started to make wooden boards of Oregon pine which, along with other forms of wooden boards, were eventually made to an accepted standard length of sixteen feet and twenty inches wide. Unfortunately, the boards that were in constant use lasted only a few short months before breaking. A new version of the board was developed when Brandstein and four-time Olympic Coach Fred Cady developed a wooden board that tapered at one end which allowed for more spring and later on produced a board tapered at both ends. Unfortunately, both of these boards were short in existence because they broke too often.

This wooden board was upgraded in the 1940' s when Ray Daughters from Seattle, Washington made a laminated wooden board which meant the board was made with thin strips of wood glued together the full length of the board. The board was tapered at the diving end which reduced its weight and made it springier. Laminating the board in this fashion not only gave it better performance but it also lasted longer than any previous wooden board. The Daughters board was also used exclusively at the 1948 Olympic Games in England. Wooden diving boards covered with fiberglass were later made but never were accepted for competition because they proved to be too heavy which offered less spring than the standard wooden boards.

A Primative Wooden Diving Board
(end covered in cocoa matting)
Photo 4

A great change in diving boards occurred soon after the 1948 London Olympic Games that revolutionized competitive diving. Norman Buck, a maker of aluminum step ladders and also from Seattle, Washington read in a newspaper that Ray Daughters diving boards were to be used in the Olympics. Having no background or previous knowledge of diving boards, Buck figured that making a diving board out of aluminum would be ideal because it would be lighter, more durable, and would offer more spring than wooden boards. With thirty-two tons of war surplus aluminum in his garage, Buck decided to construct an aluminum board using "I" beam extrusions with aluminum tubing on the sides all of which were attached with steel rods. This new version was brought to Ohio State University to be tested by Bruce Harlan, Johnny Simpson, and me. The board proved to be successful except for a very strong torque action that caused the diver to cast to the side when taking off. Buck went back to his garage and corrected the problem by placing a three-foot long thin metal plate cushioned with a rubber strip around its edges on the diving end of the board. This eliminated the torque and restricted the noise when the diver dived from the board.

Buck also added another feature to the performance of the board by developing a non-skid material that was baked on the board's surface. This new version eliminated the need for cocoa matting so there was no need for the boards to be elevated. Thereafter, the boards were installed on a level plane. The leveling of the boards proved to be a very important change for it reduced the chance of divers hitting the board when performing reverse and inward dives. One other feature of the Buck board was that it was the only board ever made that could be repaired if broken. When one of the beams broke, the rods could be removed, and the broken beam could be replaced with another beam. Other versions of aluminum boards were marketed at that time such as the Patterson and Clark boards, but none could compare with the Buck board until the late 1950's when another great change in diving boards appeared.

Ray Rude, an aeronautical engineer in Arcadia, California, discovered a new way of making a superior diving board almost by accident when a friend of Rude's was giving a party one evening that included a diving exhibition. The friend painted the wooden diving board for the show, but it didn't dry in time for the exhibition. So, Rude went to his shop and cut a section off of an airplane wing and used it as a diving board. The substitute proved to be a tremendous success which convinced Rude that this new version had great promise as a competitive diving board. He immediately constructed a board called the "Duraflex" which was designed after an airplane wing. Because it offered more spring than any other competitive board, it quickly became the most popular board used in competition throughout the world. New improvements of the board soon followed with the first called the "Maxiflex" board. This board was tapered at both ends which reduced its weight and offered greater spring. The next improvement was made by drilling perforations near the end of the board which, again, reduced its weight. This again increased the spring making it the best board ever made. Most people believed that the holes were bored to allow the air to filter through the board to reduce air resistance, but that claim was unfounded. The Maxiflex Model 'B' has probably reached the maximum amount of spring that can be obtained from any diving board because divers can now put the tip of the board into the water when diving from the one-meter level. A board any springier would result in divers putting a great part of their legs in the water before its recoil which would not be desirable (photo 5 below)

The Maxiflex Model "B" diving board
Photo 5

Diving Stands

The change in diving stands was almost as great a change as in diving boards for the first stands were made of wood and quite shaky when used with fixed fulcrums during the early part of the twentieth century. The fulcrum on these wooden structures was usually in the form of a block of wood or a metal bar that was covered with a rubber tubing to absorb the force of the board and reduce the sound as it bounced off of the fulcrum. If one wished to move the fulcrum forward or backward, the board had to be lifted to make the change. The back of the board was usually anchored to a steel bar sunk in a block of cement (Photo 6 below).

A primitive diving stand and board with a fixed fulcrum
Photo 6

Over a thirty-year period, these primitive stands were gradually replaced with metal stands in the form of a steel pipe structure anchored in cement that was used and produced for both one- and three-meter competitions. Sometime in the 1930s a moveable fulcrum was added to the diving stands by putting metal cogged tracks on the top of the steel stands which allowed the fulcrum to be moved with the use of a metal wheel (photo 7).

This kind of stand and fulcrum was popular throughout the world until 1949 when the aluminum Buck diving board was created. Though this board was soon used world-wide, there was no improvement in diving stands and fulcrums until the late 1950s when the Duraflex diving board replaced the Buck board along with a new version of a diving stand and fulcrum. Besides making it possible for divers to give a better performance than from any past diving facility, the new modern stand, known as the Durafirm Stand, offered a very firm foundation for the divers which was not found in previous stands. It also presented a fulcrum that was easy to move back and forth on smooth runners all of which gave a long-lasting service. The Model "B" board and Durafirm diving board standard has left little room for improvement in springboard facilities.

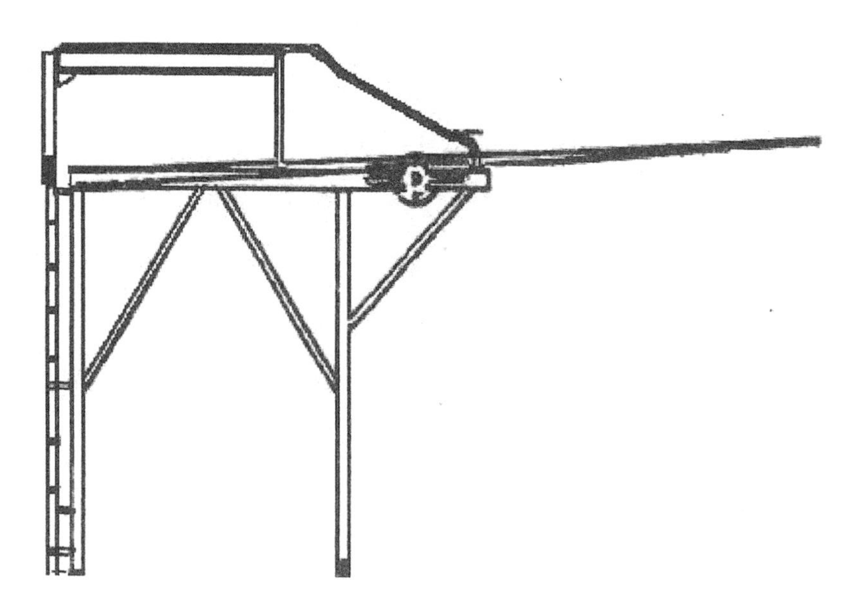

An early three-meter diving stand with the first movable fulcrum

Figure 7

Duraflex diving stands at one and three-meter levels

Photo 8

Duraflex also developed a fulcrum box called a "short stand" that can be installed on cement platforms at both the one-meter and three-meter levels as well as on one and three-meter stands.

The railings around the platform are not only used for safety reasons but also to avoid law suits resulting from a diver falling off the platform (Photo 9).

The Durafirm short stand
Photo 9

CHAPTER 6

TEACHING AIDS

The use of teaching aids for the sport of diving has been largely responsible for the vast improvement in the performance of divers in recent years. Some of the advantages teaching aids have offered divers include:

* Have made it possible for divers to learn and perform dives that otherwise would have taken years to perfect without their use.

* Have increased the safety of performers when practicing, training, and competing.

* Have helped divers reach goals, develop confidence, reduce fear, prevent and rehabilitate injuries, compete better, and be more motivated.

* Permits divers to take part in diving programs from the time they learn to walk up to the time they are ninety years of age and perform dives that were at one time mere fantasies or dreams.

* Allows divers to perform dives in competition from heights ranging from three to thirty-two feet with little chance of injury or pain.

* Helps divers from little tots to the experts to be guided through the performance of sequential moves that are used in the performance of all dives.

* Protect the performer from harm by offering support when performing some sort of stunt in the air or when making contact with the surface of the water.

* Have made it possible for persons to take part in a diving program where they all can safely enjoy the sport as a form of recreation and competition.

Some of the most popular teaching aids are:

The trampoline

With the exception of the sand pit board, most of the teaching aids used for diving were perfected and introduced to competitive diving just before and after World War II. One of the most important teaching aids produced at that time was the trampoline which is believed to have been first developed in circuses in France as far back as the eighteenth century. It is also believed that the idea for the trampoline came from the safety nets used by trapeze artists while performing stunts and as a means of dismounting at the end of a performance. The use of trampolines then spread throughout Europe and later on to the United States where they were used in circuses such as the Ringling Brothers and Barnum and Bailey. Their popularity increased when they were used in acts found in night clubs, fairs, and theaters. Then in 1938, George Nissen and Larry Griswald from Cedar Rapids, Iowa formed a company that developed and marketed trampolines and other various kinds of gymnastics equipment that were soon distributed to Y.M.C.A.' s, various athletic clubs, colleges, high schools, and gymnastic centers all over the world.

Since few people knew anything about trampolines, they were first used as a form of amusement and recreation by persons, mostly children, who performed various simple stunts with basic landing positions. Their use suddenly changed with the outbreak of the war when the military services discovered that trampolines could be used to physically condition the service men. The value of the apparatus increased when it was also found that with good instruction, the service men could learn, with the support of spotting and safety belts, aerial dynamics, body control, balance, visual perception, endurance, and body awareness while rotating in the air. Following the war, interest in trampolines flourished and was soon in demand by schools, colleges, and sports clubs that used them in gymnastic classes as a form of recreation. It didn't take long before such exposure led trampolines into the competitive gymnastics programs as an exciting new event.

The value of the trampoline and spotting rigs as a teaching aid for competitive divers

After the trampoline was introduced to the public divers discovered that the apparatus could be a tremendous aid in learning all kinds of new stunts and diving techniques. It didn't take long for divers to find that with the use of spotting rigs, many of the difficult stunts used in diving could be safely learned on the trampoline.

Other features that helped divers when using the trampoline were:

* One can continue training without having to go into the water due to a cold, while ill, or when recovering from certain injuries.

* Develop greater concentration and emphasis on body control and movements when performing certain difficult stunts.

* Better communication between the coach and diver because the coach can get nearer to the diver than when coaching in the pool.

* With the use of spotting rigs, learn the proper mechanics used in performing the approach and take-off from the diving board, the desired body positions used in the performance of basic and difficult dives, and learn all the lead-ups needed when learning new dives with little or no chance of injury.

* Reduces the fear of learning dives and certain moves used in the performance of difficult dives.

* Makes it easier for the coach to move around the area to observe the divers' movements from different angles.

* Allows the performer to repeat stunts quicker than when diving from a board or platform. It is a great time saver.

* Makes it easier for divers to learn aerial rotation, orientation, and "spotting" certain areas when rotating in the air.

* Offers a source for developing physical fitness.

* Provides a fast means of warming up before starting a physical activity.

* An easy means to store the equipment

* Repeat stunts and movements quicker than when diving from a diving board or platform this is a great time saver.

Trampoline competitions were not offered in the United States or other parts of the world until after World War Two. After that period, many divers learned stunts on the trampoline that were similar to and usually more difficult than stunts performed on the diving board. Unfortunately, divers could not use the new difficult stunts in diving competitions because they were not listed in the rule books. However, with the induction of diving Degree of Difficulty Formula in the early 1980s, divers were allowed to perform dives in competitions that were not yet listed in the rule book if accepted by the rules committee.

At first, most of the performers on the trampoline were divers for it was found that it took little to change the actions used in diving and, with a little adjustment, to perform them on the trampoline. Nearly all of the national champions on the trampoline were Olympic divers such as Bruce Harlan, 1948 gold, Skippy Browning, 1952 gold, Bobby Clotworthy, 1956, gold, Don Harper, 1956 silver, and Tom Gompf, 1964 bronze. These divers, all from Ohio State University, soon recognized that the trampoline was an ideal teaching aid for learning new stunts that could performed from the diving board and platform. This new approach to competitive diving could also be used for improving diving technique and, with the use of safety rigs, divers were able to learn difficult dives quicker than when trying to learn them on the springboard or diving tower.

The transition from one sport to another

Surprisingly, most divers did not have much difficulty changing actions performed from the springboard to those used on the trampoline. But gymnasts who wished to compete in diving had much trouble in making the change from the trampoline to the springboard or tower. Though the acrobatic movements performed by athletes from both sports were very similar, the landing positions of the stunts were just the opposite. Divers more often enter the water head first at the completion of most dives while the gymnasts usually land on the bed with both feet at the completion of a stunt. With this difference, gymnasts had no difficulty with landings on the trampoline when learning with safety belts but found it to be a problem when landing head first with no use of safety belts when diving. Fortunately, the problem has become minor because a safety belt can now be rigged over the one-meter springboard to be used when learning new dives.

Other differences in the transition of stunts from one sport to another are noted when performing twisting somersault dives. When somersaulting or twisting during a somersault, divers usually rotate one-half more or less than gymnasts when performing on the trampoline. For example, when gymnasts perform one, two, or three forward somersaults, they twist ½, 1 ½, 2 ½ times so they can site the trampoline bed upon landing. Divers, however, perform a forward 1 ½ or 2 ½ somersaults with one, two, or three twists so they can site the surface when entering the water. Gymnasts also perform back one, two, or three somersaults with one, two, or three twists while divers perform 1½, 2 ½, or 3 ½ twists when performing 1 ½ or 2 ½ somersaults in a backward or reverse direction. Some divers also perform 1 ½ or 2 ½ twists when performing a back somersault from the one- meter springboard and enter the water feet first which does not offer the diver a very clear view of the water upon entering. Therefore, divers sight the water in front of the rotation of a stunt when rotating forward or backward and gymnasts sight the bed or floor behind the rotation of a stunt when performing twisting somersaults that require a feet first landing. Recently, many gymnasts perform back somersaults with ½ or 1 ½ twists in floor exercise events which make sighting the floor difficult. However, they have little difficulty sighting the floor when performing back somersaults with one or two twists. Whatever the differences in landing, it still appears to confuse, frustrate, and scare the gymnasts more than the divers when making a transition from one sport to the other.

The structure of the trampoline

The trampoline used for gymnastic competition and as a teaching aid for diving is a steel rectangular apparatus six by ten feet in diameter that stands approximately four feet from the ground. It features a flat taught nylon bed attached to the frame with steel springs (Photo 1).

The trampoline
Photo 1

Early trampolines did not fold up when first made so they had to be dismantled when moved from one area to another or when being stored. Nissen later made a better version where the trampoline could be folded up and moved on wheels. The first steel springs attached to the bed from the frame had sharp edges which injured any performer who landed on them after an uncontrolled maneuver. Nissen attempted to solve the problem by replacing-the springs with shock cord. However, he discovered that the shock cord lost its elasticity within a short time, so he changed back to steel springs which were tapered on the ends and no longer injured a performer and produced a better spring. These springs are still used and now have pads over them to prevent anyone from falling between the springs.

The first trampoline beds were made of two solid canvas covers, one on top of the other and sewn together on four sides. With a lot of use, the bottom cover was found to tear which was followed by the tearing of the upper cover which resulted in a replacement with a new bed. Later on, Larry Griswald, a circus performer and known as the finest clown diver in the land and also a close friend and partner of Nissen, developed a webbed bed. This bed permitted the air to filter through the webbed strips which greatly reduced the air resistance and gave greater spring for the performer. The canvas strips were later replaced with thinner nylon strips which further reduced the weight of the bed and air resistance which offered greater spring. This bed was used for years until it was improved on by an Australia company in the form of a perforated nylon mat that was again made better by a Canadian firm and is presently known as the best bed made for trampolines.

When trampolines became a gymnastic event in the late 1940s, the competitors performed stunts for a three-minute period taking as many free bounces as they wished between stunts. Jumping for that period of time often resulted in many performers passing out so the time period was reduced to two minutes which still caused many of the jumpers to feint. Eventually, the time period was reduced to one minute that required the jumper to perform no more than ten stunts with no free bounces between stunts. This format is still used for competitions and appears to be the best system for choosing the winner.

The safety of the trampoline

During the earlier stages of the trampoline, nothing was available to protect the performer from harm other than persons standing around all four sides of the apparatus to catch anyone who fell off. If a performer went flying off into space, one of the persons (called spotters) standing at the side of the trampoline would try to 'catch' the performer before he or she hit the ground. As the trampoline became more popular and challenging, accidents often occurred causing injuries to those landing on and off of the apparatus. This led to the use of spotting belts or safety rigs similar to those used by circus performers when performing difficult stunts on the trapeze, high wire, or other aerial acts. The spotting rigs used on trampolines consist of a strong leather belt wrapped around the performers waist with ropes attached to both sides of the belt. The ropes are strung up over the top of the trampoline with pulleys attached to steel poles or to the ceiling (Figure 2 & 3).

The late Charlie Pond, the gymnastics coach at the University of Illinois for forty years, developed a belt that allowed the performer to twist as well as somersault when performing stunts in any direction with no chance of injury. This belt contained steel ball bearings encased in a metal ring around the performer's waist which virtually eliminated injury from these types of movements. The ropes then pass through pulleys attached to the poles about twenty feet high that are clamped on both sides of the trampoline. The ropes that pass through the pulleys are held by the instructor who stands to one side of the trampoline and guides the movements of the person performing stunts (Figure 4).

Spotting belt for somersaults Figure 2	Spotting belt for twisting somersaults Figure 3
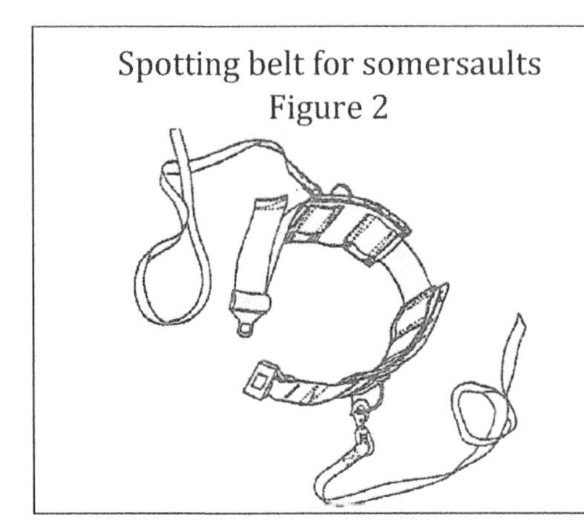	

Trampoline with spotting rig
Figure 3

Although misuse of trampolines and neglect of instruction has resulted in injuries and law suits, they have prevailed because when conducted under proper supervision, they offer a safe activity. The trampoline has been used in world, national, international events and more recently in the Olympics, and it has always received tremendous support from fans for it is an exciting event to watch. Recently, the trampoline created enough interest and excitement as a sport to include synchronized trampoline events as a part of the gymnastic program. This new event has two persons performing identical routines of ten difficult stunts on trampolines stationed side by side. Synchronization requires perfect timing and body control.

More recently a new innovation of the spotting belt has been devised as a teaching aid that does not require any assistance to help the performer when jumping on the trampoline. The belt has bungee cords adjoined to ropes that pass through the pulleys attached to the tops of metal poles that are spanned above the trampoline. The performer simply stands in the center of the trampoline and begins to bounce up and down, guiding the performance by the manner in which he or she jumps.

The bungee rig
Photo 5

The bungee cord apparatus offers much more spring with less effort than the conventional trampoline and allows the performer to perform multiple somersaults and twists that are self-controlled with no chance of injury (Photo 5).

Dry land boards

Prior to 1965, this kind of dry land equipment was known as "the sand pit" because most of the divers jumped into a pile of sand or sawdust from a wooden gymnastic springboard or a diving board mounted on a metal stand set on the ground or floor (photo 6). Though the sand or sawdust gave some cushion for the diver when landing feet first, it was hard enough to cause injury to the diver's legs or ankles. This kind of landing material was used up until 1963 when a dramatic change occurred the also affected many other sports.

Sand Pit
Photo 6

A dry land board is a one-meter stand with a stationary or moveable fulcrum and a diving board which is set up in a gymnasium, field house, pool deck, or an outside area. Obviously, the diver takes off from the board, performs some sort of diving maneuver, then lands on his or her feet, stomach, back, or knees atop a large foam rubber casing. Divers use the dry land board to perfect approaches, take-offs from the board, basic stunts, lead up stunts for difficult dives, and difficult dives. Divers can perform stunts in four different directions while in a safety belt which *must be used* when performing more than one somersault. Twisting stunts also can be performed if the diver uses a twisting belt.

With nine divers injured by jumping into a pile of sand from a mounted one-meter diving board in the field house at Indiana University, I believed there had to be a way to prevent such injuries. I soon came up with the idea of digging a hole in the ground in the field house and filling it with foam rubber which I obtained 'free' from a local furniture company. After filling the hole with foam rubber, the divers were able to jump into the pit landing on their back, stomach, knees, and seat with no fear of injury because the foam rubber acted as a shock absorber. Obviously, jumping into the pit head first was not an option. Unfortunately, I never thought of putting a liner in the pit before filling it with foam rubber, so the divers looked like they were climbing out of a coal bin after landing in the pit. One of the divers whose roommate was majoring in journalism stopped by to watch practice one day and was so awed by what she saw that she decided to take some pictures and write an article on our activity for the school paper. The article in the school paper attracted the attention of the local newspaper, then was picked up by the Indianapolis Star newspaper, and finally ended up in the *"Stars and Stripes"* which was then a national newspaper.

I believe that a firm in California saw the article in the paper and thought to take this new version of a landing surface a step further by encasing the foam rubber in a plastic bag which would eliminate the need for digging a hole in the ground. The first plastic casing with various dimensions came on the market around 1965 and was filled with chunks of polyurethane foam covered with a net over the top. The original version was later modified to include blocks of foam and a mesh top that allowed the air to escape from its cell structure Photo 7.

Once the compression was made by the diver landing on the cushion, air was immediately drawn back into the cells which allowed the process to repeat itself. A plastic cover was used to protect the foam rubber and meshed casing from erosion and moisture. The new soft-landing pad, along with overhead spotting devices, made the teaching and coaching of diving, gymnastics, track and other sports involving aerial activity much safer. This allowed athletes to perform stunts that were before out of the question to attempt, and land on a soft surface with little chance of injury.

At the same time this cushion was manufactured, another way of making such landings was presented which was in the form of an "air bag". These two companies competed with each other for the best and the safest to use until an athlete landed on an air bag that had a leak and was injured. The air bag is now used by firemen and other groups that involve jumping from heights by filling the air bag with air at the site which is not always possible when using the rubber cushion method.

Foam landing pad encased in plastic casing.

Figure 7

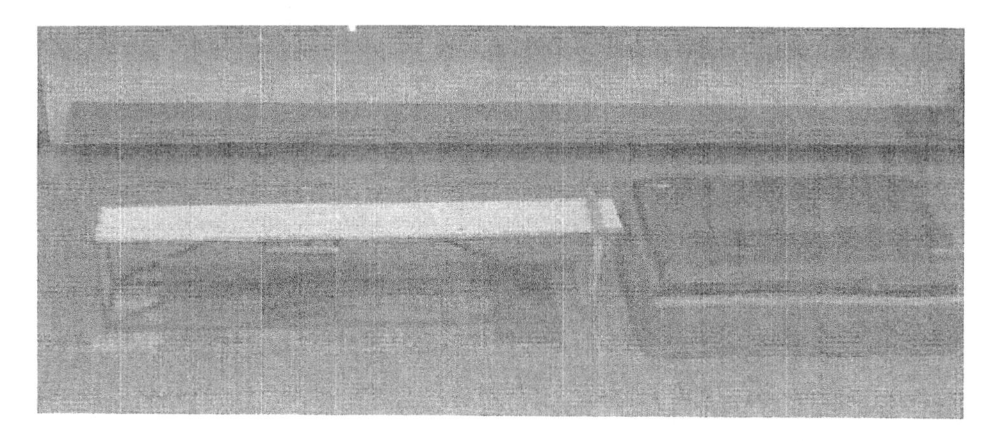

Portable dry land stand with board

Photo 8

Features of the dry land board

Benefits of using the dry land board are essential because divers can:

* Practice board work without going into the water.

* Learn all of the basic movements used in diving including the approach, the take-off, the dives, and all of the difficult dives.

* Practice faster than when diving in the pool.

* Work with spotting rigs which not only act as guides in learning but also offer safety from injury.

* Learn aerial orientation used in somersaults and twisting stunts.

* Easily communicate with the coach.

* Receive instructions from different angles by the coach. Some dry land boards can be moved and/or stored with little difficulty from one area to another for convenience.

The "bubbler"

Another training device was introduced to competitive diving in 1971 that allowed the sport of diving to make a breath-taking advance in the performance of difficult dives. Invented by Herb Flewelling, Alberta, Canada, this new safety feature, called the "bubbler" or "sparger" has made it possible for divers to learn intricate dives with little fear of injury or pain when landing on the surface of the water from heights up to ten meters. The bubbler uses tanks of stored air from an air compressor, and the air is projected through a metal and/or plastic pipe positioned on the bottom of the pool slightly in front of the diving boards and/or platforms. Air is released through small holes in the pipe which forms an air bubble as it jets out and rises to the surface. This process filters the water and offers a soft cushion for the divers by reducing the impact on the diver's body when landing on the water's surface. The curvature of the water caused by the air bubble also decreases the chance of injury by greatly reducing the surface tension of the flat surface on which the diver lands when hitting the water (Photo 9).

Landing on the bubbler
Figure 9

When using the bubbler

The coach communicates with the diver by using a count-down system that begins before the diver leaves the springboard or platform which allows time for the air to be released. The air is cut off when the diver nears the surface of the water on the entry. This allows time for the generator to refill the air tanks which normally takes a couple of minutes. The amount of air pressure stored in the tanks depends on the horse power of the air compressor and the size of the air tanks. The bubbler is normally installed when building new pools but can be installed in pools that are already built. If not for the invention of the bubbler, it would have taken years for competitive diving to reach the high point of excellence it now enjoys.

The mini-bubbler

The standard bubbler is very expense, but a "mini" bubbler can be made and installed in any pool that is at least ten feet deep. This kind of bubbler can be easily assembled and disassembled, placed in any area of the pool, requires no pool plumbing, and is particularly used for age group and high school diving programs. The mini bubbler produces a ten-foot diameter bubble and is generally used beneath one- and three-meter springboards but can also be used under most platforms on the diving tower. At a cost of well under a thousand dollars, the mini bubbler provides benefits that are identical to those of the standard bubbler. The bubbler has proven to be far and away the most valuable aid for learning new dives. above any other teaching aid to be the most valuable aid for the learning of new dives because it reduces the fear of performing dives and the chance of possible injury. Teachers and coaches also find that they can teach divers many times faster with its use.

How to make your own mini bubbler

The parts needed to make your own bubbler can be purchased at any hardware store.

1. An air compressor with an air tank with at least a three horse-power motor that holds 200 pounds of air or more. Most air tanks have a one-half inch outlet.

2. A high compression one-inch in diameter rubber hose with a length that can reach from the tank to the edge of the pool area where it will be inserted into the water. It is possible to use half- inch high compression hose if a one-inch is not available.

3. A control valve that regulates the flow of air from the tank to the hose.

4. A plastic two-inch in diameter pipe that can be inserted in water to the bottom pool area in front of the springboard or platform. The pipe should protrude at least four feet above the water surface to be controlled by a person standing on the deck.

5. An adapter is attached from the end of the one-inch hose to the two-inch pipe. A fifteen- pound weight can be attached to the end of the plastic pipe by drilling holes near the end in order to keep it from rising when the air is released from the tank. Plastic covered weights used in weight training are ideal for they won't rust or scratch the pool tile.

This kind of unit requires two people: one, to control the air for the bubbler and the other to hold the plastic pipe in place until the diver is in the air. At that time, the pipe is pulled back to eliminate any chance of the diver hitting the pipe. I used this kind of aid for twenty- five years and never had any kind of injury. Even if the diver should hit the pipe, no injury occurs because the near vertical slope of the pipe offers little to no resistance if hit by the diver.

Another attachment can be made for the air outlet which is in the form of a three or four-foot rectangle metal or plastic pipe with small perforated holes (Figure 11). This is placed in front of the boards or platform on the bottom of the pool. If plastic is used, a portion of the pipe can be filled with cement to keep it from rising while the bubbler is on. The attachment to the rectangular piece can be a high compression hose coming from the generator that can be placed down the side of the pool and weighed on the bottom of the pool. This makes it possible to detach the unit at pool level when not in use. Such a unit is not portable and must remain in a permanent position on the bottom.

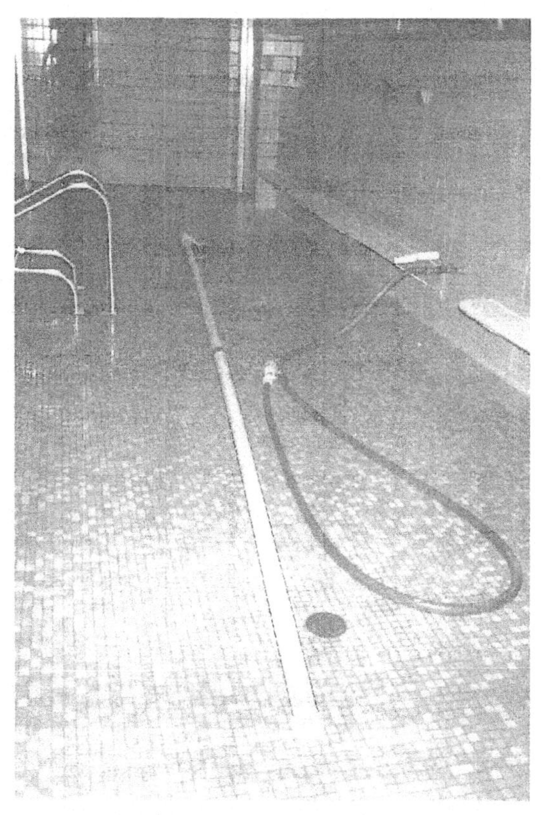

Self-made mini-bubbler
Figure 10

The safe operation of the mini bubbler

In the years the standard bubbler has been in use, the only injury I am aware of is when the force of the air bubble was too strong in its delivery and exploded like a balloon. The force of air can be regulated when using the expensive standard bubbler and to some degree when using a mini bubbler. The force of the mini bubbler is not strong enough to offer much resistance and no injury from *over-force* has ever been reported since its use. I would suggest that the high compression hose be replaced every year or two because it can wear and react from use much like a tire on an automobile.

CAUTION: The compressor should be set in a dry area away from the pool deck due to the danger of any electrical exposure to water or persons that could result in serious injury or even death.

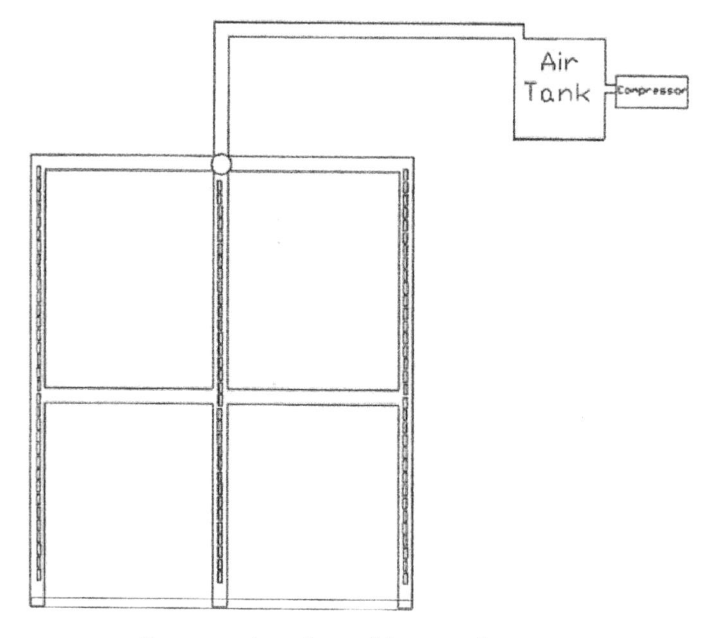

Rectangular pipe with cross braces
Figure 11

Crash mats

Crash mats are also available to divers and coaches. They are used when a diver is airborne by jumping from the floor or ground onto the mats. The mats are particularly used for single standing somersaults but can be used when approaching the mats on the run. Mats are also useful in teaching youngsters how to dive into the water forward and backward (photo 12). The mats come in various sizes and thickness some of which can be folded which can increase their thickness and also makes it easy for storage.

Mats used by youngsters learning to dive into the water
Photo 12

Video and Tivo

Not long ago, divers and coaches viewed and analyzed dives by taking movies. This was an expensive operation for it meant purchasing a movie camera, buying the film, paying for film developing, and finding a projector and screen to show the film. No wonder so few divers ever saw themselves on film or had the chance to analyze their performances. To make matters worse, it usually took a week or two to have the film developed, time to repair broken film, set up the operation, and change locations to show the film.

Video then appeared on the scene in the early 1970s which eliminated all of the expensive and tedious operations related to films. Today, all one needs is a video or digital camera that can take pictures which can be played back immediately on a screen or even on the camera without ever leaving the pool deck. The cost of this operation is very minimal and the help to the divers is priceless for they can replay and make immediate evaluations and corrections of their dives without ever leaving the pool deck.

Tivo

It is not unusual to find several cameras and video screens around a pool deck taking pictures of dives from all angles and portraying them all at one time which are shown the moment the diver leaves the water and steps out on the deck. This operation is called "Tivo". Animation is also entering the sport which has been found to be very helpful to divers and coaches in defining and analyzing movements of dives. With this kind of technology available, all that is needed is for the divers and coaches to better understand and become more educated in the science related to the movements they are observing.

Figure 13

The nice thing about video and tivo is that the diver and coach can view stop action, slow motion, and regular motion all of which makes is easy to analyze any part of the motion used in the performance of the dive. Such feedback works two ways: if the dive is well performed, it offers positive reinforcement. But if the performance is poor, it may discourage the diver and coach. Whichever way the dive is viewed, both diver and coach will have a more accurate concept of how the dive should be performed.

CHAPTER 7

SOME MECHANICAL PRINCIPLES APPLIED TO DIVING

A person cannot perform or coach a dive if one does not have a concept (mental picture) of how the dive is to be executed. To create such a concept requires guidelines for each of the movements made by the diver when performing a dive. Obtaining accurate guidelines has been a difficult task especially when looking at the competitive diving rulebooks. The only diving rulebook in the United States that has ever offered any kind of guidelines was provided by the Amateur Athletic Union (A.A.U.) - the national governing body for amateur sports for many years. The guidelines **in** that book were adopted from the F.I.N.A. rule book which is the governing body for diving throughout the world. With the exception of a written explanation of the forward dive in the layout position, the only guidelines ever offered were in the form of drawings that portrayed movements of certain dives performed in sequence.

Some of the drawings were first portrayed as far back as 1908, were later updated in 1924 and then again in the 1970s. Unbelievably, some of the primitive drawings of the dives are still displayed in the F.I.N.A. rulebook (Figure 1). It is also interesting to find that some of the dives were called "headers" in the early years because the diver entered the water head first with the arms placed at the sides of the body (Figure 1, B). Dives performed in this manner, which were later dropped from the rule books, were given higher degrees of difficulty than dives entering the water head first with the arms extended overhead (Figure 1, D). However, the term "header" continued to be used for a short time to describe dives that entered the water head first before it eventually died.

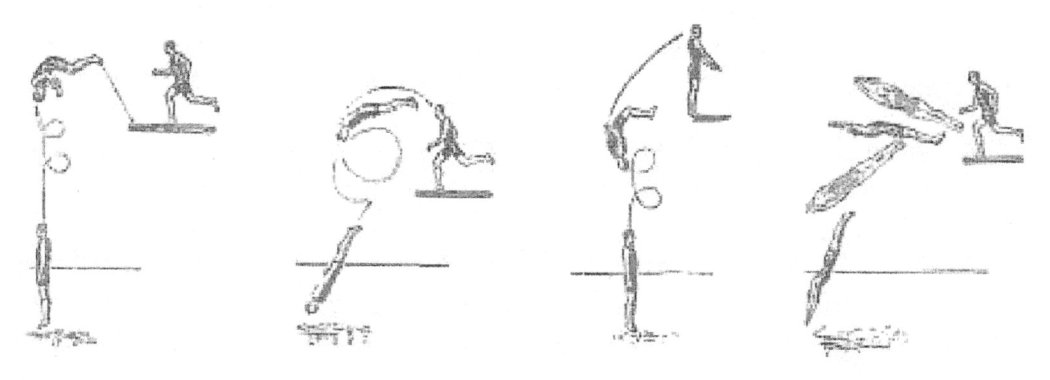

Dives from the springboard 1908
Figure 1

Unfortunately, written explanations and accurate drawings involving the movement of all competitive dives performed in sequence have never been displayed in the high school, college, and U.S. Diving rulebooks. This has resulted in a great deal of confusion and frustration for divers, coaches, and judges who, over the years, would have liked to know how dives should be properly executed. Such conditions could have been avoided if accurate and standard guidelines for competitive dives had been available years ago.

Since competitive diving offers next to nothing in terms of guidelines for the performance of dives, it may be possible to move nearer to perfection if one becomes familiar with and agrees to a hypothesis: "No move should be made in the performance of a dive unless it contributes to the execution of the dive". Stated another way, if a diver uses moves that do not contribute to the execution of the dive, then such moves should be eliminated because they do nothing to improve the dive. For example, starting with an arm at the side of the body, the easiest known way to scratch the nose with the finger is to lift the arm upward in a straight line to the nose rather than moving the arm in several directions and making different gyrations before reaching its destination. Obviously, any motion of the arm and hand away from a straight line would be a waste of energy, motion, and time and should be avoided.

To satisfy one's curiosity of why a written description of the front dive, layout was the only dive put in the F.I.N.A. rulebooks, the answer can be found by checking the rules used for the 1912, 1920, and 1924 Olympics. As mentioned in Chapter 1, an event called "Plain Diving" was offered in the Olympics that required the diver to perform two front headers in the layout position from the five meter and two from the ten-meter platforms. The diver executing the four dives with the best form, grace, and control was declared the winner. Since no one at that time had a very good idea of how to perform the header, the following written description was offered by the F.I.N.A. rule book.

"The diving illustrations serve as guides only (referring to the drawings) and it is to be noted that the position of the arms shall be the choice of the diver except in the case of the plain front header forward (front dive) where the arms must be stretched out sideways in line with the shoulders during the flight through the air. The arms must be kept still until just before the entry into the water, when they must be brought together and extended beyond the head in a line with the body."
(This refers to the execution of the Plain Front Dive only).

Though the Plain Diving event was eliminated following the 1924 Olympic Games, the explanation of the Front Header remained in the A.AU. rule book for nearly forty years before it was finally removed. Meanwhile, many of the drawings of the dives presented in those early years are still displayed in the F.I.N.A. diving rulebook.

It is very important that divers, coaches, and judges recognize what makes a dive beautiful. Beauty can be recognized when one realizes that the less motion used to reach an objective, the easier and more beautiful the motion appears. When one observes a ski jumper soaring four or five hundred feet through the air in slow motion on television, the simple stillness and accuracy of the performance is a beautiful sight to behold. The jumper looks like a soaring eagle with the arms stationed at the sides of the body while portraying little or no motion. But if the jumper should move any part of the body while in flight, the friction from the air would cause the skier to change position which could result in a painful landing none of which would be very pretty to observe. In diving, one should realize that the beauty of a dive is proportional to the amount of motion used to successfully perform the dive. When a dive is performed with no wasted movements, comments on how easily the diver performed the dive are often made.

Keeping the hypothesis in mind, coaches and divers can look to Sir Isaac Newton's Laws of Motion as the source from which the scientific approach to the execution of dives can be obtained. In Newton's Laws of mechanical principles, lie the guidelines for the performance of dives that can reveal how, when, where, and why every move in a dive should be made. The use of such principles should be applied with the least amount of motion to insure beauty in the dive. Such guidelines can not only offer direction in forming sound concepts of dives but also provide information and understanding of the body movements resulting in a greater accuracy when analyzing dives. Choices in style and technique related to the performance of dives can also be more easily recognized and evaluated which can shorten the time divers need to learn and to practice. For example, when performing backward and reverse somersaults in a tuck or pike position, the diver may extend the arms overhead and bring the legs upward toward the hands. Or, extend the arms overhead in the same manner and then circle them in a backward direction as they reach for the legs which are drawn toward the chest. Either technique is acceptable but in analyzing the two different motions, it is possible to determine which method may be more favorable to use by one diver than by another. It is important to realize that in offering guidelines, the intent is to offer direction toward a "desirable" way to execute a dive rather than the "perfect" way for few would ever agree to absolute perfection.

With the use of scientific principles, it becomes obvious that simple written explanations for all competitive dives could be offered that would reduce the confusion and frustration shared by divers, coaches, and judges over the years. Some may feel that guidelines would force divers into a lock- step style of diving that would give little or no opportunity for individual creativity. This not so because different body types require different timing patterns in movements made by each diver.

NEWTON'S LAWS OF MOTION

Isaac M. Newton was the first to offer scientific evidence that enables divers, coaches, and diving judges to better understand what, how, and why things happen in diving. His three laws of motion are the most important and widely used sources for analyzing and coaching diving; or for that matter, any sport. Newton' s Laws were somewhat overlooked in competitive diving for around sixty years. Then an English track coach and professor in bio-mechanics, Geoffrey Dyson, decided to apply Newton's Laws of Motion to many sports. In his book entitled Dyson *"The Mechanics of Athletes"* offers countless simple explanations of human movement that leave no doubt that all sports should use this approach to obtain success and perfection.

Dyson was followed by two other English bio-mechanic experts, Dr. George Rackham and Dr. George Eaves, who had differing opinions on how twists could be inaugurated when performing twisting somersault dives. Rackham won out with his book *"Diving Complete"* which describes how mechanical principles based on Newton's Laws can be applied to every needed movement used in the performance of a dive. With our present knowledge of how to relate science to diving, one can look back at their arguments with amusement while also appreciating their confusion and frustration at that time in attempting to solve the dilemma. Another English expert in the science of motion, Derek Travis, followed Rackham and took the approach of using mechanical principles a step further with a series of lectures and written articles.

Five diving coaches pioneered the scientific approach to the sport of diving in North America during the early half of the century. The first American bio-mechanics authorities surfaced in the 1960's which included Lyle Draves, Dennis Goldman, Charlie Batterman, Sam Slobonav, and Hobie Billingsley. These coaches were followed by Doris Miller, from Ontario, Canada, who is an outstanding bio-mechanics expert who wrote the book, "*The Bio-mechanics of Competitive Diving*" that greatly contributed to the improvement of diving. With the additional aid of Jan Gabriel of U.S. Diving, they performed years of scientific research using video tapes, computers, and other technical tools related to diving. Along with the coaches mentioned, they analyzed and explained the value of mechanical principles, based on the laws of motion, and how they contribute to the movements used in diving.

Some coaches are comfortable using trial and error methods and copying the performance of others and occasionally obtain good results, but not very often. Although such methods are no longer producing *great* results, too many coaches still have not awakened to the fact that there are other methods, based on scientific fact, that are more helpful for coaching and teaching diving. These methods act as guidelines and offer a scientific base in directing the actions of a diver or any other athlete. Knowledge of these mechanical principles also makes it much easier for a coach and a diver to understand the moves and forces that need be used when performing a dive. To learn these principles is not difficult for all it takes is a little curiosity and motivation to try something new. I strongly recommend that divers and coaches who wish to understand the basic physics used in the performance of dives, read over the information that is offered in this book and consult the books by Dyson, Rackham, Miller, and the other authorities that have been mentioned here.

It is suggested that you not try to digest all of the information at once; read a little at a time and let the information sink in. It's like learning a new language. Build your vocabulary word by word and when you have spoken your first "sentence," you will be off and running with eagerness to learn more as your knowledge and comprehension expands. Once familiar with the scientific principles, you will find that you have formed a scientific foundation that enables you to analyze and coach dives with accuracy and validity that will bring success to you and your program.

Universal terms

With the information gathered from the six bio-mechanical masters and many other sources acquired in recent years, an attempt is made here to discuss some of the mechanical principles that relate to the performance of dives. Such a discussion is greatly needed because competitive diving does not provide, at this time, any kind of blueprint that portrays how dives should be executed near to perfection.

In discussing Newton' s Laws, it is important to avoid meticulous and complicated jargon and keep the subject as simple as possible if any value is to be derived from the presentation. This approach requires that certain universal terms be given so as to make the topic of Newton's Laws a little clearer, consistent, and more meaningful to the reader.

* Motion - The movement of the body in a straight line or in a circle.

* Angular momentum - A measure of the amount of rotational force a body possesses by virtue of its rotation about a particular axis. Angular momentum can be created only by an external force. This means if a person were suspended in space and wanted to rotate about an axis, the body would have to make contact with some outside object such as a meteor.

* Angular velocity - The rate of rotation of a body about an axis. Normally recognized as the speed at which a body rotates.

* Inertia - The resistance required to move and an object from a state of rest and once in motion, the object will remain in motion until an external force is applied to the object which will reduce or stop it from moving.

* Force - Is the effect that one body places upon another. In diving, force is used for changing the state of motion in reference to s owing down, speeding up, going higher, and starting or stopping the motion of the body. Force equals mass times acceleration (F=MxA).

* Moment of inertia - A measure of the amount of rotational resistance about an axis. Altering the resistance to rotate will increase or decrease the angular velocity (speed) of a body. This is easy to recognize when a diver extends or reduces the radius of the body while somersaulting.

* Linear and angular motion - Linear motion is when a body that moves in a straight line while angular motion refers to a body that circles about an axis.

* Center of gravity - the point where the pull of gravity is balanced in the body. This point is located in the physical center of the body from which it may rotate. The center of gravity may be located inside or outside the mass of the body (Figures 2 & 3).

Center of Gravity

Center of Gravity

Center of gravity in the body

Figure 2

Center of gravity outside the body

Figure 3

* Vertical line - An imaginable line runs vertically through the point where the arms are attached to the shoulders when entering the water head first and a point at the hips entering the water feet first.

* Conservation of angular momentum - While in flight, the angular momentum stored in the body remains constant about the axis on which it rotates regardless of any change the diver may take relative to his or her body position. If the resistance to the rotation is increased (which means extending any part of the body away from the axis of rotation), the angular velocity of the body will decrease and if the resistance to rotate is decreased, the body will speed up (increase its angular velocity).

* Eccentric thrust - Refers to the force of the legs or the springboard pushing upward and away from the center of gravity causing the body to rotate. Eccentric may be seen as a way of being off balance.

* Mutation - A wobbling motion of the body while in the air

* Horizontal axis - A straight line passing through the center of gravity at right angles to its length on which the body rotates (somersaults) Figure 4.

* Longitudinal or vertical axis - A straight line passing through the center of gravity of the body lengthwise on which it rotates (twists) Figure 4.

The horizontal and longitudinal axis
Figure 4

* Recoil - The upward force provided by the springboard from its lowest bending point that determines the dive's height, distance, rotation, and angle when projected.

* Impulse - The lowest bending point of the diving board.

* Centripetal force - A force that moves an object close to the center of gravity as it continues to move in a circular path. The amount of force depends on the mass, distance, and angular velocity of an object.

* Centrifugal force -A force that moves an object away from the center of gravity while rotating.

* Oscillation - An up and down or back and forth movement of an object

* Kinetic energy - The energy retained by a body from a force that puts it in motion.

Though different styles and concepts of dives are practiced by divers and taught by coaches throughout the world, it is still possible to create concepts of dives based on authentic mechanical principles that can guide divers in the direction of perfection. To make such an approach requires one to first become familiar with Newton's Laws of Motion.

1. Law of Inertia - An object at rest remains at rest and an object in motion continues in motion at a constant velocity in a straight line unless acted upon by an external force. This includes a rotating body, isolated from external forces that will have constant angular momentum. This means that in performing a somersault, a person's body will continue to rotate about its axis until an external force acts upon it to increase or decrease its rotation.

2. Law of Acceleration -The rate of change of motion of an object is proportional to the applied force acting upon it and takes place in the direction in which the force is

applied. The greater the force, the greater the acceleration and vice versa. This law is usually expressed by the equation: Force on an object equals mass times acceleration F = M x A. The law applies to all forces started by divers when attempting any dive. Each body part has a mass and to accelerate it, requires an application of force. The greater the acceleration of a body part, or the greater its mass, the greater will be the resulting force. For example, when a diver takes off from the board, the body immediately begins to decelerate which will affect the height of the dive due to the pull of gravity. As the body continues to move upward while resisting the downward pull of gravity, it continually reduces its upward velocity to the point where the upward force equals the downward force causing the mass of the body to momentarily stop, then start to accelerate downward. The constant pull of gravity on the body, as it falls, then causes a proportional increase in the velocity of the body.

Therefore, the acceleration of an object is always proportional to the force acting on it. Double the force, and the acceleration doubles; halve the force and the acceleration is cut in half. Also, since acceleration has a direction associated with it, so must the force.

3. Law of Action Reaction - For every action (force) there is an opposite and equal reaction. Although nearly everyone is familiar with this law, it is frequently misunderstood because the action and reaction mentioned in the law are not two forces exerted on the same object, but rather forces exerted on two different objects. To put it more clearly, if object " A " exerts a force on object "B", then object "B" exerts an equal and opposite force on object A. With respect to diving, when a diver is ready to take off from the board or platform after exerting a force of some magnitude and in some direction, the result is for the board or platform to exert equal amount of force in the opposite direction. If the body is in the air and the arm is extended laterally at the shoulder level in front of the body, the reaction is that the body moves in the opposite direction of the arm movement with an equal force. Therefore, regardless of whether a move is initiated within the body, when in flight, or when contacting some external object, there will be an opposite reaction with equal force.

Newton's Third Law (action - reaction)
Figure 5

The diver can benefit from the use of the action and reaction in three different ways:

* The diver may initiate a motion to reach an objective when the reaction to the movement is insignificant. For example, in the preparation for the head first entry, the diver simultaneously extends the arms overhead moving along the longitudinal axis of the body. The reaction to the arm movement is for the body to move in the opposite direction which would be upward. However, this movement is not noticeable due to the gravitational force applied to the body during its descent.

* The diver may create a motion with the intent of using both the initial action and the reaction to benefit the outcome of the dive. This is observed when a diver, rotating forward, moves the arms, well within the width of the shoulders, from the waist to a position overhead in preparation for the entry. This motion of the arms moving in a forward counter-clockwise direction causes the lower part of the body to move in a clockwise direction which aids in preventing the diver to enter the water short of the vertical line.

* The diver may make an initial move to take advantage of the reaction. This objective is obvious when making certain movements with the arms while performing a dive like a reverse 1 ½ somersault. In this dive, the diver swings the arms upward and overhead to a point behind the center of gravity while also lifting the head and the chest on the take- off *before* the feet leave the board. These movements cause the feet to push back into the board which reacts by pushing the feet and the lower portion body forward and upward creating angular momentum as the diver leaves the board.

With all of this in mind, an application of Newton's Laws as they apply to certain aspects of diving can be seen in the following:

* The desirable moves used in the execution of the forward approach.

* The required moves when performing a simple basic dive such as the front dive, layout.

* The desired sequential moves made in the performance of a difficult dive such as the forward 3½ somersault in the tuck position.

* Various methods used in initiating a twist when performing twisting somersault dives.

THE FORWARD APPROACH

Starting from a stance, the forward approach requires the diver to take three or more steps forward and then perform a hurdle to the end of the board before taking off to perform a dive with movements that require rhythm, grace, balance, and strength. Obviously, the purpose of the forward approach is to project the diver from the end of the springboard with the greatest amount of force possible in order to meet the objectives needed in performing a dive. Variations of the forward approach by divers in an attempt to obtain greater projection from the board have been common for the last seventy years.

These variations emerged from the gradual change in the spring of the boards which began in the late 1940's, when wooden boards with shaky wooden stands with fixed fulcrums were replaced with aluminum boards, sturdy metal stands, and moveable fulcrums. These improvements have proven to be so effective that there appears to be little room for developing better diving facilities
without changing the sport.

The Stance

Other than the performance of a dive, there is no better way for a diver to communicate or impress a judge than by the way he or she stands on the board before beginning the forward approach. Few realize how many divers have won or lost a close competition because of the impression they made on a judge when standing on the board. Having judged diving for over fifty years at all competitive levels, I found it much easier to judge a diver standing on the board who was well groomed, wearing an attractive suit, and portraying good posture than when trying to judge one that did not display any of those qualities. Granted, a good appearance does not guarantee a good performance, but it does create a positive impression that could affect the score of a dive. If the stance can encourage better scoring from the judges, a few suggestions presented here may help the diver to be more presentable before performing a dive (Figure 6, A)

Posture

It is not necessary for a diver to stand in a military fashion before beginning the forward approach, but it does help if he or she stands with the body erect, the head level, and the eyes focused on the end of the board or platform. The shoulders should be rolled back slightly with the stomach drawn in to give a flat stomach appearance, the arms and hands extended and close to the sides, and the legs straight with the feet together. Such posture certainly makes a greater impression on a judge than a diver who is slouched over with the arms away from the sides and the feet apart.

The diving suit

Years ago, a country in Europe had some very good divers performing in the Olympics, but they didn't score well though their performances were outstanding. From the comments made by the judges and coaches following the contests, it was found they were turned off by the ugly diving suits the divers had worn and admitted that it affected their scores. This bears out that a diver wearing an attractive suit, is more apt to score better in a meet than one who offers a poor impression by wearing an ugly suit.

The color and design of the suit can be an influence in giving a favorable impression. A dark-skinned person usually draws more favorable attention when wearing a light-colored suit and, in contrast, a light skinned diver normally looks better in a dark colored suit. Either way, the color contrast compliments the diver's figure. A suit that fits female divers a little snug usually brings out the best in their figure. Since there are so many designs and styles of suits these days, it is suggested that the diver obtain the opinion of other divers, coaches, and friends as to which suit makes for the best appearance.

Grooming

Though hairstyles change from time to time, many judges feel that it is more difficult to judge divers who have long and uncombed hair, a mustache, and/or a beard, than it is to judge one who is clean shaven with well-kept hair. If a diver feels their personal appearance is being violated, they should at least groom the hair to make their appearance more presentable. The female diver with long hair should crop or braid the hair to keep it out of her face while performing a dive. One thing for sure, an abundance of hair on a male or female does little to encourage better scores from the judges.

Many divers have missed going to the Olympics or lost an important diving contest by a few hundredths of a point which may justly have been due to the performance of the dives. However, it also may have been the impression they made while standing on the board or platform. Since the name of the game is to win, and the diver is in a sport that involves human judgment, he or she should make the best appearance possible when performing. Such is seen in figure skating where the outfits worn by the skaters can turn a judge on or off when they perform in a contest.

A diver should remember that with a diving judge, he or she doesn't get a second chance to make a first impression.

The Forward Walk on The Board

The great improvement in diving equipment has resulted in many changes on how divers walk when executing the forward approach. During the years when cocoa matting covered wooden boards that projected upward to allow the water to drain off, the rules stated that the forward approach be made with the divers taking at least three steps in a "running fashion" so they could reach the end of the board following the hurdle. When wooden boards were replaced with aluminum boards, the coca matting was replaced with a baked non-kid material on the surface that resulted in the boards that made it possible to mount the boards on a level plane.

These changes in the diving equipment resulted in discarding the old rule of running toward the end of the board and replacing it with a rule that states divers take no less than three "normal" steps which should be smooth, straight, and forceful prior to the hurdle.

Once the aluminum boards replaced the wooden boards, constant improvements were made by making them thinner and lighter in order to give the divers more spring. These changes increased the oscillation wavelength of the board when force was applied. The slower movement of the board led divers and coaches to believe that divers had to walk slower in order to catch the rhythm of the board. Coaches and divers were convinced that the board oscillated more and more with each step when starting from the stance, walking over the fulcrum, and continuing until performing the hurdle. However, close observation has shown that there is no oscillation during the walk because there is no downward force applied to the board during the walking process. Although it is clearly noticeable that there is a slight downward bending of the board caused by the diver's weight as he or she passes over the fulcrum and continues to move toward the end of the board, no oscillation of the board occurs (Figure 6, A-F).

In analyzing the walk, when one leg steps forward, the hind leg pushes the ball of the foot backward into the board. According to Newton's Third Law, the board then pushes the back foot forward in the opposite direction with the same amount of force causing the body to move forward. During this process, the heel of the forward foot makes contact with the board which creates force in a linear direction with no measurable downward force to cause oscillation. The distribution of the diver's weight and the forces created by the legs when walking remains constant in a forward and backward direction because both feet are always in contact with the board at the same time. Although the center of gravity of the body moves up and down slightly during the walk, it is not negligible. It can then be concluded that, with the exception of the speed of the walk and the length of the last step prior to the hurdle, the forward walk has little or no influence in creating a downward force on the board that would cause the body to lift when performing the hurdle.

The most popular walk on the board when performing the forward approach is with the diver taking four steps before the hurdle. Starting from the stance, the diver takes the first two steps with the arms hanging at the sides which does nothing to create any movement that would influence the approach (Figure 6, B & C). The arms then swing forward in front of the body as the diver takes the third step (Figure 6, D). Once the foot of the third step is planted, the arms begin to swing backward to a position behind the divers back as the fourth step is made (Figure 6, E).

The speed of the walk

The speed of the walk may affect the performance of the hurdle. To a point, the faster the diver walks on the board, the more momentum can be transferred from the walk to an upward direction when taking the last step prior to the hurdle. A similar effect occurs when athletes perform the high jump and the long jump in track. In the high jump, all athletes approach the high bar with a slow run at a slight angle from the side of the jump pit. The speed of the run then increases a few steps before the jump to generate more forward momentum. When the jump upward toward the bar is made after planting one foot on the ground, the momentum created from the forward run is transferred to a force that moves the jumper in an upward direction. Needless to say, no jumper could possibly match any jump performed this way by simply walking up to the high bar before jumping.

A similar transfer of momentum occurs when performing the long jump. The one quality that all long jumpers possess is their ability to run fast for the faster they run, the further they can jump. This is clearly seen when jumpers sprint down the runway and plant a foot on the take-off board in preparation for the leap forward. At this moment, the forward momentum from the run is transferred to an upward direction, allowing the jumper to jump high while using the momentum from the run to carry him or her over the jump pit. Therefore, the distance a jumper can obtain not only depends on how fast they can run but also how high they can jump. In doing so, much of the forward momentum transferred from the run on an upward direction causes the jumper to be in the air for a greater amount of time. Again, it is obvious that a jumper could never jump far when walking up to the take-off board then when sprinting down the run way. The objective of the athletes who perform in these two events is to produce an upward force as high as possible which is obtained by accelerating the athlete's mass (Newton's Second Law).

Relating to the movements of the high jumpers and long jumpers with divers, if one wishes to jump as high as possible when performing the hurdle, they can create a greater force for the jump by walking fast rather than walking slow. In doing so, most of the force created by the forward momentum of the walk is transferred into an upward direction after planting the last step on the board before the hurdle. Obviously, divers can walk too fast causing a loss of body control and/or balance when performing the hurdle, so the speed of the walk must be adjusted accordingly. Conversely, if the diver walks too slow, little force can be transferred to project the body upward. How high a diver can jump in a hurdle depends on the amount of strength the diver possesses in his or her legs and the amount of downward forces applied by the body to the board. As when performing the high jump, some divers walk slow for the first two or three steps then suddenly speed up the last couple of steps to perform the hurdle which offers the needed transformation of momentum to perform the hurdle. However, this kind of walk does not follow the rule for the forward approach in diving that states that when performing the forward approach, the walk to the end of the board shall be *smooth,* straight, and forceful.

When asked why so many divers walk slow on the board, the only answer to that question that I have been able to offer is because Greg Louganis walked slow in his approach and everyone likes to copy the champion. In reality, Louganis could have jumped well above six feet from a stand on the board so walking slow appeared to have little effect on how high he could jump in a hurdle. In observing the Chinese and Russian divers, it is found that they all walk faster than most divers from other countries for the reasons already stated which may give cause for much of their success.

The length of the last step before the hurdle

Another point of concern concerning the forward walk is the length of the last step prior to the hurdle (Figure 6, E). The length of this step determines the position of the diver's center of gravity which can have a significant effect on the performance of the hurdle. If the last step is considerably short, the center of gravity remains high and away from the board which makes it easier for divers with limited strength in the legs to jump upward. Conversely, if the diver takes a long last step prior to the hurdle, the center of gravity drops closer to the board which requires great leg strength to lift the body upward to successfully perform the hurdle. The low center of gravity also makes it difficult for a diver with limited strength to place the center of gravity of the body over the forward leg when jumping upward. It is therefore suggested that divers with *limited strength* keep the last step relatively short before the hurdle, and divers with strong legs take a long last step making it possible for them to jump higher in the hurdle.

In recent years, many divers have used a hop or skip step into their hurdles believing that it creates oscillation of the board *before* taking the last step prior to the hurdle. Some divers using these methods have succeeded in moving the board up and down to generate greater height. Unfortunately, this style appears to look a little peculiar and has caused many divers to be off balance or out of control when performing the hurdle and the take-off to perform the dive.

Another concern of divers who wish to walk faster during the walk is their tendency to overstep the board when performing the hurdle that often causes difficulty in performing the proper take-off from the board. In most cases, this error occurs because the hurdle leg is not lifted high enough when planning to perform a difficult dive or the diver get too anxious when planning to perform a dive. Therefore, lifting the knee higher in the hurdle creates more traction from the foot that pushes forward and downward into the board resulting in a reduction of the forward motion of the body. It should be understood that lifting the leg in the hurdle does not cause the upper torso to bend forward as long as the other foot remains on the board. To prove this point, one may run in place and lift the knees high to find that the upper body will not bend forward as long as one foot is on the ground. However, the body will bend forward if the hurdle leg is lifted to extremes, like up to the chin, or if the diver's "push off leg" has left the board while lifting the hurdle leg.

A B C D E

The stance and the walk in the forward approach
Figure 6

The approaches used by most divers in competition

* A slow, normal, or fast walk with a hurdle about the length of a normal step

* A slow, normal or fast walk with a long or short hurdle.

* A walk where the steps change speed before performing the hurdle.

* A walk that has a hop or skip before performing the hurdle.

* A walk where the diver moves the arms in various directions before the hurdle.

The Hurdle

The purpose of the hurdle is to project the body as high as possible in the air so the diver can alight on the end of the board in balance with the greatest amount of force before the take-off. The kind of hurdle made depends much on how the last step in the walk is planted on the board prior to the beginning of the hurdle (Figure 7, F). When taking this step, a transition of force occurs that pushes the board downward due to the arms swinging forward and upward in unison with the lifting of the hurdle leg and the extension of the push off leg (Figure 7, F-G). When the board is pushed to its lowest point (impulse), it then begins to recoil as the arms continue to swing upward to form a fixed " Y" position slightly in front of the head. The hurdle leg also continues to move upward bent at the knee to form a right angle and the push off leg extends as the board passes a level plane and projects the diver into the air (Figure 7, H).

As soon as the diver leaves the board, the hurdle leg is immediately extended to meet with the extended push off leg while the arms remain in a fixed position until reaching the peak of the hurdle (Figure 7, H). A quick extension of the hurdle leg is desired because it gives the diver more time to use the arms to make any adjustment or correction of balance if any poor movement is made when the hurdle leg extends. Extending the leg immediately also gives the diver more time to focus on the take-off and the dive to be performed. When reaching the peak of the hurdle, the arms begin to circle backwards behind the body as it begins to descend (Figure 7, I & J). The arms are in a position slightly behind the hips and the legs are slightly bent when the feet make contact with the end of the board (Figure 7, K). The board continues to move downward as the arms swing upward and the legs begin to extend (Figure 7, L).

A problem with beginner and novice divers is found when they don' t place the arms in a fixed position at the peak of the hurdle. Instead, they begin to circle the arms before the legs come together. Circling the arms too soon greatly reduces the force applied to the board prior to the take-off and also creates an unbalanced hurdle.

When performing the hurdle, some divers have difficulty in obtaining the proper rhythm, tempo, and timing when landing on the end of the board prior to the take-off. This is usually known as "stomping the board". In an effort to correct this problem, most divers will move the fulcrum forward or backward, change the standing position, or change the length of the hurdle. Many don' t realize that it is not the board that is out of timing but rather it is the divers. When one really thinks about it, the problem involves the correct timing of the arm swing from the peak of the hurdle in preparation for the take-off. Leaving the arms in the fixed position at the peak of the hurdle for a longer or shorter period of time before starting the circular swing backward, changes the timing of the force to be applied to the board that is oscillating. In this way, the tempo and rhythm of the body meeting the board can be synchronized by changing the timing of the arm swing (Figure 7, J-L) rather than trying to change the tempo of the board.

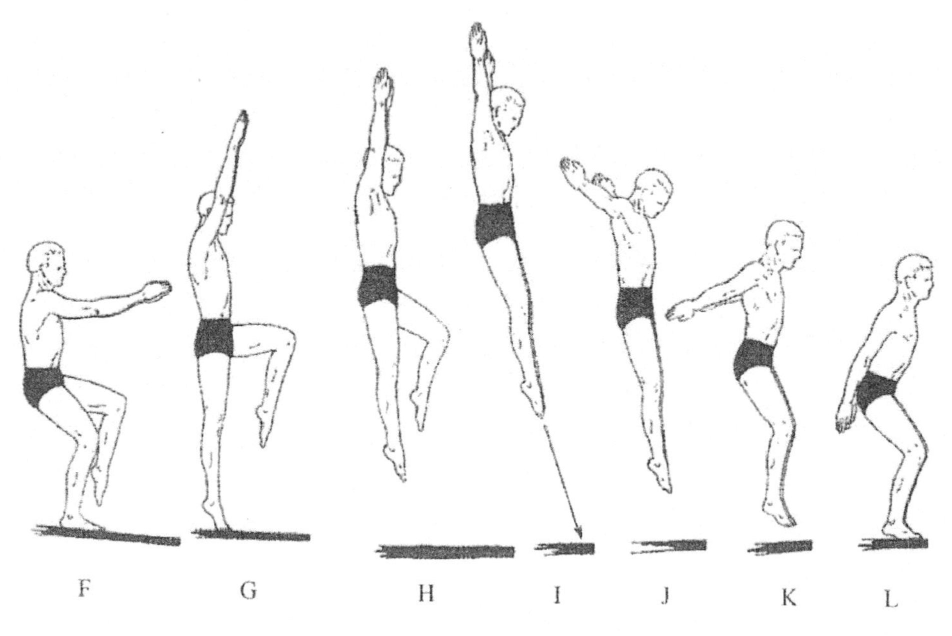

The hurdle in the forward approach
Figure 7

The distance of the hurdle

The distance of the hurdle to the end of the board can have a significant effect on the height obtained by the diver when projected from the board on the take off. The American divers seem to find the distance of the hurdle to the end of the board to be about the length a normal step which they believe they can do with balance and control. The Chinese divers usually use a hurdle shorter in length because of their small size and light weight. They figure that the closer to the end of the board they apply a downward force, the more the board will bend so they perform the hurdle close to the end of the board to capitalize on more spring. Furthermore, they found that if they walk a little fast and perform a short hurdle, they can take off from the board in a near vertical direction and let the kinetic energy from the fast walk and the pitch of the board carry them away from the board while obtaining maximum height; which appears to make a lot of sense.

Another type of swing that will create more force when performing the hurdle is to swing the arms in a full circle prior to the beginning of the hurdle. This kind of swing starts near the end of the third step and is performed as quickly as possible to take advantage of creating more force by accelerating a mass. Swinging the arms in a full circle increases their velocity which generates more force to the jump when performing the hurdle. One may think that the diver would experience less balance and body control when using this type of swing but, on the contrary, those who have perfected the full arm swing state they can jump higher in the hurdle with balance and control than when using the half swing.

For years I have never been able to understand why athletes in such sports as golf and baseball swing the club or bat at least 360 degrees to develop maximum force to hit the ball and the discus and hammer throwers rotate their bodies 360 degrees to obtain the maximum force to make a successful toss, while divers rotate their arms only 180 degrees to create force when performing the hurdle. Some feel that such an action is unorthodox but after observing the action for a short time, one begins to accept the motion as orthodox and the half-circle arm swing as unorthodox. In other words, it is a movement that can offer maximum force in the hurdle and take-off if divers are willing to accept something new and adapt to the change (Figure 8).

The full-arm swing hurdle
Figure 8

The Take-off

There is no doubt that the take-off from the springboard or platform is the most important phase in the performance of a dive because it is from this point on the end of the springboard or platform that determines how, when, and where the dive will be performed. Similar to the objective of the hurdle, the purpose of the take-off is to project the body from the springboard or platform into the air with the greatest amount of force possible to obtain enough height and movement to successfully perform the intended dive. The preparation for the take-off begins when the board reaches its lowest bending point (impulse) and begins to recoil upward as the legs extend and the arms continue to swing upward to a point overhead (Figure 9, M & N).

Circling the arms prior to the take-off is to generate centrifugal force which is transferred to the springboard or platform and used to offer resistance to the legs, ankles, and feet as they extend and push into the board or platform when the diver is taking off. The arm swing is normally synchronized with the extension of the leg parts to obtain the best results in the take-off. The greatest amount of force from the arm movement when they swing upward to push the board downward, is when they are fully extended and shoulder width apart.

The position of the diver on the board or platform at the point of take-off depends much on the dive to be performed. Whatever the dive, when diving from the springboard, the arms first extend overhead to a near vertical position after swinging them in a full circle. In fact, all dives begin with the arms extended overhead regardless of the style or technique which, incidentally, includes the arm stand dives. Nearly all of the moves made with the arms when performing dives begin before the feet leave the point of take-off.

The center of gravity of the diver differs when performing dives that take off from the board in different directions. For example, when performing a dive that rotates forward or inward, the center of gravity is slightly in front of the diver.

M N O P

The take-off from the springboard
Figure 9

However, when performing reverse and backward dives, the center of gravity is located slightly behind the body.

THE FRONT DIVE IN THE LAYOUT POSITION

In discussing the front dive, layout, it should be clear that the diver be in complete balance to successfully control the force of the board's recoil when taking off. That is, when the board reaches its maximum impulse (lowest downward bend), the body should be positioned with the hips of the diver directly over the feet and the body at a slight angle as the legs begin to straighten. The arms also extend overhead and outside the width of the shoulders, the head remains erect, and the center of gravity is slightly in front of the feet.

As the board begins to recoil upward, the first move in the dive is made when the diver pulls the arms down laterally from a "Y" position to a lateral position slightly in front of the head and at the level of the shoulders *before* the feet leave the board (Figure 10, A & B). Since the body will rotate a little less than 180 degrees to perform the dive, pulling the arms down laterally with the body at a slight angle on the take-off causes the feet to push forward into the board which in tum pushes back in the opposite direction with the same amount of force (Newton's Third Law). This action-reaction with the feet creates enough angular momentum for the diver to perform the dive. The early placing of the arms in a lateral position before leaving the board places the diver in a balanced position before leaving without affecting the height of the dive because the board is already loaded with the force to be recoiled. However, if the arms are placed in position once the diver is airborne, there is a good chance that the diver may have to counterbalance the body by moving some other body part. Therefore, there is more to be gained in the consistency of balance when leaving the board with the arms already in position than trying to pull the arms down to a lateral position while in the air which will vary from dive to dive.

After leaving the board, the diver rotates about an imaginary plane on which the body is balanced while it follows a line of flight, or projection, in the form of a parabolic arc. The length of the arc for the performance of this dive should be about four or five feet from the end of the board. Experience has proven that the shorter the parabolic arc of the diver rotating in the air when performing this dive, the more difficult it is to control the rotation the body.

When the diver nears or reaches the peak of the dive, a second move is desired but not always possible particularly when the body is rotating too slowly to complete the dive. This move involves moving the head in a downward direction near the peak of the dive causing the lower part of the body to move in the opposite direction of its rotation (Figure 10, D). The reaction to the head moving downward will occur only for a moment after which the body will return to its normal rotational state. The head movement not only gives the diver a chance to sight the water in preparation for the entry, but it makes it easier for the diver to control the motion of the dive. If the head moves downward at the peak of the dive when there is not enough rotation to complete the dive, the reaction will be for the diver to be shorter on the dive, which is not desirable. A greater reaction will occur if the head is dropped down near the beginning of the take-off because the downward rotation of the head is increased, creating greater resistance to the rotation of the body and, in turn, decreases its angular velocity that making the dive enter the water short of vertical.

The arms remain in a fixed position throughout the dive until just before making the entry into the water (Figure 10, B-E). At this moment, the arms extend overhead laterally in a direction slightly in front of a vertical line (Figure 10, E &F). If the dive continually goes over or short on the entry, the diver should adjust the width of the arm position on the take-off before pulling them down laterally to a fixed position at shoulder level. Widening the arms will create less angular momentum on the take-off while narrowing the arms will create more angular momentum.

If the arms move on the body's long axis when reaching for the water, no resistance to them will occur to change the position of the body. In reference to the hypothesis "No move should be made in a dive unless it contributes to the execution of the dive", it is seen that no more than three moves are made throughout the dive to properly perform the dive with beauty, grace, and consistency.

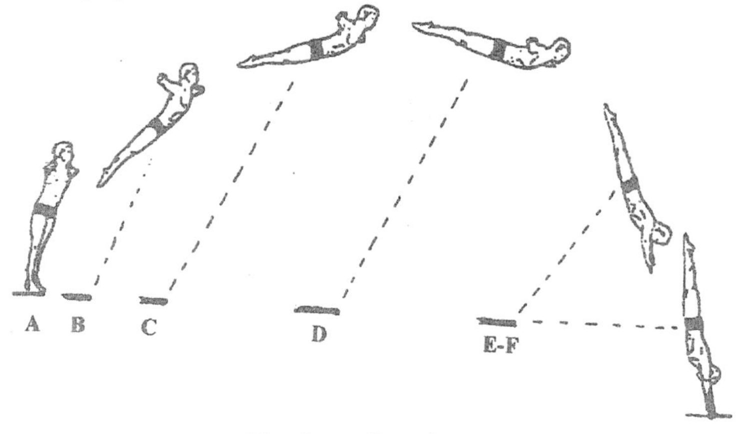

The front dive, layout
Figure 10

THE FORWARD 3 ½ SOMERSAULT IN THE TUCK POSITION

To understand how the forward 3 ½ somersault is executed requires one to know how the diver initiates rotation (angular momentum). Obviously, such a difficult dive requires a great amount of rotation and, as with any dive, the body movements needed to acquire adequate rotation must be created while the feet are still in contact with the board. The needed angular momentum can be obtained from four different sources each of which is discussed at some length because of its importance in performing many other dives requiring similar amounts of rotational force.

1. Overbalance of the body (lean) - George Rackham's (1975) book *"Diving Complete"* probably says it best stating, "When a body is in flight, it is a 'closed' system and no force within the system can cause it to rotate if it is not already rotating" (Figure 11, A). He further states that "two opposing forces must be applied to a body to start it rotating. To be effective, these two lines must be in opposition to each other and may not coincide. They must be off-set to form what is technically termed a 'couple'. For example, if a board is balanced on a fulcrum and the downward force of gravity equal on both sides, the board will not rotate in either an upward or downward direction (Figure 11, B). But if a force is applied to the top or bottom of the board any distance away from the fulcrum the board will then become unbalanced and it will rotate in the direction of the applied force" (Figure 11, C)

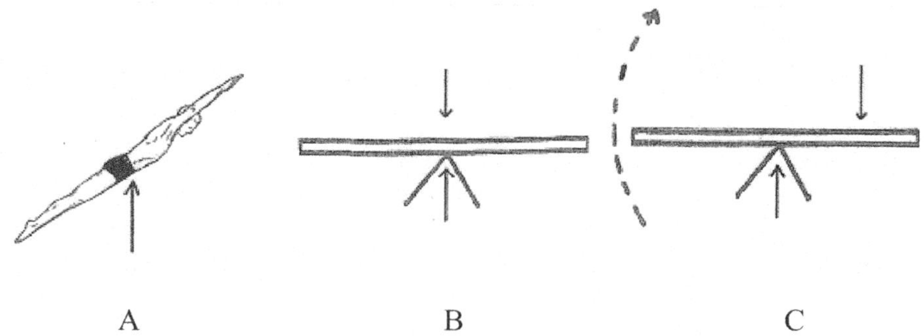

A — Body balanced in the air; B — Opposite forces in line; C — Opposite forces set off

Figure 11

Likewise, if the diver stands straight up on the board, the body is balanced and will not topple (Figure 12, A). But, if the diver should start to lean, the earth's surface will react by pushing upward through the feet and outside the body's center of gravity causing the diver to topple (Figure 12, B). If the diver continues to lean, the body will rotate from the vertical to a horizontal position which means the diver will land flat on the earth' s surface.

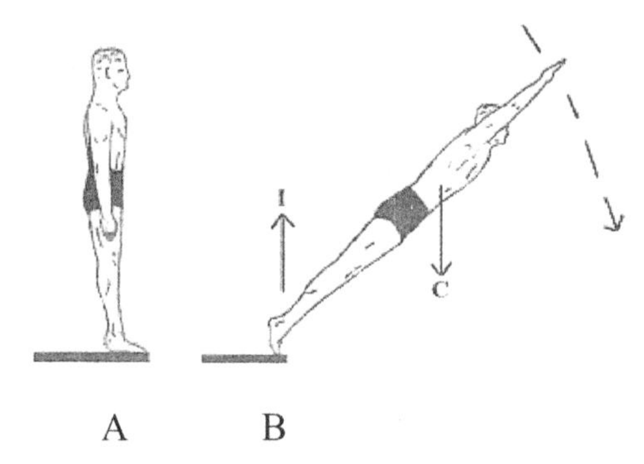

A B

Body balanced and off-set on land
Figure 12

If a similar movement is performed from the springboard, the extra height from the board will enable the diver to fall far enough and turn enough to enter the water head first. Therefore, a lean on the board will initiate rotation needed for the execution of forward and backward dives. Attempting to create rotation by leaning away from the board on the take-off when performing reverse and inward somersault dives is not feasible because any lean will incite angular momentum in the wrong direction.

2. The transfer of momentum of the arms and upper trunk to the lower part of the body when performing forward somersault dives -The angle of lean is measured from the line projected from the line projected from the toes through the center of gravity (Figure 13, A). As the body bends downward at the waist, the arms begin a vigorous forward and downward thrust as the board nears a horizontal level while continuing to recoil upward. The arms move faster than the upper body and no wider than the width of the shoulders as they establish the largest arc possible. The force created from the arm and body movements are then transferred through the extending legs to the feet which are still in contact with the board. This force is then exerted in a forward direction which reacts by pushing in the opposite direction with the same amount of force causing the board to rotate as it leaves the board (Figure 13, B).

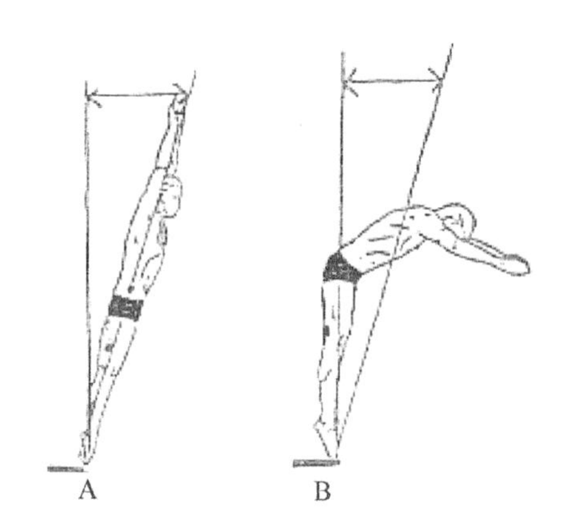

Transfer of momentum from arms and upper body
Figure 13

3. Eccentric thrust of the legs -As the arms and upper trunk of the diver are pushed downward at the hips (b) or (c) or the back is rounded so the body's center of gravity lies in front of the hip joint at the completion of the leg thrust, an off-center or eccentric turning force will be applied, causing rotation of the body about its center of gravity in addition to the upward motion. On the take-off, the legs extend powerfully while pushing the feet into the board. Rackham explains "If, during the take-off for a Forward or Inward Dive, the body is bent forward, the greater will be the distance between the hip joint and the center of gravity. When the legs straighten at the take-off, the thrust is along the line projected upward from the toes passing through the hip joint causing the body to rise, but there will be no rotation from this action (Figure 14, A).

   If during the take off for forward and inward dives the body is bent forward at the hips so That the center of gravity lies in front of the hip joint at the completion of the leg thrust, the body will then commence to rotate. This occurs because an effective off - center or eccentric turning force is applied causing rotation of the body about its center of gravity in addition to upward motion (Figure 14, B & C). The angular momentum will also be greater creating greater momentum, but less force will be available to project the body upwards and vice versa."

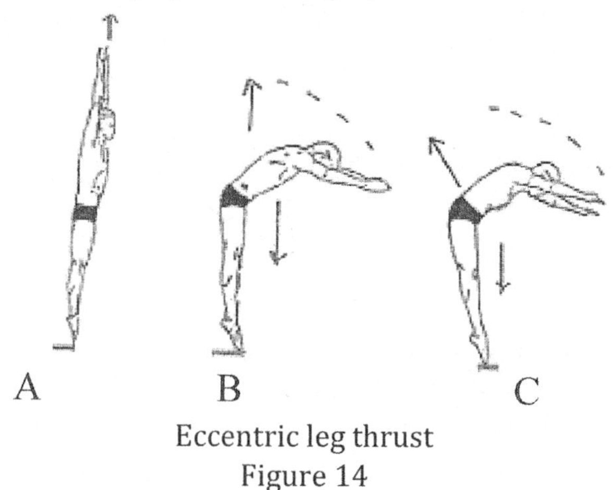

Eccentric leg thrust
Figure 14

4. Eccentric thrust of the board - When a force is applied to the end of the diving board, the line of thrust is at right angles to its surface. However, if at the moment of take-off, the line passes outside the diver ' s center of gravity, a rotating force is initiated. The rotation for forward and backward dives will be in a forward direction off the board (Figure 15, A). and in the opposite direction, executing an eccentric thrust from the board will create angular momentum but less force will be used to project the body upwards and vice-versa. This method is closely related to that which happens when the diver leans or is overbalanced when performing forward and backward take-offs.

The effect the radius has on the angular velocity of a rotating body

Angular momentum cannot be altered by any action of the diver unless it comes from an external object, which most likely will be the water. Realizing that angular velocity (speed of rotation) of a dive is the product of its angular momentum in the air, the moment of inertia (resistance to rotate) would be produced proportionately by the radius of the rotating diver.

A B

Eccentric board thrust
Figure 15

Therefore, if a diver rotating in the layout position with little angular velocity and with a great amount of inertia, suddenly changes to a tuck position, the angular velocity will increase and the resistance to rotate proportionately will decrease while the angular momentum remains constant. Conversely, the farther away the body parts are away from the center of gravity, the slower will be the rotation of the body while the angular momentum remains the same (Figure 16).

Center of gravity of the diver (0)

Radius of body	Moment of inertia	Angular velocity
Layout position	-------------------0-----------------	Slow
Pike position	-------------------0-----------------	Medium
Tuck position	-------------------0-----------------	Fast

Angular velocity based on change of radius
Figure 16

The forward 3 ½ somersault, tuck

All four ways of creating angular momentum are used in the performance of a forward 3 ½ somersault. The degree to which each of these methods is used will determine the success of the dive. The four methods are initiated after the diver performs the hurdle, lands on the end of the board in an upright position with the arms extended overhead and is ready to take off to perform the dive. At this point the diver is in an eccentric position for he or she is ready to leave the board with a slight forward lean. As the board begins to recoil upward, the legs extend and the upper body bends at the waist, led by the arms which are driven downward crating. At this point there is a transfer of momentum from the arms and upper torso to the lower torso. The reaction to this movement is for the feet to push forward into the board which pushes back with the same amount of force - creating angular momentum as the diver is projected up and away from the board (Figure 17, A).

As the diver is projected from the board, the extended legs begin to bend at the knees and hips as the upper body continues to move downward, bent at the waist (Figure 17, B). The arms move faster than the upper part of the body and should be no wider than the width of the shoulders in order to create the largest arc possible to exert the greatest force. As the legs continue to bend, the arms grasp the shins slightly below the knees as they are drawn in toward the chest to form a tight tuck position (Figure 17, C-J). Since the diver can increase the angular velocity (speed) by decreasing the body's radius, he or she tries to tuck the body in as tight as possible pulling the knees close the chest and pulling the heels in to the buttocks by spreading the knees while keeping the feet together. The spread of the knees is known as a "split" tuck helping to pull the feet closer to the buttocks when in the tuck position. Most of the divers who compete today use this type of tuck position.

Divers and coaches should be aware that the success of this dive and other multi-somersault dives depends on how tight the tuck or pike is made while performing the "first" somersault. If the tuck or pike position is loose, the following somersault(s) will also be loose. It is very rare that a diver can close up a tuck or pike position after performing the first somersault is performed loosely. This is due to the force caused by the added radius of the legs and the existing centrifugal forces placed in the body while rotating.

After somersaulting about 3 ¼ times, the diver releases and extends the legs while lifting the head slightly to sight the water (Figure 17, J). Once the legs are released and the body begins to straighten, the arms begin to reach in a semi-circular motion in the direction of the water about six inches in front of vertical (Figure 17, K). The diver enters the water slightly short of vertical about four and half feet away from the board. With no change in the angular momentum, the diver should enter the water slightly short of vertical because the body is still rotating as it enters the water. If the diver attempts to enter the water in a vertical position, the continued rotation will cause the lower part of the body to wash over as it passes through the surface of the water.

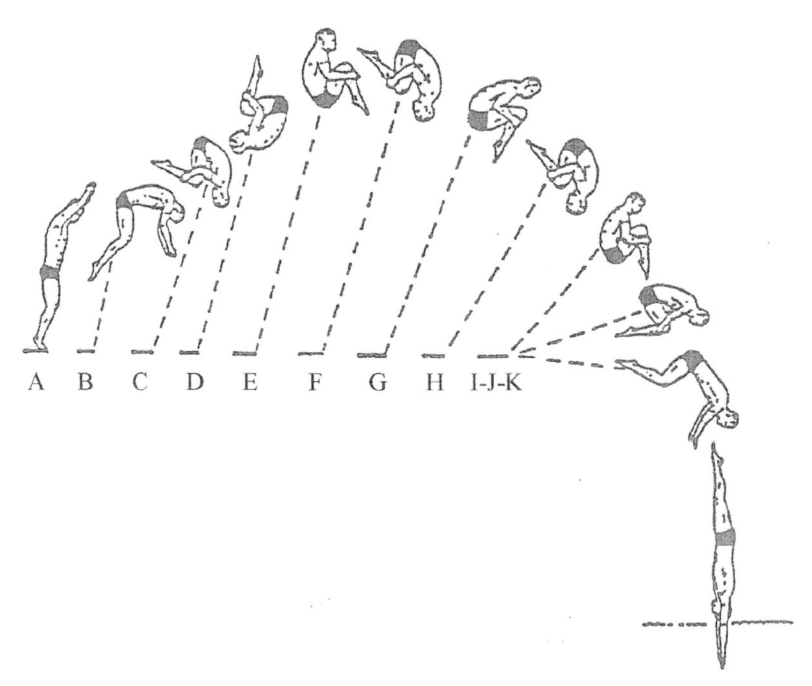

Forward 3 ½ somersault, tuck position
Figure 17

The standing take-off

Since a forward and reverse dive performed from a stand on the springboard are nearly non-existent, there is no need to include them in this text. Obviously, the main objective in performing the take-off for standing backward and inward dives is to obtain a maximum force from the springboard to execute a dive. To obtain this objective, it is necessary that the diver perform certain moves with various parts of the body.

The Take-off for Backward Dives

When performing all backward rotating dives, the diver first stands backward on the end of the board in an upright position with good body alignment and with the center of gravity of the body over the tip of the springboard (Figure 18, A). While standing backward, the feet are together with the toes near the end of the board, the balls of the feet are spread slightly to form a base for a balanced take-off, and the heels positioned slightly higher and together to form a "V" which helps the diver maintain balance when jumping from the board. The diver usually has the arms at the sides of the body or has them spread laterally at shoulder level while in the stance.

The take-off begins with the diver leaning slightly backward from the board as the arms lift above the shoulder level and begin to circle backwards (Figure 18, B-D). As the arms continue to circle and near the buttocks, the legs begin to bend while the upper torso remains in an upright position and the head erect (Figure 18, E). The legs continue to bend, and the arms begin to circle upwards as the board nears its lowest bending point (Figure 18, F & G). As the board begins to recoil, the arms continue to raise overhead, and the legs continue to extend (Figure 18, H).

The lean not only prevents the diver from hitting the board, but it also places the diver in an eccentric position which off-sets the body from its center of gravity causing it to rotate. As the arms continue to circle to a near vertical position, the legs quickly extend to create a jump before the feet leave the board. The circling of the arms is synchronized with the extension of the legs to create the greatest amount of thrust from the board (Figure 18, I).

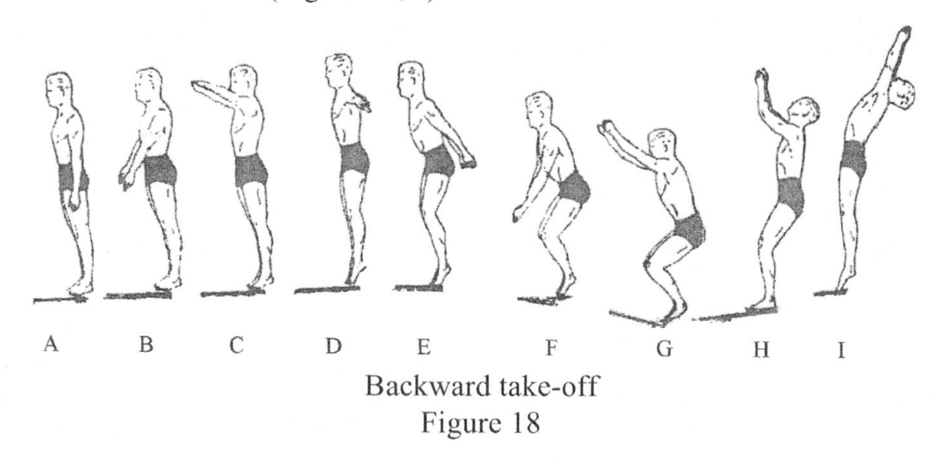

Backward take-off
Figure 18

Inward take-off

With the body in an upright position, all inward dives start with the arms lifting upward laterally to a position at shoulder level or higher (Figure 19, A & B). The arms then circle backwards with the center of gravity slightly over the board (Figure 19, C). The arms continue to circle upwards to or near a vertical position overhead where they stop. They then start in the opposite direction and move forward and downward in front of the body, within the width of the shoulders. This arm movement causes the feet to push forward into the board which reacts by pushing the feet in the opposite direction causing the body to rotate forward as it is pushed upward and away from the tip of the board which prevents him or her from hitting it (Figure 19, E).

Upon leaving the board, many divers believe they are going to hit the board as they are projected upward and are not aware that the body is going to move on a parabolic arc away from the board. Therefore, it suggested that the teacher and/or coach inform the divers that they should not reach for the board once in the air because in doing so, they may reach out and grab the end of the board and cause an injury.

A B C D E F

Inward take-off

Figure 19

An error that often occurs when performing inward dives from the springboard or platform is when the diver anticipates performing a dive and fails to place the arms completely overhead. Failing to do so results in a reduction in the arc of the arms which reduces the angular momentum needed to perform the dive (Figure 20).

Arm overhead vertical Arms short of vertical

Figure 20

If the timing of the arms and upper torso are applied *after* the feet have left the board or platform, the motion of the lower torso will be in the opposite direction of the rotation in the air which will greatly reduce the diver's angular velocity and make the completion of the dive difficult (Figure 21). One should note that the flexion of the legs, ankles, and insteps is not as deep from the platform as from the board because the platform does not provide any springing movement.

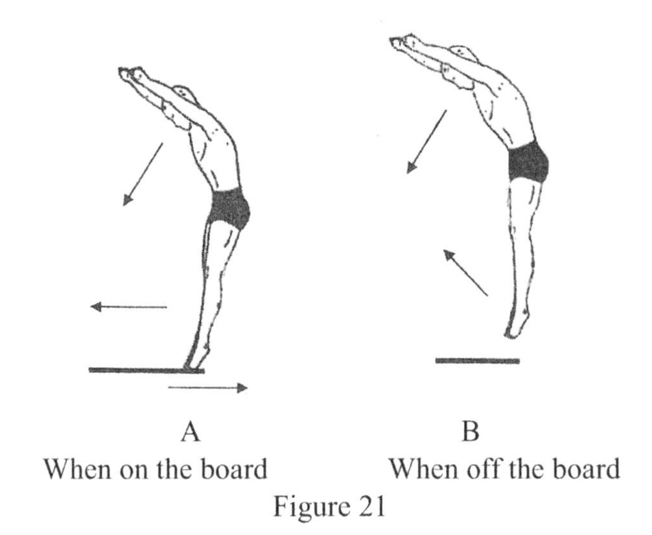

A When on the board B When off the board

Figure 21

The manner in which the diver creates angular momentum when taking off the springboard in four different directions.

Regardless of whether the diver takes off the springboard from a stand or after performing the forward approach, certain movements made by the body determine the direction, the amount of force created, and the amount of angular momentum that will be applied to the dive.

Since the diver can take-off the springboard in four different directions, each take-off requires certain movements from the upper and lower body to create the necessary forces. These forces are created by moving the upper torso and arms off the longitudinal axis that cause a reaction in the opposite direction and with the same amount of force to the lower torso. The part of the lower torso most effected by the reaction concerns the feet and lower part of the legs.

In viewing Figure 22, it is noted that the reaction to the movement of the upper torso has the lower torso moving in the same direction. So, if the upper torso moves backward, the lower torso also moves backward. However, with the feet still in contact with the springboard, they push forward or backward into the board that reacts by pushing back in the opposite direction with an equal force. In doing so, the angular momentum of the diver created by the board has the rotation of the body moving in the same direction as that of the upper torso.

Two techniques used when performing back and reverse somersault dives

After taking off the board or platform to perform backward and reverse somersaults in the tuck and pike positions, the diver can use two different techniques when grasping the legs to initiate the somersault.

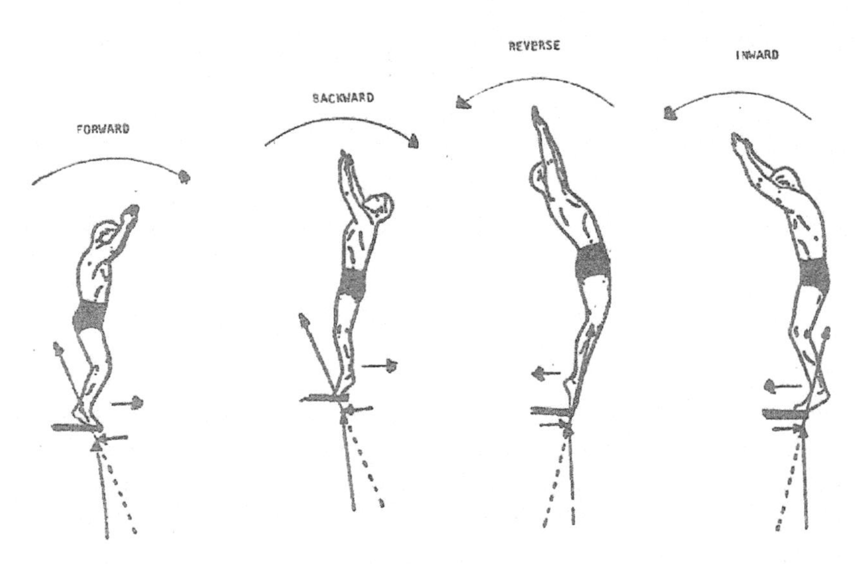

Rotations and movement of dives
Figure 22

The diver can reach overhead to a fixed position while the legs are pulled up to the hands which grasp the shins for dives in the tuck position and the knees for dives in the pike position (Figure 23), or after reaching overhead, continue to circle the arms and grasp the legs as they are lifting upward toward the upper body (Figure 24).

The advantage of using one technique over the other lies in the size of the diver. If the diver is short and has short arms, he or she can circle the arms fast enough, after reaching overhead, grasp the legs while the legs are moving upward toward the body. In doing so, the diver can grab the legs as the somersault is being formed. However, if the diver is tall and has long arms, the length of time needed to circle the arms and grasp the legs is greater which means the somersault will have rotated further before the legs are grabbed. The delay in grasping the legs later in the somersault makes it more difficult for the diver to control the dive before preparing for the entry. Whether tall or short, reaching vertically and bringing the legs up to the hands is very workable for both parties.

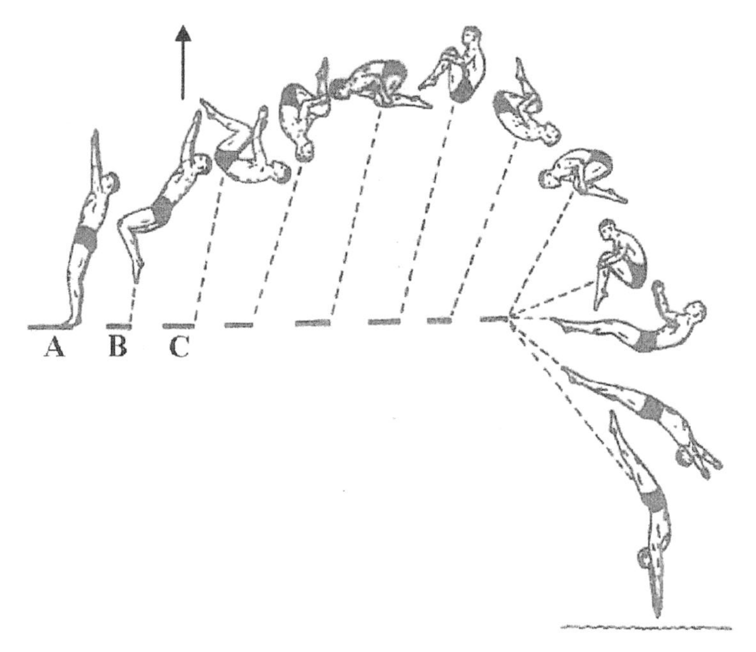

Reaching vertically in a back 2 ½ somersault
Figure 23

Another technique used in performing backward and reverse somersaults in the tuck or pike position is when after the arms circle and reach overhead before the feet leave the board, the arms will circle again as the legs are immediately drawn up to the hands. The flexibility of the shoulders and the length of the extended arms will determine their angular velocity as they circle. (Figure 24).

Reaching overhead then circling the arms in back and reverse somersaults
Figure 24

* Some back and reverse somersault dives require *an extended* reach beyond the vertical line to obtain the needed angular momentum to successfully perform a

dive such as found when performing a back or reverse 1 ½ somersault, in the layout position (Figure 25).

Reaching past vertical in back 1 ½ somersault, layout
Figure 25

SOME TECHNIQUES USED WHEN INITIATING TWISTING SOMERSAULT DIVES

The Perry Winkle

With no record as to when the first somersault with a twist was ever performed, it is believed that it was perfected somewhere between 1908 and 1915. From that time until 1947, the most difficult twisting somersault dive listed in any diving rule book was a forward 1 ½ somersault with one twist in the *pike* position and was called, for reasons unknown, a "Perry Winkle" (Figure 26). Since divers always copied the actions of the champions (and still do), they basically performed the dive in the same way, and no one thought to execute the dive otherwise. It should be remembered that the diving equipment in those days was quite primitive and the thought of perfecting more difficult dives was rarely considered plus the fact that dives not listed in the rule book could be used in competition. To induct a new dive into the rule books usually took years which did little to encourage any growth in the sport.

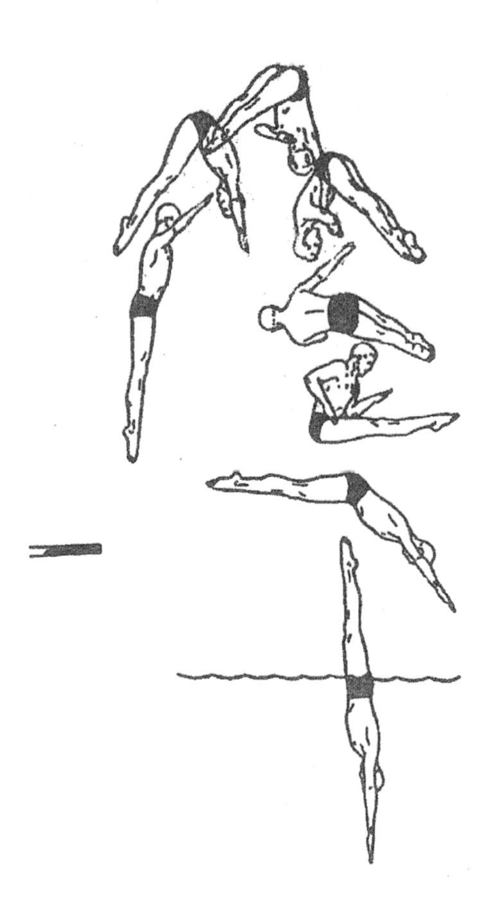

The Perry Winkle
Figure 26

It is really hard to believe that the Perry Winkle was the most difficult twisting somersault dive performed in competition worldwide for nearly forty years for no one had a clue as how to perform the dive any other way. The dive was performed by twisting about an axis while the diver remained in the pike position. This position caused the body to wobble from side to side throughout the entire dive. Divers at that time did not realize or even consider that the arms had to be raised above the center of gravity to straighten the body while performing the twist in the somersault.

During that period, the United States had some outstanding divers who performed difficult dives that were not yet in the rule books. Jim Patterson, the first great diver from the Ohio State University dynasty, was the first diver to ever perform a forward 3 ½ somersault in the tuck position which was performed from the ten-meter platform in 1931. He also was the first to perform a forward 4 ½ somersault which was executed in 1941 from the same height. Albert Root, who placed second on the ten-meter platform in the 1936 Olympics, was famous for his double twisting double somersault from the three-meter springboard and ten-meter platform. Another great acrobat and circus performer, Larry Griswold, performed multi-twisting somersaults from a trapeze over the water in water shows back in the 1930s.

The Clark Technique

The Perry Winkle technique of twisting continued throughout the world until 1940, when a new innovation of twisting in a somersault was presented by Earl Clark of Ohio State University. This new version of the twist in the somersault amazed everyone for the twist was performed at a sizzling speed compared to the old wobbly Perry Winkle. Hence, the Perry Winkle style was rapidly discarded by most divers and replaced with this new technique. Basically, this new version of twisting changed the whole concept of twisting while somersaulting and has never again been improved upon.

Clark began the full twisting 1 ½ somersault in an open pike position, and then performed the twist *while* straightening the body after which he again assumed the pike position before entering the water. How Clark learned this new technique was never revealed for years. One day in the 1960s while we were performing in the Al Sheehan Aqua Follies in Minneapolis, I asked him how he had learned such a unique twisting technique. He humorously replied that one day while diving off a springboard to perform a front dive 1 ½ in the open pike position, he was stung on the neck by a bee. When lifting his arms in the direction of the bee sting, the body began to straighten as he performed the twist. Later just before he passed on, I asked him again. He told me that he was jumping up and down on the board one day. Losing his balance, he flew off the board to perform a front dive with a full twist. When he realized that he was over rotating in the somersault, he quickly decided to pike over to prevent from landing on his back. Instead, he miraculously landed feet first in the water. Finding the mistake pretty neat, he decided to intentionally try the action again using a 1 ½ somersault which he did with amazing success.

Not knowing at the time, the reason for the body straightening, he had applied Newton's Third Law by first taking off the board in an open pike position (Figure 27, A), and then placed one arm, bent at the elbow, over the head while the other arm moved across the area of the chest. (This was the proper way a front dive with a full twist in the layout position was performed.) Moving the arms above the body's center of gravity caused the body to begin to straighten. Placing the arms in this position while the body was still in a partial pike position also created resistance to the lower torso causing the body to start twisting (Figure 27, B). The angular velocity of the twist continued to increase as the body straightened because the radius of the body on the long axis was reduced resulting in less resistance to the twisting motion (Figure 27, C & D).

With the body straight and twisting faster than ever seen in any dive before, Clark stopped the rotation at the completion of one twist by pulling the upper arm down to a lateral position while the other arm also moved into a lateral position from the chest position (Figure 27, D & E). Pulling the arm and upper body down created an action- reaction response by pulling the lower part of the body upward thus placing the body in an open pike position. The increase in the radius of the arms when placing them in a lateral position and moving the lower torso to a position at right angles to the diver's long (twisting) axis created enough resistance to stop the dive at one twist. Preparing for the entry, the arms then moved laterally when reaching overhead for the entry (Figure 27, G-I).

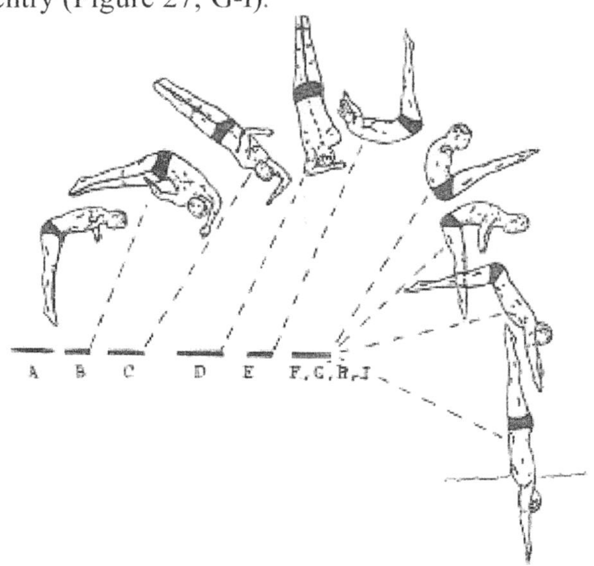

Clark's version of the forward 1 ½ somersault with one twist
Figure 27

Clark performed this dive at the 1940 National A.A.U. Championships while competing against his teammate, twenty-time national champion, Al Patnik, and received perfect scores from all the judges which helped him dethrone the "king" of diving. The dive was so spectacular that it was featured in sequence, in *Life magazine*. Naturally, every diver from that time on tried to emulate Clark's technique which led to another breakthrough. Miller Anderson, another great Ohio State diver and teammate of Clark perfected a seemingly impossible dive in 1945when he executed a forward 1 ½ somersault with two twists by using Clark's technique. This new dive was put into the rule book in 1947 after World War II.

The development of new twisting somersault dives

The development of many new twisting somersault dives that occurred during that period of time can be credited mainly to the influence of the trampoline. Competition on the trampoline became a gymnastic event and with the aid of spotting belts, divers were able to perform various forward and backward twisting somersaults that had not yet been performed from the diving board. Strangely, using the trampoline as a teaching aid for diving was long in coming until a belt was made that permitted one to twist while somersaulting. During that time, many divers performed on the trampoline for gymnastics teams which encouraged the innovation of new stunts many of which were eventually used in competitive diving. One of the divers who competed on the trampoline was Bruce Harlan, the 1948 Olympic Champion from Ohio State, who, as previously mentioned, introduced the reverse 1 ½ somersault with 1 ½ twists and the back 1 ½ somersault with 2 ½ twists to diving after first learning the stunts on the trampoline. Coincidentally, the last dive mentioned was also perfected by Skippy Browning, the 1952 Olympic champion from Texas, at the exact time as when developed by Harlan. With the aid of the trampoline, dives that were considered impossible to perform in the earlier part of the century soon became a common occurrence. The greatest contributor of new twisting somersault dives in modem times was Dick Kimball, the diver and coach from the University of Michigan, who introduced several multi-twisting somersault dives from the ten-meter platform in the early 1960s. Unbelievably, it took nearly forty years for these dives to be accepted which are now used in our present diving competitions.

During this period of growth, twisting somersaults could be executed in different ways, some of which confused the coaches and divers for no one knew how they worked. Up until the early 1960s it was generally believed that twists performed in all twisting somersaults dives were created from the diving board or platform. But when divers began to perform forward somersault dives with a twist in the second somersault it became questionable as to whether or not the twist was started from the board or while the diver was in the air. Finding that a twist could be created while the diver was in the air was brought to light when Jim Patterson, the Ohio State great diver, performed a forward 3 ½ somersault in the tuck position from the ten-meter platform, and added a full twist on the end of the dive before entering the water. Never performed by any other diver up to the present time, Patterson' s dive made it quite clear that no diver could possibly perform three somersaults and somehow conserve a twist started from the board or platform before applying it to the end of the dive. With the aid of such bio-mechanics experts as Geoffrey Dyson and George Rackham, many of the puzzles concerning the techniques used in twisting somersault dives were eventually solved.

Before discussing the different methods used in creating twists in somersaults, it should be noted that twisting somersaults occur with the body rotating about two different axes simultaneously. So, what is said concerning rotation about the horizontal (somersaulting) axis is equally true for rotation about the longitudinal (twisting) axis of the body. It is also true that the angular velocity with which a body will rotate about the axis depends upon the amount of rotational inertia (resistance to turning) is applied to a given force. Therefore, if the arms are extended laterally while the body is turning on the long (twisting) axis, the resistance from the long radius of the arms causes the body to twist slowly. Then when the radius of the arms is reduced by holding them close to the body, the angular velocity of the body is increased due to the reduced resistance to the turning force (rotational inertia). The same actions and reactions occur when a diver is somersaulting about the horizontal (transverse) axis. For example, changing the length of the radius of some part of the body will affect the velocity of rotation on either axis while the angular momentum remains constant.

Four methods used in creating twists in somersaults

*** Initiating a twist from the diving board or platform**

In the beginning, the Perry Winkle dive was performed with the twist started from the diving board. This was accomplished by throwing the upper torso of the body downward, while the arms were thrown to one side of the body. Since the reaction to the force applied to the lower torso was in the opposite direction of the upper torso, the feet on the board were pushed side wards into the board in the opposite direction of the upper torso. The board then pushed the feet and legs back with equal force in the same direction as the upper body and the arms.

Thrusting the body forward and downward with the feet still on the board created Angular momentum for the execution of the somersault, while the movement of the shoulders and arms thrown to the side of the body caused the body turn in the same direction as the arms that were originally thrown down to one side (Figure 28 A-C).

With the exception of twists performed in the second somersault, all back and reverse twisting somersault dives are performed by initiating the twist from the board or platform (Figure 28, B-C). Twisting somersaults in these two groups are performed by swinging the arms overhead and behind the center of gravity with an arched back to create angular momentum. The arm and shoulder on one side of the body then pull back and downward while the other arm and shoulder move in the same direction while the feet are still in contact with the board. The force created by any move made by the diver while still in contact with the board or platform will react by applying a force with the same magnitude in the direction of the arms and shoulders.

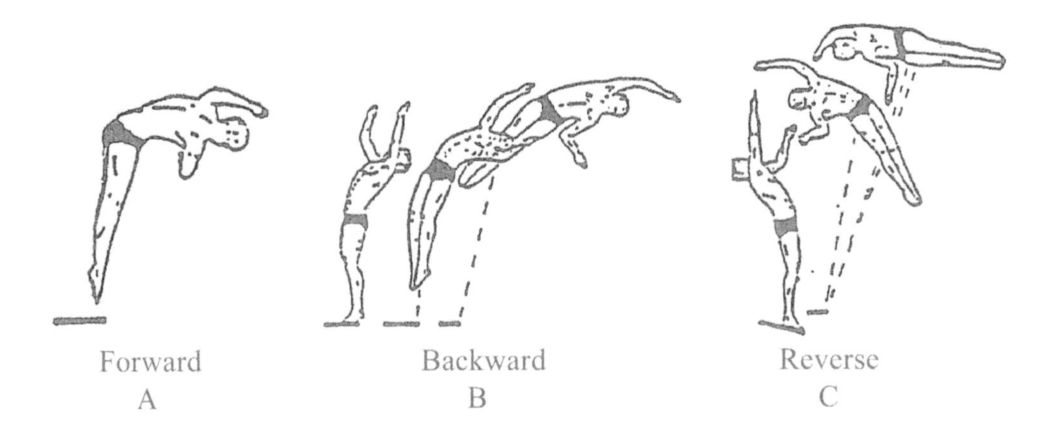

Creating twists from the board or platform
Figure 28

*** Initiating the twist with the use of arms with the upper torso**

Whether obtaining the twist from the board as found in back and reverse twisting somersaults or creating a twist in the air when using the Clark method, neither manner of twisting will normally occur without the aid of the movement from the arms and shoulders. The resistance needed to create the twist in the air is formed when the lower torso of the diver is offset from the longitudinal axis in the form of a pike position. The arms and shoulders then create a rotating motion as the diver begins to change from the pike position to the layout position (Figure 29, B & C).

Some coaches believe that a twist can be created by starting a forward somersault in the pike position, then snap out to a layout position ***before*** attempting to twist by rotating the upper torso and arms. This approach is not workable because there is no portion of the body off the longitudinal axis to form resistance from which the diver can initiate a twisting force. when in the layout position.

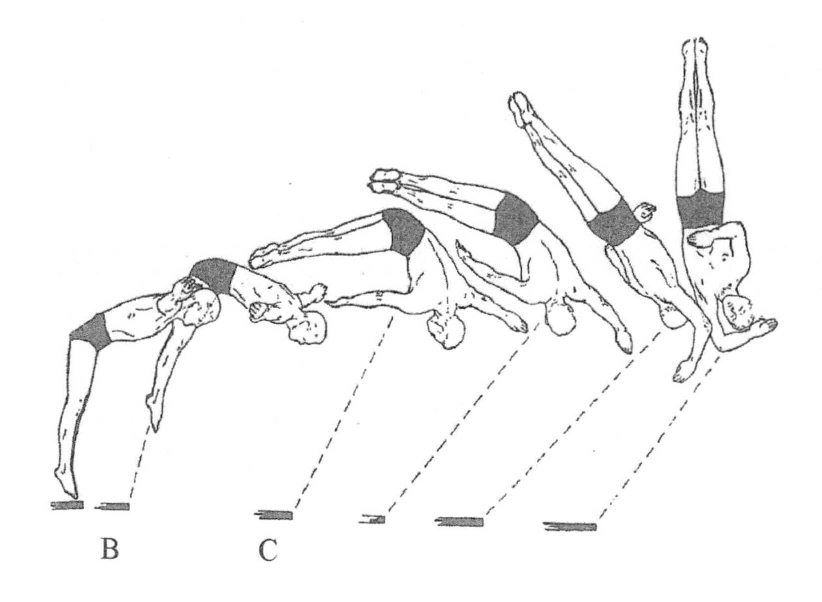

Creating a twist with the arms and upper torso
Figure 29

*** Using the Cat Twist Method to create a twist in a somersault while in the air**

To fully understand how the Cat Twist method is applied to creating a twist in the air, Doc Counsilman, the late world-renowned swimming coach from Indiana University, and I used two cats and a puppy in an experiment. Cats and a puppy were used because of their similar anatomical structure to the human body. We first took a cat with a long tail and cut its nails, so it wouldn't scratch us. We then held it upside down by its four paws and dropped it from about three feet high to a soft mat on the floor. The cat immediately twisted around and landed on its feet. We then dropped the same cat from different heights but found it to always twist around for a safe landing on all four paws. We then took the other cat, without a tail, and went through the same procedure, only to get identical results.

This told us that the tail of the cat had nothing to do with the cat twisting around and landing on its feet. With a similar anatomical structure as a cat, we tried the same experiment using the puppy, but it failed the test. When dropped from any height, the dog wiggled a lot before landing flat on its back on the mat. This brought up the question of why a cat could twist around and land on its feet when the dog could not turn over at all.

In photographing the experiment of the cat in slow motion, it was discovered that when the Cat was dropped by its paws (Figure 30, A), it immediately went into a pike position (Figure 30, B). From this position, the cat turned the upper torso about 180 degree in one direction, where it could see the floor while the lower torso of the cat twisted only a few degrees in the opposite direction. This was due to the lower part of the cat now positioned at nearly right angels to its longitudinal axis which created a great amount of resistance to the twisting action (Figure 30, C). With the aid of muscular force, the cat then straightened its body by pushing the hind legs away from upper torso and into alignment with the upper body (Figure 30, D). This movement greatly decreased the radius of the lower torso which reduced the rotational inertia and eliminated its resistance to twist in the opposite direction (Figure 30, E).

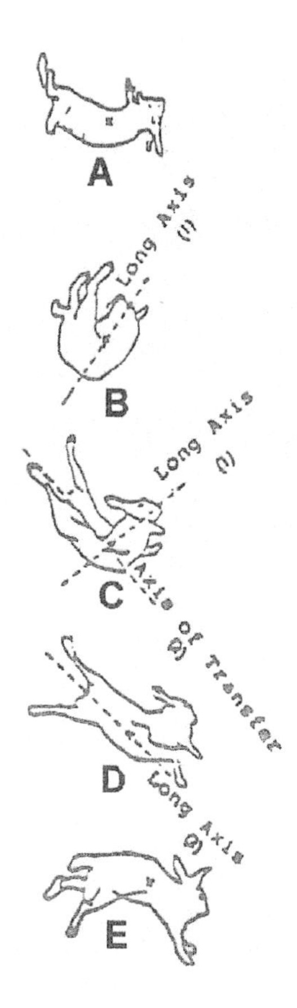

The Cat Twist
Figure 30

The cat twist maneuver can be easily observed when a diver performs a forward 2 ½ somersault and applies a twist in the second somersault (Figure 31). This is not so when somersaulting backward due to the fact that the arms cannot be used much against the resistance to that part of the body that is arched.

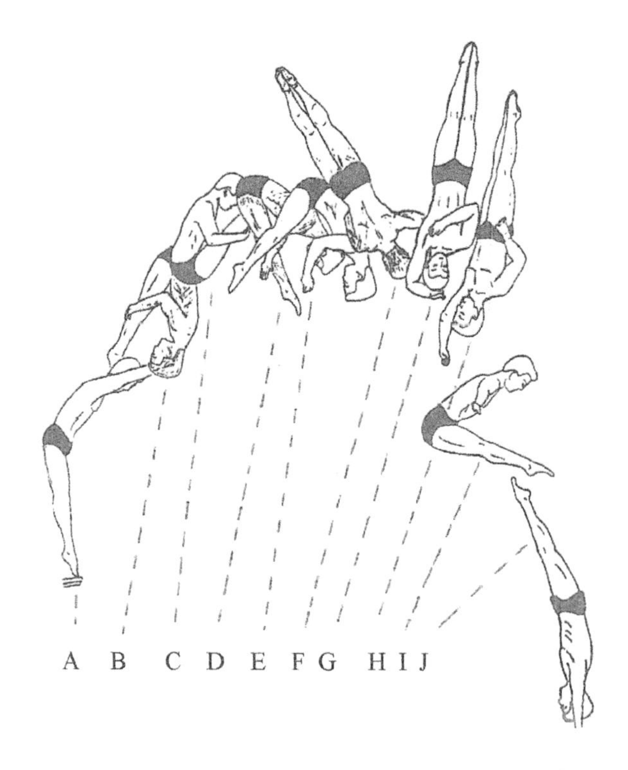

Creating a twist in the second somersault
Figure 31

*** Tilting the body to initiate a twist while somersaulting**

It was believed for some time that there were only three ways to initiate a twist when the diver performed a somersault, but further exploration found that there was a fourth and fifth way. The fourth way to create a twisting action was eventually recognized when it was seen that the lower torso of the body was off set from the vertical plane when leaving the board or platform, and/or while somersaulting about the horizontal axis in the air.

Studies soon showed that when the legs were off-set while somersaultingthe tilting position created a twisting action. The twist occurred when the diver, still in a pike position, attempted to tum the body on the longitudinal axis in one direction with the lower torso moving in the opposite direction (Newton' s Third Law). However, with the legs off-set from the longitudinal axis while still in a pike position, a resisting force to the turning of the upper torso was created. This caused the body to tilt which prevented the lower torso from twisting in the opposite direction of the upper torso (Figure 32, A & C) Then as the lower body moved from a pike position to the layout position, the resistance to upper body twisting was eliminated - causing the lower body to twist in the same direction as the upper body. In creating a twist by tilting the body, energy is taken away from the somersaulting motion and is transferred to the twisting motion. This is called a double axis displacement because energy from the horizontal axis is transferred to the longitudinal axis. The more the body tilts the more rotational inertia to the somersault is formed and the more energy is transferred from the body rotating on the horizontal (somersaulting) axis to the long (twisting) axis. This transfer results in the diver somersaulting slower but twisting faster.

If the resistance to the somersault would cause the body to tilt 90 degrees, the diver would be twisting instead of somersaulting without any change in the direction or magnitude of the angular momentum (rotating force) created from the board when taking off (Figure 32, B). Whatever the amount of tilt, no amount of energy transferred from one axis to another will change the center of gravity of the body as it rotates and twists about two different axes.

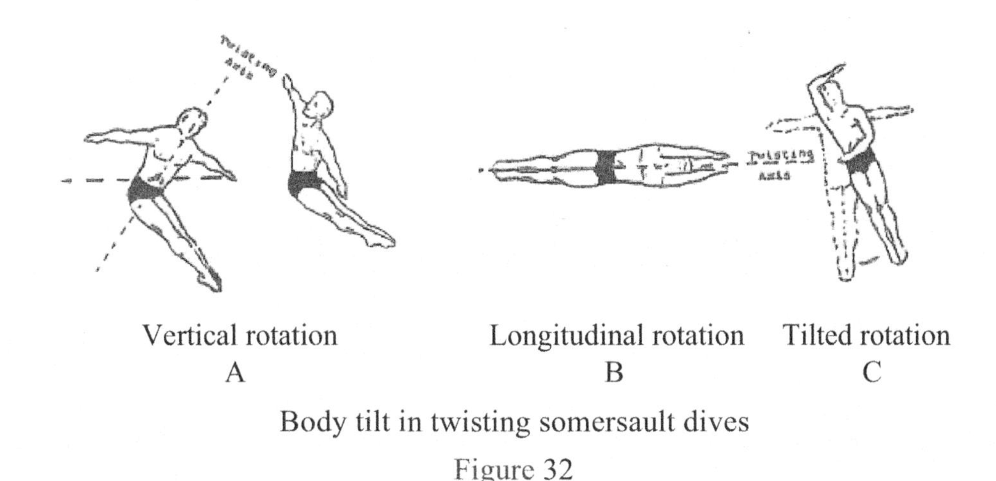

Vertical rotation A | Longitudinal rotation B | Tilted rotation C

Body tilt in twisting somersault dives

Figure 32

Using the tilting action has revealed that the greater the angular momentum obtained when performing somersaults, the easier it is to perform twists. For example, a diver finds it much more difficult to perform a forward dive with two twists than to perform the same number of twists when performing a 1 ½ or more somersaults in a dive. The difference in the ease of performing these two dives obviously relates to the transfer of motion from one axis (somersaulting) to another (twisting axis). Therefore, the difficulty when performing only a front dive with two twists is due to the body rotating only a half somersault which offers little resistance for the transfer of motion whereas, tilting the body from its horizontal axis when performing one or more somersaults during flight creates resistance from which force is formed to perform a twisting motion. Studies have shown that the tilting action can be created in two different ways:

* **Tilting from the board**

Tilting the body as it leaves the board or platform requires an action from the upper torso where the shoulders dip and the arms move downward and slightly sideways toward one side of the board which causes the feet to push into the board sideways. The board or platform then reacts by pushing the feet in the opposite direction which tilts the body as it leaves the board or platform. This can be clearly seen in the execution of the forward, back, and reverse twisting somersault dives when observing the dives from behind or in front of the diving board or platform (Figure 33).

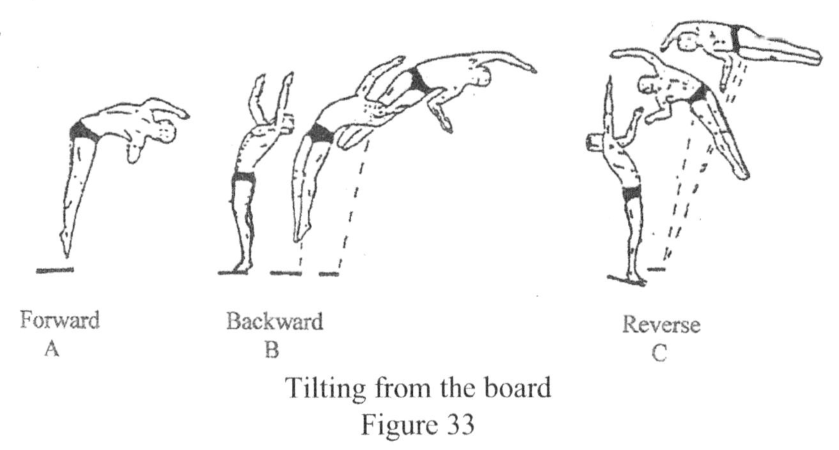

Tilting from the board
Figure 33

*** Tilting in the air**

To better understand these movements, we may look to Newton's Third Law and how it works when a person, suspended in the air in an upright position, pulls an arm upward and overhead in a lateral direction while the other arm is pulled down laterally from overhead. towards the arm that is pulled down. When, let's say the left arm lifts upward and overhead in a lateral direction, the lower body will move to the right. Conversely, when the right arm overhead is pulled down laterally to the side of the body, the lower body also moves to the right which places the body in a tilting position (Figure 34).

Creating a tilt with the arms
Figure 34

Creating a tilt of the body while it is somersaulting in the air can be seen when a diver performs a dive like a forward 1 ½ somersault with a full twist (Figure 35).

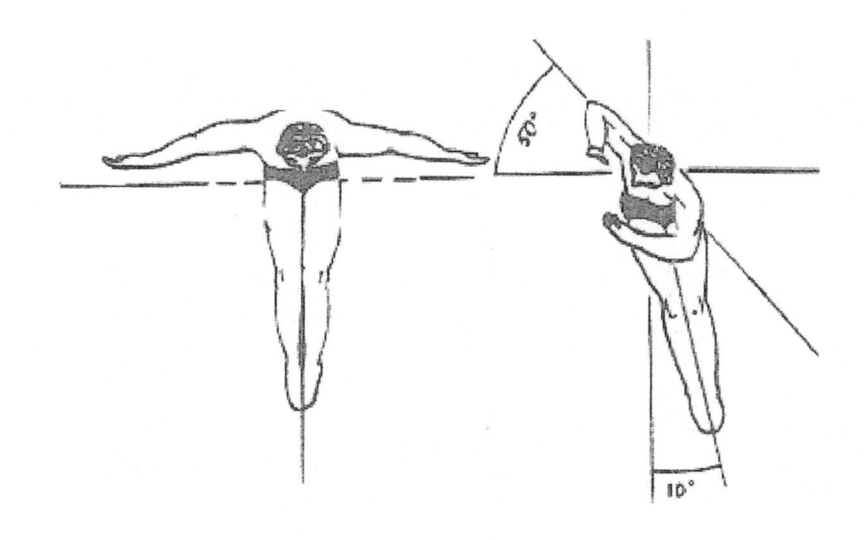

Tilting while in the air
Figure 35

Arm positions when performing a twist

Two different arm positions are normally used when performing a twisting action. The diver can place one arm across the chest while the other arm is placed overhead bent at the elbow. The arms are usually placed higher when twisting backward with the head up or even tipped a little Backward (Figure 36, A). Another position is for diver to place both arms, bent at the elbows, close to the body at chest level and pointing upward (Figure 36, B).

A B

Position of arms when twisting
Figure 36

All four of these methods are used when initiating twisting somersaults from the board and platform and three methods when somersaulting in the air. For example, when performing a back 1½ somersault with 1 ½ twists, the diver swings the arms overhead, shoulder width apart to establish rotation. This movement causes the diver to leave the board with an arch in the back which creates the cat twist (Figure 37, A & B). The upper torso immediately begins to tum to one side as one shoulder and arm pull back and downward as the other arm begins to cross the body at chest level (Figure 37, B).

Upon leaving the board with the body beginning to turn, a tilt is created when the body bends on its side which off-sets it from the long axis and offers resistance for the diver to twist (Figure 37, B). During this process the arms switch position as the top arm overhead pulls down and crosses in front of the chest and the lower arm moves upward, over the head bent at the elbow (Figure 37, C- F). Obviously, one method for creating a twist can be more effective than another in the performance of certain dives, but being aware of the four methods, makes it easier for the coach and diver to recognize and analyze which methods need be emphasized when performing certain twisting somersaults.

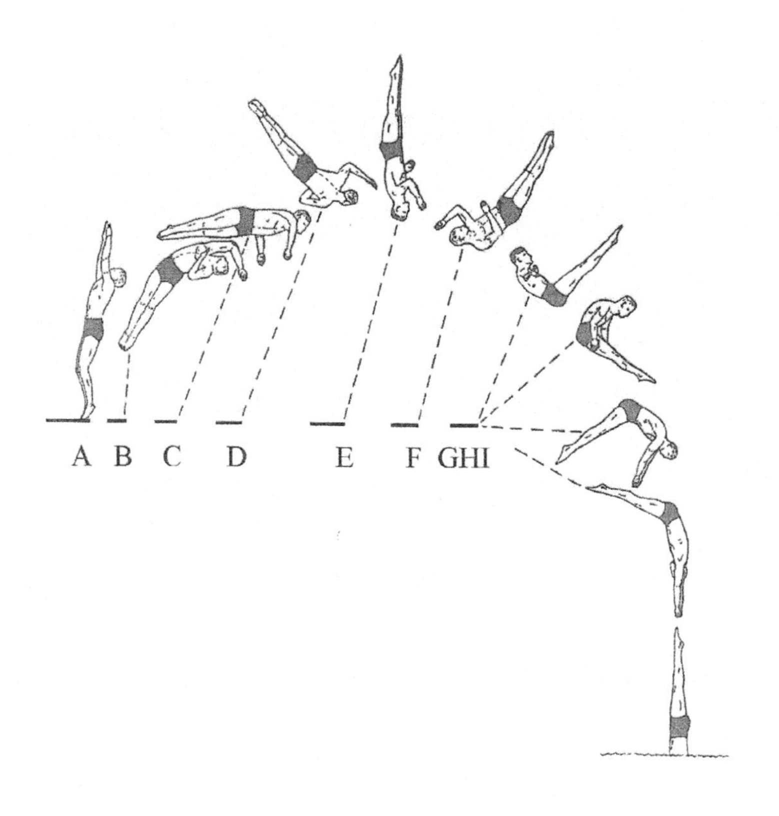

Back 1 ½ somersault with 1 ½ twists
Figure 37

Changing the body from the pike position to the layout position to perform the twist in a somersault reduces the angular velocity of the somersault because the radius of the body is increased, and the transfer of energy moves from the somersault to the twisting action. The amount of angular momentum needed to perform twisting somersault dives is a very important point. Many divers and coaches do not realize that the longer the body is in the layout position the slower is the somersault (Figure 38, A & B). This bears out that the greater the angular momentum generated to perform somersaults, the easier it is to execute twists. So, when a diver executes a dive like a one and half somersault with two twists, he or she must generate enough angular momentum on the take-off to make up for the reduction of angular velocity of the somersault while the twists are being performed in the layout position. From this the diver and coach can reason that the difficulty in performing twisting somersaults dives is not in the execution of the twists but in creating enough somersault action to complete the dive.

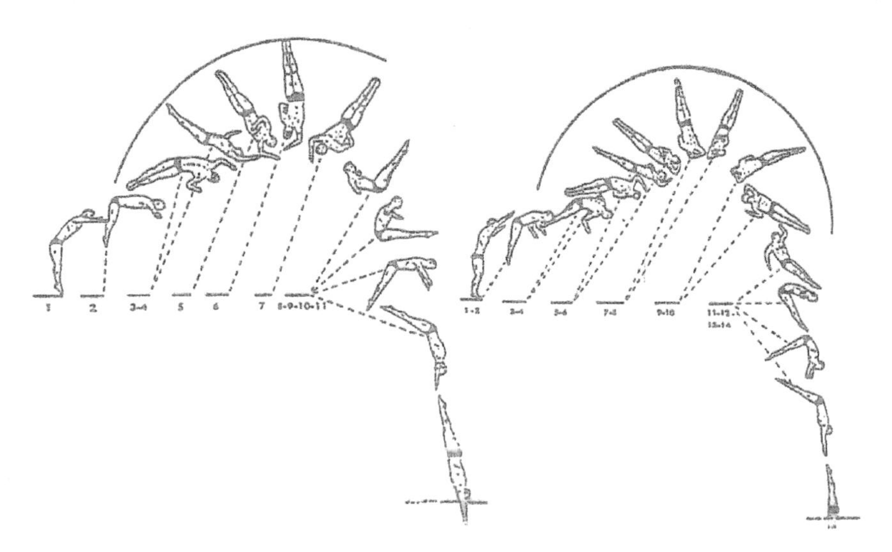

Forward 1 ½ somersault with two twists Forward 1 ½ somersault with 3 twists
Figure 38

Motions used for head first entries at the completion of twisting somersaults

A certain style concerning the finish of twisting somersault dives was used by nearly all divers as far back as the early 1900's when such great divers as Dick Degner, Marshal Wayne, Al Patnik and more recently divers such as Olympic Champions Skippy Browning and Pat McCormick along with many others, finished twisting somersault dives by reaching over "one" shoulder for the water with "both" arms. This body position making it very difficult to align the body for the entry (Figure 39, A). Eventually, this poor technique was replaced with Clark's method, developed in 1939, which was performed by pulling one arm downward from overhead in a lateral direction while simultaneously moving the other arm across the chest at shoulder level to form an open pike position with arms at the level of the shoulders (Figure 39, B).entry was used when performing the Perry Winkle dives which invited an awkward body

Pulling the arm down from overhead permit's the body to move from a layout position to a pike position. In doing so, the increased radius of the body from the extension of the legs and both arms placed at right angles to the longitudinal axis of the body, creates enough resistance to stop the twisting motion. Having returned to a pike position during these movements, the diver's angular velocity in the somersault increases which is used to complete the performance of the dive. Realizing the success of performing twisting somersault dives when using this method, makes one wonder why so many top divers in the world continued to use the old technique of entering the water head first throughout their diving careers when a better method of entering the water was available to them all along.

Before continuing, the fifth way to initiate a twist need be mentioned which is known as the hula hoop method. This method has a person circle the hips, like when twirling in a hula hoop, and the gyrations cause the body to rotate at the hips in one direction which causes the body to react about the longitudinal axis in the opposite direction. The hula hoop method of creating a twisting motion is not found in diving because the diver cannot create enough rotation in the short time that the body is in the air. Much like the cat twist, the hula hoop method is initiated with the use of internal muscular force that changes the body position without rotation. or contact with an external force such as the diving board or platform. Therefore, to my knowledge, the hula hoop maneuver is not related to diving so there is no need to discuss it in this text.

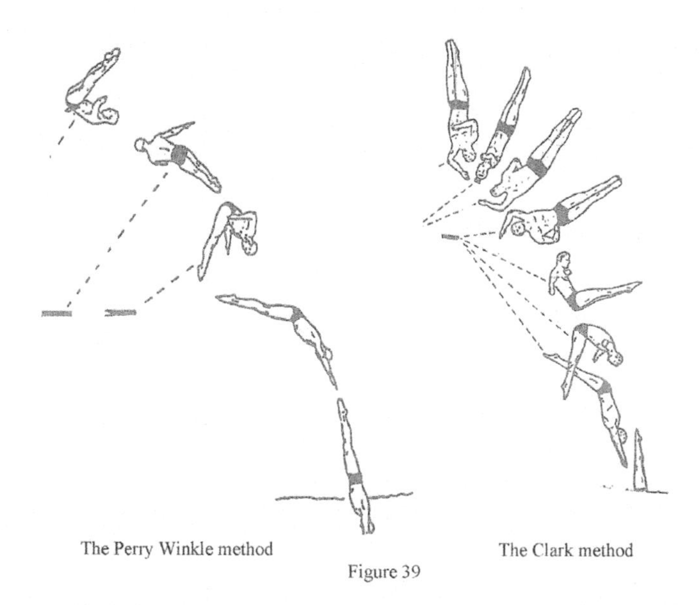

The Perry Winkle method The Clark method

Figure 39

Some helpful suggestions when teaching twisting somersault dives

* It is suggested that the beginner learn to perform and control a forward somersault in the open pike position from the one-meter springboard before attempting to perfect the forward somersault with one or more twists.

* Once the open pike position is learned, the instructor should physically aid the diver in placing the arms in the proper position when twisting while standing on the deck. That is, one arm bent at the elbow, placed overhead while the other arm, also bent at the elbow, is crossed in front of the chest at shoulder level and just below the chin. Neither arm should touch the body.

* Due to the positioning of the arms, instruct the diver to perform the full twist in the somersault rather than a half twist.

* Teach divers to keep the arms high, at least at shoulder level, to keep them from getting lost in the air. If the head or arms drop down while performing the twisting action, the body will begin to pike causing it to wobble causing the diver to lose control.

* Whatever twisting somersault is performed, one arm must lift above the head when nearing the completion of the dive. From this position, the arm pulls down laterally to the level of the shoulders causing the body to pike and stop the twisting action so the diver can align the body for the entry.

* Since the most difficult movement needed when performing backward twisting somersault dives is a strong somersault, it's advised that the diver learn to perform back and reverse somersault dives in the layout position. These two lead-up dives require the diver to tilt the head upward with the back arched after the arms begin to swing overhead before leaving the board or platform. The arms then continue to reach behind the body while the head remains tilted backward and the back arched until the somersault is nearly completed. The diver will find it much easier to perform the dives if he or she tries to lift the chest upward before the feet leave the board or platform. Those who cannot perform the two lead- up dives well, find it difficult to complete twisting somersault dives.

THE VALUE OF MECHANICAL PRINCIPLES

These principles are nothing more than basic rules, based on the laws of motion, that act as guidelines in directing the actions of a diver or any athlete. Principles based on fact make it much easier for a coach and a diver to understand which moves and forces should be used when performing a dive. To learn the methods is not difficult for all it takes is a little curiosity and motivation to try something new.

Two books are available for anyone who wishes to understand the basic physics used in the performance of dives. Geoffrey Dyson's book *"The Mechanics of Athletics"* and *"Diving Complete"* by the late George Rackham. It is suggested that one not try to digest the information offered in these two books all at once. Take in a little at a time and let the information sink in. Soon, you will find yourself off and running, eager to learn more as your knowledge and comprehension expands. Once you are familiar with the scientific principles of movement, you will find that you can actually analyze dives with accuracy and validity because you know that your analysis is based on scientific fact.

The use of mechanical principles is also helpful in teaching one to become more knowledgeable and appreciative of what should and should not take place during the performance of dives. The use of mechanical principles does not only affect the performance of divers and coaches, but it also relates to improving the making of diving equipment such as diving boards and stands; teaching aids such as the trampoline, dry land board, bubbler, spotting belts, etc. all of which are designed to offer better safety and performance for the performers. Once the coach and diver understand how these facilities interact, they can analyze the diver's motions and teach movement patterns with greater accuracy, validity, and efficiency.

To express the importance of learning and using such scientific principles, I was able to develop many divers who were first recognized at best as mediocre but "quickly" went on to become national and international champions. No attempt is made here to take credit for their accomplishments because they were the ones, called "Hobie' s Heroes" who were willing to accept the scientific knowledge that was offered them. The intent here is to impress you with how quickly these divers learned when using scientific laws. Some of their accomplishments often appeared to be miracles; but in approaching the sport scientifically, it quickly became evident that this approach to learning was far superior to that when using other methods.

Some divers who used scientific principles.

Rick Gilbert - when entering Indiana University as a freshman in September 1961, Gilbert had no experience diving from the 3-meter board. He learned to do a full list of dives at that level in a little over a month which included a 3 ½ somersault; back, reverse, and inward 2 ½ somersaults; and a back 1 ½ somersault with 2 1/2 twists which then were dives just beginning to be performed by elite divers in the sport worldwide. Since the N.C.A.A. did not permit freshman athletes to perform in any college sport at that time, Gilbert could only compete in competitions that were offered outside the university's jurisdiction. Gilbert's first attempt at competing from the 3-meter board was at the National A.A.U. Championships in Bartlesville, Oklahoma on April 7, 1962. Diving against four Olympians and three national champions, he won the contest by the highest score and widest margin ever recorded in a national competition up to that time.

Tom Dinsley - from British Columbia, Canada, never qualified for the finals in any national championship meet. While attending Indiana University, he won the 1963 Pan American Games gold medal in San Paulo, South America, by beating his two Indiana teammates Rick Gilbert and Kenny Sitzberger who took second and third. The win made Dinsley the first Canadian diver to ever win an international contest.

Ken Sitzberger - was outscored by his Olympic teammate, Frank Gorman from Harvard University, on nine out of ten dives at the 1964 Olympic Games in Tokyo, Japan. Ken made up a total of 62 points on one dive when Gorman missed a back 2 ½ somersault badly and Ken performed a remarkable reverse 2 ½ somersault. There is no record of anyone ever accomplishing such a feat in any diving contest at any competitive level anywhere.

Lesley Bush - a 17-year old who also never made the finals at any senior national contest. Bush, with no experience in competing from a ten-meter platform, learned a list of dives in six weeks while training with us in the summer in 1964 at Indiana University. After taking fourth on the 3- meter board at the 1964 Olympic trials in New York, she placed second on the 10-meter platform on her first attempt at diving from that level. She then went on to win the 10-meter event at the Olympics in Tokyo, Japan, beating Ingrid Kramer, the diving sensation from East Germany. Kramer had won both springboard and tower events in the 1960 Olympics in Rome and had just defended her three-meter title in Tokyo. Due to an injury to her back and shoulder during practice before the meet, Bush lost all confidence in herself and was expected by everyone, including the American diving coaches, to place no better than last in the contest. However, she accomplished the impossible by beating Kramer on every dive, who was favored to win the 10- meter event even if she should miss a dive completely. In winning the event, the American Press called her father in Princeton, New Jersey at three o'clock in the morning to inform him of her amazing performance and he replied that it was a heck of a trick to play on someone in the middle of the night and hung up only to have the AP again call and confirm Lesley's victory. This shocking win had to be one of the greatest upsets in Olympic history, but being a non-revenue and minor sport, no one ever recognized what she had accomplished on her second attempt at ever competing from that height. She later attended Indiana University and went on to win several international and national one, three, and ten-meter events in her career.

With only one scholarship available for diving each year, seven divers from Indiana University dived in the 1967 one-meter finals at the National A.A U. Championships in Fort Worth, Texas and placed first, second, third, fourth, seventh, ninth, and eleventh which matched the performance of the Ohio States divers in 1951 who also took the first four places at the National A.AU. Championships.

Cynthia Potter - having never won a national gold medal while competing between the ages of thirteen to eighteen, Cynthia won 28 national championships after attending Indiana University which is the greatest accomplishment made by any female diver in the United States. Cynthia was recognized two times for being the world's greatest female diver and made three Olympic teams one at which she won a bronze medal.

Brian Bungum, Mark Virts, and **Amy McGrath** learned to dive from the 10-meter platform during the summer of 1979 at Indiana and all went on to make the 1980 Olympic team on the ten-meter platform which was boycotted so they were never given the chance to compete in the Olympics. Bungum and McGrath went on to win national titles on the springboard and tower and Virts won several national titles on the tower. McGrath won the 10-meter national title after learning to dive from that height in *two* weeks.

Niki Stajkovic - one of the great divers in the world for many years, Niki made the 1972 Olympic team for Austria at the age of thirteen. He started to train in the summer at Indiana where he later attended school. He went on to compete in four more Olympics but only made the finals once which was the 1980 Olympics in Moscow, Russia. Strangely, it was found that Niki had never learned to dive springboard before entering Indiana. Giving a full scholarship to a diver who had never dived springboard when tower diving was not yet a N.C.A.A. event, nearly cost me my job. However, he eventually learned to dive springboard, placed second in the N.C.A.A. Championships, and went on to win many international three-meter titles over the years.

Robbie Bollinger- a gymnast who had terrible form, flat feet, and showed little to no ability to dive. Robbie was forced on me by his father who was a close friend and cheerleader with me at Ohio State University. Showing no possibility of ever becoming a good diver, Robbie was not recruited by any university, including Indiana. Because of his father's insistence, I finally gave in and after overcoming his physical problems through hard work, he won two N.C.A.A. and two Big Ten diving titles.

Win Young - a protege of Dick Smith before attending college. Win attended Indiana and showed little promise of becoming a national champion until it was found that he had very poor eye sight. I sent him to the doctor who suggested that he attempt to wear contact lenses when diving. The doctor believed that if Win would close his eyes when entering the water, it was possible that he could wear them while diving. It is believed that he was the first diver to ever use contact lenses when diving. This made it possible for Win to garner several 3-meter and 10-meter national titles, a gold medal at the Pan American Games, and a bronze medal at the 1968 Olympics.

Rick Early - a teammate of Win Young. Rick was recruited to Indiana by Doc Counsilman, the world-famous swimming coach. Having never met him before attending Indiana, I found that Rick was extremely strong with great acrobatic ability. He didn't appear to be adaptive to diving, but he was adaptive to instruction. With a lot of hard work, he went on to win the two national 10-meter titles, a Pan American gold medal, and took fifth at the 1972 Olympics in Munich.

Mark Lenzi - an obscure wrestler who showed little sign of ever becoming a good diver. Mark Lenzi at the age of eighteen, was brought to my attention by Paul Lenihan, a former diver at Indiana. Lenihan had seen Lenzi dive at a local pool where he displayed good somersault actions, but nothing more for he had no concept of how to perform dives, particularly in the twisting category. Receiving only one scholarship every four years, I offered Lenzi a full ride, sight unseen, to attend Indiana University which I quickly believed was the worst mistake in my coaching career. For the first six weeks Lenzi showed no promise that he could learn to dive. Exasperated, I finally informed him of my belief and told him that if he couldn't learn to correctly perform a forward approach on the board and learn to get into the water clean in six weeks, he should take up a new sport such as golf. Soon after, a very small spark of talent appeared which began to grow. By the beginning of the season, he was badly performing a list of difficult dives with a maximum degree of difficulty from the three-meter board. The coaches in the Big 10 Conference laughed when they saw him dive in the dual meets, but not for long.

Within the next three years, Lenzi went on to win several World, international, and national titles topped off with the 3-meter 1992 Olympic gold medal in Barcelona, Spain. After retiring, he decided to return and try out for the 1996 Olympics in Atlanta, Georgia where he took the bronze medal. Through this whole ordeal, I was led to believe that I could not recognize talent if I fell over it. It may be worth noting that I had never met Rick Early, Tom Dinsley, Brian Bungum or Mark Lenzi or seen them dive before they walked onto the Indiana Campus.

Though boring as it may be for the reader, these accomplishments were made through the use of mechanical principles based on laws which I believe should be passed on to up-coming coaches and divers. I realize that in this text, I have continually made a great effort to try and convince divers and coaches to move in the direction provided in this book. The reader must realize that we all live in a life of technology which does not refer to only material things. If divers and coaches do not reach out to the scientific approach to compete in this sport, I see no other way the American teams can successfully compete with the divers world-wide. When a Canadian diver can score 813 points from the three-meter springboard in the World Championships, it appears to me that coaches and divers should change their ways if they wish to compete with divers who perform that well.

Many of us claim to be masters of our trade and become quite content with the knowledge we have already gathered about the sport. Most coaches have acquired their knowledge from personal diving experiences and information passed down to them from their coaches who, in turn, obtained their knowledge from those who coached them. In any case, most of the information passed down from coach to coach over the years is based more on trial and error than on sound scientific principles. The refusal to bear an open mind has prevented many involved in the sport from setting guidelines that could offer them the information needed to execute near perfect dives. Instead, we have a situation where one coach teaches and coaches diving according to his or her concept of perfection while another coach offers information that provides an entirely different concept. Unfortunately, it is often found that in neither case are their concepts based on scientific fact. To make matters more ridiculous, many persons who judge diving believe they are experts in the field based on their own concept which is created from watching divers perform. However, having little experience in analyzing the movements used in the performance of dives, they have difficulty matching their efforts with other judges who are well educated in the sport.

As shared in this chapter, certain basic concepts of motion have been explained with supportive reasoning based on simple scientific laws presented by Isaac Newton, none of which are difficult to understand or transmit into diving motion. In fact, if a coach and/or diver would keep the laws of motion in mind when participating in a diving activity, they would be amazed to find how much clearer their concept of dives would become. This approach to diving will someday offer the greatly needed guidelines for all dives which will help all coaches and divers move in the direction of perfection. Such an approach in no way tends to standardize diving by forcing divers to execute dives in the same way for there is more than ample room for divers to be creative and express style and technique while remaining in the confines of Newton's Laws. Only through Newton's Laws can a dive be properly performed, and it remains unbelievable how long it is taking so many diving coaches to realize it.

CHAPTER 8

ANALYSIS

With respect to diving, analysis means distinguishing between desirable and undesirable movements used in the performance of dives. The purpose of analysis is to offer accurate information that can help guide the divers' movements toward perfection. Accurate analysis of dives requires the acceptance of the hypothesis mentioned many times in this text: *"No move should be made in the performance of a dive unless it contributes to the execution of the dive."* Therefore, the analysis of a dive is concerned with movements that involve:

The approach	The execution of the dive	The entry into the water
walk – hurdle- take-off balance and power	what moves are made how-when-where	body alignment feet and head first entries

Concept and principle

To analyze dives effectively, coaches and divers must first realize that competitive diving is divided into two sectors; concept and principle.

A concept of a dive is the mental picture of how a dive is to be performed in the mind of the diver and coach. The concept includes basic guidelines in the form of sequential movements used in the performance of the dive. With no guidelines for the performance of dives found in any of the rulebooks, many coaches and divers have created their own concepts of how to perform dives which, more often than not, are different than the concepts of others. The differences can be attributed to:

* Exposure to various levels of competition

* Different coaching and competitive backgrounds

* Different geographical locations

* The use of trial and error, and/or copying the methods used by other divers

* The technical knowledge acquired

* Experience in coaching and teaching diving

The use of video makes it possible for divers and coaches to observe every move made in dives. Such observational technology has greatly reduced the coaches and diver's differences in concepts related to the proper movements used in the performance of dives. However, many differences still occur among coaches because of invalid reasoning in forming their concepts of dives.

One of the biggest problems that lingers in competitive diving is how to get everyone to form similar concepts of the moves used in the performance of dives which, obviously, cannot occur without the use of guidelines. The question is, if everyone has a different idea of what movements should be used in a dive and how they should be executed, then how is it possible to coach, judge, and perform dives accurately. The answer to that question seems to be in making a gradual change from the old methods of coaching diving to the new method of using scientific mechanical principles. Thankfully, the concept of how to properly perform dives has greatly improved over the years due to technological / bio-mechanical review of dives and the increased exposure of the sport worldwide. Much of the improvement was possible through standardizing diving facilities and equipment that no longer require major changes from one competition to another.

To move on, the principles used in the performance of dives refers to the movements performed in sequence that are matched with the concepts of the dives created by the coaches and divers. Therefore, the concept of a dive created in the minds of coaches and divers depends much on how much they are aware of the laws of motion and how they can be applied. Up until the breakthrough in using a scientific approach to the performance of dives, no substantial source was available to accurately analyze dives because no one knew in what direction to go to obtain perfection. Now, it appears that an accurate and scientific analysis of dives can be offered by implementing the right concepts of the dives in the minds of the coaches and divers. With the use of mechanical principles, coaches, divers, and judges can now distinguish between desired and undesired movements used in the execution of dives... if...they are willing to adjust their concepts of how dives should be scientifically performed.

The performance of dives depends on:

1. The diver's profile:

    a. Physical qualities in terms of strength, physical condition, flexibility, body structure, coordination and rhythm, acrobatic ability, and awareness in space, and ability to relax.
    b. Psychological make up including motivation, desire, fear, confidence, emotional control, competitive attitude, etc.
    c. Mental qualities regarding the capacity to concentrate and focus, to plan moves in advance.
    d. Spiritual reliance, because many athletes look for external forces such as religious beliefs, to help them perform well.

2. The proper concept the coach and diver have of the dive to be performed.

3. The coach's understanding of mechanical principles used in the analysis of a dive, so the proper instruction can be offered.

4. The proper assessment made by the coach of the diver's talent and innate ability to perform certain desired movements when performing a dive.

5. The level of knowledge and amount of experience the coach possesses in analyzing dives.

6. How well the diver can respond to the information given by the coach which is obtained from his or her analysis of dives.

The analysis of dives depends on the proper assessment of:

* What movements are made and how they are implemented in the performance of a dive.

* When the movements are made.

* Where the movements are made.

* Why the movements are made.

The criteria used in analyzing dives

It appears that coaches spend about ninety percent of their time and energy working with movements, forces, technique, and style used by divers. Actually, this area is only a fourth of what is really involved in the execution of a dive. Nearly everyone will agree that body mechanics are very crucial in the performance of dives, but when, where, and why the movements are made is more crucial than making the initial moves needed to perform a dive. This is born out when one realizes that standard movements for the performance of all dives and why they are used can be proven with the use of scientific fact based on the Laws of Motion. However, "when" and "where" the moves are made cannot be standardized because they constantly change in the performance of every dive due to:

* The amount of angular momentum needed to perform the dive.

* The angle of the body on the take-off

* The angular velocity of the body while rotating in the air.

* The height and distance of the dive from the point of take-off and from the water.

I believe that the key to forming accurate concepts of dives by the coaches and divers is found through the use of curiosity. When performing or coaching a dive, if one is aware of "what," "when," and "where" such moves should be made when performing a dive, he or she should then ask themselves "why" such actions are needed. In answering the question, concepts of dives can be accurately formed with the use of mechanical principles which are also used in the analysis of dives.

An example of how the four methods are used in the performance of a dive, be easily observed when a diver performs a forward 3 ½ somersault from the ten-meter platform. If the arms are thrown downward late when leaving the platform, the legs will move forward rather than backward because the arms are still moving in a downward direction "after" the feet have left the platform which creates a negative reaction. Such forward motion of the legs occurs in all forward rotating dives when the arms are thrown down late. Unfortunately, some coaches don't see the reaction or do not understand what causes it. Conversely, if the arms and upper body move downward too soon before the take-off, the diver will cut back in toward the take-off point which effects the intended direction of the dive. These early and late movements from the take-off point cause the diver to lose some control of the dive which makes a vertical entry into the water very difficult.

Another example of where a move is made is found on when the diver grabs the legs in a closed pike position. Many divers, who grab the leg below the knees by the hands, do not realize that the further away from the center of gravity the arms move, the slower will be the rotation. Grabbing the legs low on the legs lengthens the radius of the arms which increases the moment of inertia (resistance to rotate) and reduces angular velocity of the dive. So. the further away from the knees the diver grabs the legs, the slower will be the somersault while the angular momentum remains constant. Grabbing the legs low also increases the motion of the arms which invites more chance of error. This action also takes more time and since the diver is in the air for such a short period of time, a tenth of a second can be the difference between success or a poor performance of the dive (Figure 1).

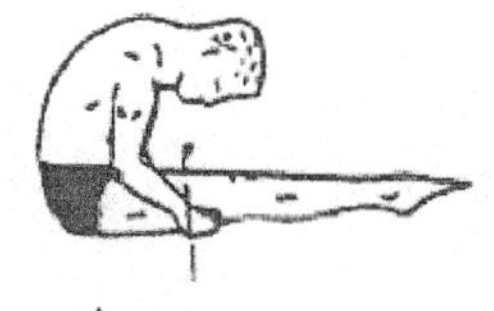

A
At the knees
(fast rotation)

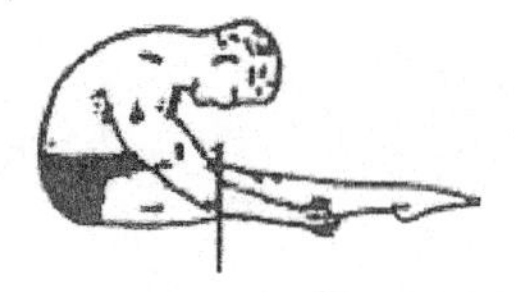

B
Lower than the knees
(slow rotation)

Closed pike position
Figure 1

CHAPTER 9

DIVING ENTRIES AND SAVES

The manner in which a diver enters the water after the performance of a dive has much to do with how successful the dive will be judged in competition. Obviously, the objective in competitive diving is for the diver to enter the water with good body alignment, as little splash as possible, and within a reasonable distance from the take-off point. To simplify some explanations that refer to the movements made by divers when entering the water, the diving entries are divided into the following two areas.

* Movements made with the arms *before* entering the water head and feet first.

* Movements made by the diver *after* entering the water.

Before the entry

Reaching for the water when performing head first entries

To perform a successful entry into the water, requires a diver to adjust the angular velocity of the dive which can be done by increasing or decreasing the radius of the body. As known, the angular momentum cannot be changed unless the rotating body is met with an external force such as the water or the diving board. With the use of Newton's Second Law, the control of the entry can be made by moving the arms in the same or opposite direction of the rotating body which will increase or conserve its angular velocity. Keeping these facts in mind, the kind of moves made with the arms and when and where they reach for the water to obtain the correct position for the entry depends on:

* The amount of angular momentum generated from the diving board or platform.

* The angle of lean by the diver when taking off from the springboard or platform initiates angular momentum.

* The amount of angular velocity of the body which is determined by its radius (tuck, pike or layout) as it rotates in the air.

* The height from the springboard or platform when the diver performs the dive.

* The height from the water when the reach for the water with the arms is made.

Head first entries

In preparation for head first entries of dives that rotate forward or inward, the arms move from a given position, such as the shins or knees, to a point overhead as the diver nears the surface of the water. With the body rotating about the horizontal (somersaulting) axis, the arms extend for the entry in three different ways:

* Moving the arms in front of the body, overhead, and in an extended position within the width of the shoulders.
* Extending the arms overhead outside the width of the shoulder in a complete or semi-lateral direction.
* Drawing the arms, bent at the elbow, close to the upper body and clasping the hands together. The arms then straighten near the longitudinal axis of the body and reach overhead for the Water.

The vertical line

All dives entering the water do so around a vertical line. The imaginary vertical line is one that passes through the point where the arms meet the shoulders (Figure 1) when entering the water head first. The success of a dive depends greatly on the direction the arms move as they extend overhead relative to the vertical line. If the diver should reach short of the vertical line *before* entering the water (Figure 1, A), the legs will move in the opposite direction of the body's rotation (Newton's Third Law). And if the arms reach short of the vertical line when making contact with the water, the reaction is for the body to increase its rotation due to the resistance of the water across the arms (Figure 1, B).

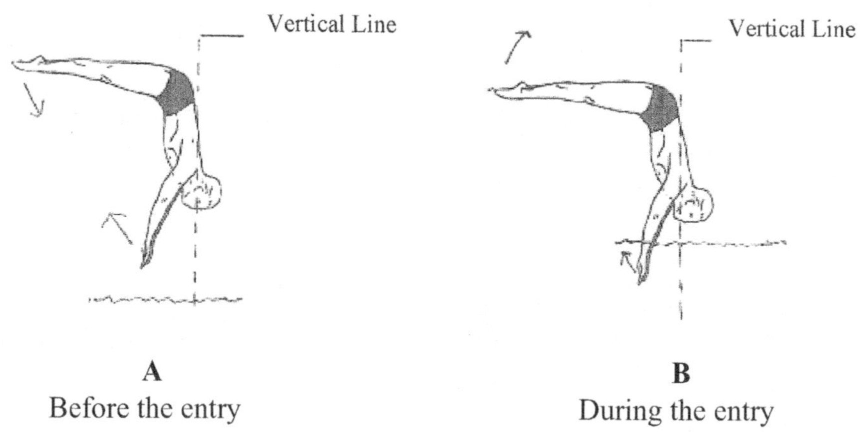

Reaching short of the vertical line
Figure 1

A desired entry for all forward rotating dives requires that the arms reach to or slightly in front of the vertical line.

Coming out of somersaults in the tuck position for a head first entry when performing dives in all four directions involves three sequential moves - "kick, look, and reach". Similarly, when preparing for the entry for somersaults in the pike position, the diver releases the legs, looks for the water, and reaches overhead for the entry while straightening the body. These sequential moves have been used in competitive diving since the beginning of the sport and are still used throughout the world by most divers.

Performing dives from Group 1 (forward dives)

When performing forward dives from the springboard or platform, the manner in which the arms reach overhead for the entry depends on the dive being performed. For example, when performing simple forward dives that require little angular momentum, the arms can reach overhead from a given position and remain within the width of the shoulders because little resistance is offered from a dive that requires little angular momentum. The forward movement of the arms when reaching causes the legs to move in the same direction as the diver's rotation which increases angular velocity of the dive. However, much of the added angular velocity caused by the forward movement of the legs is offset by increasing the radius of the diver ' s body when the arms extend overhead (Figure 2). If the dive is rotating a little too fast or begins to over rotate, the diver can spread the arms outside the width of the shoulders to control the entry.

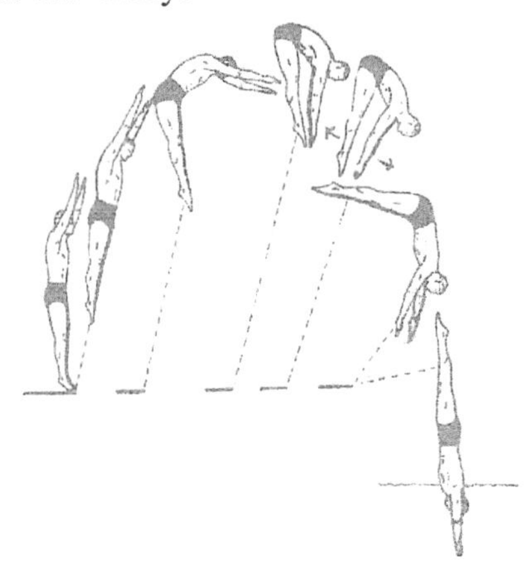

Forward dive pike
Figure 2

When performing dives that require more angular momentum, such as forward 2 ½ somersaults, the arms reach overhead for the water by circling outside the width of the shoulders. In doing so, less force is applied to the forward rotation of the dive than when reaching forward with the arms within the width of the circle. The wider the arms circle, the less force is applied to the forward rotation of the body. Therefore, the less force added to the rotation of the dive created by the forward movement of the arms, the easier it is for the diver to control the entry (Figure 3). Obviously, if the diver is rotating too slow, the diver should then reach for the entry by keeping the extended arms within the width of the shoulders.

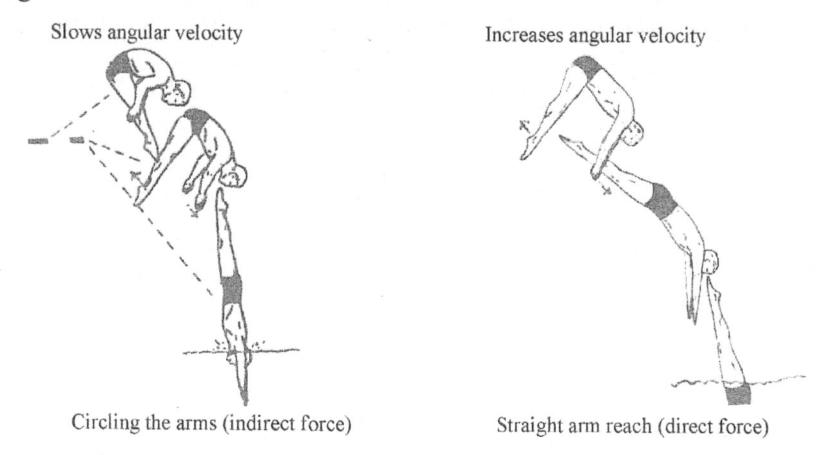

Reaching overhead for the entry
Figure 3

Some divers prefer to use the method of reaching for the water by drawing the arms, bent at the elbows and close to the chest before extending them overhead. This movement, which is generally used when the diver is somersaulting, nearly eliminates any resistance to create more forward rotation. The reason for this is that the arms do not move away from the longitudinal axis of the body which would increase its radius and create a resisting force (Figure 4).

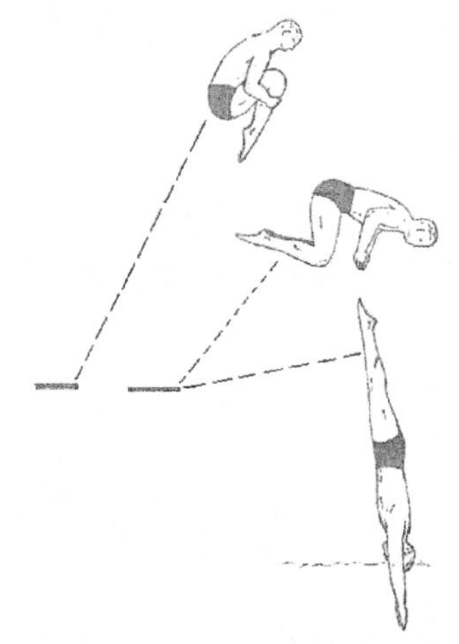

Drawing the arms to the body before extending them overhead
Figure 4

The diver and coach should be sure that the arms always reach in front of the vertical line for the entry when performing dives that rotate forward. How far the arms should reach is determined by the amount of angular momentum, angular velocity, and the distance from the take-off point. If the diver reaches too far in front of the vertical line, the dive will enter the water short of vertical. Normally, the best distance to reach in front of the vertical line for the entry is from one to six inches.

If the arms are placed behind the hips or the center of gravity when coming out of a forward or inward rotating dive, and the reach for the water is within the width of the shoulders, the rotation of the lower body will increase which generally causes the diver to over rotate when entering the water (Figure 5).

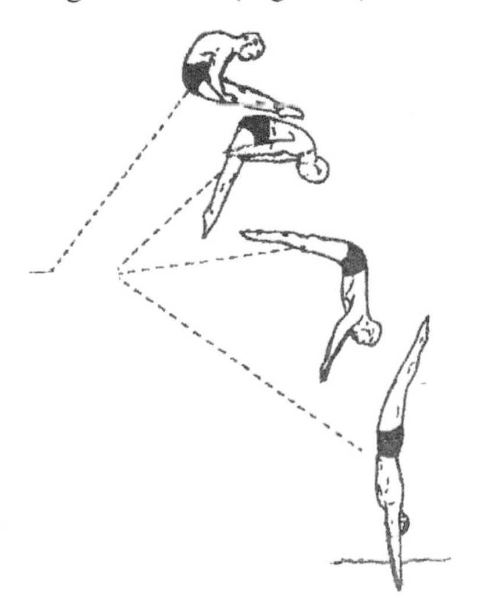

Moving the extended arms from behind the legs to in front of the vertical line
Figure 5

Reaching for the entry when performing dives rotating forward in an open pike position has the arms move from a lateral position at shoulder level to one that moves along the longitudinal axis of the body as they reach overhead (Figure 6).

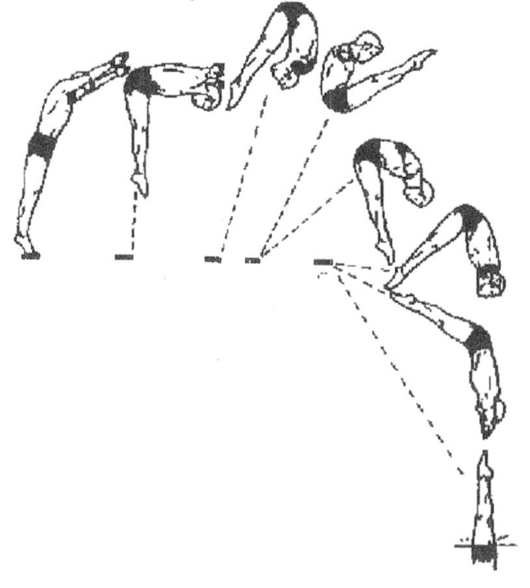

Reaching for the entry from an open pike position
Figure 6

Performing dives from Group 4 (Inward dives)

The entry for inward dives is handled a little differently than those performed in Group I. The difference involves the length of the parabolic arc on which the dive is performed, the direction of the body while passing through the parabolic arc, and the absence of a hurdle when diving inward. The parabolic arc through which the diver passes when performing dives from Group I, normally ranges from three to six feet from the end of the take-off point (Figure 7, A). The parabolic arc performed by dives rotating inward usually ranges from one to three feet because the diver is facing the board or platform. This means that the diver is moving backwards while rotating forward in order to miss the edge of the board or platform. Such a maneuver requires the diver to stay close to the take-off point if success of the dive is to be accomplished. Consequently, the more the diver moves backwards, the more difficult it is for the diver to rotate forward and enter the water properly (Figure 7, **B).** Dives moving backwards while rotating forward do not require the diver to reach in front of the vertical line in preparation for the entry. Not reaching in front of the vertical line is not desirable because the parabolic arc for inward dives is shorter than when performing dives from the forward group.

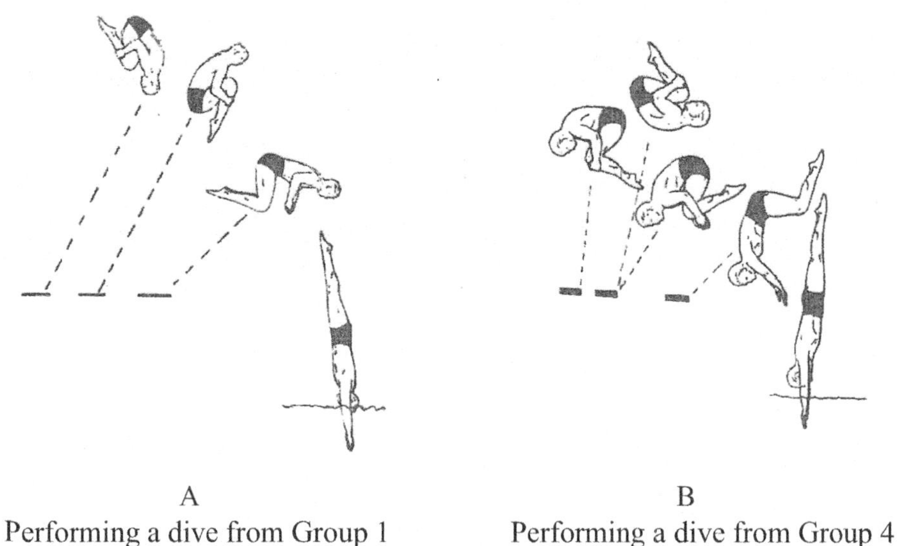

A
Performing a dive from Group 1

B
Performing a dive from Group 4

Figure 7

Performing dives from Groups 2 and 3 (back and reverse dives).

The amount of angular momentum needed to perform dives rotating in a backward or reverse direction depends on the kind of dive performed. The angular momentum will increase in proportion with the number of somersaults performed and the body position (tuck, pike, or layout) used when performing the dive. As is found in the performance of most dives, the greater the angular momentum, the more difficult it is for the diver to control the angular velocity needs to successfully perform the entry. Therefore, when performing dives that rotate backward and require a minimal amount of angular momentum, such as back and reverse dives and 1 ½ somersault tuck, the arms normally reach for the water in a lateral direction (Figure 8, A).

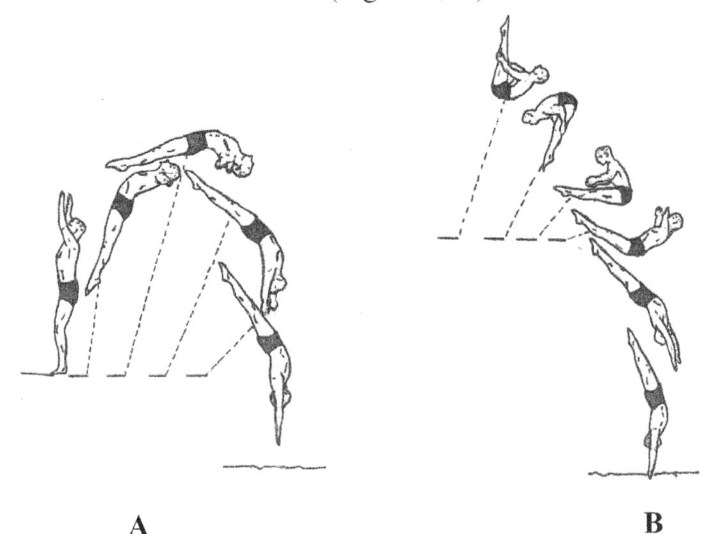

A
Back dive, layout position

B
Back 1 ½ somersault in the pike position

Figure 8

Moving the arms overhead *laterally* is the only method used where the arms do not move off the longitudinal axis of the body to create resistance. The lateral movement makes, it much easier for the diver to control dives that contain minimal angular momentum. However, dives that require more angular momentum, like a back 2 ½ somersault, generally requires the diver to control the angular velocity in preparation for the entry by extending the arms in a narrow position as they pass overheard to create as much resistance as possible to the body's rotation (Figure 9).

Back 2 ½ somersault tuck
Figure 9

A reverse 3 ½ somersault normally requires the diver to reach overhead with the arms bent and close to the longitudinal axis which is the quickest way to get the arms in position for the entry. This method is necessary due to the little time before the diver enters the water (Figure 10).

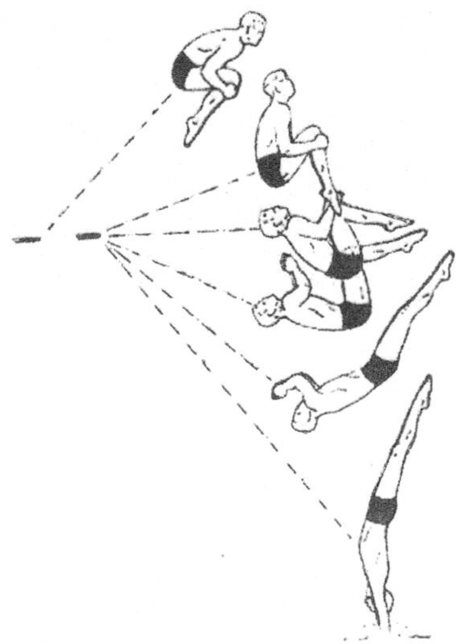

Reverse 3 ½ somersault
Figure 10

When performing backward and reverse dives and entering the water head first, the diver can move the arms in a lateral, semi-lateral, shoulder width direction, or draw the arms close to the chest and extend them overhead in line with the body. All four of the styles are used but not for all dives because some dives can be successfully performed using one style, but not when using another.

Performing the back and reverse 1 ½ somersault in the layout position also requires a lot of angular momentum and is more difficult to control than when performing the dive in the tuck or pike position. On leaving the board or platform, the arms swing upward and beyond the head before quickly moving in the opposite direction to a position close to the front of the body. This Action creates more angular velocity by reducing the radius of the body and also using an action- reaction with the arms. In swinging the arms overhead, the head remains up and back with the back arched which permits the diver to sight the water near the completion of the somersault (Figure 11).

Control of the diver's rotation before the entry is accomplished by placing the arms in a particular position on the front side of the body while somersaulting. Such an adjustment depends on the amount of angular momentum that has been created on the take-off. If the diver feels comfortable with the rotation of the dive, the arms are normally placed in the middle the body throughout the performance of the dive. If the div r is rotating too fast the arms are placed low on the body and if rotating too slow, the arms are placed high on the body due to the length of the radius of the arm when reaching for the entry. When preparing for the entry, if the arms are low on the body and reach overhead while extended, the reaction will be a considerable reduction in the dive's angular velocity. Conversely, if the arms are positioned high on the body, bent at the elbow, they will extend overhead close to the long axis.

If too much angular momentum has been created, the diver can place the arms low and in front of the body; and if too little angular momentum has been created, the diver can place the arms high and in front of the body. As the diver nears the end of the dive, the control of the dive for the entry can be determined by the difference in the length and/or arc of the arms when they reach overhead within the width of the shoulders. A long arc with the arms creates more resistance to the rotation of the body then the shorter arc which is how the dive is controlled.

Obviously, the diver will place the arms near the center of the body during the execution of the dive if he or she feels that the correct amount of angular momentum has been provided for the dive. The amount of arch in the divers back often depends on the amount of angular momentum, the angular velocity of the dive, and the height and length of the trajectory the diver follows while passing through the air.

Reverse 1 ½ somersault layout
Figure 11

The same movements can also be made when performing other backward somersault dives that possess great angular momentum. In such cases, if the diver feels that the dive is rotating too much or too fast, he or she can push the arms downward in front of the body to create a greater arc when reaching overhead for the entry. The longer arc will offer more resistance to the rotating body and allow for better control of the dive and vice versa.

In contrast, when performing dives that rotate forward with great angular momentum, the control of the entry is made by moving the arms in a lateral or semi-lateral direction to reduce their resistance to the body's rotation as they reach forward for the entry. However, when performing dives with great angular momentum that rotate backwards, the rotation of the body is slowed down to control the dive for the entry by extending the arms overhead within the width of the shoulders.

All four of the methods are used for controlling the entry but not for all dives because some dives can be successfully performed using one method but not when using another. Which method to use when rotating backwards depends much on the angular momentum needed to perform the dive and how much the diver may arch the back while in flight or when preparing for the entry. Which method to use may be decided by the diver when rotating too fast, too slow, over rotating, or when too close to the water to use the intended method. It should be realized that when performing dives with a minimum of angular momentum the arms need not be used to a great extent in controlling the rotating force. However, the arms are vital in controlling dives that require an abundance of angular momentum and angular velocity.

When the moves should be made

The timing of the reach overhead is crucial because the entry depends much on the amount of rotational force needed to successfully perform the dive. When performing simple dives that require little rotation, the diver can reach for the water at the diver's discretion which means before or after the body is aligned for the entry. As mentioned before, aligning the body and extending the arms overhead in preparation for the entry increase the radius of the body on the longitudinal axis. This, in turn, creates resistance that reduces the angular velocity of the dive's rotation. Keeping this in mind, the reach for the entry when performing dives requiring great rotational force is usually made much later and closer to the surface of the water than when performing dives requiring little angular momentum or rotational velocity: This is not to say that the arms should be extended just before entering the water but they should extend from a position low enough where a reaction to an undesirable may not occur soon enough to affect the entry of the dive.

If the reach for the entry is made too early for dives having great angular velocity, little can be done to control the dive or make corrections for errors once the arms are extended overhead. Such an early move is like a boxer stepping into the middle of the ring and throwing several punches only to find that his opponent is still sitting on his stool in the other corner. The only time a diver should reach early with the arms in preparation for the entry is when it is realized that the dive is going to over rotate. If the dive is rotating too slowly, the reach with the arms should then be made at the very last moment before the entry. If the dive is going to be short on the entry, the diver should reach overhead with the arms narrow when rotating forward and wide when rotating backward to add rotation for the dive. In either situation, the diver should attempt to first align the body then decide how, when, and where the arms should reach overhead for the water.

Where the moves should be made

To perform a successful dive requires the diver to perform the dive at preferred distances from the board which has been discussed earlier in this chapter. For example, inward dives need be a short distance from the diving board and platform while other dives, like the front dive, layout, the front dive with a half twist, etc. need be performed away from the board to best control the dive. The reason for the greater distance on some dives is to allow the diver to project the body in a parabolic arc that is easy to control. A narrow parabolic arc makes a dive rotating forward and rotating 180 degrees in the layout position very difficult to perform. Backward and reverse dives need not move far away from the board or platform because the back can be arched to control the line-up for the dive. Needless to say, these dives should be performed far enough away to prevent any part of the body from hitting the board or platform.

When performing forward rotating dives in the tuck or pike position, the distance from the take- off point should increase as the amount of angular momentum in the dive increases so as to allow for more control of the rotational forces. This is shown when performing a simple dive such as a front dive in the pike position when the diver can remain close to the board or platform due to the minimum amount of rotation needed to perform the dive. However, dives with greater rotational force, found in forward 2 ½, 3 ½, and 4 ½ somersaults, require a greater parabolic arc to control the rotating forces.

Moving any part of the body in the wrong direction can be disastrous in the performance of the dive. For example, moving the arms laterally rather than in front of the body on the take-off will not create any angular momentum ; moving the head in the wrong direction at any time during the dive can be crucial to the success of the dive; or reaching on the wrong side of the vertical line when entering the water will certainly affect the performance of the dive. Again, the success in the performance of all dives depends on the movements made by the diver, the time the movements are made, and where the movements are made. Any deviation made from any of these areas will result in lower scores for the dives.

Chinese and American styles of performing back and reverse dives in the tuck or pike position

The American and Chinese divers use two different styles in preparing for the entries when performing back and reverse dives. For example, when performing back and reverse dives in the pike position, everyone agrees that the diver should swing the arms forward and upward, shoulders width apart, to a position overhead and with the head in a level position. Keeping the arms in a vertical position, the diver then pulls the legs up to meet the hands and the eyes sight the knees or the feet at or near the peak of the dive. At this point, it appears that the diver has stopped rotating and is momentarily suspended in mid-air. The different methods used by the Chinese and American divers come into play as the diver begins to descend toward the water.

The Chinese Version

After touching the feet, the upper body pushes away from the lower part as the arms slide to the sides where they remain until the body is completely straight. The head is also tucked in with the chin near or on the chest allowing the diver to sight the position of the body. At this point, there is no movement of the body until the diver continues to descend and the arms begin to extend overhead near the width of the shoulders. The head then tilts back slightly and sights the water as the diver prepares for the entry (Figure 12).

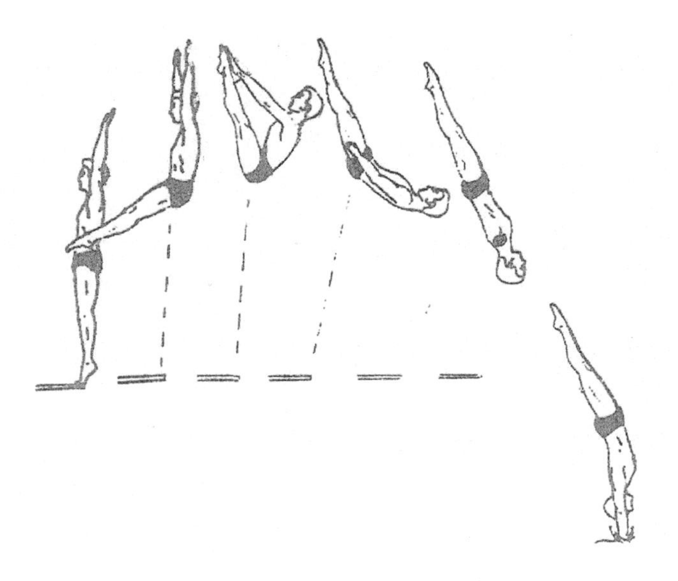

Chinese back dive, pike
Figure 12

During the short time that the arms are at the sides after dropping from the peak of the dive, there are no moves made to control of the body while it continues to rotate. Though dormant only for a split second, loss of control at this stage can affect the performance of the dive. This Chinese style is used by many divers from other countries. Not particularly attractive aesthetically nor easy to perfect, this style is used by many divers from other countries. Though not a common occurrence for the Chinese who practice up to eight hours a day every day, most divers using this version have the tendency to over rotate. The Chinese use this style in preparing for the entry when performing nearly all back and reverse dives in the tuck and pike positions.

The American Version

After touching the feet near or at the peak of the dive, the diver tilts the head back to sight the water as the arms begin to spread laterally along the longitudinal axis of the body. Dropping the head back aids in making the upper half of the body pull back and away from the lower torso while the arms continue to move late rally. When the body has straightened, the diver spots the water and the arms continue to extend overhead in preparation for the entry (Figure 13).

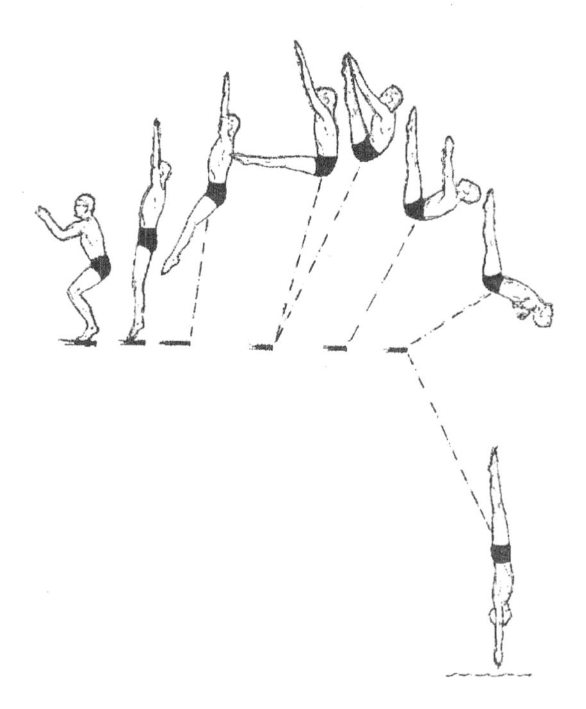

American back dive, pike
Figure 13

Moving the arms laterally offers no resistance that would change the position or rotation of the dive. The lateral position of the arms is used to balance and adjust any undesirable move made by the diver. If the arms should deviate from the long axis of the body and cause some loss of balance, the error can be corrected by slightly arching or straightening the back. Though it is a matter of taste, I personally like the American version for I believe that the movements of the diver are more graceful, picturesque, and easier to control.

Adjusting to new versions of dives

It is extremely difficult for divers, coaches, and judges to accept change when new versions of performing dives and other ideas are presented to the diving world. Those who don't wish to accept change either don't try them to see if they work or they think the movements are unorthodox while using no reason or logic. Not long ago, the Russians came up with a new version of performing the front dive with a half twist which at first was performed in jerky movements. But soon, after making some adjustments, they performed the dive with grace, beauty and control which caught the eye of many divers from other parts of the world - who copied this new version. Unfortunately, after compulsory dives were eliminated from diving competitions, few divers perform the dive anymore. The point here is that when a new version of performing a dive or someone comes up with a new idea, such as the bubbler and D.D. formula, they are first seen as unorthodox; but with time and development, what appeared to be unorthodox becomes orthodox.

The Russian divers also performed the back and reverse dives in the pike position by touching the knees rather than the feet or ankles at the Olympic Games, and received poor scores, so they dropped this new innovation. It was later found that the reason for the low scores was because they touched their knees in a rough and ungraceful manner. Unfortunately, no one realized that touching the knees was more aesthetic and correct than touching the feet. In analyzing the dive, it is seen that the distance in touching the knees with the hands is less than when touching the feet. This allows for less chance of error because of the difference in the length of the reach with the arms. Moving the arms a shorter distance also offers more beauty. As mentioned before, the less motion used in the performance of a dive the more beautiful it gets. Therefore, had the Russians touched the knees gracefully and received high scores for the dive, the divers in the rest of the world may have copied this new style. A similar scenario pertaining the clasping of the knees when performing somersaults in the pike position can be found in Chapter VIII.

Feet first entries

Few dives entering the water feet first are rarely performed from the three to ten-meter levels. Female divers still perform dives entering feet first from the one-meter level because of the slim selection of dives offered by the rule books for that level and an inward double somersault in the tuck position from the three-meter board. Feet first dives are still common in age-group competitions, especially those that are found in Group 1, the forward dives, and Group 5, the twisting dives. It has been found over the years that performing dives feet first from the one meter or three-meter springboards rarely receive high scores from the judges. One reason for the judge's lower scores is found in the difficulty to create a rip entry from the two different springboard heights. Although rip entries for feet first dives performed from the 7 ½ and ten- meter platforms are very common and often receive high scores, few divers use them in the present competitions. With over sixty years in competitive diving, I cannot remember ever seeing a diver receive over a score of eight for a feet first entry dive when performed from the springboard.

Better entries from the high platforms occur when the divers flatten their feet just before entering the water it creates a non-seething entry. Some divers who perform dives entering the water feet first do not have a very good concept of how to control the body for a straight entry, especially when performing feet first twisting somersault dives. Therefore, a few hints are offered here to aid those who have difficulty in performing dives that require a feet first entry.

Forward and inward dives

Most divers complete the dive by extending the legs from a pike position or kick the legs out from a tuck position. Those who extend the legs from the tuck position often extend the legs to form a pike or layout position in preparation for the entry. Whatever method used, most divers do not see the water or the pool until they start to pass through the surface of the water. Since it is basically a blind dive, the divers must guess how to place the legs for the entry and in doing so, rarely align the body at the proper angle for the entry. Placing the legs in the right position for the entry is often difficult because of the angular velocity of the dive and the height of the dive from the water or the distance from the take-off point. It is suggested that when extending the body for the entry, an attempt should be made to:

* Place the feet slightly in front of the vertical line to account for the continued rotation of the body when entering the water.

* Straighten the legs completely when coming out of tuck somersaults so as to better control the rotation of the dive.

* Keep the head erect with the eyes focused on the other end of the pool after straightening the body. No attempt should be made to move the head, or even the eyes, downward because it usually results in the diver over rotating on the entry.

* Place the *straight* arms slightly forward on the thighs to give good body alignment when extending the legs towards the water. Placing the arms in this position hollows the shoulders and prevents the diver from arching the back when making the entry. It also gives an illusion that they are at the sides of the body. Many divers have the arms bent at the elbow that project behind the body when entering the water which does little to better their scores. The diver should kick out strong and stand upright even if entering the water at a poor angle because the body will be aligned and will score better (Figure 14).

Forward

Inward

Front inward somersault, tuck with feet first entry
Figure 14

Straightening the body for feet first entries when executing a twisting somersault dive is difficult for nearly all divers. To simplify the entry, the diver should attempt to make sure, after performing the twist, to pull the top arm down at right angles from overhead and make sure that the eyes sight the other end of the pool. Moving the top arm in this fashion helps keep the legs and feet together and also prevents the body from casting or twisting when entering the water. Again, when making the entry, the diver should place the hands near the thighs to keep the arch out of theback.

Feet first entries in backward or reverse dives

Entering the water feet first when somersaulting in a backward or reverse direction is much easier than when rotating in a forward direction because the diver can sight the water before the entry. In seeing the water, the diver can adjust the body for the entry and place the arms in the same position as when entering the water rotating forward. As previously mentioned, the diver should not make any effort to look down at the water when entering the water rotating forward but the diver can look at the water just before entering the water when rotating backward.

When entering the water rotating backward, the diver should be conscious of placing the head in an erect position to avoid entering the water in a pike position. It is not easy to obtain the proper body alignment when entering the water in the backward or reverse direction (Figure 15). Few divers perform dives rotating backward or reverse that enter the water feet first from the three-meter springboard, but many novice and beginner divers perform backward somersault dives entering the water feet first from the one-meter board. Years ago, three of the four required dives performed from the ten-meter platform required feet first entries. But since then very few dives performed from that height enter the water feet first.

Feet first entry when rotating backwards
Figure 15

After the entry

Before World War II, most of the swimming pools were rarely deeper than eight feet for one- meter and ten feet for three-meter springboard diving. Most divers hit the bottom of the pool with their hands to prevent hitting their heads. In those days, little was known on how a diver could enter the water without a splash other than drawing the knees to the chest when over rotating on backward or reverse dives and "scooping" the entry when rotating forward. When deeper pools were built after the war, different ways of entering the water were developed leading to the present day with divers entering the water making little or no splash.

Saves

The moves made by divers after they submerge beneath the surface of the water to avoid making a splash when performing head first entries are called "saves". These saves reduce the resistance of the body making contact with the surface of the water which makes for less splash. Over a period of time, saves have been improved to the point where very little or no splash occurs which are now known as "rip' entries. Such entries are made when a diver enters the water in a near vertical angle or when a dive is over rotating. Obviously, it is not possible to use most saves when the dive has not been completed. When saves were first used by divers, it was believed, by some, that their use in competition was unfair. However, in reviewing the rule that states "any movement made by a diver under the surface of the water will not be taken into account when judging", saves have been accepted and are now commonplace. Some of these saves are:

- **The somersault (roll) save** - This save is used by divers when performing dives that rotate in a forward or inward direction. Upon entering the water, the diver performs a forward somersault in an open pike position. The somersault maneuver moves the legs in the opposite direction of the body's its rotation preventing them from moving past the vertical line that could cause a splash. This save also makes it safer for the divers when diving into shallow pools by turning the body over into a sitting position as it nears the bottom.

The roll save

Figure 16

The success of the roll save depends on when and where the save is performed, the angle of the body when entering the water, the angular velocity of the dive, and the distance from the point of take-off. The following drawing suggests how deep the diver should plunge before applying the roll save to make it effective (Figure 17).

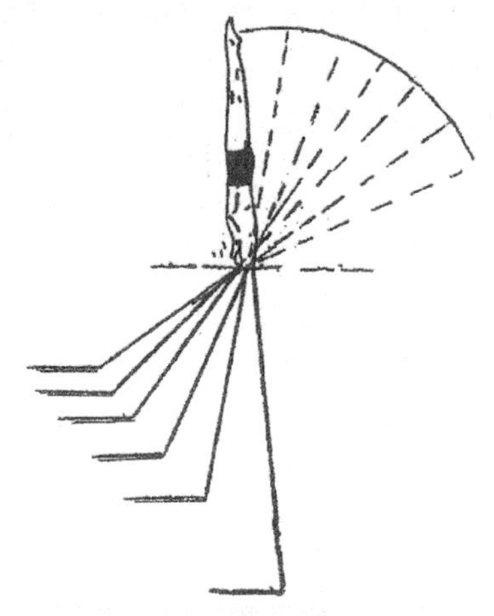

When and where to use the role save
Figure 17

Some divers perform the roll save near the bottom of the pool when the dive has entered the water at a near perfect angle. The reason for saving a dive when no error has occurred, is in anticipating the save. The diver will not arch the back during the entry which keeps the diver's body in the correct alignment.

* **Knee save** - used for dives that are over rotating when performing backward or reverse dives. This save is performed when the arms pull in toward the knees which are rapidly drawn in toward the chest as the diver enters the water (Figure 18). The timing of this action is critical because the bent legs are drawn in just as they pass through the surface of the water to avoid splashing.

Knee save
Figure 18

* **Scoop save** - is used when backward and reverse entries over rotate. As the diver begins to over rotate when entering the water, the arms pull down in front of the body towards the waist while lifting the head and arching the back (Figure 19). This causes the legs to move in the opposite direction of the body's rotation which aids in preventing them from moving past the vertical line and causing a splash. Since this movement is made just as the upper body enters the water, the diver will submerge only a short distance from the surface. As in the knee save, the legs can bend slightly just after they break the surface of the water which gives the illusion that the diver entered the water in a near vertical line.

Scoop save

Figure 19

* **Reverse somersault save** - It has already been stated that there is no way to save a dive that has not been completed. But divers performing back and reverse dives can perform a movement that makes the dive *appear* as if it was completed. Though not easy to perform due to the need of exact timing, the diver performs a front somersault in the open pike position when entering the water which causes the legs to move in the same direction as the rotating body (Figure 20).

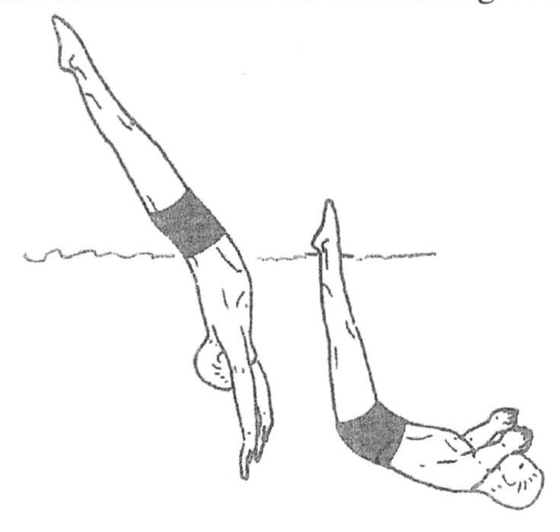

Reverse somersault save
Figure 20

Rip entries

Rip entries are merely a sophisticated means of performing saves that reduce the splash of an entry to a very minimum which often creates an impressive sound for the audience to enjoy. The rip is to give the illusion that the diver is entering the water in a near vertical position. The name "rip" is used because it is characteristic of the sound made when the diver is cleanly entering the water. Jan Gabriel of U.S. Diving in her study "Characteristics of Entries in Competitive Diving" states that there are two types of rip entries: seething and non-seething. A seething rip entry offers a boiling or churning affect produced by swimming and rolling, or swimming and scooping out of the entry. The "swim" portion of the rip creates low pressure areas while the roll/scoop movements produce a turbulence that rises vertically to the surface and makes a "rip" sound with little or no splash. The "swim with the arms' creates an early seething and the roll/scoop produces a delayed seething. Looking at the surface following rip entries, one finds that the disturbance caused by the rip is in the form of a triangle. The non-seething rip entry usually displays a minimal, if any, turbulence on the surface. In non-seething entries, divers do not swim out of the entry but rather hold their entry position to the bottom of the pool. Only a few divers have been found that can rip the entry when using the non-seething method.

The rip entry was first developed by divers from Europe and Asia in the early 1970's. During that time, the American coaches, including myself, watched divers from Russia and other European countries walk up to the five-meter platform and fall off to perform a front dive in the open pike position. None of us Americans were aware of why they were doing such a thing that took so much time and energy. We later found, that those from other countries *thought* the Americans already knew why they were performing these simple maneuvers. American divers and coaches finally figured it out soon after the 1972 Olympics when Vladimere Vassin, of Russia, broke the American 3-meter springboard dynasty that began at the 1920 Olympics. Vassin won the gold medal when entering the water short of vertical on nearly every dive while ripping every entry. Later, with the aid of Doris Miller of Canada, Jan Gabriel and Lawrence D. Abraham did a thorough study on the characteristics of the rip entry which gave the American coaches and divers a better understanding of how the rip entry works. Their studies pointed out that:

* There were no overlaps in data between the seether who rolled (Ducking under into a forward somersault in the pike position), the non-seethers, and non-rippers who rolled.

* Divers who were seethers rolled earlier than the non-seethers and non-rippers.

* The depth of the roll/scoop determined the timing and intensity of the delayed seething.

* There was no difference in cavity velocity between rip and non-rip divers, but the roll did influence the velocity of the cavity nose between non-seethers and seethers.

Their summary explains that water is not as compressible as air in a water mix. When diving into the water, the body descends through an air cushion in the water, which the body displaces, then the cavity collides as it seals back together forming an air-water mixture. This results in the height of the ensuing up-jet splash that displays characteristics between a rip and non-rip entry.

How to rip an entry

Learning to rip an entry is an art. That is, it takes a lot of practice to develop the proper actions to perform the rip with consistency. From experience, I would say that a person who practices three to five days a week performing thirty to forty line ups each day, can learn to perform a fairly good rip in four or five months. Lineups are generally known as simple dives performed from a three-meter springboard or a three-meter to five-meter platform that are used to learn the rip entries. Dives most often used for line ups include the standing forward dive tuck, pike, or layout; the forward1½ somersault, tuck or pike; the back-dive tuck, pike, or layout; the reverse dive, tuck or pike; and the inward dive tuck or pike. Divers can also perform back lineups by sitting on the edge of the platform and roll off backward in a tuck or pike position. They can also bend over facing the platform with the legs straight then jump up as they fall backwards and grab the knees and pulling them upward to a closed pike position. Some divers also fall backwards in a straight position with the arms extended overhead. A reverse dive in the tuck position is usually used to perform the reverse lineups. Inward dives in the tuck or pike position conclude the manner in which lineups are performed. Lineups can also be used when performing forward 1 ½ somersaults in the tuck position from these heights.

* Lineup dives require the diver to form good body alignment after leaving the take-off point by extending the arms laterally along the longitudinal axis of the body when reaching for the entry. When entering the water, the diver should get the body in proper position before making a role save (Figure 21).

Forward line ups
Figure 21

* Body alignment - The diver should place the body parts as close to the longitudinal axis as possible so as to streamline the body and create as little resistance to the water as possible when entering the water. This means that the

body should be erect with a straight spine, head in line with the body, drawn in stomach, straight legs with no bend in the knees, extended ankles, and a good toe point.

* Following the performance of the simple dive, the arms should move along the longitudinal axis of the body so that their movement does not create any body resistance that would cause a reaction resulting in some form of body change. The extended arms should squeeze the ears when reaching overhead for the entry.

* Divers usually stand or sit on the edge of the board or platform when practicing forward lineups and perform a forward diving in the tuck, pike, or layout position as they leave the platform or three-meter springboard (Figure 21). Some divers jump from the platform or springboard and perform a front dive in the tuck or open pike position or perform a forward 1 ½ somersault in the tuck position. Divers normally perform an inward dive in the tuck or closed pike position.

When entering the water while rotating forward or inward with the upper part of the body already underwater, the arms may pull down laterally, semi laterally, or straight in front of the body as the diver rolls, or the arms may collapse completely and let the water direct their movements. Which arm action works best depends on the diver so he or she may have to try any or all of them to find which one works.

* When performing backward line ups, divers can squat or sit on the edge of the board or platform and roll off and perform a back dive in the tuck or pike position. The diver can also perform a standing back dive in the layout position (Figure 22). Others stand in a closed pike position and pull the legs up to a tight pike position after leaning from the board or stand upright and fall backwards with the arms overhead. The reverse line up normally usually is done by performing a reverse dive in the tuck position.

When performing lead-up dives that rotate backwards the diver should attempt to sight the point of entry by tilting the head backward. When some divers don't see the water straight down but can spot the water a few feet behind the point of entry (Figure 21). The diver positions the body for the entry then scoops the entry after the body is submerged. Nearly all divers roll or scoop the entry to acquire a rip. It is rare for a diver, who does not use a save, can rip.

When entering the water, the arms normally pull down in front of the body as the diver scoops the entry by pulling the head and shoulders back arid arching the back. Applying the movements of a rip to a dive has resulted in some injuries due to the motion of the arms and the added resistance of the body to the water caused by the increase in the angular momentum needed to perform the difficult dives. As observed earlier, divers use so much tape on their hands and wrists that it is difficult to know whether they are divers or boxers.

Backward line ups
Figure 22

The following suggestions may be helpful in learning to rip an entry:

* Practice forty line-ups that require ten in each direction requires about an hour of time, which is difficult to do when trying to take part in all the other activities in the diving program. But performing an entry in competition with little or no splash is essential if a diver wishes to seriously compete with other divers.

A suggestion is offered here for those who wish to perform a back dive and/or reverse dive in the tuck position as a line up but don't know how to perform the dives. The diver should start by standing on the end of the one-meter board with the fulcrum pushed forward as far as possible. When jumping from the board, swing the arms overhead to a fixed position while drawing the legs up to the chest. In this motion, sight the other end of the pool until the legs are in the tuck position, then release and extend them above the horizontal line of the body while still looking forward. With the legs pulled upward well above the horizontal plane, release the legs, and look over them sighting the other end of the pool before entering the water. If the dive enters the water short or beyond the vertical line, repeat the dive and adjust the legs by pulling them up higher or releasing them lower until the proper position is acquired.

Once these dives are learned on the one-meter springboard, the diver can then repeat these dives from the three-meter springboard or the three or five-meter platform if he or she can perform the dives a little short of vertical at a lower level. This prevents a diver from over rotating in the dive and landing on their stomach when entering the water. Progressively performing the dive in this manner can allow the diver to jump from nearly any height with little danger or chance of injury.

Back dive, tuck
Figure 23

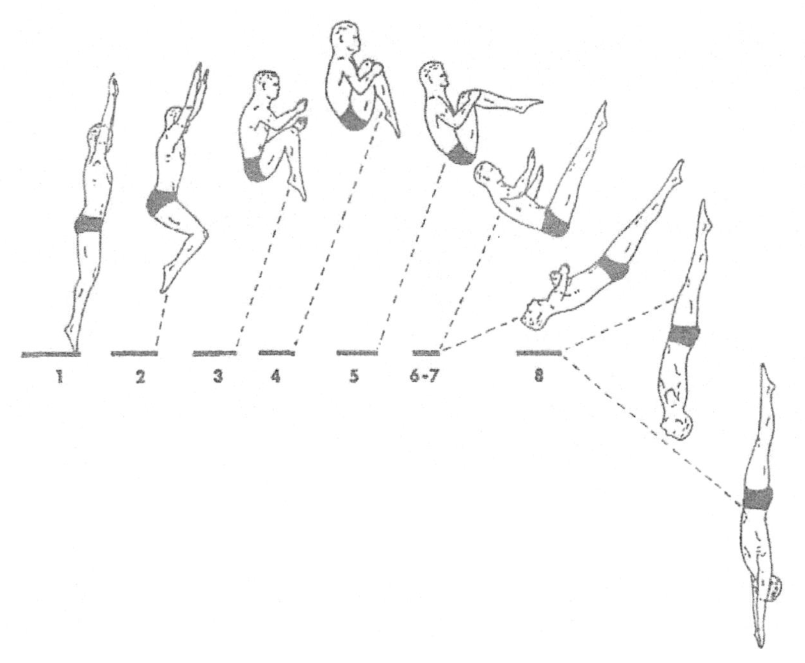

Reverse dive, tuck
Figure 24

CHAPTER 10

COMMUNICATION

No single behavior in competitive diving is more important than communication between the diver and the coach. There is little doubt that poor communication is one of the most common problems found in a diving program. Communication means the conveying of information between two or more persons which in the sport of diving is done in various ways:

* Auditory- Sounds that can be made verbally or in some other form such as blowing a whistle, clapping the hands, etc.

* Non-verbal - Involves the use of body movements, video, books, etc.

* Kinesthetic - Movements by direct or indirect contact with the body such as when the coach places the diver's arms in a particular position or spots a diver with the use of a belt.

* Cognitive - when a person communicates with oneself.

If the diver is within hearing distance of the coach, the communication between the two is normally auditory and non-verbal. While talking, the coach often uses body language, like the hands, arms and other parts of the body to make gestures, in the attempt to get the point over to the diver. Kinesthetic communication is more common with beginner divers than with advanced divers. Most kinesthetic contact is made on gymnastic mats, on the trampoline, on a dry land board, and in some cases with a rig over the one-meter diving board. If the diver is out of hearing range, communication by the coach with the diver is usually in the form of some sort of body language such as arm, hand, or facial movement. Whatever means, without understandable communication between the coach and diver, the diver has little chance of improving his or her performance.

Communication in competitive diving includes a " concept" and "principle" to be applied to the dive. Choosing the correct sequential movements at the proper time and place in the performance of each dive requires good communication between the coach and diver. Through good communication, the diver and coach can successfully relate, plan, and compare concepts that concern the movements used in the successful performance of dives. From this understanding, coaches and divers can work together to correct and eliminate moves that are not properly executed.

The concept/principle scenario is extremely important in the performance of dives for, with the aid of the coach, once the divers establish an image of the dive in their minds, they can then mentally perform the dive in sequence many times before actually performing the dive. This mental rehearsal of a dive prior to its actual performance is known as *imagery*. The purpose of mentally rehearsing a dive again and again, is for divers to cement the desired movements of it in their minds. Imagery also helps divers focus on the performance of the dives and not on something else that could cause harm to the performance of the dive or to the diver. This form of imagery was not recognized by coaches and divers until a few years ago, when the performance of dives is visualized in various other ways.

AUDITORY COMMUNICATION

Although verbal communication between the coach and the diver is obviously the best method used in competitive diving, this form of communication often presents many problems. For example, it is amazing how often a coach verbally relates information to the diver only to find later that he or she did not have the first clue of what the coach was talking about. This confusion often occurs when a diver engages a new coach who often has a whole new vocabulary in the way of expressing his or her views. What makes it worse is the diver is usually afraid to ask the coach to explain himself or herself. Some coaches are brilliant in verbally expressing themselves while others, many of whom are experienced in competitive diving and possess a great knowledge of diving, cannot convey their valuable knowledge because they don't know how to communicate.

Having observed and listened to hundreds of coaches converse with their divers over the years, I have yet to find any two coaches using the same terminology when coaching. In most cases the coaches communicate by using terms heard from someone else or by making up their own. Whatever terms used, the most important point is that the coach and the diver understand each other. Let it be clear that no attempt is made here to simplify the way coaches express themselves to the divers, but it is important that some kind of terminology be used that is familiar to both parties, so they can understand one another. Although most terms used by coaches and divers are basic and generally used universally, many common terms have different meanings to different coaches and divers.

A list of traditional terms normally used by most coaches in directing, discussing, coaching, explaining, and exchanging information is offered here to aid the reader in becoming more familiar with terms. These may make it for those in the sport to communicate a little easier. However, these terms need not be used in their entirety, for many coaches and divers have their own vocabulary which their divers already understand.

* Action - Movements used when executing a dive.

* Approach - Beginning from a stance, the walk on the diving board or platform and the hurdle to the end of the board before that the take-off.

* Balk - A false start before attempting a dive.

* Blow - A movement in the performance of a dive or the entire dive that is poorly executed.

* Board - Usually refers to the springboard.

* Capping the knees - Grasping the top of the knees with the hands in the tuck position.

* Cast - When the body is out of line of its normal projection during a dive.

* Checking - Stopping or trying to control a movement during the execution of a dive.

* Check this out - Normally a request by the diver for the coach to observe a dive or a particular movement made in a dive.

* Closed tuck - When the knees are together and drawn tightly into the chest with feet together and the heels pulled close to the buttocks.

* Control - A state in which the diver has complete command of the actions which include psychological, emotional, physiological, as well as physical.

* Cowboy - When the knees and the feet are spread apart when performing dives in a tuck position. This position makes a diver look like he or she is riding a horse.

* Crimping - The bending of the knees while the diver is in the pike position.

* Crow hop - The lifting of one or both feet from the board when raising the arms upward to depress the board when performing a standing take-off facing the board or platform.

* D.D. - Refers to the "degree of difficulty" given to each dive that can be performed in competition.

* Diver - Anyone who dives from a springboard or platform and survives.

* Drop - The decent of the diver or any part of the body from an upper position.

* Early - A movement by the diver that is made prior to its need to acquire the intended objective.

* Entry - The passage of the body, head first or feet first, through the surface of the water.

* Faded out - A diver performed too far away from the board or platform.

* Failed dive - Failure to perform an intended dive.

* Firm or firm up - Muscle contraction of some part of the body.

* Free - Related to twisting somersault dives in which the body changes position before and after the twisting action is executed.

* Fulcrum - That part of the diving standard beneath and near the center of the board that is used as a pivot to cause the board to bend and become a level to project the diver upward.

* Give up - to quit making the effort to succeed when performing a dive.

* Good, great, okay, etc. - Some hackneyed comments made by the coach when communicating with the diver.

* Got paid - The response to the diver from the opposition who receives scores from the judges that are believed to be too high for the dive.

* Heavy entry - An entry into the water that creates a lot of splash.

* Hitching the hurdle - Pulling the lower portion of the hurdle leg back behind the knee at or near the peak of the hurdle.

* Hurdle - The jump to the end of the board or platform following the walk or run when performing the approach.

* Kick out - A strong and explosive extension of the legs from the tuck position made by a diver performing a somersault in the air.

* Killing the spring - A bending at the knees while the board recoils which reduces or eliminates the upward spring of the dive.

* Late - A movement made by a diver that is not made in time to obtain the intended objective.

* Layout - A basic body position in which the diver's legs are straight with noforward bending of the upper torso.

* Lead ups - Dives practiced with less rotation than the difficult dives when preparing to perform a difficult dive. For example, practicing backward double somersaults in preparation of performing a back 2 ½ somersault.

* Lift - The upward projection of the diver when leaving the board or platform.

* Line ups - The execution of simple dives when learning to properly align the body for entering the water with little or no splash.

* Long - An over rotation of the body before entering the water.

* Lost - A diver who loses control of the body in the air and has no idea of where he or she is going which often results in a sickening crash.

* Missed - The failure of the diver to make the proper move in the execution of a dive resulting in performing the dive improperly.

* Optional dives or voluntary dives - The difficult dives chosen and performed by the diver with no D.D. requirements or limitations.

* Palming the entry - Where the diver turns the palms of the hands away from the body, so they will hit the water flat upon entry. Some divers use this technique to help them enter the water with little splash.

* Pike position - A basic body position where the body is bent at the waist with the legs straight.

* Press - The downward push of the body on the board resulting in a recoil to project the diver.

* Punching the entry - The diver makes fists with the hands when entering the water.

* Reach - The extension of the arms at the beginning of the dive and at the end of dives that enter the water head first.

* Required, compulsory, or involuntary dives - Dives that have certain requirements that involve total degrees of difficulty.

* Rip - A diver entering the water with little or no splash.

* Save - A movement made by the diver above or below the water surface that alters or adjusts the body position for a straighter entry.

* Scoop - The arching of the back when entering the water head first either in a reverse or backward motion.

* Short - A term used when the body does not rotate enough to complete the dive for the entry.

* Sitting down on the take-off - The backward drop of the hips while the diver is still on the board in preparation for the take-off when performing back or inward dives.

* Split tuck - A body position where the legs are apart when performing somersault dives in the tuck and pike positions. The feet may be together or also apart when executing this technique.

* Square out - The arms positioned laterally at the level of the shoulders when the diver is in a pike position after coming from another position when performing a dive.

* Stance - The position taken by the diver on the board or platform before beginning to move to performing a dive.

* Stomp the board - When the diver lands on the end of the board following the approach and is not in rhythm with its oscillation or recoil.

* Stretch - Extending the muscles of the body or some of its parts.

* Stuck or hung up - A position of the body in the air in which the diver is helpless because there is not enough rotation to complete the dive.

* Swimming out of the entry - A breaststroke motion of the arms used by the diver to make a rip entry.

* Take it up - An expression used by the coach when telling the diver to get on the board or platform and perform a dive that is at a higher level.

* The coach - Good looking, great personality, rich, always friendly, never yells, never wrong, warm hearted, God, and sees every dive. Always has complete control of his or her temper, never lies, always makes good calls on hard dives, and dresses well. Never late for practice, sympathetic, never plays favorites, always gives short and easy workouts, and accepts suggestions from the divers and their parents on how to coach. Never has divers do hard dives, much better diver than anyone on the team when young, loves parents and other coaches, always listens and seldom talks, and always has emergency kit on deck. Never drinks alcohol or smokes, always gives divers credit for their accomplishments and always takes blame when things go wrong, never tells dirty jokes, and is well organized. Has many paid vacations, lets divers sleep in every morning, never gets nervous at meets, gives every diver on college team a full scholarship, has all divers memorize 911, encourages divers to applaud the performance of opposing divers when competing, and doesn't let anyone know where he lives.

* Throw - Refers to a vigorous thrust of the arms when attempting to create more rotation of the body.

* Tight - Can be used when a diver has come too close to the board or can refer to drawing the legs in closer to the body.

* Tower - A solid stand that usually offers one to five platforms that include one, three, five, 7 ½, and ten-meter heights. Platforms are normally 20 feet long and seven to ten feet wide which permit divers to dive from a stable base with no spring.

* Tuck - A basic body position in which the body is bunched into a tight ball, the legs bent and with the knees drawn close to the chest, the feet pulled into the buttocks, the head in line with the body or pulled down toward the chest, and the arms bent with the elbows close to the body.

A breakdown in communication frequently occurs when the coach makes negative comments to the divers such as, "I can't talk to him. He doesn't hear a word I say"; "I have told him a hundred times but....;" or other similar statements with negative connotations. Divers may also complain that the coach, "doesn't talk to me; he never explains what he means; he is always hollering and shouting but..., or I don't understand him." These comments clearly show that communication between the coach and diver is lacking, and such things as leadership, motivation, learning, teaching or coaching performance, organizing the program, self-control and strategies cannot be effective. Communication can also be distorted due to distrust, fear, conflict, bias and other such factors. Other reasons for not communicating well can be attributed to the lack of skills or knowledge, failure to listen or speak, and most often the failure of coaches and athletes to understand each other's behavior patterns.

The manner in which the coach talks to the diver can greatly affect the performance of the dive. Some coaches can enchant the listener while others can talk all day and the diver hears or understands little to nothing that the coach says. One thing is certain, effective verbal communication requires the speaker and the listener to be on the same wave length. Some divers ignore the coach when a comment is made concerning a particular dive and this can be very irritating and frustrating to the coach. This seems to be the nature of some divers and it should not be taken too seriously by the coach. More attention from the diver can be acquired if the coach occasionally changes his or her frequency by using different words or synonyms when making comments about diving.

Most divers turn the coach *"off"* when they have heard the same explanations or commands stated the same way time after time. A very successful approach to eliminating the problem is to put the desired information in the form of a question rather than making it a command. The logic when attempting to explain or dictate certain movements. The logic here is that divers have been told what to do from the time they were old enough to understand their mothers, to the present moment. However, when the coach offers the information in the form of a question, the diver cannot respond unless the question is heard. Asking a question also *challenges* the diver which is not apt to occur when the coach gives a command. This approach need not be used for everything the coach says but can be very helpful when wishing to make an important point at a particular time in the performance of a dive.

When attempting to instruct a diver to focus on a particular move in performing a dive, coaches often fail to realize that the reason why some divers do not respond to such commands is because they still haven ' t learned the movement; a situation that often tries a coach's patience. Such was the case when I instructed one of my divers to put his head up when performing a front dive. I continually repeated the comment to the diver throughout the performance of the walk, the approach, the hurdle, and the execution through the peak of the dive. After the dive was completed, I asked the diver why he didn't lift the head up after 40 commands during the actual dive... and he replied that he forgot. The reaction to such a comment would make one believe that it is not possible for a diver to forget a simple command that was repeated constantly throughout the entire approach and dive. With some thought, I realized that the diver had not forgotten my constant demands after all. The real reason for not responding was because he had not learned to replace an old movement with a new movement.

Some divers are easier to communicate with than others for they listen to the given instructions and have the capacity to internalize every detail without distraction. In doing so, they can concentrate completely on what moves should be made to successfully perform the dive. Others hear the instructions externally along with a lot of noise, none of which penetrates the divers thinking capacity. Thus, the coach's suggestions are usually taken as vague and unclear and are often ignored which results in the diver having great difficulty concentrating on the moves needed to perform the dive.

The confidence in the coach by a diver can be in jeopardy when the coach admits not having seen the dive performed; which, in some instances, can occur quite often. When this occurs, it is suggested that the coach never admits not haven seen the dive but merely tell the diver to do the dive again in order to get another good look at it. In this way, the diver does not place blame on the coach for ignoring his or her performance. Every coach has gone through the ordeal where the diver asks the coach to comment on a dive just performed that the coach did not see. Rather than admitting not seeing the dive, the coach will comment on certain movements made in the forward approach, the take off, and the dive when suddenly the diver informs the coach that he had just performed a *back* dive. Another point worth mentioning is that the diver and coach not get into any long discussions about a dive in the middle of a workout because it takes the attention away from the other divers. Therefore, it is best to have such discussions after practice.

Oft times, the coach will make a casual remark about a particular move rarely made by a diver who, out of nowhere, picks up on the error and turns it into a gigantic problem. For example, a diver may have performed a back dive, layout hundreds of times and never once twisted when entering the water. The coach then makes a casual comment about the twist which has never occurred before and the diver suddenly becomes very concerned about twisting on back dives. When divers make such isolated or infrequent errors, it is best for the coach to not mention such infractions until the errors occur frequently.

The interpretation of the information offered by the coach often affects the performance of the dive in the wrong way; for what the coach says and what the diver "thinks" the coach says can be two different matters. In many cases when the coach assumes that the diver understands exactly what is said but in actuality, the diver may have interpreted the comments to mean just the opposite of those given by the coach, potentially resulting in injury or great disappointment. An example on how the interpretation of a comment can be understood in two opposite ways can be seen in the picture shown here of the lady who is either a witch or a beautiful damsel (Figure 1). The picture shows how easily a simple misinterpreted comment made by the coach can change the entire relationship between the coach and the diver.

The tone of the coach's voice can also affect the diver's performance. When the coach has mastery of his or her voice in commuting information that includes emotions, motivation with authority, and confidence; there is little doubt that the attention of the diver will be captured. However, if the coach has a soft voice or has a tendency to mumble, the communication between the coach and diver can be difficult. Consequently, it is often not "what" is said, but "how" it is said that steers the diver's reactions.

What the coach said (pretty girl) — What the diver heard (witch)

Figure 1

Comments made by the coach need to be made at a certain time and/or place if they are to be really heard by the divers. Divers seem to hear the coach best when in some state of stress or danger such as when attempting a difficult dive from the ten-meter platform for the first time or when having just landed on the stomach or back. Obviously, this is the time when the diver wants to be in ' synch' with the coach who is trying to guide him or her to a safe and painless entry.

Encouragement is needed if a diver is to be successful. It appears that the less experienced a diver is, the more need there is for praise and encouragement, so inspiring comments should be offered consistently. Naturally, it is helpful for the coach to verbally correct the diver's mistakes but if too many corrections are offered, the diver may take the instruction negatively and ignore nearly everything said. More often than not, everyone wins when the coach corrects the diver's mistakes and especially when the instruction is positive and motivating. It is important that the comments made by the coach are not taken as personal criticism of the diver, who should understand that the comments are to improve the dive. Therefore, the best way to coach a dive may be made by commenting on what was wrong with the dive followed by some positive reinforcement such as: "You went out too far, your legs were a little crimped in the pike and your feet came apart at the entry, but the hurdle was well executed with a perfect takeoff and the dive had a great entry."

NONVERBAL COMMUNICATION

Nonverbal communication is a means of conveying information in a manner other than with the voice. Since there are so many ways of communicating in this fashion, an attempt is made here to elaborate only on communications that have a direct influence on the performance of dives. A person can communicate with another person by sharing thoughts, feelings, information, attitudes, etc., without uttering a word. A coach may use body language such as making arm gestures, using facial expressions like smiling or frowning, and making eye contact, all of which may be transmitted without saying a word. It is amusing to attend a diving competition and watch coaches use different arm and hand signals when not in a position to verbally communicate with a diver. Naturally, these nonverbal gestures are intentional but not always interpreted correctly. Sometimes the slump of the shoulders, throwing the arms and head up, or throwing a towel on the floor seem to indicate a moment of despair or disgust when actually, the person' s feelings are just the opposite. Some non-verbal actions occur in radically different circumstances. Sometimes a person cries when in pain but also cries when overjoyed, persons yawn when fatigued but also yawn when confronted with anxiety or fear. Though body language can support verbal communication, it can also be used to hide or falsify feelings and attitudes that contradict verbal statements. Thus, one often finds it difficult to interpret people's feelings by virtue of their body language.

One needs only to attend a football or basketball game to understand how silence can convey a nonverbal powerful message. One look at the bench of the losing team shows few people talking to each other while others have towels over their heads trying to hide from the defeat or poor performance, and the coach is staying away from the entire team. There is no question which side of the stadium represents the losing team for all these spectators are quiet enough to be attending a funeral. In such moments of defeat, coaches often become so angry or frustrated that their behavior patterns change from normality to one completely out of character like throwing chairs, breaking yard markers over the knee, or yelling at everyone including their assistant coaches and players. In such instances, the verbal, nonverbal gestures, and the presence of silence easily explain the situation.

Then, when observing the winning team, teammates are seen hugging each other, jumping up and down and generally acting like they won the lottery. The coach is all smiles while hugging the athletes and assistant coaches as one big happy family. The spectators on the winning side of the stadium are waving their arms at the team and hugging each other like relatives at a family reunion. As can be expected, few people try to get near the members of the losing team while everyone from the winning side can't get close enough to their heroes.

KINESTHETIC COMMUNICATION

Coaches normally do not use kinesthetic communication as much as they should. This form of instruction is very effective when teaching and coaching the basic moves needed to successfully perform a dive. Physically directing the movements of the diver is a stronger technique than when directing movements through the use of the voice or when using gestures. Though the message may be external when applying kinesthetic communication, the internal feeling allows the diver to compare one sensation of feeling with that of another. So, when making a particular movement one way while the coach kinesthetically directs the movement in another way, the diver can feel, evaluate, and correct the contrasting movements. For example: when a diver places the arms too high when performing the front dive layout, the coach can take the arms of the diver and go through the movement needed to position the arms correctly. When doing so, the diver will begin to resist placing the arms in the correct position. Both the diver and the coach will feel the resentment made by the diver which will help him or her understand where the correct arm position is. This means of communication also enhances quick physical memory which is the essence of physical performance. Communicating with the diver also kinesthetically eliminates much of the fear when performing certain movements for the coach is controlling the actions. The sensation experienced by the diver in these situations is similar to that of holding someone's hand when in a state of danger.

In contrast to direct kinesthetic communication, when the coach has physical contact with the diver, indirect kinesthetic communication makes use of devices such as spotting rigs. These rigs are made up of belts, ropes, pulleys and metal poles that are attached over trampolines, dry land pits, mats, and one-meter diving boards. They are used to control body movements and teach body awareness while the divers are performing in the air. They also minimize and/or prevent errors from happening that could cause injury to the performer. Other devices used for indirect kinesthetic communication include ropes and poles that are elevated so that divers can jump over them when performing dry land hurdles or in obtaining desired heights and distances when diving from the one-meter board.

COGNITIVE COMMUNICATION

Although most communication is between two or more persons, it is possible for a person to communicate with oneself. This mode is referred to as cognitive communication and involves two types of thoughts; conscious and subconscious. Conscious thinking is mentally talking to oneself. Divers use this method when trying to talk themselves into a good performance, warning themselves of particular dangers, thinking of the sequential movements needed to perform a dive, and so on.

Sub-conscious thinking is often difficult for divers to identify or relate to because it is that little voice one hears in the head when performing that warns the diver of a move that may be dangerous or point to disaster. This voice usually occurs just before or during the performance of a dive. Unfortunately, the diver has no control of when, what, how, or where that little voice in the back of the mind will pop up. Usually the subconscious voice arises in response to fear.

When engaged in conscious thought, a diver will often think of too many things which can distract or hinder the performance of the dive. It is not unusual for a diver to change his or her mind just before or during the performance of the dive which often results in disaster and/or pain. "Over thinking" might be avoided if the diver thinks of only two or three moves needed to perform the dive. This kind of mental preparation is controllable and has proven to be very successful when practicing and competing in meets. When a diver develops this process, that little voice from the subconscious mind is not heard from so often.

A negative form of subconscious communication appears to be more prevalent in those who have great fear, little confidence, difficulty in focusing on what they are attempting to do, have had previous experiences involving failure, pain, confusion, poor instruction, or have no knowledge of how to perform a particular dive.

The subconscious mind often activates with the purpose of protecting the diver from disaster or harm for it will come to light when the diver strays from what already has been successfully learned. Divers should not look upon the sub-conscious mind as a bad thing but rather a time when the mind is trying to warn them of danger. Unfortunately, many divers do not make any attempt to control or understand this mode of communication, so they continue to have problems with it.

Spotting

Spotting is a technique used by divers to orient themselves in the air during the performance of a dive. By spotting certain objects in the pool, such as the water, wall, ceiling or some other object that can be easily seen, divers can detect where they are when somersaulting in different directions. Up until the early 1960s, with the exception of the forward and inward 2 ½ somersault dives, most divers worldwide did not perform dives that rotated more than 1 ½ revolutions. Since little angular momentum was used to perform the dives, the need to sight anything while rotating was not apparent. Most divers "felt" their way while rotating and used their sight only when preparing for the entry. At that time, the only difficult dives in which the diver spotted the water while performing were the back and reverse 1 ½ somersaults in the layout position. When performing these dives, the diver spotted the board or the water when completing one somersault. However, when divers started to rotate 2 ½ or more times in dives from all five groups, more angular momentum was needed to increase the angular velocity of the somersaults. The increase in angular velocity made it necessary for divers to start spotting some object while rotating to determine where they were going and when to prepare for the entry into the water. Divers discovered that by spreading the knees, they could see the board or some other object on the first and/or second somersault when performing backward somersault dives, and other parts of the pool when performing reverse multi-somersaults.

Divers at that time did not believe they could spot something when rotating forward because their legs prevented them from seeing the water below. However, as more divers started to perform forward multiple somersaults from all competitive heights, they eventually found that the water could be spotted by spreading the knees while keeping their feet together. Spotting in this manner not only aided the divers in seeing where they were going, but it also reduced the fear of getting lost while rotating.

Divers have learned to spot by keeping the head still or moving it into various positions while rotating in the air. Which method to use varies with different divers and depends on the kind of dive being performed. Most divers learn to spot on the trampoline and/or dry-land board where, with the use of a safety harness, they are suspended in the air while performing various somersaults. Others have learned to spot when performing simple dives with little rotation and with practice, learned to spot more difficult dives that require more angular momentum and angular velocity.

Since the angular velocity of the body when twisting is normally much greater than when somersaulting, the possibility of spotting an object while twisting is minimal. However, the diver can still obtain some orientation if the eyes remain open during the twisting process. Common sense tells us that we can determine where we are going much easier in flight with the eyes open than when shut. When the eyes are closed, one must rely on their kinesthetic senses to determine direction in flight. At any rate, spotting particular objects at a given moment in flight offers the divers guidance and direction which makes it easiest for them to perform intricate dives.

When the coach should communicate with the diver

The first communication between the coach and the diver usually occurs when the diver is standing on the board at which time one tells the other what dive is to be performed. This moment provides the coach the opportunity to offer suggestions to the diver, based on previous performances of the dive. In other words, the coach gives the diver a "game plan" for the way the dive should be performed.

Since the diver often has different concepts than the coach on how the dive should be executed, it is important that the coach converse with the diver about what is desired when performing the dive. It is not necessary for the coach to go into any great detail about the dive, especially if the diver is already familiar with the movements used. It is helpful if the coach reminds or confirms the movements that are desired, so both can expect what is to occur. Many coaches would be surprised if they could read the minds of some divers before they perform a dive; for many divers often have little idea of what they are planning to do.

Some coaches prefer to talk to the diver while he or she walks toward the end of the board in the forward approach or while standing backwards on the end of the board in preparation for the take- off. This coaching technique has been questioned by some divers who believe it interferes with their concentration. Others feel that the coach' s comments helps them to develop the same thoughts shared by the coach on how to perform the dive. When divers told me that talking to them when walking on the board interrupted their thinking, I would tell them that I would stop talking when their thinking coincided with mine.

Another time a coach can communicate with the diver is when the diver is performing a dive. This hardly seems possible when the average time a diver is in the air is around one and five eights of a second. Obviously, if the coach is to communicate with the diver in such a brief period of time, the commands need be concise. However short the airborne time, it has been found that the coach can actually control many of the diver's movements with verbal commands that not only improve the diver's performance but also reduce the time needed to learn.

The old cliché, "kick, look, reach" has been used in diving for nearly a century, and is used when a diver is coming out of a somersault in the tuck position and entering the water head first. The movements are performed in sequence with the legs coming out first which diminishes the angular velocity of the somersault by lengthening the body's radius about the horizontal axis. The second move is to search for the water after kicking out with the legs. The third movement is made as the body begins to straighten and the arms extend overhead in preparation for the entry. If these moves are not executed in the proper sequence, the dive is usually performed unsatisfactorily.

When talking to a diver at a precise moment in the dive, the coach may instruct the diver to respond to the command "look", at which time the diver moves the head in a given direction. The diver may or may not respond to the command at first but will learn when he or she becomes used to hearing the command. In this way, the diver develops a "conditioned" response to certain verbal commands. A few other verbal commands are offered here that may enable the coach to communicate better with the diver while in the air:

1. Look - Sight a particular object when in the air or turn the head in a specified direction.

2. Reach - Extend the arms in a given direction such as overhead, toward the water, etc.

3. Stretch - Lengthen the body or a portion thereof when completing a dive in preparation for the entry.

4. Hold on - Remain in the tuck or pike position when performing multiple somersaults or when the diver is passing too close to the board or platform.

5. Out - Release of the legs and the extension of the body when performing a tuck or pike somersault.

6. Squeeze - Tighten the tuck or position when performing a somersault.

7. Square - Place the arms at shoulder level on each side of the body.

Some commands are made for the sound rather than for the meaning of the word or words. Coaches may use different expressions when having divers make particular moves none of which have any identity with the motion of the dive. For example, when I wished a diver to extend the arms overhead when coming out of a particular dive in preparation for a head first entry, I used. the expressions L-5 - which instructed the diver to move the arms late rally, G-4 - calling for the arms to move semi-laterally, S-2 - for the arms to extend and move in front of the body shoulder width apart, and B-3, which meant to draw the hands close to the chest then extend the bent arms overhead. Actually, none of the numbers or letters has anything to do with the desired motion of the arms. The commands were made up by the divers and, at first, I thought it was all a joke until the divers suddenly started to respond to the sounds which made it possible for me to control some of their movements while in the air. Credit can be given for winning several national and international championships by Indiana divers when using this method of communication for nearly thirty years.

Particular credence for this method of verbal cueing occurred at the National Championships in Fort Worth, Texas in 1971. After arriving for the meet, my divers were chided by some of the coaches for using the "L-5 mumbo jumbo," as they called it. At the conclusion of the one-meter event, the Indiana divers had placed first, second, third, fourth, seventh, ninth, and eleventh with only three of the divers on scholarship. As I walked away from the event, I turned to the coaches that had chided us and said "not bad for a bunch of guys using the L-5 mumbo jumbo. Coaches and divers can make up their own verbal commands for directing body movements made in the air. This method of communication, which has been proven, to work, can be very helpful in developing better diving skills and it makes the coaching of diving more entertaining for the divers and the coaches.

The final occasion the coach can communicate with a diver is after the diver has completed the dive. After viewing and analyzing the movements made in the dive, the coach can then discuss the execution of the dive with the diver. The conversation may include suggestions and questions from the diver's view which encourages the diver to think about what happened rather than relying completely on the opinion of the coach.

Overall, there are three different times a coach can communicate with the diver in the performance of a dive and that is before, during, and after the dive is completed. The coach should be aware of the three methods and use all of them as often as possible. The least amount of time the diver receives when communicating with the coach is when the diver is in the air and the coaches should realize its importance.

Some communicative suggestions when coaching:

Coaching twisting dives with the use of the clock image

Starting with the direction in which the diver is facing, assume that the 12 o'clock position is straight in front of the diver when entering the water. If the diver over twists to the left or right, the coach can calculate approximately how much twist occurred and match the amount of twist by the familiar concept of the clock. For example, if the diver should twist around 30 degrees to the right when entering the water, the coach need only say to the diver "12:05." Since a circle is 360 degrees and the diver twisted one twelfth of a circle, the time would be five minutes past twelve. Likewise, if the diver twists 90 degrees to the left, the coach need only say to the diver " 11:45." This way of communicating with a diver is particularly helpful when a coach has a lot of divers at one time for it saves a tremendous amount of time and it offers an accurate correction for the error.

Using hand signals related to distances

When performing dives with forward rotation, it is not desirable for the diver to reach behind the vertical line with the arms when entering the water because such an action will cause the lower part of the body to over-rotate. So, when a diver is performing a dive with little angular momentum, the reach should be about two or three inches in front of the vertical line. But when performing a dive requiring greater t angular momentum, like a 3 ½ somersault, the reach should be a little further in front of the vertical line to account for the additional angular velocity of the rotating body as it enters the water. The coach can inform the diver, before or after the dive is performed, where he or she should reach for the water by holding up the number of fingers that relate to the number of inches the diver should reach in front of vertical when performing the dive. Again, when this system is used for a while, the diver and coach can communicate quickly without discussion which is very helpful when the coach is working with a large number of divers at one time. This action can also be used if the diver has reached behind the vertical line for the water. When this occurs, the coach can flash a certain number of fingers in a downward direction to the diver to indicate that the reach for the water was in the wrong direction.

The three areas of discussion when communicating

Having discussed "when" the diver and coach can communicate, it is now important to consider "what" they talk about when discussing a dive. With some research and observation, I have discovered that the coach's discussions with the divers involved only three issues. . .*period.* One issue involves "movement," such as communicated in comments like "lift the leg, turn the head, squeeze the tuck, do a somersault with a twist, etc." Actually, discussing the diver's movements receives much more attention from the other two issues, that are concerned with "when" and "where" the movements in the dive are to be made. If the diver performs a dive as instructed by the coach and it matches the coach's concept, it would then appear that the diver performed a near perfect dive…at least in the eyes of the coach. However, this may not be the case for if the diver performed every move perfectly, but not at the proper time or in the proper place a flaw in the dive will occur. Like in the game of baseball, if the pitcher delivers a perfect pitch and the batter makes a perfect swing at the ball, nothing occurs if the swing is made when the ball is only halfway to the plate or if the catcher has already caught the ball before the batter swings. In diving, little or no success is accomplished if the diver touches the feet too soon, somersaults too late, dives out too far or close to the board, or any number of other mistakes.

In summary, in the sport of competitive diving: auditory, non-verbal, kinesthetic, and cognitive are the four learning modes of communication that divers have with their instructors, their coaches and themselves. The more the diver and coach know about how to communicate, the better are the chances of success. It is recognized that communication between the diver and coach can be accomplished in many different ways all of which should be considered at all times. It is also recognized that the quantity and quality of the information communicated between the diver and coach can have a proportional effect on the success of their performances.

CHAPTER 11

COMPETITION

According to the dictionary and Thesaurus, the word "competition" simply states to mean "rivalry." To me competition means matching the performance of one with that of another. Competition can range from persons competing with themselves or with something else which could be a person or some other form such as time, space, groups of people, etc.

Competing with someone or for something starts at an early age and continues through our entire lives. Starting from the beginning, a baby begins to compete as soon as it is born by competing for a time to be nursed, fed, and for attention. The time needed for these chores often conflicts with the time father and mother want to spend with each other. This form of competition with the two parent's increases with growth for as the baby develops into childhood; it learns many little tricks that can get the attention of the parents and the things it wants or needs. This is especially seen when in the presence of other children, such as brothers and sisters. Parents normally identify this form of behavior as selfishness when in reality it is a form of competing with one another.

Then when attending grade school, most children immediately begin to compete with others while playing such games on the school playground as skip rope and tag. They also compete in the class room for grades, the attention of the teacher and others, and acceptance and approval of their peers. Competitive behavior also occurs during times before and after school. These competitive patterns are recognized as simple behavior because little if any of the activity is planned. During this period, some youngsters have natural competitive instincts and just dig in and go at while others don't, so they have to be coaxed, badgered, and awarded or motivated in some way to get them to compete. It is also found that the highly competitive children are usually the most popular with their peers.

When the children advance to the middle and high school level, the mode of competition suddenly changes from a simple form to one of complexity. At this level, they participate in sports and other organized activities that involve planning, preparation, strategies, self-control, philosophy, confidence, leadership, loyalty, dedication, self-sacrifice, honestly, etc..."Wow! Quite a change from competing for mom's attention." How well the children respond to such challenges at the higher competitive level depends much on the motivation, confidence, focus, physical and mental preparation, and instruction they receive. A good instructor or coach can direct the competitors to a high state of performance if good communication takes place and the competitor accepts the environment in which he or she is placed.

My oldest daughter decided to go out for the swimming team when she was a little tot and her first competitive race was the fifty-meter breaststroke. Like any father, I was walking along the side of the pool encouraging her to swim faster and when she neared the end of the pool, she suddenly stopped and stood up on the bottom of the pool. A little surprised, I told her to touch the wall for she would take third place and her reply was "Dad, I don't want to beat anybody". When I helped her out of the pool, I told her that I understood, but that was the end of her competitive athletic career. Nancy is now in a business that is very competitive, and I would not wish to compete with her now for she is one of the best in the business. This story is to point out that some people may not be competitive in a certain area or at a certain time in their lives, but suddenly change and become very competitive in another area or at another time. It seems that some are born with a competitive attitude which may blossom at any time or under certain circumstances while others must learn to be competitive with the aid of outside sources.

In sports, one of the big goals when competing is to win, to be number one. But it may be asked just what is really gained by winning and for that matter what is lost or gained by losing? Normally, the athlete who wins has reached a certain transitory goal for the moment and often relaxes and/or becomes complacent over the victory. Self-confidence is certainly maintained or increased but usually the only motivation derived from winning is in trying to win again the next time around. The thought of dominance over others may also be a motivating factor and even addictive, for beating others often provides a sense of being better than the opposition which offers personal satisfaction. One needs only observe Tiger Woods when he is playing well to recognize this point. But what of the loser? Oft times, persons can learn more from losing than in winning for they become more motivated and focused in defeat to take the challenge to win which becomes more pressing and important than ever before. In defeat, the athlete may question his or her abilities, talent, training habits, attitudes, goals, etc. and if self-confidence can be retained, the desire to compete better may improve and be stronger than before. Unfortunately, some become despondent over losing which can affect their entire view of their abilities and talents which may only be temporary, or it may be long lasting. Whatever, the decision as to which way to handle a loss is entirely up to the individual. As a coach, I would often remind my divers when they lost a close contest that it was only a game and even the New York Yankees don't win every game.

Obviously, the desire to compete is based on the individual's wants, needs, and goals. Strangely, it is found that some individuals don't need the aid of others to compete for they will do so within themselves as is seen when they compete against such things as the clock. It is also found that the intensity of the competition often depends on how important the prize or goal is to the one competing. For example, if Notre Dame was to play Ann Arbor High School in a game of football, it is doubtful that the Notre Dame players would be too excited about the contest. They probably would do little preparation for the game and show about as much enthusiasm as when watching the movie "Heidi". Then when looking at Ann Arbor High School, the whole town would probably spend months preparing for the game with great zeal, spirit and excitement. In perspective, the Ann Arbor ball players would be yawning a lot before the game due to fear. Excitement and anxiety while the Notre Dame Players would also be yawning because of boredom and lack of zeal. Thus, the quality of competition for Notre Dame would be very poor and require little motivation while the Ann Arbor team would be highly motivated and feel this to be the greatest game of their lives. Regardless of the outcome of the game and who competes well or poorly, there is going to be a winner and a loser which is very important to those competing at the time. The most important factor is not which team wins or loses, for it is obvious who will win, but how well they perform which will offer more reward or disappointment to the players than anything else. Either way, most will find the activity healthy with the Ann Arbor players and spectators never forgetting the game for the rest of their lives while the Notre Dame players would probably forget the whole episode within a few short days.

Competing in the sport of diving

Naturally, to get a diver into the best possible condition to compete in a contest requires a great deal of preparation. The quality and quantity of the preparation depends much on the kind of program the diver is engaged in at the time. The quality of the diver, the coach, the facility and the environment will decide the success of those who are competitively involved. So, it appears that the key to success depends much on how competitive the diver and coach are, given that the other areas of the program offer a favorable means for reaching their goals.

Preparing a diver to compete

Success in the sport also requires divers to develop certain standards. As is known, people can compete in the sport of diving from a very young age to the time they can no longer walk which is borne out by observing the age group and masters competitive diving programs. When a person wishes to participate in a competitive diving program as a diver or coach they can successfully do so if they address certain conditions.

First, it is suggested that the participant read and discuss the material found in the diving rule book so as to understand how the diving contest is conducted and what is required of them to participate in the various areas of the diving competitions. Those who are involved in the sport for a time are often amazed to find how many of those who compete have never read or studied the rules which is especially noticeable with those in age group programs. The penalty for failing to read the rule book is indicated by the problems and misunderstandings that often occur and disrupt the whole contest. Unfortunately, some will attempt to twist the meaning of the rules around to meet their favor and sometimes get away with it when others have failed to read or check the rules. Not only do some divers not read the rule book, they also depend on their coaches, other divers, and parents to take on many of the responsibilities that are often found in a well-organized competitive program. Such incidents that can and do occur are:

* When they fail to make out the diving sheets and/or turn them in on time or check their list of dives with the coach to make sure they are performing the right dives and in the right order.

* When on trips, the divers neglect or forget to call their parents to inform them where They are and how they can be contacted in case of an emergency.

* Fail to get directions to the pool site.

* Arrive at the pool late and find their event already in progress.

* Fail to check the times for practice sessions.

* Neglect to pick up credentials and passes for getting into the pool.

* Fail to bring money for food.

* Forget to check the time or place of the teams meeting.

* Fail to check out of the hotel where they are staying.

* Forget or neglect to inform their parents when and where to pick them up upon returning home.

Some, but not all of the incidents that occur to divers in preparation for a competition are the responsibility of the coach. Some can be blamed on the divers and parents due to the pressures caused by the meet. But, regardless of who is to blame, the divers should be taught to accept responsibilities that not only simplify their involvement in the sport, but also make it better for others participating in the sport.

Divers should give themselves ample time to get to the pool before a contest. This is not a problem for those who do not wish to practice or to watch the swimmers compete in conference or championship meets. Not having ample time to practice or get used to a different facility can be a problem when competing away from home in a dual meet and the team arrives a short time before the meet. Divers should anticipate this problem and be prepared to practice as soon as possible when arriving at the site, so they can have time to select the dives to be performed in the meet. In some meet, when the divers are not going to do any more than warm up prior to the contest, they should not arrive at the pool any sooner than an hour before their contest so as to not stand around for any length of time waiting for the meet to start.

It is suggested that the coach and divers who are competing in championship meets arrive on the site no sooner than three days before they perform. This suggestion is made from experience. Divers seem to tire and get stale before competing which is caused by practicing more than normal or diving four or five days at the site prior to the meet Being around the opposition for a long period of time also makes it difficult to hold a psychological edge which often diminishes after watching the other diver's practice. Divers should not dive more than normal during this time to avoid fatigue and allow mental preparation.

Most divers associated with an age group or high school program, usually have some idea of what to expect when preparing for a contest. However, since the season is devoted to getting the divers into the best condition possible to compete in important meets that are usually staged near the end of the season, some preparation is necessary which includes:

Physical preparation

Divers will rarely perform well when not in good physical condition, so this is a very important goal for divers to meet before competing in important contests. Such physical training requires exercises and activities that are conducive to their physical needs and should be performed consistently and in different stages of intensity which are determined by the kind and importance of the meet. The training should be well planned and organized with suitable resting periods to allow the body to rejuvenate itself and help avoid injuries. Over training can be disastrous when trying to copy the training methods used by others such as the Chinese and Russians.

Psychological and mental preparation

The coach is in the best position to get the divers into the best physical, mental, psychological and spiritual condition possible to compete in meets. Though the coach cannot solve all of the problems that confront divers from time to time, he or she is closer to the divers than anyone else so is the one who can motivate, persuade, and lead them as far as possible in their quest for success.

To encourage the divers to compete to the best of their abilities requires them to first form certain goals that are realistic and well within the range of their abilities. The goals should be based on the quality and competitive level of the competitions in which the divers will participate. When divers and coaches set goals beyond reality, the goals become nothing more than dreams or fantasy. The next step is for them to develop a positive attitude that relates to their willingness to pay the price needed to fulfill their goals. The price to be paid is by taking part in well planned physical workouts that require continuous disciplined efforts. It also includes sacrificing activities that interfere with training, giving up junk food in favor of a healthy diet, and missing the Friday night parties in order to get a good night's rest before a Saturday competition.

Divers should realize that they will not perform well in every training session and should accept adverse conditions as part of their training experience. Controlling the temper, being disciplined, and acknowledging training standards, working out with intensity while showing patience are all very important when attempting to meet the intended goals. When things don't go well, it is best to back off and change the setting by engaging and focusing on some other part of the program. They can spend more time doing line ups for better entries, practicing approaches on the dry land board, doing more conditioning exercises in the areas of weakness, watch video tapes of themselves and others, etc. If the diver feels stress and pressure when training, it may be best to walk away from the activity for a short time like a day or two, and then return with a good relaxed and positive attitude.

Divers with a positive attitude and personality will not only generate a positive approach to diving but also give a positive affect to others on the team. To illustrate this point, years ago, one of my top divers who was basically moody at times, came into the pool for practice with his head hung low and with an attitude like he had just flunked out of school. When he approached me, I asked him if he could read the sign above the door at the other end of the pool and he replied that the sign read "exit". Pointing at the door, I then told him to obey the sign. After going through the same routine for two or three days, he went to his teammates and complained about his situation with me and was very upset for he wasn't able to practice. Finally, one of his teammates suggested that maybe I didn't like his attitude. The next day, he came into the pool whistling and gave me a friendly greeting which I acknowledged and told him to start practice. At the end of the workout, he came to me and asked why I had him miss all those days and not let him practice. I explained to him that whenever a leader like him came into the pool displaying such a poor and negative attitude, the whole team would be affected resulting in a poor practice for everyone...including the coach. I also stated that I would not tolerate such a bad attitude and if he didn't change, he could stay out of the pool... and maybe for good. That was the last of his negative entrances when coming to practice and when performing in any meets.

It is not a very good idea for a diver to encourage the opposition to beat him or her when competing. Divers do not help themselves by clapping for the opposition who has just performed an outstanding dive. Divers may think they are displaying good sportsmanship and showing all that are present that he or she is a good sport. Frankly, no one cares what kind of sport the diver is in the middle of the contest. To me, as a coach, any diver who encourages the opposition in any way wants the other diver to win.

A few years ago, one of my divers at the Big 10 Championships suddenly got up from sitting next to me on the bench in the middle of the contest and ran around to the other side of the pool to congratulate an opposing diver for performing a great dive. When he returned to sit next to me again, I congratulated him for losing the Big 10

Championships. When he asked why I would say sucha thing, I told him that in making sucha blatantmove he had just told everyone in the pool that he wanted the other diver to win...which he did by a very narrow margin. The rationale for my comments is based on the fact that nowhere have I ever attended a contest where everyone stood up and cheered when the opposing football team scored a touchdown or won the game. Ialso have never heard of a boxer after getting smacked in the nose, stop in the middle of the fight to congratulate the opposition for the blow that just broke his nose. In such cases, they wait until the fight is over to congratulate each other for a great fight and this also goes for divers.

A diver who displays a bad temper when competing has an excellent chance of losing. Slapping the water when surfacing or throwing a towel down on the pool deck, glaring at the judge for giving a low score, climbing out of the pool with a scowl on the face is no way to encourage good scores from the judges. One who loses it should go into the locker room with no one around and regain composure before returning to the pool.

Being a good team member is important because it encourages everyone on the team to develop a positive attitude and give more of themselves. Nearly everyone performs better when they know their team is behind them. Normally, the success of a team depends much on how unselfish, loyal, and dedicated the members are on the team to the coach. When a team member breaks such a bond, it affects the whole team which more often than not results in failure to win. Being a team member when competing in a national or international meet can be difficult for it is not possible for a diver to be at the pool for a long period of time to cheer for his or her teammates from day to day without losing the edge to compete. It makes sense that divers on a team are at a meet where the events are strung out for a long period of time, not spend much time in the pool area. It is not possible for one to walk into the pool with a good psychological edge and maintain it while sitting around the pool watching others for days and expect to compete well. Divers should realize that once an edge is built up for an important engagement and it is lost, it takes a long time to regain another edge. Team member or not, I would recommend that three days of practice at the site before competing in an important meet is enough. Any other time should be used for resting and/or staying away from the site so as not to lose the psychological edge to compete well.

Teaching a diver to be mentally and psychologically prepared to compete in a contest is much more difficult than trying to work a diver into top physical condition. Once a diver has developed good physical condition, retaining such condition throughout the rest of the season is rarely an issue. This is not so when working with diver's heads for their mental and psychological state can change instantly or change several times during a season. To correct such changes that hinder the diver's mental or psychological state requires a lot of time, understanding, effort, and patience. I have not only seen changes occur during the season, but sometimes right in the middle of a dive in a contest. Such a change happened to Scott Downey, the silver medal winner in the 1992 Olympic Games in Barcelona, when in the middle of a hand stand dive at the Goodwill Games in

Texas a year later, he suddenly came down from the controlled position and walked down off the ten-meter tower and scratched from the contest offering no clue as to what had happened. With his mother sitting right behind us judges, she asked him what happened, and he stated that he no longer had any interest in diving tower. That was the last time he ever dived tower. Thankfully, he went on with his springboard diving and took fourth place at the 1996 Olympics in Atlanta. Strange that he would change his mind in the middle of a dive when competing in such an important contest.

On occasion, divers will prepare to compete in a meet only to suddenly realize that they are unable to perform a particular dive which usually is some sort of twisting somersault dive. This usually occurs when the diver is uncertain of oneself and feels the pressure of failure mount to the point where it develops great fear develops. Most of these mental blocks take a long time to overcome... if ever. What causes a diver to "psych out" is not really known except most occur when a diver is competing under anxiety, fear, or great pressure. Such situations often cause the divers to go "vertical" which means they become light headed and don't know up from down when in the air.

Another example of over doing it occurred to two of the most dedicated divers in the country. In their attempt to train for the up-coming Olympic Games, they decided to train as hard as the Chinese divers which meant they were going at it seven or eight hours a day. I had the chance to observe their training enthusiasm while attending a clinic in Florida and decided to offer some advice. I told them that they were not Chinese and could not possibly train like them since the Chinese begin their strenuous training at a very young age. I continued by saying that if they continued, to try and train like the Chinese, the body would eventually break down which could be for a temporary or long period of time. I then suggested that they take a long rest period to allow their bodies to rejuvenate, making it clear that the rest shouldn't be for a day or two but rather for a week or more. They ignored my comments and a short time later, one developed vertigo and the other dislocated a shoulder which put them both out of commission for nearly a year.

Any change in the environment that relates to a diver's preparation to compete normally does not affect his or her physical condition unless an injury occurs. However, any happening in the environment can change the mental and psychological make-up of the diver without warning. Usually the diver has no clue as to what caused the change or what could be done to change it. Most of these times, the change in the diver's mental state is unintentional with no thought of hindering a performance. Then there are times when incidents happen, or comments are made that *are* intentional to "psych out" an opponent. Such comments as "In what direction do you twist?" Or, "what a shame that you are having so much trouble with your hurdle", or worse yet when in the middle of a contest a person comments, "that crow hop you have is just killing your scores too bad", are obviously unfair and damaging to nearly any diver but they do occur. Such damaging remarks have often shook-up divers to the point where they lost their competitive composure causing them to perform poorly or even change to their list to perform easier dives.

Incidents such as being embarrassed or yelled by the coach or embarrassing a diver in front of everyone, the coach playing favorites while ignoring other teammates at an important meet, or finding another diver wearing his or her clothes or swim suit when told not to, have upset divers to a point that it has greatly interfered with their diving performance. Witnessing another diver get injured by landing flat on the water or hitting the diving board also does little to improve the mental and psychological state of a diver in a meet. Such occurrences often confuse or create fear for a diver which can affect his or her performance which makes it questionable if a diver should watch the other divers perform during the contest.

It has already been mentioned that coaches sometimes push a diver's button, and causes the diver to respond with an outstanding performance. Pushing someone's button means that the coach makes a comment to a diver before a dive or sometime during the meet that motivates the diver to give a good performance. Years ago, one of my divers placed eighty-third on the one- meter board at the National Collegiate Championships at Brown University. Not displaying my normal reaction to such a poor performance, my comment to him was "well Brian, you at least beat one diver. I know that you will do better tomorrow on the three-meter board". The next evening, he won the three-meter contest which astounded everyone present...including me. The next year, Brian was defending his title in the same meet staged at Cleveland State University and was several points behind the leader going into his last dive. Needing no less than nines on a triple twisting one-and-a-half somersault, I tried to figure out what I could say to motivate him into giving a great performance. After some thought, I confronted him just before the dive and told him that everyone who saw him win the title the year before after taking eighty-third on the low board believed it was a "fluke". I then asked him if it he really thought it was a fluke and walked away. He scored nine and half points from five of the seven judges and won the contest.

It is not uncommon for divers to perform miserably before an important contest then get up and perform one the best lists of dives in their career. On the other hand, some divers, in fact a whole team may dive like gold medalists in practice before a big meet then land all over the pool in the meet. What causes such changes in a performance, especially in such a short period of time, is a real mystery for both the divers and the coach.

All of these incidents are not to say that the coach cannot teach a diver how to mentally and psychologically prepare to compete, but it does indicate that no matter how well a diver is prepared there is no guarantee that his or her performance will be favorable. However, it can be said that a diver who is physically, mentally, and psychologically prepared to compete has a much better chance of performing well than one who is not prepared.

In most cases, the divers look to their coach for direction, motivation, confidence, assurance, compassion, and favorable instruction that will assure them of a good performance. Positive reinforcement will help a diver in one incident only to have no affect at another time regardless of how much assurance is offered. Likewise, a diver may respond favorably to negative reinforcement in one instance but crash when placed in a similar situation at another time. Oft times, no assistance at all will offer a better or worse performance from the diver. So, the dilemma is how, when, and where should a coach attempt to prepare the diver's mental and psychological state for an up-coming contest. As has been mentioned before, if coaches knew the answer to that question, they all would be wizards.

Competitive anxiety

Studies have shown that a competitive environment creates competitive anxiety and stress on those who engage in some form of competitive activity. This emotional state experienced by divers is usually caused by the uncertainty they put on themselves and the intensity they attach to contests in which they take part. The uncertainty the diver feels can be created not only from within himself or herself but also from many different sources which includes the input from other people. Since the coach is the closest person to the diver when competing, he or she can unintentionally install uncertainty within the diver, particularly when both coach and diver are under stress and pressure at the same time. The coach can lose control when in such a state and make negative comments or remarks to the diver that are damaging, ambiguous, or misunderstood, which may cause a poor performance from the diver. A similar response can occur when the coach unintentionally creates an incident that, under normal conditions, would be overlooked by the diver. Such incidents as leaving a diver home when going to an away meet, not greeting the diver's parents when they visit, showing no concern for a diver's scholastic difficulties, etc. can cause damage to the diver-coach relationship. Therefore, parents, coaches, and teammates should be careful on how they treat divers who are preparing for a meet because they can cause divers to be uncertain of themselves through poor communication.

The reaction to competitive stress placed on the diver and coach

Divers react in many different ways when competing in a meet and particularly in major meets. The difference in the anxiety and intensity felt by the diver and the way they react to such pressures depends much on how important the meet is to them. This was observed at a national championship one time when the winner of the contest was between two of my divers. On the last dive I noticed one my other divers, who wasn't very talented, appeared to be just as excited about performing his last dive, as was the other two top divers. When he placed twenty seventh, I suddenly realized that his last dive was just as important to him as it was to the two champions.

When divers compete, and the outcome is questionable, it is at that moment that some become aware that they are comparing their abilities with those of others. Others don't appear to be aware of the pressure created by the meet but still react in many different ways. Some divers bite their fingernails, chew their towels, listen to music, read a book, hide from others, seek out a teammate or friend, etc. Whatever their reactions, most athletes experience competitive anxiety and stress that cause mental and psychological changes and react in their own way.

Showing how emotional stress can affect the performance of a diver is seen when one of the divers from Indiana University made the 1963 Pan American team along with two of his teammates. He was a good diver from Canada but had never made the finals in any big meets such as the Big " 10", the N.C.A.A. or the A.A.U. national championships. Therefore, nothing was expected of him when competing in this prestigious meet. After having a terrible week of practice in San Paulo, South America, he totally lost his confidence the day before the meet and worked himself into such a state that he was going to scratch from the meet and go back to Indiana. His two teammates managed to talk him out of leaving and told him he had nothing to lose by competing, so he decided to give it a shot the next day. He astonished everyone by not missing a single dive and won the gold medal by beating his two teammates who were second and third. That was the only time in his entire career that he made the finals in an important meet and ever beat his two teammates Incidentally, his gold medal was the first ever won by a Canadian in an international contest.

Similar incidents occurred to Lesley Bush at the 1964 Olympics, and Bernie Wrightson and Sue Gossick at the 1968 Olympics when all three had given up on themselves and believed that they were going to disgrace their country, their families, their teammates, their coaches, and themselves. Fortunately, all three did a complete reversal in their mental state within a very short time before their events and went on to win the Olympic gold. These reversals had nothing to do with their parents, teammates, coaches, the environment or any other noticeable outside influence. It appears that the change came from within when all of the pressure, tension, anxiety, and fear had suddenly exploded and was released after being cropped up inside of them for a long period of time. Such a release permitted them to become stable and focus on their dives with control and confidence when they were put under great stress. In one lasting example, Mark Lenzi was given a negative remark from a television commentator just before competing on the three-meter springboard in the 1992 Olympics in Barcelona that disturbed him so much that he changed his whole competitive attitude just before competing which made it possible for him to win the gold medal.

It is often difficult for a coach to recognize or identify the stress a diver experiences when under pressure for some show no signs of anxiety at all. Others may have little or no pressure placed on them when competing but may suddenly react to fear brought on by the uncertainty of what may happen to them during a dive. All and all, regardless of how experienced or educated a coach may be, recognizing the quality and quantity of the competitive anxiety a diver may be experiencing in a competition is very difficult. However, it does help a coach to know which divers compete well when thriving on the pressure and the importance of the competition and which have great difficulty performing under similar conditions.

A recent study showed that only ten percent of a group of high school diving coaches could recognize any form of anxiety experienced by their divers before a diving contest. Most coaches will admit that there is no worse feeling than watching a well-prepared diver suddenly fall apart under pressure. However, some of the pressure may be reduced in practice sessions. For example, with most divers repeating the performance of dives several times in practice, the coach might select a practice where after a short warm up, the divers have only one attempt to perform the dives they will use in a meet which should be done before the practice session.

Preparing a strategy

When preparing to dive in competition, divers should know what dives need be performed that will match the degrees of difficulty of the dives performed by the opposition. It doesn't take long for divers to realize that if they use easier dives than their opponents, the chances of winning the contest are slim no matter how well they perform the dives. Therefore, when the divers decide which dives need to be changed, they should prepare to do so as quickly as possible by:

* Selecting the lead up dives for each dive to be learned by becoming familiar with and learning the sequential moves that are involved in performing the dive.
* Deciding whether or not they have the ability to successfully perform the dive based on their physical strength and power.
* Checking to see if the necessary teaching aids and facilities needed to learn the desired dives are available. The teaching aids may include the trampoline, dry land equipment, the bubbler, a one meter and three-meter springboard, and an instructor or coach who is familiar with the correct performance of the dive.

Following the first dive, the diver gradually works toward the dives that may be questionable to perform well. The diver should then finish the competition with a dive that can best put him or her in a position to win. From experience, female divers may consider performing some other dive other than an inward 2 ½ somersault, tuck from the three-meter competition as their last dive in a competition. From what I have seen, most divers in the past got so wound up to perform the dive, that they over rotated on the entry which cost them an Olympic medal.

Competing in a contest involves more than just climbing up on the board or platform. It is important that divers perform their dives in a strategic order which may be different from diver to diver. Since most divers are a little nervous and not yet settled down for the contest, starting with a competent dive that offers the most consistency helps the diver settle down for the competition and establish a favorable impression on the diving judges. Psychologically, it is best for a diver to start the contest with a dive that he or she has the most confidence in performing well. they should make a good start by performing the dive they perform with the most consistency and performing a list of dives because the order in which the dives are performed has much to do with the diver' s success in the performance. The order of dives may change from diver to diver because of the certainty and confidence the diver places on the dives to be performed. Since some divers get nervous when they begin to perform in the contest, they may consider using a dive that can be done with the most consistency, confidence and assurance. From experience, I would suggest a diver select a dive from the forward or inward groups because the back and reverse groups of dives are usually less consistent to perform well. Dives from the twisting group also do not usually score well from the judges at the beginning of a contest. If a choice from one of the two groups mentioned can be made without reservation, I would suggest performing a dive from the forward group because it usually offers more controlled action than dives performed from the other groups. However, if a diver has any difficulty in performing a good hurdle, the diver should consider performing a dive from the inward group which requires a backward take off.

Several national and international contests have been won by Indiana divers by placing the dives in the order that offered them their best performance. This was found to be particularly effective in meets that required a preliminary, semi-finals and a final. When the divers had to qualify by performing well in the semi-final round to make the finals, none of my divers ever performed the back and reverse somersault dives in the preliminary or semi-finals because, percentage wise, dives from these two groups proved to be the easiest to miss. It was found that when divers saved their best dives for the finals, they usually watched the finals from the bleachers. Again, divers should perform the dives with the highest degree of difficulty that can be performed with the most consistency first so as to be sure of making the cut and the finals.

The psychology used in selecting the best dive as the first dive is for the diver to perform a dive that shows the judges the most confidence, assurance, and consistency. Performing the best dive first also reduces the nervousness often possessed by the diver that usually dwindles as the contest progresses. Another reason for starting the contest with a good dive is to make a good impression on the judges the first time around. If a diver starts the contest by performing a poor dive, good scores from the judges will not be given which may occur on the divers next dive since he didn't impress anyone on the first dive. Missing the first dive also results in the diver losing self-confidence right from the beginning which is difficult to recapture throughout the contest.

The second dive to be performed in the contest should also be a dive that the diver feels he or she can perform well with little difficulty. This dive may be followed by the weakest dive in the diver's list for the diver has now lost most of the nervousness while retaining the strength and power to perform the dive. This dive could also be used as the last dive in the divers list where it offers more of a challenge to the diver to perform it well. The fourth dive should be a dive that gives the diver little concern in performing it poorly which is then followed with the fifth and/or sixth dive which is normally twisting somersault dives. Performing these dives at the end of the contest usually score better than when used earlier in the contest. Remember, I offer these suggestions based on sixty some years of experience which may not be agreed to by others.

To better show this point, one year, the best diver on my team who was an Olympian decided to use a back 2 ½ somersault as an optional dive in the semi-finals of the N.C.A.A. championships so that he could have a more consistent list of dives for the finals. I told him I was totally against this strategy because it was possible for him to miss the dive and not qualify. After his constant plea to do the dive, I finally consented which resulted in the only time in his career he ever missed diving in the finals of any meet while attending Indiana University. You can be assured that I made it real plain to him who was coaching our diving team after that little episode.

It has also been proven that executing the same dive over and over in practice does little to guarantee an improvement in the consistency of the dive. Once the diver has performed the dive three or four times, further practice of the dive only makes the errors of the dive more effective and that much more difficult to correct. By performing a dive three or four times the diver can also conserve more time and energy to complete the full list of dives that are to be used in competition.

Divers should also understand that performing in an important meet is not the time to gamble on a dive that could be easily performed poorly. Some divers believe that though they miss the dive three or four times out of five attempts in practice they will be more apt to successfully perform the dive in the meet because of the added supply of energy to challenge themselves in successfully performing the dive-- wrong. In most cases, though on occasion they do perform the dive successfully, they will not perform the dive any better than what was done in practice. More clearly a diver, who can complete a forward 2 ½ somersault dive only two times out of five performances in practice, will likely not complete the dive in a meet. But if the diver can perform the dive four out of five times, then there is a good chance the diver will successfully perform the dive well in the meet. The diver must learn to play the percentages in his or her favor and not gamble unless they are willing to accept the consequences. This means, that in some situations, it is better to perform an easier dive well, than to perform a difficult dive poorly.

It is also suggested that divers perform the more difficult dives early in work outs while they still have the energy and strength. Practicing very difficult dives near the end of a workout when becoming fatigued can be psychologically and physically damaging to the divers. Another suggestion concerns the attitude of a diver after poorly performing a dive in a contest. Anything can happen in any contest and the diver should never give up on himself or herself for "all" of the divers could miss a dive. This has occurred in two Olympic Games when the favorites of the contest missed a dive badly and opened the door for the other divers who also could have missed a dive but the chances of winning or placing well were realistic. Cynthia Potter, winner of 28 National championships, missed an optional dive for twos in two different Olympic tryouts, but came back to make the Olympic team both times because she refused to give up on herself. The point is "don't quit trying" for no one knows what the opposition will do.

Divers should focus on one dive at a time in a contest. Once a dive is performed, the diver should immediately begin to focus on the next dive to be performed rather than dwell on the performance of the dive just executed. In watching coaches comment on a dive his or her diver has just performed in the meet has always confused me for nothing can be changed or gained by thinking about the dive just done. However, a lot can be gained by thinking about the dive that is to be done in the next round of dives. Finally, it is well not to watch the opponents' dives or listen to the scores given because it can often affect one's performance.

The following is an article presented in part to a group of American Olympic hopefuls at a training session. The coaches requested that I write this article to better prepare the divers in readiness for the up-coming Olympic tryouts. Since most of the information given to them has already been discussed in this book, a couple of excerpts are offered that may be helpful to you when preparing your divers for an important contest.

Getting Ready to Compete in A Major Diving Competition

This presentation is given with the purpose of improving what is above your shoulders more than what is below them by trying to get you mentally, psychologically, and spiritually prepared to give a top performance in a major diving contest that is coming up soon. It is recognized that us coaches cannot solve all of the problems that can guarantee you a top performance in these meets for if we could do that, we would all be Gods. However, we are here to give you some guidance and a few tips for you to consider that may lead you on to a successful competition.

Coach's believe that you are physically ready to compete in almost any meet at hand, but from experience, we have some concern about whether or not you are mentally and psychologically prepared to take on the task of giving a top performance in a major meet. We wonder if you are willing to take the next step which is to develop an attitude to not only make the Olympic team and win a medal, but to win the gold. As you know, we have drastically fallen from the depths of supremacy in international competition to a position where we have won a slew of fourth places and have been close, but not close enough, to break into the medal arena. So, we are gathered here to see if we can create some realistic goals and plan what it will take to obtain them. Coach's believe that several of you could actually go all the way if you put your mind to it and do all that you can to prepare for it. If our objective is to medal or win the Olympic gold medal, then let's take a good look at what it will entail to make it possible to go all the way.

First it is realized that you divers are going to have to be in the best physical condition possible. This means you have to be flexible, strong and explosive, and develop an endurance that will withstand long training periods which are needed to succeed.

Secondly, you must realize that you have to perform the difficult dives that are needed to win. This has been a major problem when performing in major contests in the past, but we have gone far since then to resolve the problem. You must also be aware of the amount of time that you have to perfect such dives and if you cannot match the difficult dives performed by the opposition, then your chances of beating them are slim to none.

Thirdly, you will have to learn to perform all of the dives with consistency. This does not mean that you must perform all of the dives perfectly, but it does mean that you cannot blow a dive and expect to win. You can be a little off on a dive and still have a good chance of placing high or winning but a real miss is fatal. The important point here is to not give up on you no matter how bad things appear. Two of our best divers had a very poor performance in the last Olympic preliminary round but did not quit on themselves and, because they performed some of their difficult dives well, were able to qualify for the finals and go on to win a medal.

Strategy

It is also important that you make up your mind to make the team and even the finals "now". If you do not make such a decision now, it is highly unlikely that you will walk into the meet with a positive attitude. Everything you do every day up to the time of that meet is important. This means you train hard, rest a lot, eat the right foods, avoid activities that can disrupt your training schedule, etc. In other words, you must make certain sacrifices and begin to physically, mentally, and psychologically prepare yourself for the big show. Obviously, it is extremely difficult to stay focused on one objective for such a time, but this all depends on how much you want it. Warning: do not let this objective get completely out of hand. You have to accept this quest while remaining in control of your anxiety, staying calm and relaxed as you train for the big days ahead.

We all know that your outside interests may or may not influence your training habits or your competitive attitude. A broken love affair, failing in school, or a death in the family are some examples of problems that may occur, but these have to be handled only by you and must be separated from what you are trying to accomplish. Not easy, but necessary.

Though some of you dive springboard and tower that may include synchronized diving, you might consider focusing on one event with the possibility of including synchronized diving in order to obtain the best possible performance in a major meet. China and Russia are leaning toward this scenario with divers competing in no more than two events, with a few exceptions, so they can focus and practice with greater intensity to obtain a certain objective.

It is also helpful if you do the list of dives each day that you plan to perform in the meet and keep a log of what dives give you the most trouble and dives that score well. If you do this daily, you should have well over a 150 scoring lists which would certainly point out your weak and strong dives.

Training

Set up a training program that is realistic, well planned, organized, and within your abilities. You must plan to train hard, but it is very important that you also take time off to rest and let your body maintain a normal state. Taking a few days off from time to time will not hurt you. The coaches realize that training all the time is not much fun and can eventually burn you out, so they will keep a close watch on you.

If you are on a team, you must learn to carry your load which includes team unity, being a good team member, cooperate with your peers and coaches, and stick together to help one another while still seeking out your own individuality. One member on the team can upset the whole group which can even affect a diver's performance. When everyone pitches in to help, then everyone has a good time which promotes a good positive atmosphere. One selfish inconsiderate member on the team can cause damage to the behavior of the whole diving program. Though being a team member, it is suggested that you train at the site of the meet no longer than three days before competing so that you can retain a good competitive edge. Any longer has been found to be psychologically damaging.

Before and during the meet

Some divers prefer to be alone and spend time with themselves during the meet while others like to be with another diver. To be truthful from a coach' s view, it is extremely difficult to know how to handle some divers when nearing an important meet. What makes a diver give a top performance at a given time cannot be predicted so we coach's try to be very careful on how to handle certain divers at that time. Pampering a diver to death may not result in the diver performing well any more than being tough with a diver. There simply is no way to consistently motivate a diver to perform well so we, as coaches try the best we can to help. As a coach, it is probably best for us to be as we always are and not disrupt a diver's focus on the meet.

Since everyone is keyed up for the meet, it is suggested that the coach avoid making waves over trivial things that cause unneeded concern with the divers such as being late for practice, forgetting your diving trunks, etc. This is the time to avoid that kind of stress. Some divers like to warm up before a meet while others do not. This is a time when the coach should let the diver decide what he or she wishes to do in preparation for the contest which may change from time to time.

Conduct of the coach and diver during a competition

Personally, when attending major diving contest, I always gathered the divers together and told them where I would be during the contest and if they wished my aid, to come to me for suggestions. I would tell them to remember that I taught them to "think" how to perform a dive and now that I had done my job, it was time for them to do theirs. I also made comments like the following to prepare them for a competition.

* Know what motivates you.

* Focus on the sequential moves you wish to do when performing the dive.

* Do not anticipate how to perform any future dives and forget the dives you have already performed. Focus on the next dive to be performed.

* The last thing you can do once you visualize the dive, is to let go and let the body do the dive.

* When performing the dive, try to duplicate exactly what you have been doing in practice. No changes need be made unless suggested by me.

CHAPTER 12

SAFETY AWARENESS IN COMPETITIVE DIVING

The following two statements offered by United States Diving clearly point out the level of safety eminent in the teaching and performing of diving at the recreational and competitive levels. These two comments alone stand far and above any that can be made by other contact sports such as gymnastics, soccer, cheerleading, ice skating, football, basketball, etc. It is also quite clear that every measure is being taken by those in competitive diving to make it possible for anyone who wishes to dive competitively to do so with confidence and assurance while safely enjoying the sport.

"In over a hundred years of competitive diving in the United States, there is no record of a catastrophic injury connected with any supervised training session or diving competition."

"Competitive diving has suffered from a poor image through the association with accidents involving a dive into the water but has no connection with the sport itself."

Those who become active in diving quickly learn that it is a contact sport that has the body projected into the air where it makes certain maneuvers before plunging downward until making contact with the water. The manner in which the body enters the water has much to do with the success and comfort the diver experience when performing the dive. It doesn't take long for the
diver to recognize that water seeks its own level which presents a flat surface. If the diver makes contact with the surface with the body extended in a horizontal position, the outcome is usually painful which means "flat on flat equals pain." When such occasions occur, the diver suddenly becomes susceptible to taking instruction more seriously than before the mishap.

It is important to note that hitting the diving board or the bottom of the pool rarely causes serious injury to those who are safety conscious of the hazards involved and have received proper instruction in protecting themselves when in harm's way. Great improvements to diving boards and diving pools have led to a huge decrease in these types of occurrences. When the change from wooden to aluminum diving boards occurred in the early 1950s, the new boards not only offered more spring but also made it possible for them to be mounted at a level plane without cocoa matting (due to a new process of baking a non-skid material on the surface of the board). Leveling the boards made it easier for divers to dive away from the end of the board, making it a rarity to strike it. The present diving boards are extremely flexible and if a diver should hit the board, it absorbs the force applied and reduces the possibility of injury. However, divers can receive a cut or abrasion when contacting the edge of the board. Most diving areas are now deep enough to prevent anyone from hitting the bottom with any great force. The bubbler has also reduced the impact of a diver hitting flat on the surface of the water to such a degree that pain is nearly eliminated.

Such new developments have brought about a great reduction in diving accidents. With so few diving coaches in the world prior to World War II, diving received little guidance in developing safety habits. Since then, instruction by well qualified teachers and coaches is available for those diving at nearly any competitive level. However, many more qualified instructors and coaches in safety education are still needed.

When Greg Louganis hit his head on the end of the 3-meter board performing a reverse 2 ½ somersault pike at the 1988 Olympics in Seoul, North Korea, had he hit the board three or four inches back, the impact may have been enough to cause death. Instead, the injury was minor due to the flexibility of the board which allowed him to continue to dive and win the contest. Unfortunately, the media played up the accident by showing the incident over and over for years which has done little to convince people that competitive diving is not a dangerous sport. I have been in the sport for 65 years and know of only two deaths that involved competitive diving which is a lot less than those that have occurred playing table tennis.

Despite Louganis' s unfortunate accident, exposure of diving through the media, television, video, and the movies along with the great expansion of competitive diving for all age ages, has created a great interest in diving where more and more people wish to participate in the activity. They are beginning to realize that anyone, from the tiny tot to the senior citizen, with some physical ability, and proper instruction, can safely engage in an activity with little or no fear. Teaching aids used today can guide those who wish to perform challenging dives, that at times caused pain, to where the chance of injury is minimal. Diving can offer much to the individual in developing creativity, emotional soundness, concentration, the control and understanding of fear, a challenge to oneself, a sense of accomplishment, self-esteem, confidence, a respect for the sport, an opportunity to participate in a social activity, and experience the thrill of success or the agony of defeat to mention only a few. Like people who drive automobiles, fly airplanes or make hundreds of parachute jumps in a life time without a single mishap, diving can be safer when developing sound safety habits.

Starting with the beginner and advancing to the expert, when passing through the learning stages of competitive diving, many physical, emotional, mental, psychological, and social experiences occur that can offer success or disappointment to the diver from time to time. Naturally, the intent of any person diving is to improve their performance and enjoy the experience which can be obtained if the diver practices with some consistency, determination, and safety in mind. In doing so, it becomes apparent that the safer the diver feels when diving, the more enjoyable the activity becomes.

Actually, all of the dangers in diving can be found in two areas and it is important that they be recognized and understood.

1. **Facilities** - the kind and condition of the facilities available can greatly affect the safety of the diver. Some of these include:

   A. Diving equipment

      Diving stands - Stands should be sturdy and well serviced. Lose, rusted, and faulty parts such as the fulcrums, railings, anchor bolts, and board hinges should be checked out at given times during the season. Maintenance concerning the cleaning fulcrum parts, the fulcrum tracks, greasing the roller clamp, lock nut, anti-rattle lock nuts, and the fittings of the roller every two weeks.

      Diving boards - The manager should inspect the surface of the board at the beginning of each season to make sure it is in good non-skid condition. He should also check for cracks in the board which would indicate that the board is broken. The cause for the board to be slippery is found when dirt is gathered from the environment including weather, excessive wear from years of use, and excessive alkalinity or excessive minerals in the water. It is suggested that the board be taken out of service if it becomes slippery and contact the manufacturer or Joe Greenwell in Brandin, Florida, to have it resurfaced. Do not try to paint the board with sand because it does not work. The extruded rubber channels on the underside of the board should be inspected for wear monthly. Do not use the board if a rubber channel is missing because the board will break. Change the channel that exposes metal wear. The hinges at the anchor end of the board should receive two drops of #10 oil every two weeks.

   B. Water

      Depth -The safety of a person diving into the water has much to do with its depth Years ago, most swimming pools were seven or eight feet deep which then appeared to be a satisfactory depth for one- and three-meter springboard diving. However, as the diving boards and diving stands improved and projected the dives higher into the air. Deeper pools were needed to prevent divers from smashing into the bottom. It appears that diving boards and diving stands have reached a point where no further improvement is needed. Therefore, the standard depths required to dive from the springboard and diving tower as listed in all diving rulebooks, will likely not need to be adjusted. Depths of pools that follow these standards rarely have any accidents that relate to the bottom of the pools.

Pool bottom - The shape of the pool bottom can offer unsafe diving circumstances, especially when the incline from the deep end to the shallow water end is sharp. This steep incline is particularly dangerous in the area directly in front of the diving boards, so divers often scoop the entry in a forward direction when entering the water. Drains should never be never be placed directly in front of the board or tower for it is possible for divers to get a finger caught in the drain. Sharp tiles or any articles on the bottom of the pool should be removed if possible. Divers can spot better if some sort of marking, such as longitudinal lane lines for swimming lanes or some sort of logo, is displayed on the pool bottom.

Water environment - Wherever there is diving activity, swimming lanes, life lines, rafts or boats in outside areas such as lakes, should be far enough away from the diving area to create a safety hazard. Slippery decks around swimming areas, reflection on the water from outside lighting, outdoor weather conditions, poor lighting and low ceilings over the board or platforms can present adverse safety conditions.

2. **Instruction-** Those desiring to learn to dive for any reason should seek instruction from persons who are not only qualified and experienced in diving, but are also in Life Saving and First Aid/ C.P.R. Receiving instruction from a life guard, a novice diver, gymnastics instructor, or family member who has no experience in diving can prove to be very dangerous for the learner.

The coach and instructor are in the best position to educate the diver and control conditions in the environment, so the safety of the diver is greatly dependent on how well the coach and teacher can:

* Control the behavior of the diver when practicing and performing. No horse play, showing off, or taking foolish chances should be tolerated.

* Teach the movements and techniques used in diving that relate to the safety of the diver. Use safety belts, bubbler, verbal commands, and other safety aids when teaching and coaching.

* Promote good communications between the diver and the coach or instructor to assure the diver's safety. The instructor should ask the diver from time to time if he or she understands the instructions for a misunderstanding could result in a painful experience.

Those who participate in diving should have some idea of the limitations of their ability to dive. The attempt to execute new and dangerous dives without proper instruction and safety awareness can and does result in injury. Divers who wish to dive but are not disciplined, aware of safety rules, ignore instruction, are inconsiderate of the actions of other divers, and try to dive beyond their capabilities, have little chance of learning to appreciate and enjoy the sport.

Legal suits concerning diving accidents

Those currently involved in diving are probably more aware of the meaning of safety than at any other time in history of the sport due to the legal actions that have recently arisen concerning diving injuries. Not long ago, if a diver was injured in some way, little or nothing was done with respect to legal ramifications. Currently, if a person is involved in a diving accident of any kind, it usually ends up in a law suit. Therefore, those who offer diving programs for any age or level of experience must be very safety conscious delineated for coverage of all members and training programs. It is difficult to state the number of serious accidents that have occurred in competitive diving since its induction in 1900, but it is safe to say that there have been more suits filed for diving accidents in the last two decades than in the past eighty years combined. Unfortunately, most of the diving injuries taken to court have had ' nothing' to do with springboard or platform competitive diving. Most of the injuries that have occurred in swimming pools are where swimmers have hit the bottom of the pool when diving from starting blocks in the shallow end of the pool.

A few years ago, a new starting technique was developed for swimmers diving from the starting blocks. Unlike the previous start where swimmers used to land flat on their stomachs when hitting the surface of the water, the new method has the swimmers diving underwater for a distance in the form of a scoop before coming up to begin swimming. This new version was introduced because it was found to save energy for the short distance before the athletes had to swim. A problem with the new start arose when many of the starting blocks were located at the shallow end of the pool. It was soon found that when swimmers dived off the starting block, they often made a sharp upward angle in a *pike position* and got stuck in the air. Many ducked under when entering the water and hit their back, neck, or head that often resulted in serious injuries. In cases where paralysis or concussions occurred, most insurance companies covered the medical expenses for a period of time until coverage ran out and the families had to go to their savings. This process usually took three or four years so most legal suits did not occur until the families ran out of money.

When such swimming accidents go to court, they are presented as "diving" accidents which reminds most people of Greg Louganis's accident at the Olympics, and don't realize that the accident had nothing to do with competitive diving. Competitive diving has been blamed for diving accidents associated with swimmers for years which has unrightfully caused the sport of diving to be dropped from athletic programs in many clubs, high schools, and colleges. Insurance companies have shied away from insuring any diving activity in fear that they will be subjected to large injury suits. In the meantime, this kind of accident has been modified by moving the starting blocks for swimmers from the shallow end of the pool to the deep end.

Most educational institutions and clubs throughout the country do not offer any basic courses in the teaching or coaching diving because of the scarcity of qualified instructors. Very few institutions have any program that relates to the coaching of competitive diving. Springboard diving has been eliminated from many aquatic programs for fear of law suits which in some cases, have bankrupted the program and many families. These trends need not continue if some statistical source could convince the insurance companies that competitive diving is not to blame for these injuries.

In reality, diving is probably safer than ever before because of its attempt to educate people in the use of teaching aids and safety apparatus. Great efforts have been taken by all diving organizations to make the sport as safe as possible and have generally succeeded in their efforts. I believe that it is only a matter of time before the rest of the world will recognize and accept the fact that competitive diving is as safe, if not safer, than most contact sports.

Safety rules and guidelines for diving activities

The list of diving rules below should be posted in any area that possesses diving boards and platforms. Some rules may apply to one facility, satisfying their aquatic needs, or may be used in larger diving programs that include different levels of competition and/or age levels. Not all of these rules may apply to all diving environments, but one can select those that relate to their environment.

1. No running, pushing, or horseplay on the pool deck or in the diving area.

2. Only one diver permitted on a board at a time.

3. Do not dive until the area in front of the board is clear. After diving, swim immediately to the pool side so as to clear the diving area.

4. Do not swim under the one-meter board to avoid the board from hitting you on the head.

5. Always check the water depth and the slopes on the sides of the pool when diving from a board or platform in a new area.

6. Never dive in a pool alone. Make sure a lifeguard, instructor, or coach is present to supervise the activity.

7. No swimming in the diving area.

8. No double or multiple bouncing on the diving board.

9. No hanging from the boards or railings.

10. No diving or swimming in outdoor pools when there is lightning.

11. Keep all floating objects out of diving area.

12. Never stand backward on the end of the diving board and jump up and down.

13. Never attempt a new dive without instruction from a teacher or coach.

14. Depth of the water should be clearly marked on the deck around the diving area.

15. Standard first aid kit and spine board should be within immediate distance as needed.

16. Close observation and control of the traffic on the tower platforms must be made from the deck of the pool and/ /or from a selected platform.

17. Always dive off the front end of the diving board and platform.

18. Do not attempt to dive after drinking alcohol of any kind.

19. Do not dive in shallow water.

20. Close off stairs to the platforms on the tower when not in use.

Diving Injuries

As previously mentioned, most of the injuries that have occurred in competitive diving up until the 1950' s were the result of divers smashing into a shallow bottom and hitting wooden diving boards that tilted upward. The upward tilt was eliminated when aluminum diving boards replaced the wooden boards which not only reduced the number of traumatic injuries that were caused from hitting the board, but also the intensity of the injuries. The reduction of injuries was due to the greater flexibility of the board which absorbed much of the impact when divers made the wrong contact with the board.

Acrobatic dives performed from the springboard and tower in the first seventy years of competitive diving were basically simple and did not require much angular momentum (rotational force) to perform the dives. Soon after, with the aid of the bubbler and trampoline, diving reached a new competitive level where divers were required to perform multi-somersaults and twists that required a great amount of angular momentum.

Divers, in their attempt to stop dives from rotating when entering the water, exceeded their physiological tolerance to the resistance of the water which resulted in injury. So, most competitive divers are not injured by hitting an object, such as the board or the bottom of the pool, but rather from their bodies not being able to withstand the resistance of the water. These are called "traumatic" injuries.

Another cause of injury is found when attempting to "rip" an entry. When diving from various heights, the motion used by the arms in an effort to perform a "rip" when entering the water, often causes a great amount of resistance to the shoulders, back, neck, arms and wrist. When these areas of the body are strained, an injury often occurs. Some divers are also injured when performing a dive or dives over and over again with poor body alignment when entering the water. This results in the body to become physically stressed which often results in a physical break down to some part of the body. This type of injury is known as "overuse syndrome" and can often occur without the diver's knowledge or with little warning.

When an injury occurs

* Pain in a certain area after completing an activity.

* Pain before the end of an activity.

* Pain throughout the activity which may not be intense but could affect the diver' s performance.

* Pain acquired from some other activity that is continual when practicing diving.

If a diver complains of pain during any of these time periods, the coach should assess the severity of the injury and if it appears to be acute, seek the opinion of t a trainer or some other medical authority before letting the diver continue to perform. If the injury does not appear to endanger the diver in any way, the injury may be treated by:

* Resting the area in pain, take anti-inflammatory drugs and/or physiotherapy. If the diver continues to dive while in pain, the matter will usually get worse or even create another injury.

* In the case of a bruise, ice should be used in the area swollen for the purpose of relieving the pain and decreasing the inflammatory reaction.

* The diver may engage in any stretching and strengthening exercises that do not cause additional pain.

An exercise program that has good instruction and facilities can offer much to the prevention of injuries to a diver. Exercise can not only be used to prevent injuries but also to rehabilitate divers who have been injured. When using exercises for this purpose, the diver should be cautious of what exercises are used and to what extent and have patience during the process so as not to hurry the treatment. Rest for the injured area of the body is necessary and no activity should be used as a quick fix. When returning to diving following an injury, divers do so with caution and gradually adjust the workouts according to what the boy tells them. Start slowly and gradually work back to the point where the injury occurred.

CHAPTER 13

BASIC TOWER DIVING

This chapter is offered in the text because of the great increase in competitive tower diving that includes synchronized diving throughout the world. With tower diving as an added event in colleges and universities in the United States, it is important that coaches become more familiar with how to teach the activity which can be performed from five different levels. Unfortunately, it is not possible to go into any detail on how dives are performed from the different platforms due to the limited space in the text.

History of tower diving

There is evidence that men were diving from great heights into water wells and natural bodies of water in Indian and China thousands of years ago and more recently in places like Acapulco, Mexico for at least the last 200 years. It is also known that divers performed only the front dive during these periods. Dives of an acrobatic nature occurred in the middle 1800's when gymnasts from the German Turnverein and Swedish Ling movements were not satisfied with just diving from piers and docks so began to challenge each other by diving from greater heights such as bridges and cliffs.

One can only guess when these brave souls began to perform some kind of somersault dive or even a forward 1 ½ somersault. This form of high diving soon spread to England, Canada, and a little later to America near the turn of the century. It is not clear when high diving became a competitive sport or how it was decided that ten meters would be a standard height for competition. From what records are available, competitive high diving from heights over three meters started in the early 1900's. When American G.E. Sheldon won the first gold medal at the 1904 Olympic Games in Saint Louis; it is still not clear whether he dived from the springboard or the ten-meter tower. The western and southern part of the United States produced most of the tower divers up to the second World War because they were outdoors where the weather was warmer and longer than found in the north. Near the end of the twentieth century, many of the new college pools included towers because tower diving was included in competitive college programs.

Types and construction of diving towers

The diving towers built before World War II were constructed of wood and few were very sturdy. Now, most of the regulation towers built in America are made of steel of cement that have platforms at the 1, 3, 7 ½, and 10-meter levels. Some provide platforms at the 5 and 10-meter levels and a few do not have platforms at the 1, 3, or 7 ½- meter levels due mainly to the cost of construction. The general length of the 5-meter and IO-meter platforms is 22 feet and ten feet wide because they are both used in competitions. The 3-meter and 7 ½ meter platforms are basically used for other purposes so they are sometimes shorter and narrower. The reason for the differences in length and width of the platforms is because of the traffic each has more recently, because synchronized competitions are performed from the 5 and ten-meter levels. Many diving towers are constructed where the platforms are stacked or are cantilevered. The stacked platforms have the five-meter and one under the ten meter and the three-meter under the 7 ½ meter platform. The one-meter platform is often attached to the tower but is off to the side with no platforms overhead (Figure 1). Cantilevered towers require more space in the pool area because the platforms are staggered with nothing over or under each the platforms (Figure 2).

By rule, it is necessary that the platforms extend over the edge of the pool at different lengths to prevent divers performing from other heights landing on platforms below them. When possible, the diving towers should be built in an area away from the competitive swimming area so as not to distract those who are diving. Many of the diving structures are now built with separate diving wells or in pools that "L" or "T" shaped so the diving activities do not interfere with the competitive swimmers.

A stacked tower with five platforms
Figure 1

Many modern designs are used in the construction of diving towers throughout the world with Germany having the most modern and greatest variety. Perhaps the most popular design of diving towers in the United States are those with the vertical support and rectangular in shape which rise straight up or slant toward the pool. Diving towers are normally made of concrete with reinforced steel, steel tubing, steel beams, or wood. Towers made of cement with reinforced steel seem to be the most popular for they provide very sturdy platforms. Steel tubing and steel beams have also become quite popular in recent years while wooden built towers are fast becoming obsolete because they are not as safe. Stable, or durable as those made with other materials. All of the diving towers built in outdoor facilities are attached to the ground with no needed supports. They are supposed to be built facing North and South to prevent the sun from shining directly in the diver's eyes during the early and late part of the day. Unfortunately, some of the towers built in Americas best facilities were built facing East and West by architects who were not familiar with competitive diving. The depth of the water for a ten-meter tower should not be less than 15 feet with the drains on the bottom off set from in front of the platforms to prevent anyone getting fingers caught in the drain. The bottom of the pools for tower diving should have a design or lane markers so the divers know in which direction they are diving while in the air. This is particularly necessary when the tower is built in a pool that has circular sides in front of the platforms.

A cantilevered tower with five platforms
Figure 2

Many indoor towers are attached to a ceiling or wall that often includes stairs to the different platform levels (Figure 3). Some of the modem towers have the stairs to the different levels built behind the wall which cannot be seen by the spectators (Figure 4). Some stairs zigzag while others are in a spiral shape (Figure 5). Stairs that go straight up the back of the tower are no longer made because if one should slip and fall, they could drop thirty feet to the ground. Many of the new towers include a space at the top level which is set off to the side and is a safety feature where persons can stand and direct traffic on the lower levels to prevent divers diving from different platforms at the wrong time (Figure 6). Nearly all of the towers recently built include a bubbler system under the platforms and three-meter springboards as safety feature and teaching aids.

Indoor tower attached to wall
Figure 3

A problem that has often occurred in the construction of diving towers is found in using natural lighting in the diving area of pools that casts a reflection on the water's surface that blinds a diver when performing a dive. This has caused many injuries in a pool and should be seriously considered when building indoor towers.

Indoor tower with stairs behind the wall
Figure 4

A B

Tower with zigzag and spiral stairs
Figure 5

All of the platforms contain railings to protect divers from falling from the sides. Some of the railings fan out sideways to offer more room for divers when they spread the arms laterally while performing the forward approach. The material used on the surface of the platforms to prevent slipping is made of rubber and nylon textures. These materials have replaced the cocoa matting that was used for around seventy years. The matting on outside towers usually rotted because of the weather and caused more problems than they were worth.

More towers are now being constructed at Universities that have swimming and diving programs because the tower event is now one of the events in N.C.A.A. championships meets. Clubs are also including towers because of tower events plus synchronized diving which is a 3 -meter springboard and 10-meter tower event in the Olympics and most other international diving meets.

Growth of tower diving

The growth of tower and springboard diving was slow over the years in terms of the kind of dives performed. Few new dives were put in the F.I.N.A. rule book until well after the second World War. For example, the first 3 ½ somersault ever performed from the ten-meter platform was by Ohio State University's first great diver Jim Patterson after which only a handful of divers in the world learned to perform the dive in a fifteen-year period. Patterson was also the first diver to ever perform a forward 4 ½ which was also performed from ten meters and was not duplicated until the late 1950's by the Mexican 1956 Olympic champion, Joaquin

Capilla and soon after by Dick Kimball, the former diving coach from the University of Michigan, Kimball went on to become the greatest acrobatic diver in the world from the ten meter platform in the early 1960's when he performed several multi-twisting somersault dives that were not performed in competition for over forty years.

With the introduction of the Duraflex diving boards and the Durafirm diving stands that were made standard in the late 1950' s, springboard diving took off like a rocket for this equipment added new spring to the boards that made it possible for divers to perform divers never before dreamed possible. Though there was little change in the structure of diving towers except for better padding on the surface of the platforms, tower diving went right along with the explosion in the creation of new dives which was made possible by a new safety device known as the "bubbler". This teaching aid and safety device reduced the fear and possibility of injury or pain by cushioning the surface of the water when landing improperly.

Another reason for the great increase of difficult dives was the introduction of the degree of difficult formula which was developed by an American gymnast from Rockford, Illinois. Bob Bollinger. His formula gave an immediate and accurate means of giving the degrees of difficulty for new difficult dives never before performed. The new formula also opened the doors for the new policy that would allow a diver to perform dives that were not listed in the F.I.N.A. or any other diving rule books.

In viewing competitive tower diving over the last few decades, it is hard to believe that in the Olympic Games and other national and international competitions staged for women before the late 1960' s, had them perform four required dives and three voluntary dives. Before that time, there were only three or four female divers in the world performing a forward 3 ½ somersault in the tuck position and a back 2 ½ somersault from the ten-meter platform. Few females performed hand stands at that time for it was believed that they did not have the strength to hold a hand stand long enough to show control plus the fact that most of dives in that group offered low degrees of difficulty. Most female divers performed three voluntary dives that were selected from a small group of dives that included a forward 2 ½ somersault a back 1 ½ in the layout position, an inward 2 ½ somersault in the tuck position, a forward 1 ½ somersault with one or two twists, and a back 1 ½ somersault with 1 ½ twists.

When comparing those dives with the ones performed at the present time, it is almost laughable for the females now execute forward, backward, reverse, and inward 3 ½ somersaults; forward 2 ½ somersaults with a twist; forward 1 ½ somersaults with three twists; back 1 ½ somersaults with 3 ½ twists and several handstand dives with multi-somersaults and twists. Quite a change from the 1920 and 1924 Olympics which staged "plain diving" contests that had a diver perform two front dives from the five meter and ten-meter platforms and the person performing the four dives the best, received a gold medal. It is also amazing that all of these new dives have been created from the same towers that were available to divers a hundred years ago.

Learning to dive tower

Tower diving presents one of the most thrilling and breathtaking experiences found in any sport. Diving from a platform over thirty feet high and soaring through the air while executing certain spins and gyrations before entering the water at over thirty miles an hour and making little to no splash never ceases to thrill the performer and the spectators. Such acrobatic maneuvers require one to possess courage, balance, strength, experience, concentration, instruction, and a basic knowledge about diving. Divers usually become proficient have diving from a three-meter springboard before taking on the challenges of tower diving which normally offers platform at three, five, seven and a half, and ten-meter heights.

Nearly every diver will agree that when first learning to tower dive, the most difficult part is to stand on the edge of the ten-meter platform and look down at the water and the surrounding area. But, thankfully, once learning some basic dives from the high platform, the diver finds it not to be as high as at first believed. Whether experienced or a beginner, divers always find it a challenge when learning a new dive from "the top". It helps if the diver tries to make a mental and physical adjustment to the added height from which the diver is to dive. Actually, the time the diver is in the air when performing from the ten-meter platform is nearly the same as when diving from the three-meter springboard because the diver springs higher when diving from the board then when diving from the platform which does not offer any spring. The greatest difference between the springboards other than the springboard offering more spring is found in the impact of the body when it hits the surface of the water. The diver can obtain much more pain or injury when hitting the water poorly from ten meters then when diving from a lower height because of the greater velocity of the falling body hitting the water.

Naturally, diving is scary for beginners when diving from greater heights because the chance of injury when hitting the water surface. Much of the fear of diving from the top can be eliminated by learning certain dives in progression. That is the diver uses of the lower platforms for certain dives that lead up to the intended dive that will be performed from the ten-meter platform. Such progression permits the diver to become more aware of the movements needed to perform the intended dive with less chance of injury.

An example for a diver who wishes to learn to perform an inward 2 ½ somersault in the pike position from the ten-meter platform may begin with first learning to perform an inward somersault in the tuck position from the one-meter platform. To prevent any chance of hitting the feet on the edge of the platform, the diver is taught to thrust the arms forward and downward within the width of the shoulders while the legs extend, and the hips push upward upon leaving the platform. Moving the arms and hips in this fashion will move the diver away from the platform which helps prevent injury. The next step is to learn to perform an inward 1 ½ somersault in the tuck position from the three-meter platform. This is followed by performing a standing forward 2 ½ somersault tuck from the three-meter springboard with the fulcrum rolled forward as far as possible to learn how to orientate the body while in the air.

When the diver feels orientated, he or she can then perform the dive inward on the springboard with a desired position of the fulcrum. If the diver enters the water a little short of vertical from the springboard, he or she should return to the three-meter platform and perform an inward 1 ½ somersault tuck before changing the position of the dive to pike. When the diver can perform the dive a little short of vertical or rotates more, he or she should then perform the inward 2½ somersault in the pike position from the 7 ½ meter platform. This height is ideal for this dive because, with a good call from the coach and the use of the bubbler, it offers little chance of injury should the diver go short of vertical on the entry. When short on this dive, the body is bent at the waist which offers no subsequent flat area to meet the flat surface of the water to cause injury. After the diver performs the dive from this height and feels he or she can control the dive, the dive can be performed from the 10-meter platform with a call from the coach on the short side of the dive and with the aid of the bubbler.

To get used to the added height, the diver performs the dive from 7 ½ meters with the aid of the bubbler and a call from the coach. This dive is ideal for learning a difficult dive from the 7 ½ or 10-meter level because there is little chance of injury if the diver enters the water short of vertical. Finally, if the diver can control the dive from 7 ½ meters and can enter the water a little short of vertical; he or she can then perform the dive from the 10-meter level with little danger.

In following the progression used in learning this dive, the diver and coach should remember the following:

* The arms be thrown forward and downward within the width of the shoulders as the legs extend and hips push upward on the take off.

* A call is given by the coach near the completion of the dive to aid the diver in knowing where the water is when preparing for the entry.

* Use a bubbler when attempting the dives from the 7 ½ and 10-meter levels.

It must be said that some dives are easier to perform from the 10-meter platform then from the three-meter springboard and vice versa.

Tower take-offs

Before discussing this area of tower diving, no attempt is made here to discuss how any dives should be performed due to the limited space offered in this book.

Because the solid platform on diving towers do not provide any spring, the diver uses different styles when performing certain approaches and take-offs in the performance of a dive. Since it is not possible to jump as high from a platform as from a springboard, the diver finds the platform more reliable and consistent compared to taking off from an unpredictable springboard. This is noted when different forces are created by the board's recoil which changes with every dive.

Forward approach and take-off

There are several styles a diver may use when executing the forward approach on the tower. The choice made by the diver often depends on the method he or she feels will provide the most lift, control, and consistency in the performance of the dive. Whichever maneuver is used depends much on the kind of dive that is to be performed and the style the diver favors. Starting from a stance around 20 feet from the end of the platform the approach to toward the end has the diver walking or trotting while the arms dangle at the sides or swing back and forth while at some time lift overhead laterally to a before performing the hurdle. The manner in which the diver places the arms overhead while making the forward approach differs with divers and normally is not judged by the style they use, but rather how smoothly they perform the motion.

Since there is no way for the platform to offer spring, the hurdle to the end of the platform is very short and low with the arms extended overhead in a fixed position. The feet normally are flat when placed on the end of the platform to create traction that can be used to perform the dive. Others may land on the end of the platform on the balls of their feet. Therefore, it is a matter of taste as to which foot position the diver wishes to take off from the platform. When taking off from the platform, the diver will either thrust the arms forward and downward to initiate angular momentum (angular rotation) or pull the arms down laterally to create an open pike or layout position. Naturally, the latter take-off is for dives that do not require a great deal of angular momentum (Figure 6).

Forward approach with arms overhead on the take-off
Figure 6

Standing take-offs

Forward rotating dives

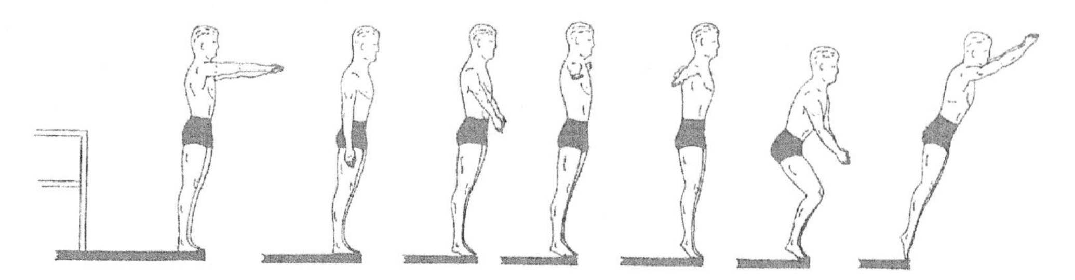

Take-off when rotating forward from standing position
Figure 7

When performing forward rotating dives from a stand, the diver usually takes off with the arms in a fixed position from overhead and with a slight lean. The lean off sets the body and places it in an eccentric position which creates rotation.

Circling the arms before taking off the platform from a stand facing forward is primarily used when performing reverse dives. In this case, the diver does not lean forward on
the take-off.

Instead, he or she diver jumps away from the platform to initiate rotation and prevents hitting the edge. The distance away from the platform when jumping is vital because jumping out too far affects the rotation of the dive and jumping too close can cause injury by hitting the platform. diver will perform front rotating dives by starting with the arms above the head (Figure 8).

Divers used to perform reverse dives by walking to the end of the platform and swinging the arms while kicking one leg up on the take-off or by taking a skip and swinging the arms while kicking one leg up, but these styles are rarely used by present divers.

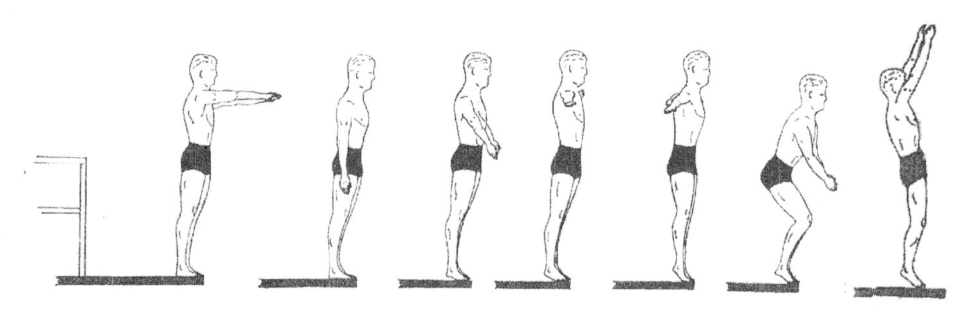

Performing reverse dives from a standing position
Figure 8

Backward

When standing on the edge facing the platform and in an erect position, the position of the arms prior to the backward swing is optional. The arms move to a position overhead as the diver leans slightly away from the platform. From the overhead position, the arms again circle and continue to reach backward which creates angular rotation before the feet leave the platform. Since the diver cannot depress the edge of the platform, the emphasis is placed on the velocity of the arm swing and the strength of the legs to generate the angular momentum needed to perform thedive.

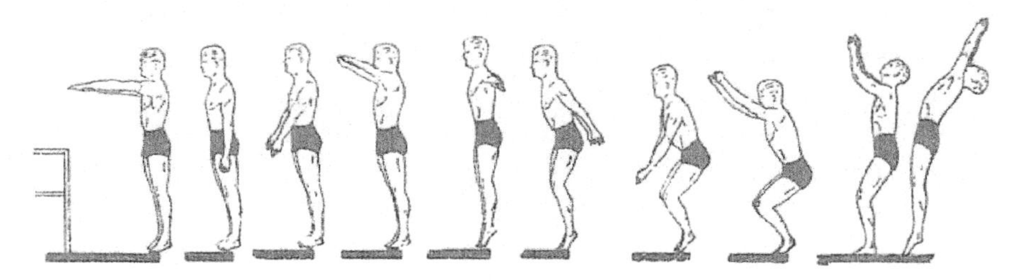

Rotating backward from a stand
Figure 9

Inward

When performing inward dives, the diver stands on the edge facing the platform with the arms extended overhead and shoulder width apart in a vertical direction. The take-off is made with the arms pushing forward and downward towards the edge of the platform as the hips lift and the legs extend before the feet leave. On the take-off, the diver pushes the arms forward and downward as the body bends forward at the waist (Figure 10).

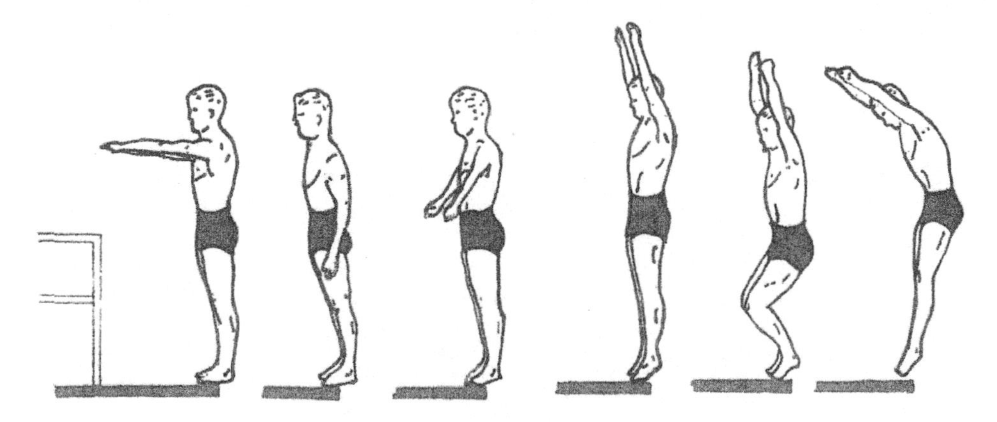

Performing inward rotating dives
Figure 10

Handstand

Dives performed from a handstand make up the sixth group of dives and are only performed from a platform on the tower. The manner by which the diver performs the handstand is not judged until the feet leave the platform. Once the handstand is made the diver must hold the position for at least three seconds to show that the performance of the handstand was under control. Regardless of facing forward or backward when performing the handstand, either way offers different methods of executing a dive.

Until recently handstand dives were only performed with the body facing forward. However, a new group of dives has been introduced that require the diver to perform a hand stand facing the edge of the platform. This new approach to the hand stand is difficult to execute because there is little room for the diver to place the feet when attempting to perform the stand.

Front handstand from squatting position
Figure 11

Front handstand from track start position
Figure 12

Front handstand from straddle position
Figure 13

A new style of performing a back handstand has been introduced that has the diver stand near the end of the platform on one side to perform a handstand by using the same motion used to perform a cartwheel. This is started with the diver facing the water and the arms overhead. The diver takes a step toward the middle of the platform while bending over sideward and placing one hand on the edge of the platform followed by the second hand which is also placed on the edge about shoulder width apart. During this process, one leg is lifted upward followed by the other leg placing the diver in a handstand position with the legs apart. The legs are then brought together to form the handstand facing the platform.

Cartwheel back handstand
Figure 14

Safety hints when diving from tower

Tower diving can be very dangerous for the beginner and expert tower diver. Much of the danger can be avoided, however, if certain precautions are taken. Some of these are:

* Swimmers should stay out of the diving area while diving activity is going on.

* Divers should always check the diving area beneath the tower before diving. He or she should also caution those on the other platforms of his or her intention to dive.
* The depth of the water should be checked, and the type and shape of the pool bottom should be explored before diving from the platforms when in a strange pool.

* Divers should not linger in the water after performing a dive. They should swim immediately to the side of the pool so that a diver on the platform cannot dive on him or her.

* It is too dangerous for any horse play on diving platforms.

* A diver should never practice tower diving unless with another dive, qualified swimmer, life guard, or coach is present.

* The steps on the platforms should be roped off with signs posted when the tower is not being used.

* The diving area should be roped off from the swimming area when the facilities are all in the same pool. This will prevent a swimmer from swimming into the diving area which could be dangerous.

* Allow only the more experienced divers dive from platforms above 5-meters.

* Divers should not practice tower diving just after eating. This can make a diver quite ill.

Things to remember when tower diving

Some hints that can be helpful in making the practice session more successful when diving from the tower are:

* Warm up with some exercises, practice some dives the low levels or the 3-meter springboard before diving from the platforms above the 5-meter platform. This will help prevent the tearing of muscles and tendons.

* Check the water area and other diving platforms before performing a dive.

* Start with basic dives then work toward the more difficult dives during the practice session.

* Concentrate on the dive to be performed before making the take-off from the platform.

* Do not change your mind once the dive has started.

* Make sure to clasp the hands and straighten the arms before entering the water on head first entries.

CHAPTER 14

JUDGING COMPETITION DIVING

The rules and regulations used to conduct competitive springboard and platform diving contests have remained generally the same since the introduction of the sport around the turn of the twentieth century. Naturally, in the early years, diving facilities were primitive, the number of divers were few, coaches and diving programs were nearly non-existent, and the number of dives offered for competition were meager and elementary. Though different versions of competitive diving were occasionally adopted in the early 1900s, the standard springboard and platform contests consisted of a certain number of compulsory (simple) dives and a similar number of optional (difficult) dives. After a hundred years of competitive diving, the establishment of sophisticated diving facilities, the development of hundreds of diving programs and diving coaches, the participation of thousands of competitors, and with the creation of nearly a hundred new dives for use in competition, the contests are still conducted in the same manner except for a recent move to eliminate the easy (compulsory) dives from the senior level contests. Changing the sport to include more dramatic and difficult dives seems to be a move to retain spectator interest in the sport. Such great growth in diving calls for competent, experienced, and well-educated diving judges who can accurately and fairly determine the winners of diving contests. However, due to the complexity of the dives performed today, many diving judges are no longer qualified to judge high level contests because they are not able to properly analyze the movements made by the divers.

No attempt is made here to cover the rules and regulations of a diving contest nor describe the duties and responsibilities of the diving judges and referees for this information is found in every diving rule book throughout the world. However, information is offered here that may help those who wish to be a competent and respected diving judge and/or referee.

A diving contest involves the following

* The meet administrator (not an official)
* Diving judges
* Diving referee
* Scoring table
* Announcer

Each of these positions requires people who are experienced and responsible for performing their duties in a manner that contribute to a fair and successful diving contest. An error or flaw in their performance can often result in a conflict that could affect the outcome of the competition. The following information concerning the officials is offered with the intent of portraying the importance of their duties for which they rarely receive any form of gratuity or are recognized for their services. With no schools to educate these officials, their participation is based simply on their willingness to aid those who compete.

The administrator of the diving contest is not an official. He or she is responsible for providing the facilities that are required for the diving contest. The duties of the administrator include providing information for housing, restaurants, furnish a snack bar for officials and coaches, schedules, practice times, entertainment, medical facilities, life guards, transportation to and from airport, concession stand for spectators, and many more duties.

The difficulty of judging and refereeing a diving contest

Judging and refereeing a diving contest is the most difficult part in the administration of the competitive sport for it is the only area that depends completely on the personal judgment of an individual. Judging diving is very difficult for various reasons some of which are:

* The absence of descriptions and guidelines for the dives in all the diving rule books. The manner on how a dive should be executed is based on the personal opinion of the coaches and divers.

* There has never been any attempt to ever gather the diving experts from around the world for the purpose of developing standards and guidelines on how all of the dives should be executed.

* Not everyone has been willing to accept the fact that the movements used in the performance of every dive could be proven with the use of mechanical principles based on the Laws of Motion.

* Many do not have the knowledge and/ or experience to judge diving at certain competitive levels.

* Some judges possess a bias or prejudice toward divers who perform for different countries, learning institutions, and clubs.

* Some judges do not keep up with the sport to be competent in their evaluation of dives.

Two methods used in judging dives

* Absolute scale - Which means scoring a dive the same for everyone regardless of age, competitive level of the contest, or the kind of contest one is participating in from an age group meet or the Olympic Games. This means that a person scoring

a six for a dive in an age group meet would give an identical score to a diver regardless of the age or level of competition in which the diver is competing.

* Flexible scale - Scoring a dive that is relevant to the age level of those competing from tiny tots to those at the senior level, and to divers at different competitive levels. This form of judging is desirable because it ensures a proper spread of points and makes the results more definitive. It also inspires youngsters to compete and encourages them to remain in the sport. This does not mean that judges should mislead divers by giving high scores for any kind of effort. But it does indicate that judges should be able to compare the efforts of one diver with those of another in a particular competition which should offer a greater variance in scores. With this in mind, it should be possible for a beginner diver to execute a dive in competition that would rate a superior score because it may be the best dive in the meet. However, such scores are rare because most judges are not willing to give such a score in a novice event.

Selecting a diving judge and/or diving referee

Normally, the big problem in administering diving contests is to find people who are available and qualified to judge the contest. This problem generally occurs at meets of little importance such as dual or invitational meets. When such is the case, the person responsible for the meet should delegate or select those who have had experience in judging diving. If enough qualified judges are not available, the meet administrator may seek out those who have had some judging experience with other sports such as ice skating or gymnastics.

The success of a diving competition is usually at the mercy of the diving judges, and there is no way of knowing how competent the judges are or how prejudiced they may be for any given event. Many have different backgrounds and experiences in judging, so they may have vastly different concepts of how dives should be performed. The differences may be evident when the judges come from different environments and geographical locations where dives are looked at in different ways. Some have different opinions concerning the movements, technique, and styles used in diving. Unfortunately, some judges have a philosophy concerning competitive diving that is basically set in concrete and it is very difficult for them to change the way they observe the sport.

Diving coaches are usually the most qualified to judge divers because they have much more technical knowledge about diving and are more involved in the sport than anyone else. Many possess some background in basic mechanical principles required to analyze the movements used in the performance of dives. Unfortunately, many coaches show bias when judging their own athletes because they see their divers perform in practice every day and are aware of their mistakes. Therefore, the coach may judge his or her divers based not on what they see in a meet, but on what they know the diver does in practice. For example, I know a great coach who is a very good judge... until he has one of his own divers compete in a contest. He then turns into a terrible judge especially when his divers perform poorly.

The very difficult dives performed in competitions today require judges to see a lot of diving in order to train the eyes to detect every movement performed by the divers at all heights and all levels of competition. If a judge becomes so trained, it is necessary that he or she also have some technical knowledge about the sport to make a valid evaluation of the dives performed. This requires an understanding of the movements that contribute to the execution of dives. Newton's Laws of Motion and how they apply to diving can greatly aid judges in creating basic guidelines for judging dives. Such an approach makes it easier for judges to recognize, evaluate, and analyze different basic techniques and styles used by the divers.

The number of divers and competitive level at which they compete can determine the number of judges to be used on the panel. When enough competent judges are available for championship contests, a double panel is normally used that offers more accuracy and less fatigue when judging. All diving contests should include a competent diving referee who should not be a member of the judging panel or be the announcer. An assistant referee, who is also a judge, is appointed by the referee to sit on the other side of the pool when judges are used on both sides. If an infraction by a diver occurs that requires the judgment of the referee, either or both referees should raise their hands. If the refraction is obvious, the head referee may recognize it without consulting the assistant referee but, if there appears to be any question concerning the infraction, both referees should get together, discuss the issue, and make a decision.

When judging dual meets, the use of two judges, one from each team, offers the fairest means of evaluating the performance of dives with the least amount of prejudice. The diving coaches from each team usually do the judging. When a third judge is used, that person is sometimes the swimming referee and may have a connection with one of the two teams involved, which could offer unfair bias or prejudice. However, if a person is neutral to those in the contest and is able to judge fairly, then a third judge may be recommended.

Conference or other major diving contests may use five or seven judges and incorporate two panels if possible. Nine judges, with the two top and two bottom scores eliminated, offers the fairest means of judging, but it is often difficult to find nine competent judges who are willing to judge all of the dives in the contest Nine judges also adds a burden on the people working at the scoring table because of the time it takes to announce the scores, add up and compute the scores. Whatever method used in judging major diving contests, coaches who have divers in the contest will often judge the preliminaries and semi-finals but not judge their own in the finals so as to avoid prejudice or bias. Eight judges have been used in some meets with one acting as the "designated" judge. This judge takes the place of one who is the coach or school representative of a diver competing. It is desired that neutral judges be used for the finals in all major diving events. Neutral judges do not represent any of the divers that are competing.

SUGGESTIONS FOR THE MAKING OF A GOOD DIVING JUDGE

1. In preparation for judging and refereeing a diving contest.

* Read the rules and regulations in the rulebook that refer to the competition you wish
to judge or referee. There are at least four different rulebooks that relate to different ages and associations:

a. F.I.N.A. - Delineates the rules for all international contests such as the Olympic Games, World Championships, Pan American Games, and others.

b. U.S. Diving - Covers rules for all diving contests outside of learning institutions Including those for age-group and Master's contests.

c. N.C.A.A. - Rules for all collegiate and university diving contests.

d. N.F.H.S. - National Federation of State High School Associations -Rules for all high schools in the United States.

* Dress appropriately when judging. Offer "class" to the position so everyone is aware that judging diving contests is an important matter. If a uniform is not required for judging, show that you mean business by dressing in a manner that reflects the importance of the position.

* Though the divingjudges are bunched together on both sides of the pool when possible and only one side if necessary, place yourself in a position that offers a clear side view of the dives performed. This position usually starts with one judge sitting even with the edge of the springboard or platform and the other positions move outward away from the entry area of the diver.

* The position of the diving referee should be on the side of the score table and near the judging panel so as to be quickly available if any diving infraction occurs.

* Be familiar with the dives, degrees of difficulty and the six different diving categories. Since diving rules change nearly every year, it is a good policy to review them every year to stay current.

* Learn the rules well enough to score dives under all competitive conditions. Be familiar with the dives and have a mental concept of how the dives should be performed. Compare your concept of the dives with those performed by the divers.

* Judges and referees should try to attend as many diving contests for all ages and competitive levels of performance as possible, for more experience can be acquired in doing so.

* Judges should study diving videos and try to detect major and minor flaws made by divers, and how such errors should be evaluated.

* Judges should learn how to analyze dives accurately so as to become more aware of how and why certain errors occur in a dive.

* All judges and coaches should know their duties and responsibilities and how they relate to each other and to the contestants.

* Judges should make it a point to see good diving at various competitive levels in order to distinguish good diving from poor diving.

2. *Duties and conduct of the diving judge and referee A diving judge should:*

* Listen to the dive announced and form a mental picture of how the dive should be perfectly executed based on personal experience and knowledge. Try to judge the dive on the level of the competition being judged.

* Request that the name of the dive be repeated if the dive announced was not heard.

* When a dive is performed, make a fast decision and select the score immediately without anything (such as applause) affecting the decision.

* Be aware of the different techniques and styles that a diver may use when performing certain dives. and not be quick to penalize the diver for using one that you do not favor.

* Give the score the dive deserves without the influence of scores given by other judges, the scores posted on the score board, or the response from the audience, The score by each judge should be given immediately following the dive or after the request for the scores by the announcer.

* If not able to avoid hearing or seeing the scores given by the other judges, be consistent in your judging. If your scores are higher or lower than the other judges, do not feel that you have to adjust your scores to match theirs. Do not

be influenced by those nearby who give their opinion of the score to be given. Unfortunately, there are coaches and people who deliberately try to manipulate judges in this manner.

* Judge the entire dive and not just the entry. Take into account the balance and the height of the diver when taking off the board or platform, the smoothness of the movements made in the execution of the dive, the distance from the take-off point to the water, the angle of the body when entering the water, and the amount of splash made when making the entry.

* Remember, anything performed under the surface of the water is not to be judged.

* Be able to distinguish between major and minor faults made in a dive and score the dive accordingly.

* Judge the dive and not the person performing the dive. Be fair in your judgment and disregard any personal impression a diver may make on you.

* Avoid letting the popularity of the diver, or the high **D.D.** of a dive affect your scores.

* Don't converse with the other judges or anyone else until after the contest is completed.

* In contests that have a great number of divers, try to avoid falling into the rut of awarding scores between four and six for every dive. Although it is possible in many competitions that the dives do not merit scores higher or lower than mentioned, a diver will perform a dive worth much more than a six but fails to receive the rightful scores. Don't be afraid to give the diver a high or low score in these circumstances.

* When missing to see the dive performed, inform the referee that the dive was not seen. In this case, the awards given by the other judges will be averaged.

* If you are a coach and judging on a panel where a judge gives your diver a low score, don't play revenge by giving that judge's diver a low score to get even.

* When giving a low score to a diver then after thinking about it, feel it was a mistake, don' t make up for it by giving the diver a higher score than deserved for his or her next dive.

* Avoid forming an opinion of a diver's performance of a dive by watching him or her in practice or in a warm up session. Judge only the dive seen in the contest and not what was seen at some other place or time.

* Do not try to judge so that your score is in the middle of the scores given by the other judges. Playing such games is not fair to those competing. Trying to judge so that your score won' t be counted out does not do any good for anyone. If you are judging to appear that you agree with everyone on the panel, then you shouldn't be judging.

* Don ' t play the "percentage" game. This occurs when a judge favors a certain team or diver and tries to give a high score to the diver he favors or a low score to the opposing diver that will count if another judge offers the same score.

* Be a positive judge by giving the diver the benefit of the doubt. When undecided as to whether to give the diver a score such as a 6 or a 6 ½, give the diver the higher score.

* Avoid trying to explain to a judge nearby judge why you gave a diver a certain score that was not agreeable with the other judges. There is no need for you to apologize or compromise your choice of scores to anyone...particularly while you are still judging.

* Take the task of judging seriously and vigilantly practice much like diver's practice with the objective of becoming proficient. Judging one or two meets a year is not enough to sharpen your judging talents if you are going to be a fair and qualified judge. If you are at meets and not judging, take a piece of paper and judge the contest. Then compare your scores with the other judges and see if your scores are near those given by the other judges.

* Realize that not everyone can be a good diving judge any more than anyone can be a good diver. Many who are not good diving judges fail to acquire the knowledge and experience that is required to evaluate and analyze the execution of dives. Most often, good divers do not make good diving judges because they do not interpret the performance of other performance of other divers in the way they interpret their own dives. They may also have subconscious prejudice against certain divers for they cannot accept the fact that someone else could dive better than themselves.

* Recognize that most divers can 'rip' an entry more easily from the platform than when diving from the springboard. This should not make a difference in the way a dive is judged.

* Recognize that when a diver has difficulty performing a handstand and wavers while attempting to stabilize the diving position should be penalized for loss of

control. The dive should be judged on how well the diver controls the handstand position from the time the feet leave the platform and not from when the diver finally performs a handstand.

* If a failed dive is performed and the referee does not acknowledge it as a failed dive, you should score the dive as seen. If, in your opinion the diver failed the dive, you should score the dive zero. But if you feel the dive was not failed, then score the dive as seen.

How a diving judge develops prejudice or bias

Some of the reasons why bias judgment occurs with some judges may be due to:

* Limited knowledge about diving - far too often, diving judges with a limited judging background try too hard to do a satisfactory job. They follow the judging rules so closely that they become hyper critical of the diver's every move, and thus give such low scores that the diver rightfully becomes discouraged. Again, judges should recognize the caliber of the competition at hand and not judge by comparing their efforts of one with those who are top performers and dive in the national and international championships. The judges must try to realize that these striving competitors have spent many hours each day for several months practicing and perfecting their dives in the belief that their efforts will be judged fairly and accurately in competition based on *"their level" of competition"*.

* Preconceived notions - when judging a great champion like Greg Louganis, it was difficult to give him a low score even when he performed a dive badly because it was rare that he ever missed a dive. If the same poor dive by Louganis was performed by an average diver, one would find that he or she would receive much lower scores than Louganis.

* Anticipated performance - it is important that a diver start off the contest with a dive that he or she knows will score well, for when a diver misses the first dive or the first two dives, the judges expect the diver to continue to miss dives that are to follow. But if the diver surprises everyone with a brilliant dive after missing the first dive or two, chances are the diver will not receive the scores deserved because the judges have already anticipated that he or she will miss the dive. An opposite response from the judges can happen when a diver starts the contest by giving a great performance for the first couple of dives and suddenly misses a dive badly. Realizing how well the diver has been performing, some judges may give a higher score than what the dive deserves.

This inherent fault of judging is related to the natural law of inertia--where an object in motion tends to remain in motion, and an object at rest tends to remain at rest. Likewise, some judges mistakenly assume that a diver who has missed the first and/or second dive in the contest will continue to miss dives, and divers who perform the first and/or second dive well, will continue to hit good dives. This biased preconceived interpretation of dives unfolds in the scoring results of most contests and may affect the results of the contest in a negative or positive way.

A solution to preventing prejudice and bias in judging

Recognizing predicable tendencies of judges, the solution to preventing such prejudice or bias may be for judges to not to watch diver's practice or warm up before an important contest. The judges should score what they see in the meet and not what a diver does in practice or has done in some other contest. Though it is very difficult, judges should not preconceive the performance of a dive for being human, that judge can blunder like any average diver.

Criticism of a judge often occurs when he or she gives a score for a dive that is much higher or lower than the other judges. Poor judging may not have occurred in some incidents because of the angle in which a judge observes the dive, may off r a different view of the dive than seen by other judges. It is sometimes more difficult to judge dives that are performed with split tucks and pikes, or feet coming apart when twisting from right angles of the diver than from other angles.

It is important to select judges for a diving contest that are fair and competent. Using judges who are competent but unfair or biased should be avoided when possible. A biased judge can usually be spotted when he or she consistently gives scores to a particular diver that are well above or below those given by the other judges.

Some common faults made in competitive diving that cause the greatest concern and are the most difficult to judge.

The degree to which a diving judge should deduct or award points in the following categories is not always clearly indicated in the rule books. Such differences occur due to the angle of perception of the judge, or subject to the variable interpretation of the judge.

* Split tuck or pike - where the feet are together, and the knees and legs are spread at different widths.

* Spreading the feet when leaving the board or platform - this movement may be for a very short time before they come together again for the remainder of the dive.

* The crow-hop as it compares to a double bounce when performing dives that require a back take-off.

* Excessive rocking of the board (oscillation) when taking off the springboard in a backward manner. The number of rocks by the diver before it becomes excessive.

* Degree of over twist or under twist when performing dives and/or when entering the water.

* In flying somersaults, how far the diver remains in the layout position before changing to a tuck or pike position.

* With the center of gravity four or five feet away and the body in a horizontal position when passing the level of the board or platform, the diver is often penalized because he or she appears to be too close to the point of take-off Then there are times when divers are penalized for being too far away from the board or platform when passing the board or platform in a vertical position.

* Dives that enter the water with a cast which is often overlooked or not seen by the judges. Many do not detect this fault because they have not seen enough diving, or because of the angle in which they are observing the dive.

* The diver dives to the side of the board or platform.

* Attempting to perform dives in the layout position with the head down which causes the body to develop a slight pike position.

* Wavering of the body when attempting to perform a hand stand on the platform.

* The length of time the diver holds a handstand when performing from the tower.

* A slight change in hand position when performing a hand stand on the platform.

* The degree of impact when hitting the board or platform.

* The use of rip entries has made it more difficult to judge dives. It is easy for a judge to over emphasize the value of the entry when little or no splash is made and de-emphasize the value of a well performed dive that does not rip.

A CLARIFICATION REGARDING A DIVER HITTING THE DIVING BOARD OR PLATFORM IN COMPETITION

One factor in the competition has always confused and concerned me was how to score a dive when the diver hits the board/ platform. The F.I.N.A. rule states (Page 151 and 1957, D 6.8) *"Where in any dive, the diver touches the end of the board/platform or dives to the side of the direct line of flight, the judge shall deduct according to individual opinion."* Unfortunately, this rule is not interpreted that way for high school competitions. Their rule states that regardless of how hard the diver hits the board, the judge cannot score the dive more than two points.

Divers often "tip" the board/platform with a finger or a toe and receive scores that range from two to six or seven points and in some cases even eight points. Such a range occurs because judges giving such scores have different views about the seriousness of tipping the board. One judge may feel that the diver was too close to the board/platform causing him or her to hit it. Another judge may believe the diver hit the board/platform because his or her body was in an extended lateral position while passing the tip of the board. The latter judge may have also been aware that the diver ' s center of gravity was an adequate distance from the tip of the board. Whatever the cause, it is apparent that the body was in the wrong position at the wrong time which caused the incident.

Divers hit the board/platform at various times with varying degrees of impact. For example, a diver may hit the board with the hands, head, or feet and still perform the dive in some fashion. When this occurs, I for one, have often been confused as to how to award the dive and hoped that my score would be similar to the ones given by the other judges. After several such incidents, I began to think that there must be a way of getting rid of the fallible guess work when scoring such dives. I finally concluded that made a lot of sense to me that when a diver hits the board with any degree of contact, the judge should first score the performance of the dive and ignore the fact that the person hit the board. Then after deciding on the score for the dive, deduct one-half to two points before entering the score, depending on the amount of impact made by the diver on the board/ or platform.

In this way, if the diver just tips the board with a finger, toe, or whatever, such little contact with the board may hardly affect the performance of the dive so the diver can still receive a respectable score for the dive. Therefore, the greater the contact with the board/tower, the more affect to the performance of the dive, and the greater will be deduction of points for hitting the board. For example, if a diver tips the end of the board and the score for the performance of the dive is an eight, the judge should deduct from a half to a point for making contact with the board. The divers final score for the dive would then be a seven or seven and a half. Similarly, if the diver hits the board with a greater impact, the more effect it will make on the performance of the dive, making the score for a dive around a six. The judge then deducts from one to two points which means the diver will receive a score between a five or a four for the dive. Naturally, if the diver hits the board hard enough to score around three or two for its performance, the judge may give the dive a score of one half or one.

Judging a diver hitting the board in this manner at least places the judges in a position to be fair and consistent while eliminating confusion and guess work. It is also necessary that the decision of whether or not the diver actually hit the board remains with the judges for if such a decision is given to the referee, that person could be in error. Keeping the decision with the judges may or may not offer a unanimous agreement as to whether the diver hit the board or platform, but it will at least make for a fair assessment.

Observers of diving have complained for years about the judging of competitive diving and many have devoted much thought to figuring out methods of eliminating, or at least reducing, the element of human error. Granted, judgment can change with the weather but one factor that makes the judging of diving extremely difficult is the absence of information in the diving rulebooks pertaining to the "desired" actions in the proper execution of dives. With the absence of such information in the rulebooks, divers and coaches throughout the world have had to develop their own techniques and methods for performing dives.

One may first believe that divers should have the freedom to perform dives using whatever techniques and styles they choose. If this were permitted, judges would be placed in a position to try to recognize and distinguish between different styles used by divers undoubtedly inviting chaos in the judging. In all fairness, the present judges are already given the responsibility of evaluating different methods used by divers that are, and sometimes not, within reason. This point is seen when divers use a hop or skip step before the hurdle in the forward springboard approach as compared with the conventional three to five step approach. Different techniques and styles has been increased in the last few years when divers found that certain difficult dives could not be successfully performed unless they used a particular technique, such as the split tuck, which in most cases has been accepted by the judges.

Check List for Organizing and Administering Diving Contests

The following check list is offered as an aid in the organization of any diving contest. Simply check those items that are needed for your particular meet.

✓	Check all that apply
	Local map - showing airport and pool location.
	Names, addresses, phone numbers and price lists for of nearby motels and restaurants.
	Hospitality accommodations for officials and coaches. Needed when events require that coaches remain at the pool all day.
	Towels - adequate number of per diver.
	Towel dryers.
	Dressing rooms - should be clean, well ventilated, attractive, with soap, adequate security systems for diver's clothes and valuables.

	Chairs and benches - for judges, officials, coaches, divers, and spectators with good view of diving area.
	Desk for officials - should seat at least five persons (under an awning if outside) near the diving area with good view of diving boards and platforms. Include electric outlet if possible.
	Sound system with microphone – for diving announcer.
	Score cards and/or electronic scoring system -for judge's awards.
	Diving score calculators - as needed.
	Diving score forms - including degrees of difficulty.
	Pencils - fifty or more with a pencil sharpener.
	Musical tapes to play during practice and meet time.
	U.S.A. flag - for national anthem and possible ceremony before meet starts.
	Diving awards for the divers who take top places.
	An award stand for recognizing the place winners in the meet.
	Concession stand access.
	Spectator seating for at least a conservative number.
	First aid facilities - including a spine board, stretcher, flat bed, plus emergency telephone numbers for ambulance and hospital.
	Ticket takers, parking area monitors, security guards, etc.
	Programs - including dates of competitions, pictures of divers, events, and past winners.
	Sponsors and adds to help pay for meet expenses.
	News media for meet coverage - local newspaper and T.V. coverage of events.
	Scoreboard for accumulated scores and places for each event - the finals are more dramatic if accumulated scores of the events are posted for the competitors and spectators.

A NEW VERSION FOR JUDGING COMPETITIVE DIVING THAT OFFERS MORE ACCURACY AND FAIRNESS FOR THE DIVERS

The new diving century offers an opportunity to improve the old system of scoring diving which has been in antiquated effect for over a hundred years. The tremendous improvement in the performance of dives and the great increase in the number of difficult dives, as well as the advanced development of the judging capacity of diving officials, calls for a more accurate means of judging diving. This call may be answered by incorporating "quarter points" to the current judging system. On nearly every occasion as a diving judge at all levels for many years, I have heard the same comment made by judges over and over say, "That dive wasn't worth a six or a six and a half, it was worth a six and a quarter."

Unfortunately, without the judging option of awarding quarter points, dive awards have been rounded out to a less accurate score. Traditionally, the judge has had to award the diver a score higher or lower than the intended score, a situation that is not fair to the divers. Everyone has seen contests won or lost by only a few points that could have been more accurately accumulated that would have possibly changed the results. From preliminary tests made in many diving contests at various competitive levels, it has been confirmed that the use of quarter points has not presented any complications in announcing the dives and scores, judging the dives, tabulating the scores at the scoring table, or announcing the scores of the dives performed. Those who have judged using the new system have all basically commented, "Where have we been for the last fifty years?"

Judging dives with score cards and technical scoring systems

Since hand held score cards with quarter points were never considered because the number of cards would have tripled making their use cumbersome, awkward to handle, and more time consuming, a change in judging was never considered. Now, with the presence of new technical scoring systems (which find no difficulty in changing their systems to include quarter points) and the improvement in plastics, using quarter points are no longer a problem. Thirty scoring cards can be made to be the same weight as ten score cards and are just as durable and easy to work with as the half point score cards. The proposed changes do not require and "retraining" for the diving judges, because all judges already recognize being " stuck" in their evaluation decision between a whole number and the half number.

Tabulating the scores using quarter points

In testing the quarter point system, a scoring sheet was made that included small square boxes in the upper right-hand corner of each scoring sheet. This was to allow those working at the scoring table to place a 1, 2, or 3 in the box to indicate the number of quarters given for a dive by each judge. Nothing was written in the box for dives that only scored whole points. When a judge wished to score a dive by giving a 6 ¾, the scoring table placed the 6 in the large opening, and a 3 in the small box. The event recorder then simply added up the diver's whole and quarter scores for the total points of the dive. This was followed by the traditional calculating of the total scores with the degree of difficulty to obtain the score for the dive (Figure 1).

If using a small box is not available on a scoring sheet. The quarter points can be written on the conventional score sheet separating the whole number using a dash or period (6-3 or 6.3) causing no interpretive concern for anyone working the scorer's table.

A simple key was made to convert the quarter scores to a metric system making it very easy to add up the total score. It was found that adding up the quarter point scores was quicker than when using the half point system.

No. of quarter points	Metric value
0 - - - - - - - - - - - - - - - - .00	8- - - - - - - - - - - - - - - - - 2.00
1 - - - - - - - - - - - - - - - - .25	9- - - - - - - - - - - - - - - - -2.25
2 - - - - - - - - - - - - - - - - .50	10- - - - - - - - - - - - - - - - - 2.50
3 - - - - - - - - - - - - - - - - .75	11- - - - - - - - - - - - - - - - - 2.75
4 - - - - - - - - - - - - - - - - 1.00	12- - - - - - - - - - - - - - - - - 3.00
5 - - - - - - - - - - - - - - - - 1.25	13 - - - - - - - - - - - - - - - - -3.25
6 - - - - - - - - - - - - - - - - 1.50	14- - - - - - - - - - - - - - - - -3.50
7 - - - - - - - - - - - - - - - - 1.75	15- - - - - - - - - - - - - - - - - 3.75

This key is functional for the judging of all contests that include:

- 2-3 judges - all scores count
- 5 judges - high and low scores are eliminated
- 7 judges - two high and low scores are eliminated
- 9 judges - three high and low scores are eliminated
- 5 judges - all five judges count at 3/5ths value per judge

Sample of using quarter point cards with 5 judges

Scores of 5 judges	Total quarter pts.	Metric	Total pts.	Judges pts.
6-2 6-3 7-1 7 6-1	7	1.75	22	23.75

Meet ______ NCAA DIVING SCORE SHEET
Date ______ Order ______
M W 1M 3M Platform

Position (S,P,T,F)	D.D.	Judges' Awards 1	2	3	4	5	6	7	8	9	Judges Total	Cumulative Total Award
S	1.4											

A typical scoring sheet when using quarter points
Figure 1

When testing the quarter point system in dual, state, and conference meets, the only difficulty found was in the feeling of *change* from one system to another. No real difference is made except in the range in which the diver can be judged and with greater accuracy. After using the same scoring system for 100 years, one is bound to find a feeling of change but once the judge uses the new system for a meet or two, the change is accepted and the realization of a better method of judging is recognized.

The electronic quarter point system

When confronting the Electronic Scoring System companies in the United States, all of them said that it would only take a minor change to include the quarter point system in the electronic score boards. It was found that all that was necessary was to activate the "2" and the "7" so when a judge punches in a score such as 7.2, 7.5 or 7.7 the score board would show 7.25, 7.50, and 7.75 respectively. This addition of quarter points does **not** interfere with any present meet function and is performed with no additional effort.

Announcing at contests using the quarter point system

When first testing the quarter point system using score cards, it was found to be very boring and strung out when the announcer expressed the scores that had various quarter points. This problem was immediately corrected when the announcer gave the scores for dives as 6, 62, 71, 63. and 72. This manner made it very easy for the scoring table to tabulate the scores with quarter points. And when the announcer informed the audience that the second-number they heard for each score was the number of quarter points, no one was confused. The scores are the same as when the name of a dive is announced using numbers and letters. When using the electronic system, nothing needs be explained to the spectators for the scores are indicated on the score board.

A POSSIBLE SOLUTION TO THE PROBLEM OF JUDGING COMPETITIVE DIVING

FORMING A SCHOOL FOR THOSE WHO WISH TO BECOME CERTIFIED DIVING JUDGES

Due to the lack of judging criteria available, as related to the approach, the take-off, the desired execution of the dives, and the entries into the water, there is little about diving that can be precisely annotated. This leaves the door open for a great deal of criticism and also invites prejudice and bias on the part of many judges. Judging a sport with the absence of guidelines for the desired manner in which dives should be performed is practiced by many who are limited in their knowledge and experience which leaves much to be desired when offering the divers an accurate and fair evaluation of their performances. The absence of knowledge when judging competitive diving and a reduction in bias and prejudice could be greatly improved if a school for those who wish to judge fairly and accurately was offered.

ORGANIZING A SCHOOL FOR JUDGING DIVING

Some countries, such as Canada, have already formed a Judging School for competitive diving which is well organized and has developed some very competent diving judges. It would be beneficial if such a school was offered in the United States, so that the American judges could improve their judging status at home as well as abroad

Forming a school for persons to be educated in judging diving contests would require the aid from a group of experts who are experienced in competitive diving at all levels of competition. A guess at the time needed to educate and certify those who wish to be diving judges appears to be at least four or five days, but not more than seven days. The daily meetings for those attending would range from six to eight hours a day. The school should be offered twice a year; just before the summer and winter seasons. The location of the school and the number and kind of instructors needed to cover all of the subjects and stations should be chosen by a national governing committee of diving experts. The proposed judging program should be responsible for creating areas that concern job descriptions, teaching and coaching schedules, teaching materials, diving facilities available, educational videos for competitive levels of competition, lodging accommodations, hospitality for participants, food preparation, teaching aids, and diving equipment needed, etc.

Applications and qualifications for admission to attend the school also need be made available. Applications should include the applicant's experience, and background related to competing, teaching, coaching, and judging. The forms should also include the levels of competition and age-groups in which the applicants wish to qualify to judge. A pamphlet containing the school criteria should be offered along with the names of the instructors and administrators. It may also include a directory of those who have already been certified so that meet administrators can notify them for judging events.

Lectures and other instruction will be given concerning the rules and regulations for competitive diving, watching video tapes, participating in actual judging situations, and group discussions. Several exams relating to the rules, the analyses of dives, and an understanding of basic principles based on the laws of motion as they relate to judging diving will be given at various times during the school operation. The tests will be offered in a written and practical manner and graded by a representative from that school. If one wishes to qualify to be certified in more than one competitive level, it may be possible for the competitive levels to be offered on different days or times.

Those who do not pass the established criteria will be permitted to take the course again at other times. Persons who become certified but do not remain active for a given period of time will be required to take a written and practical test again to be reinstated.

The inactive period of time will be decided on by the school officials. A class for anyone who wishes to update his or her judging or consult with an expert on judging problems might be arranged at given times.

Once the school is created, videos of the school's activities could be made to offer more schools in various parts of the country. Whatever its growth, a school is sorely needed not only in America, but also in competitive diving areas all over the world.

In summary, it is hoped that the judging of diving with quarter points will increase the accuracy of judging dives and widen the range of scoring when added to the present scoring system. And finally, schools should be created to educate and certify persons to judge competitions at all competitive levels.

Made in the USA
Coppell, TX
19 December 2022